Corporate Governance after the Financial Crisis

Edited by

P.M. Vasudev

Faculty of Law, University of Ottawa, Canada

Susan Watson

The University of Auckland Business School, New Zealand

Edward Elgar

Cheltenham, UK • Northampton, MA, USA

Published by
Edward Elgar Publishing Limited
The Lypiatts
15 Lansdown Road
Cheltenham
Glos GL50 2JA
UK

Edward Elgar Publishing, Inc.
William Pratt House
9 Dewey Court
Northampton
Massachusetts 01060
USA

A catalogue record for this book
is available from the British Library

Library of Congress Control Number: 2011939348

FSC www.fsc.org MIX Paper from responsible sources FSC® C018575

ISBN 978 0 85793 152 8

Typeset by Servis Filmsetting Ltd, Stockport, Cheshire
Printed and bound by MPG Books Group, UK

Contents

Tables

Contributors

Peter A. Appel, Associate Professor, University of Georgia School of Law.

Aishah Bidin, Professor of Corporate and Insolvency Law and Dean, Faculty of Law, National University of Malaysia, UKM, and Member, Malaysian Corporate Law Reform Committee (CLRC), Companies Commission of Malaysia.

Franklin A. Gevurtz, Distinguished Professor and Scholar, University of the Pacific, McGeorge School of Law; Director, Pacific McGeorge Global Center for Business & Development.

T. Rick Irvin, Adjunct Professor, Interdisciplinary Program on Toxicology, University of Georgia.

Trish Keeper, Senior Lecturer, School of Accounting and Commercial Law, Victoria University of Wellington, New Zealand.

Yu-Hsin Lin, Assistant Professor, College of Law, National Chengchi University, Taiwan.

David Millon, J.B. Stombock Professor of Law, Washington and Lee University, Lexington, Virginia.

Aviv Pichhadze, Ph.D. candidate, Osgoode Hall Law School, York University, Toronto.

Leonard I. Rotman, Professor, Faculty of Law, University of Windsor, Windsor, Ontario, Canada, and Visiting Scholar, Hennick Centre for Business and Law, Osgoode Hall Law School, York University (2010–11).

Lynn A. Stout, Paul Hastings Distinguished Professor of Corporate and Securities Law, UCLA School of Law, Los Angeles, California.

P.M. Vasudev, Assistant Professor, University of Ottawa, Faculty of Law, Common Law Section.

Susan Watson, Professor of Commercial Law, The University of Auckland, New Zealand.

Peter Watts, Professor of Law and Associate Dean (Postgraduate), Faculty of Law, The University of Auckland, New Zealand.

Acknowledgments

As with any other project of this kind, we owe a debt of gratitude to a number of persons and institutions for their support and cooperation. We received valuable support both for the *Corporate Governance in the Post, Post World* symposium hosted by the New Zealand Governance Centre at The University of Auckland in April 2010 and in bringing out this volume of the papers presented at the symposium. In particular, we are grateful to The University of Auckland for providing financial support for the symposium. Funding from the Law Foundation of Ontario and The University of Auckland was helpful in securing student and editorial support for this volume, and we express our thanks.

Michelle Boodhoo and Marissa Kirsh, law students at the University of Ottawa, and Julie McMeikan of Auckland, New Zealand, provided invaluable help by carrying out style and citation checks and proofreading. Their assistance made our editorial task simpler and more enjoyable. We have valued working with Ben Booth and John-Paul Macdonald at Edward Elgar Publishing, who have been supportive and encouraging throughout.

Lest we forget, we owe enormous thanks to the contributors to the volume. We have been fortunate in having a wonderful working relationship with all of them since October 2009 when we began our planning for the symposium. Working on the several interesting articles written by a wide range of scholars from different jurisdictions was a truly rewarding experience for us. It is satisfying that our combined efforts have resulted in this volume, which we trust will make a meaningful contribution to the ongoing debate on corporate governance.

P.M. Vasudev, Ottawa, Canada
Susan Watson, Auckland, New Zealand
July 2011

Tables of cases and legislation

TABLE OF CASES

TABLE OF LEGISLATION

European Union

Conventions

Introduction

P.M. Vasudev and Susan Watson

CORPORATE GOVERNANCE – AN OVERVIEW

For a short while in 2008–09, as the wave of the Global Financial Crisis swept over us, it seemed that the world might change. The tenets that underpinned our economic systems were called into question, and faith in the invisible hand of the market wavered. When speculative credit derivatives business began to unravel at many large financial institutions, it threatened to destroy giant companies of long standing, such as Citigroup and American International Group (AIG). This sparked fears about a systemic collapse at the global level. The disaster, largely of human making, was averted by the 'bailouts' organized by the government of the United States in coordination with the Federal Reserve. Once the immediate crisis had passed leaving the rescued institutions intact, the immediacy of the need for fundamental change also seemed to pass.

Several years on, the world looks much the same. The clean-up after the acute emergency of the sudden meltdown continues. To cynics, the international response to the Financial Crisis has had a dreary predictability: much hand wringing, and regulatory responses that addressed symptoms of the Crisis without touching the underlying malaise. Indeed, writing in 2008 just before the onset of the Global Financial Crisis, La Porta et al. compared and contrasted the policy-implementing focus of civil law jurisdictions with the market-supporting focus of common law jurisdictions – to the latter's advantage. The paper concluded:

> The world economy in the last quarter century has been surprisingly calm, and has moved sharply toward capitalism and markets. In that environment, our framework suggests that the common law approach to social control of economic life performs better than the civil law approach. When markets do or can work well, it is better to support than to replace them. As long as the world economy remains free of war, major financial crises, or other extraordinary disturbances, the competitive pressures for market-supporting regulation will remain strong and we are likely to see continued liberalization. Of course, underlying this prediction is a hopeful assumption that nothing like World War

> II or the Great Depression will repeat itself. If it does, countries are likely to embrace civil law solutions, just as they did back then. (p. 327)

In fact, and as predicted, the response to the Financial Crisis of 2008–09 and the underlying events has been legislation. The US Congress enacted the *Dodd-Frank Act of 2010* – a formidable tome of over 1500 pages of closely printed text. The *Dodd-Frank Act*, reflecting its motivating drivers, targets a number of issues related to the Financial Crisis. These include setting up an agency to protect consumers against abusive lending practices, and regulation of credit rating agencies, trade in derivatives and hedge funds.

The sweep of the *Dodd-Frank Act* also extends to corporate governance. This can be interpreted as a strengthening of the trend for federal regulation of public corporations. The *Dodd-Frank Act* has adopted the principle of shareholder empowerment. The areas selected for reform are shareholder nomination of candidates for director positions (section 971) and a non-binding shareholder vote on executive compensation, or 'say on pay' (sections 951–7).

The principle of shareholder empowerment in the *Dodd-Frank Act* is, by and large, consistent with the theme of federal regulation since the 1930s. The concern of federal securities regulation has traditionally been with 'investors' – who are essentially shareholders. Federal regulation may be viewed as an attempt to set right the imbalance created under state incorporation laws that endow directors with most of the corporate powers. In this setup, federal securities regulation has generally made interventions on behalf of the shareholders.

The Securities Exchange Commission (SEC) has framed Rule 14a-11 to implement the directive under the *Dodd-Frank Act* to provide access to shareholders in nominating directorial candidates. But the rule has come under legal challenge by the US Chamber of Commerce and Business Roundtable, which have filed an action in the US Court of Appeals for the DC Circuit. These business groups attack the rule, among other things, on the ground that it does not consider the effects on 'efficiency, competition, and capital formation' (Allen 2010). Pending the decision of the court, the SEC has agreed not to implement the rule.

The other element in the *Dodd-Frank Act* is about shareholders having a 'say on the pay' of senior executives. This measure is significant for a number of reasons. First, it represents a response to the longstanding complaint that the executives, in effect, determine their own salaries. Recent innovations such as compensation committees of the board of directors and a majority of independent directors are apparently not considered adequate. Secondly, it reflects the idea that shareholders are the principals and managers are their agents. If this is so, then it is quite appropriate that shareholders are involved in determining executive pay.

Finally, there can be an economic justification for involving shareholders rather than anyone else in determining executive pay. Shareholders are the residual claimants in solvent corporations, as economic theory stresses. Executive pay is a charge on the residue and it is logical for shareholders to have a say on the quantum of the charge.

However shareholder intervention in executive pay – indeed the theme of shareholder empowerment – presents some difficulties. For instance, there is a complaint that shareholders' major concern is with share prices (see, for example, Ryterbrand 2010). Targeting share prices, they often act with short-term motives and might persuade managers to follow their bidding. Another issue is why shareholders should be treated any differently from other 'stakeholder' groups, such as employees or lenders. Stakeholder theorists argue that there is no justification for the proprietary idea associated with shareholders and for granting them special rights.

The difference that the 'say on pay' provision in the *Dodd-Frank Act* will make to the culture of high executive pay and the recent growth in imbalances in pay structures between the lower and higher levels in corporate organizations (see, for example, McDonnell 2008) remains to be seen. Compensation committees with independent directors have been around for several years, and they are mandatory under the New York Stock Exchange Listing Rules (NYSE Rules 2010). To be fair, these mechanisms have had some impact but there is obviously a considerable distance to travel. There is now regulatory intervention in executive compensation through the non-binding shareholder vote provided in the *Dodd-Frank Act*.

In dealing with sensitive issues such as executive compensation, the character of business corporations and our understanding of the subject are crucial. A sound theoretical underpinning is essential in coming to terms with the phenomenon we call business corporations. We need greater clarity in our understanding and perception of these devices. To illustrate, in theorizing about the regulation of executive compensation we must necessarily consider a number of other longstanding issues. These include questions about the public or private character of business corporations, their relationship with the state, the legitimacy of regulation and its extent or reach. Finally, there is the issue of the impact of regulation on business initiative and enterprise and, consequently, general economic welfare.

The current round of governance failures in the financial companies has occurred just a few years after the equally sensational collapses seen in Enron, WorldCom and other companies in the early years of the new millennium. Similar to the discussion and debate that occurred after Enron, the Global Financial Crisis of 2008–09 presents an opportunity to examine afresh our assumptions about the prevailing economic framework. This examination may also cause us to ask whether Enron and the recent Financial Crisis were isolated events or in fact portents of a bigger wave to come.

The business practices, indeed the business culture, at the affected companies is a material issue in the Financial Crisis of 2008–09. Excessive leverage and risk taking, bonus payments to executives based on annual performance figures with little regard to the medium or long term, and failure to understand the complex derivative instruments properly are some factors that contributed to this crisis. The events underlying the Crisis have triggered a fresh round of debate about corporate governance.

Granted, the Financial Crisis was not just about corporate governance. It had its roots in the climate of financial liberalization and permissiveness which facilitated the financial industry to develop exotic and complex derivatives and trade in them in large volumes. Yet questions remain. Could the phenomenon have grown in size and seriousness to the extent that it actually did if better corporate governance had exercised a moderating influence? In other words, could an environment that emphasized a greater sense of responsibility in corporate governance have helped in avoiding the Financial Crisis, or at least mitigated it to some extent?

This book is a study of corporate governance in the emerging world. It explores potential new directions in corporate governance. It contains a collection of the papers presented at the *Corporate Governance in the Post, Post World* symposium hosted by the New Zealand Governance Centre at The University of Auckland, New Zealand, in April 2010. The title of the symposium reflected that we now live in the post-Enron, post-AIG world, and posed a question about the lessons learnt from these sobering experiences. The chapters included in the volume deal with a wide variety of subjects such as shareholder primacy, enlightened shareholder value, directors and their position, the stakeholder principle in corporate governance and business ethics. The range of jurisdictions covered is quite wide as well. The chapters deal with the United States, Canada, the United Kingdom, New Zealand, Malaysia and Taiwan.

Since the 1970s, the emphasis has been on private ordering as the best means of promoting economic efficiency. The shareholder value maxim, lack of restraints on executive compensation, and an emphasis on aligning the interests of managers with shareholders through stock options are among the more prominent prescriptions in the corporate governance discourse. Recent events call into question the validity of many of these ideas. They present an opportunity – indeed, an imperative – to revisit these principles of corporate governance which have been influential in the last few decades.

There is now a need to explore possible alternatives including a greater role for law and public regulation in shaping the governance practices of companies. Recent events also cause us to question several assumptions that are implicit in the discourse on corporate governance. These assumptions have influenced policy and practice. For example, is the relationship between shareholders and boards in fact agency based, and is shareholder primacy a gold standard ideal? The recent legislative attempts to boost the powers of shareholders as a check on management excess may prove to be misguided and futile if, in fact, the corporate entity does not benefit from increased shareholder control. In this volume, a chapter by Professor Lynn Stout raises these questions about the prevailing paradigm.

The aim of this volume is to introduce the new ideas animating the emerging universe of corporate governance in the post-Financial Crisis world. To understand the present better, looking to the past is essential. The chapters included in the volume are written from diverse perspectives and seek to accomplish a variety of goals. Some attempt to chart the path for the future, while some point out the limitations of the ideas and concepts that have proven to be influential in the recent past. A third set examines how globalization is promoting homogeneity in corporate governance and shaping the regulatory regime in countries like Malaysia and Taiwan.

THE CHAPTERS AND THEIR CONTENT – AN INTRODUCTION AND ANALYSIS

The volume has a total of twelve chapters and is divided into four parts. The first part deals with the 'Great Debate' in corporate law over whether directors should consider the interests of shareholders only (usually termed the 'shareholder primacy' rule) or a wider constituency of stakeholders that includes employees and consumers (the 'stakeholder principle'). Part I has seven chapters, just over half the number of chapters included in the volume. The next part examines the effectiveness of the private remedy model that is largely relied on in corporate law. It has a chapter that uses the decision *In re Citigroup Inc Shareholder Derivative Litigation* (2010) as a handle to analyse the issues with the private remedy model.

Part III is about globalization and its impact on corporate governance. It has two chapters that deal, respectively, with recent developments in Taiwan and Malaysia. The fourth and last part of the volume presents studies on recent developments in business ethics and corporate responsibility. It has two chapters. We summarize below the chapters included in the volume and, in doing so, also explain their contextual significance.

Part I – The 'Great Debate'

The 'Great Debate' in corporate law is over whether directors should consider the interests of shareholders only ('shareholder primacy') or a wider constituency of stakeholders that includes groups such as employees and consumers. It must be surprising to persons new to corporate law that such a fundamental question still remains unsettled. Equally, for those running companies it must be difficult to know who they should be thinking about when they make decisions. The messages are mixed, even within jurisdictions. For example, the UK is considered, more or less, a bastion of shareholder primacy. This is justified, in part, by the source of the powers of boards in UK companies being through the articles of association rather than being statutory, which is the case in most other jurisdictions. But it is the UK that has adopted, in section 172 of the *Companies Act 2006*, a statutory provision that appears to entertain stakeholder principles and, at the very least, adopts principles of enlightened shareholder value. Conversely in the US, directors derive their powers from statutory provisions. Nevertheless agency theory holds sway in the US.

The first part of the volume examines different dimensions of the Great Debate and has seven chapters.

Chapter 1: Lynn A. Stout – New thinking on 'shareholder primacy'

The first chapter, by Professor Lynn Stout, poses a trenchant challenge to shareholder primacy. The chapter is based on the keynote address delivered by Professor Stout at the *Corporate Governance in the Post, Post World* symposium in New Zealand. The chapter argues that shareholder primacy thinking, which reached its high watermark at the beginning of the new millennium when it acquired a quasi-scientific patina from law and economic theorists, is on the wane. The logical inconsistencies in the shareholder primacy model (for example, shareholders do not have ultimate control over directors, directors do not always seek to maximize share price) are borne out by empirical studies that reveal that it is in fact directors who run companies. The rights granted to shareholders are limited in scope and they do not enable shareholders, as a matter of fact or law, to insist that managers act as their agents serving only their interests.

US law does not give shareholders the power to control the board. Often promoters establish companies that weaken shareholder powers to a greater extent than is the case under the so-called default statutory provisions; yet shareholders, who from a shareholder primacy perspective are the owners, do not object. The chapter by Professor Stout sets out several theoretical arguments against shareholder primacy. It concludes that, given the serious flaws in shareholder primacy theory, regulators and policymakers should not move to boost the powers of shareholders in the belief that this will serve investors' interests. Incidentally, this prescription goes against the efforts made in the *Dodd-Frank Act*, outlined earlier, to enhance shareholder participation. According to Professor Stout, for the serious issues experienced with the way business corporations are run by their directors and managers, it is not a solution to expect shareholders to provide the correctives. Professor Stout also argues that the US should not export its shareholder-oriented model to other jurisdictions.

Chapter 2: Peter Watts – Shareholder primacy in corporate law – a response to Professor Stout

In the second chapter, Professor Peter Watts presents a brief response to Professor Stout's chapter. Interestingly, there is a degree of agreement between the two scholars. Professor Watts agrees with Professor Stout that shareholder involvement in day-to-day decision making should not be compulsory. Rather, his argument is for a model of the company that gives shareholders a choice to be so involved. Refuting the arguments against shareholder primacy, Professor Watts asserts that the rule of shareholder primacy is alive and well. Indeed he argues it is not just a post-1980s phenomenon, but dates back all the way to the nineteenth century.

Chapter 3: Susan Watson – Derivation of powers of boards of directors in UK companies

The third chapter, which is written by co-editor Professor Susan Watson, deals with an important dimension in the shareholder primacy framework. This is about the relationship between shareholders and directors in companies. In the conventional shareholder primacy model, shareholders are treated as the 'owners' of companies and assimilated to the position of principals. Directors, who are elected by shareholders, are quite logically understood as the delegates or 'agents' of the shareholders. There is a significant difference in this respect between the corporate law prevailing in North America and company law in most parts of the British Commonwealth. In North America, directors generally derive their corporate powers from the statutes. Therefore, their powers can be viewed as original and 'un-delegated'. In the British Commonwealth, however, directors' powers are usually granted under the articles of association, which are treated as contracts among companies and their shareholders. An issue is whether this feature in UK company law defines the position of directors as delegates of shareholders.

Professor Watson's chapter critically questions the true significance of the source of boards' powers in UK company law, and argues that the non-statutory source is more a historical anomaly. It does not speak to a fundamental difference in UK company law. The chapter makes a historical inquiry to determine the origin of the phenomenon and traces it to the deeds of settlement that existed before general incorporation became possible in UK under the *Joint Stock Companies Act 1844*. The statute provided for compulsory registration of the deeds of settlement.

During subsequent legislative amendments, the clause in the 1844 statute on boards' powers was simply adopted from the pre-existing deeds of settlement and included in the model articles of association appended to the statutes. This occurred in the late nineteenth century. The result is of no great significance, it is argued. Indeed boards of directors and their powers were clearly understood in the UK at the time without reference to the articles of association of companies. The result, Professor Watson argues, is that the powers of directors in UK company law are original and un-delegated – in no way materially different from the position across the Atlantic in North America.

Another important trend in this context is the 'enlightened shareholder value' model included in the *Companies Act 2006* (UK). Although the structure of UK company law is seemingly based on shareholder primacy, section 172 of the *Companies Act*, which enshrines the concept of enlightened shareholder value, requires directors to act in a way they consider will 'be most likely to promote the success of the company for the benefit of its members as a whole' while having regard to matters such as the interests of the company's employees and its business relationships with suppliers, customers and others.

Chapter 4: David Millon – Enlightened shareholder value, social responsibility and the redefinition of corporate purpose without law

The fourth chapter is by Professor David Millon, who has written about corporate purpose and a potential role for law in defining it. The chapter outlines the ideas emerging in the US about enlightened shareholder value (ESV). Enlightened shareholder value, which stresses the long-term value for the corporation, would naturally benefit shareholders. But the emphasis on the long term ensures that corporations are not driven by 'short termism' and a desire to stimulate rises in current share prices. Instead they develop policies and strategies that promote long-term corporate value, which automatically includes due consideration for other stakeholder groups such as employees, consumers and the environment.

More specifically, Professor Millon explores how market pressures are weaning American transnational corporations from 'narrowly focused shareholder primacy'. The chapter explains how risk management practices are helping in reinterpreting the corporate goal and in promoting the consideration of stakeholder interests in ways that resonate with notions of corporate social responsibility (CSR). Myopic labor and environmental policies that reduce operating expenses in the short term may carry litigation and reputational risks. These can lead to sizable litigation and settlements costs, as well as negative reputational effects in product, labor and capital markets. The result of the ongoing process, Professor Millon predicts, 'may be a richer, more socially-oriented notion of the corporate objective, shaped by public opinion rather than legal intervention'.

Having made the prediction about responsible governance impelled by market compulsions, the chapter by Professor Millon concludes on a note of caution on how far these pressures alone can shape the corporate objective. Quite probably, the policies and actions of business corporations will still be driven by considerations about the bottom line and little else. This might not be adequate to foster an acceptable level of socially responsible behavior. As a result, public policy and legislation may yet have a role in influencing corporate behavior if only to minimize the externalities of the operations of business corporations.

Chapter 5: Leonard I. Rotman – Re-evaluating the basis of corporate governance in the post, post-Enron era

Professor Rotman's chapter also provides a challenge to shareholder primacy orthodoxy, in particular the basis of Henry Hansmann and Reiner Kraakman's seminal 2001 article that the shareholder primacy norm had triumphed over all other conceptions of the company and that corporate history was at an end (Hansmann and Kraakman, 2001). Professor Rotman argues that subsequent events are inconsistent with that view and also challenges the arguments used by Hansmann and Kraakman. Presenting the Canadian angle, the chapter refers to *Peoples Department Stores v Wise* (2004) in which the Supreme Court of Canada expressly affirmed a broad, stakeholder framework of business corporation.

Hansmann and Kraakman assert that the five key characteristics of companies – namely, legal personality, limited liability, shared investor ownership, management delegated to a board, and transferable shares, which have existed in every major jurisdiction since 1900, provide for a firm that is strongly responsive to shareholder interests. Professor Rotman queries why, if these characteristics have been in place since 1900, has shareholder primacy triumphed only relatively recently? Also, Professor Rotman points out that it is especially ironic that the Hansmann/Kraakman article was published in the same year that Enron failed – a collapse which more than any other highlighted the failures of the shareholder primacy model. More significantly perhaps, the issues that have plagued corporate law such as corruption and abuse of managerial power have not been resolved with the supposed triumph of shareholder primacy. Also, the gauntlet thrown down by the 'end of history' article, with its assertion that progressive corporate law scholarship had become redundant, has been picked up by an increasing number of scholars, not just in the US but around the world.

Professor Rotman highlights the problems seen in Enron where market pressures and managerial incentivization cause directors to take unwarranted risks that benefit management and shareholders in the short term, but may ultimately lead to the demise of the corporation. Professor Rotman argues that shareholder primacy unduly skews the focus of corporate directors. A corporation is, as a matter of law, separate from its shareholders and theirs are not the only interests that should be considered.

The final section of the chapter by Professor Rotman has a discussion of corporate personality and a close examination of the *Dodge v Ford* (1919) and *Revlon* (1986) cases. In *Dodge*, the Michigan Supreme Court held that a business corporation is organized and carried on primarily for the profit of the stockholders. But Professor Rotman points out that the court also said that plans must be made for a long-term future and made several orders that sacrificed short-term profitability. These orders were not consistent with a short-term interest in maximizing shareholder profits under the shareholder primacy model. Also the context in which the decisions were made was important; investment in improved infrastructure and increased salaries would ultimately improve the competitive position of Ford Motor Company. The case should therefore be read as support for the view that the pursuit of shareholder profits does not exist in a vacuum.

In *Revlon* the directors engaged in defensive tactics that the Delaware Supreme Court held were improper because their focus should have been on obtaining the highest price for the benefit of the stockholders. The *Revlon* duties require directors to shift their focus from the best interests of the company to maximizing shareholder value when a company breakup is inevitable. As Professor Rotman points out, this necessarily means that in circumstances where the corporation is *not* under threat of a hostile takeover, the directors' duties are not restricted to a sole focus on shareholders.

Professor Rotman concludes that foundational corporate law issues around corporate identity and corporate purpose remain unresolved – the 'end of history' is not yet upon us.

Chapter 6: P.M. Vasudev – Corporate stakeholders in New Zealand: the present, and possibilities for the future

The contribution by Vasudev, co-editor of this volume, widens the discussion of the stakeholder principle to jurisdictions outside the US. A survey carried out in New Zealand showed that 91 of 130 companies listed on the New Zealand Stock Exchange had documentation that evidenced recognition of stakeholder interests in some form. Vasudev argues that a mechanism exists in the *Companies Act 1993* whereby companies could give stakeholders rights. That mechanism is the ability given to companies to extend the categories of entitled persons in their constitutions. Entitled persons have the right to bring actions for oppression and for unfairly discriminatory and unfairly prejudicial conduct. The court has access to a wide range of remedies, including regulating the future conduct of the company and ordering the payment of compensation.

Vasudev also discusses the stakeholder regime and its variants, in particular the directors' duty approach prevalent in the UK and the US, and the remedy-based version available in Canada. In the 'directors' duty' version of the stakeholder corporation, which has been developed in legislation since the 1980s, directors are authorized in statute to consider non-shareholder interests. One notable exception is Delaware – but the Delaware court has, in cases such as *Unocal* (1985) and *Paramount* (1989), recognized the stakeholder principle at times. However, other cases, such as *Revlon* (1986), which is also discussed by Professor Rotman, are inconsistent with a stakeholder conception of the company. But Vasudev argues that these cases are fact-specific and the inconsistencies highlight the risks in relying solely on judicial decisions to form corporate theory. Vasudev advocates public policy statement in the area through legislation, understood as the considered expression of the society, with due regard to all interests involved. In the UK, the position appears to be settled with the enshrining of stakeholder consideration in section 172 of the *Companies Act 2006*, discussed above.

Vasudev moves to a discussion of the stakeholder remedy approach seen in Canada. Non-shareholder groups can bring derivative actions and also actions for oppression. The Dickerson Committee in 1970 described the idea of giving shareholders some of the powers exercised by directors as misconceived. Shareholders were not viewed as having proprietary rights, nor were directors considered to be their elected surrogates. Despite the recommendations of the Dickerson Report being enshrined in the statute, and despite the Canadian Supreme Court's apparent affirmation of the stakeholder vision in *Peoples Department Stores v Wise* (2004), Vasudev questions if the outcomes in this and other cases have in fact endorsed the stakeholder view. He therefore discusses a third alternative – representation and empowerment of stakeholder groups as seen in Germany. The idea was rejected by the Dickerson Committee in Canada and has not been seriously considered in the US. The chapter concludes with a modest proposal for New Zealand – for the adoption of a stakeholder principle reflecting the unique features of the corporate landscape in New Zealand.

Chapter 7: Aviv Pichhadze – Institutional investors as blockholders
The concluding chapter in Part I, which deals with shareholder primacy, deals with another significant thread in the debate on this subject. This chapter by Aviv Pichhadze is about institutional investors as shareholders. Institutional investors, in particular pension funds, have been at the centre of the corporate governance debate for several decades now. In 1976, Peter Drucker proclaimed the 'unseen revolution' and the advent of 'pension fund socialism' in America. More recently, evidence of a similar spirit can be found in the work of Hawley and Williams (2000) about 'fiduciary capitalism'.

The chapter by Aviv Pichhadze offers a contrary perspective. Characterizing institutional investors as blockholders, Pichhadze points out that institutional investors are oriented towards capital markets. This can raise questions about their engagement in the governance of the corporations included in their portfolios. Proponents of the shareholder model of corporate governance usually refer to the emergence of institutional investors in recent decades and stress their potential to play the role of 'responsible' shareholders in accord with the democratic framework provided in corporate law. The chapter by Pichhadze presents the Market Oriented Blockholder Model (MOBM) as a more appropriate perspective for interpreting the dominant shareholding pattern in the US, and argues that the interests and priorities of institutional investors as blockholders do not necessarily coincide with those of other shareholders. After stressing the significance of the MOBM, the author cautions against failing to take note of the blockholder concept and developing policies that do not reflect the phenomenon, which may introduce systemic risks into the market.

Part II – Private Remedy in Corporate Law and Its Limits

This part consists of a chapter by Professor Franklin Gevurtz that examines the efficacy of the private remedy in corporate law. Specifically, it is about the law and the court of the state of Delaware, which is the preferred jurisdiction for public corporations in the US. Professor Gevurtz has selected the recent decision of the Delaware Chancery Court *In re Citigroup Inc Shareholder Derivative Litigation* (2008), rendered specifically in the context of the Financial Crisis and the derivatives business of Citigroup, to test the thesis about the private remedy in corporate law and its efficacy.

Chapter 8: Franklin A. Gevurtz – The role of corporate law in preventing a financial crisis – reflections on *In re Citigroup Inc Shareholder Derivative Litigation*

Delaware has an open structure of corporate law that permits corporations a high degree of freedom and flexibility, which has drawn complaints for a long time now (see, for example, Cary 1973). Within corporations, powers are significantly concentrated in the directors. In addition to these features, another important advantage Delaware is perceived to possess is 'a sophisticated and expert judicial system and bar, modern and flexible business entity laws, [and] a wealth of well-reasoned case law . . .' (Conaway 2008, p. 789).

The chapter by Professor Franklin Gevurtz deals directly with the Financial Crisis. It starts by explaining how unreasonable risk taking by financial corporations was a primary factor in producing the Financial Crisis, and then reviews the five basic methods by which law attempts to prevent such unreasonable risk taking – through banking regulation and corporate governance rules. These include control over compensation, liability of management for unreasonably risky conduct, and selection of management.

The chapter links the failure of corporate law to curb unreasonable risk taking by financial companies to other major themes in the book. It uses the decision of the Delaware court *In re Citigroup Shareholder Derivative Litigation* (2008) as a predicate for asking why laws regulating corporate governance are as weak as they are. The chapter advances the thesis that weakness in corporate law stems from its shareholder primacy orientation and this ties in with the debate in the prior part of the book. Corporate law, for example, allows shareholders to waive director liability for unreasonable risk taking, even though unreasonable risk taking harms depositors, taxpayers, and the broader economy. In addition, the chapter ties shareholder primacy in US corporate law to the ability of managers to choose the state that sets the rules of corporate governance, subject only to consent of shareholders. This concern with allowing selection of corporate laws in a marketplace of competing jurisdictions, in turn, segues into the discussion of globalization and corporate governance in the other parts of the book.

Part III – Corporate Governance and Globalization

Globalization is an important development of recent decades. Liberalized international trade, mobility of capital and the opening up of hitherto insular economies such as China, India and Russia have greatly altered the economic landscape. An important element in the process of globalization has been the rise of the stock market as a key institution and the adoption of the corporate form of business organization in countries the world over. To be fair, over the last two centuries the British Empire laid the foundation for this by spreading the company form in Asia and Africa. The current round of globalization has carried the process further.

The third part of the volume consists of two chapters which explain how ideas formed in Western countries are shaping regulation in emerging countries. Chapter 9 by Yu-Hsin Lin is about independent directors in Taiwan, and Chapter 10 by Aishah Bidin traces the developments in corporate law – in particular, corporate bankruptcy and insolvency – in Malaysia in response to the forces of globalization. Interestingly, an issue raised by Professor Stout in Chapter 1 about the wisdom of transplanting the American system of corporate governance into other regimes also animates the chapter by Yu-Hsin Lin about independent directors in Taiwan and their efficacy.

Chapter 9: Yu-Hsin Lin – How public regulation changes corporate governance practice – corporate board reform in Taiwan

This chapter by Yu-Hsin Lin examines how the mechanism of independent directors functions in Taiwanese companies. The role of independent directors in a traditional corporate governance framework informed by shareholder primacy views is to ensure that the board monitors the management of the company on behalf of the shareholders. Yet the evidence of the effectiveness of independent directors as a corporate governance mechanism is mixed at best. Empirical studies do not show that board independence improves performance (Bhagat and Romano, 2007).

In addition, the appointment of independent directors may not be appropriate or effective in regimes that are not characterized by strong stock markets with dispersed shareholding – an imperative for maximizing shareholder value. Research on corporate governance in emerging and mature economies as a result of the crisis has revealed that widely held corporations are rare outside the US and the UK. Many companies outside these two jurisdictions are family controlled. The reason why family control may not necessarily be a corporate governance problem is that close relationships between the business and political elites can equally develop in systems with widely dispersed shareholdings. In fact, as seen in Asia in the preceding 30 years and as seen in continental European countries, family dominated systems can work well. Family-owned companies perform as well as ones with dispersed shareholdings and professional managers.

The International Monetary Fund and the World Bank suggested that a major cause of the Asian financial crisis of the 1990s was, at least in part, the low level of development of the stock markets in the region, which forced corporations to borrow from banks. Despite high debt–equity ratios, it has been argued that close relationships between borrower corporations and banks meant that the banks did not carry out the monitoring role normally performed by a share market. For that reason, policies were introduced to boost investment in the share markets. These included generally accepted good governance measures like independent directors and independent audit committees (Glen and Singh 2004).

Ysu-Hsin Lin looks at the legal transplantation of independent directors into Taiwan, which has a two-tier board system. To align itself with the reforms introduced in the US by the *Sarbanes-Oxley Act of 2002*, the Taiwan Stock Exchange moved to encourage the appointment of independent directors. Yet in September 2011 – the date of study by Yu-Hsin Lin – 56.8 per cent of listed companies did not have independent directors.

The chapter discusses the characteristics of corporate governance in Taiwan, highlighting the fact that corporate ownership in that country is concentrated and family dominated. Business groups, in particular family business groups, dominate corporate ownership. The statutory responsibilities and the practice of independent directors in Taiwan are outlined before the chapter moves on to an interesting analysis of interviews with independent directors. The importance of *guan xi*, which roughly translates into connections or relationships, is highlighted, and the integrity of controlling shareholders and managers is seen as a key criterion for putative independent directors. Assessment of integrity is usually built on the personal relationships between the controlling shareholders and independent directors, but it raises issues about the true independence of the independent director. Conversely, it also means that companies usually select independent directors whom they know. In the survey only seven of the 40 independent directors interviewed did not know the controlling shareholders or other inside directors before they decided to join the board. The chapter concludes with a discussion of the risk of unintentional bias; the growing awareness of the impact of personal relationships on director independence makes this an issue not just in Taiwan but also in other Asian countries where similar links between controlling shareholders and independent directors are common.

Chapter 10: Aishah Bidin – Corporate law reform and corporate governance in Malaysia – responses to globalization
Professor Aishah Bidin turns the spotlight on to Malaysia with a chapter setting out the corporate governance reforms currently undertaken in her jurisdiction. These reforms are driven by the Malaysian Corporate Law Reform Committee and, unlike earlier 'piecemeal' amendments, are intended to result in a systematic and coherent review of the *Companies Act 1965*. The chapter begins with a discussion of the history and regulatory framework of company law in Malaysia, highlighting the influence of English common law, which provides the foundation of Malaysian company law. The corporate governance provisions that have been in place in some form since the enactment of the *Companies Act 1965* in Malaysia are modeled on practice in overseas jurisdictions such as the UK (Jenkins Committee 1962) and Australia (Eggleston Committee 1967). These are discussed. In Malaysia, a two-pronged approach has been adopted for the reforms involving amendments in the short term followed by a fundamental review of the core company law provisions in the long term. Again, practice in other jurisdictions will be used to refine and fine tune the reforms.

The second section of the chapter shifts to a discussion of the corporate rehabilitation framework. The current legal framework for corporate insolvency in Malaysia is discussed and some of the problems with that system, such as delays in the courts, are highlighted. The section explains mechanisms introduced after the Asian Financial Crisis of 1997, such as special administration, which operate outside the court system, and the Corporate Debt Restructuring Committee that acts as an intermediary in negotiations among creditors, banks and debtor companies. The corporate rehabilitation regimes in other jurisdictions – namely, Singapore, the UK and Australia — are discussed. The chapter concludes with an interesting discussion of the importance of corporate vehicles as the engines of growth for Malaysia. The influence of the state on business and the interrelationship between transplantation and evolution of corporate law are also highlighted by Professor Bidin in this chapter.

Part IV – Corporate Ethics and Responsibility

Ethics and social responsibility have emerged as significant themes in corporate governance. The trend was particularly strengthened after the revelations of accounting fraud and unethical business practices at Enron and a host of other companies during 2001–02. These events increased the level of sensitivity to the ethical dimension in business. Responsible governance is another related stream in contemporary governance. It stresses the importance of corporations adopting responsible business practices without being driven completely by myopic approaches and narrow profit motives. Corporate responsibility is about companies taking the initiative to do things right, even though it might have a financial cost in the short term. The final part of the volume covers the interrelated themes of ethics and responsible governance. The two chapters in this part both adopt an empirical approach to the study of corporate governance, although they deal with different jurisdictions, namely, the US and New Zealand.

Chapter 11: Peter A. Appel and T. Rick Irvin – Public regulatory encouragement to the adoption of private ordering systems to achieve environmental protection through sustainable commerce

Professors Peter Appel and Rick Irvin present a case in this chapter for a 'public/private' approach to the issues of environmental responsibility and sustainable commerce, particularly in the context of corporate governance. Pressures of the financial markets, supported by the law of corporations, encourage business enterprises to underperform in the increasingly vital area of environmental care. Faced with environmental issues, the US government has traditionally responded with 'command-and-control' regulation. There are problems with this variety of regulation that relies, predominantly, on coercion to achieve the desired ends. To begin with, it is archaic and outmoded. Secondly, its efficacy as policy is questionable. To be fair, Professors Appel and Irvin concede that the penalties provided in US environmental law *do* have a considerable deterrent effect. The question posed in the chapter is whether traditional methods of command-and-control regulation and adversarial litigation in tort are, by themselves, adequate.

Professors Appel and Irvin present 'sustainable commerce' as an emerging concept that has gained significant traction in recent times. At once, it captures the environmental concerns that become stronger every day and highlights the importance of balancing these concerns with the needs of business. The concept of sustainable commerce is about products and practices that minimize environmental impacts and optimize commercial value while also meeting environmental benchmarks, both private and public. In other words, it is about reducing the environmental impact of business operations and promoting products that are eco-friendly.

Many corporations are now aware that sound environmental practices can enhance their profitability. Professors Appel and Irvin point out that this sensitivity persuades corporations to be proactive in reducing the environmental impact of their operations and products, because they understand the advantages from a business standpoint. The chapter presents some case studies that demonstrate how enhanced environmental consciousness among businesses is making a real difference.

Murray Industries of Tennessee, a case cited by the authors, overhauled its production systems to meet the environmental standards stipulated by its UK buyer. Having climbed the learning curve, Murray Industries now applies the same systems for the products it sells in the US market as well. This has resulted in overall environmental improvement in its operations. Wal-Mart, which is another case discussed by Professors Appel and Irvin, has announced steps for independent verification of its efforts to reduce its carbon footprint. In a similar spirit, the Los Angles Port Authority has initiated action to ensure the quality of the trucks that enter its premises for delivery and pickup of cargo. This is to be achieved by the use of new zero-emission technologies. But this effort of the Los Angeles Port Authority to check emissions has run into legal complications and litigation.

Professors Appel and Irvin argue that the limitations of command-and-control regulation do not mean that the state has no role to play. They point out that the government is an effective agency to harness the power of the market to impel improvement through means such as setting aggressive standards for government procurement and requiring greater information exchange and disclosure. The chapter envisions a partnership between the government and private actors in which they work together in addressing environmental concerns. The chapter presents the public/private paradigm in the area of environmental governance, and it remains to be explored how far the model can be applied in other aspects of corporate governance.

Chapter 12: Trish Keeper – Codes of ethics and corporate governance – a study of New Zealand listed companies

The final chapter in the volume concerns New Zealand. Ethics has emerged as a major strand in corporate governance, although this development is not free from controversy. In any event, most leading jurisdictions now formally include ethics and ethical business practices among the benchmarks of good governance. In New Zealand, the Securities Commission and the New Zealand Stock Exchange Listing Rules deal with the issue of ethics. The Securities Commission requires listed companies to disclose in their annual reports how they achieve the goal of ethical behavior, and the Stock Exchange Listing Rules have included the adoption of a code of ethics in the checklist of 'best practices'.

Trish Keeper traces the development of codes of corporate ethics in the United States since the 1970s and she explains how over the subsequent decades companies in Canada, Germany and the UK have also increasingly adopted such codes. The chapter points out that the *Principles of*

Corporate Governance formulated by the Organisation for Economic Co-operation and Development (OECD 2004) provides a comprehensive framework of ethics for business corporations. These developments prepared the ground for New Zealand to adopt measures to promote ethical business behavior.

Trish Keeper is critical of the ambiguities of the 'soft law' regime on corporate ethics in New Zealand. She finds some inconsistency in the language between the Stock Exchange Listing Rules and the Best Practices Code, which is an appendix to the Rules. The rule that companies must merely disclose non-compliance with the prescribed benchmarks, which include having a code of ethics, is less rigorous than the 'comply or explain' rule prevailing in the UK and Australia. From a review of a limited number of codes, the chapter finds that they tend not to be robust. These codes are found to be rather formalistic and confine themselves strictly to the matters specified in the Stock Exchange Rules and Best Practices standards.

The chapter includes a survey of companies listed on the New Zealand Stock Exchange to determine how many of them have a code of ethics as recommended in the Best Practices standards. The survey found varying levels of compliance and the results are grouped into three categories – namely, substantial compliance, mid-level compliance and low-level compliance. Thirty-eight per cent of the companies fell within the 'substantial compliance' category formulated in the chapter, while 45 per cent were found to have 'mid-level compliance'. The remaining 17 per cent are placed in 'low-level compliance' category.

The chapter concludes that both the New Zealand regime on corporate ethics and the trends in companies' practices do not measure up to international standards. Hopefully, the survey and the results presented in the chapter can stimulate a debate on the issue and inspire New Zealand regulators and companies alike to consider reformative action.

CONCLUSION – THE SHAPE OF THINGS TO COME?

As we pointed out earlier, the persistent theme in corporate governance has been that corporations perform best when left alone. This idea has been vigorously advocated since the 1970s by scholars identified with the law-and-economics movement. As pointed out earlier, the tenets of the law-and-economics model of corporate governance have been thrown open to question by the developments of the last decade or so. In any case, it is now quite obvious that mono-dimensional approaches and single-point agendas, be they wedded to belief in market efficiency or 'strong' government regulation, are impracticable. Such doctrinaire notions are necessarily restrictive and they are inadequate to deal with the multifaceted character of corporations and the complexities experienced in their governance. And at all times, we must also remember the primary objective of business corporations, which is to generate and distribute wealth through enterprise. This basic function has become more challenging in this age of globalization, mobility of capital, and international markets.

While the market may lack the self-corrective qualities attributed to it, it is apparent that regulation finds it equally hard to arrive at neat solutions. An example is the ongoing controversy, referred to earlier, regarding shareholder access to proxy in director nomination which is facilitated by the US *Dodd-Frank Act*. It remains to be seen how effective the 'say on pay' mechanism will prove to be in checking excessive managerial pay and promoting greater distributive equity among employees at different levels.

An important development in recent decades is the emergence of a plethora of codes of corporate governance. They represent a new source of materials on corporate governance, falling in the category of 'soft law'. Myriad agencies have been engaged with the subject, including the OECD, stock exchanges, United Nations, trade associations, investor councils and civil society organizations. They have all taken initiatives to develop norms that can influence the management practices of business corporations.

As a result, there appears to be a codification and institutionalization trend in corporate governance. Mechanisms such as independent directors, audit and compensation committees and codes of ethics have now emerged as norms in most jurisdictions and this can be traced to the efforts of several agencies to promote healthy and responsible corporate governance. These developments reflect the need, in this age of transnational corporations and global markets, for greater streamlining of corporate governance through the formulation and codification of standards.

The universe of corporate governance is now populated – some might say overcrowded – by a number of actors. In addition to the traditional elements – namely, market forces, government actors, business and professional groups and chambers of commerce – we now have multilateral agencies, such as the UN and OECD, civil society organizations and investor councils. Interest in corporate governance is now more widespread. This is not surprising considering the reach and influence of business corporations and their impact on our lives. Hopefully, the results from this rich interplay of forces will have a beneficial effect on corporate governance and help us to understand and manage these vehicles better as we emerge from the Financial Crisis.

The title selected for the volume reflects the wide-ranging changes that have occurred in the recent decades in corporate governance and thinking on the subject the world over. It adopts the time of the Financial Crisis (2008–09) as a catalyst for review and for making a critical analysis of emerging ideas. The volume weaves together several important strands of thought in the field.

REFERENCES

Articles and Books

Bhagat, S. and R. Romano (2007), 'Empirical studies of corporate law', in A. Mitchell Polinsky and Steven Shavell (eds), *Handbook of Law and Economics*, vol 2, Amsterdam and London: Elsevier, p. 945.
Cary, W. (1973), 'Federalism and corporate law: reflections upon Delaware', *Yale Law Journal*, **83**, 663–705.
Conaway, A. (2008), 'Lessons to be learned: how the policy of freedom of contract in Delaware's alternative entity law might inform Delaware's general corporation law', *Delaware Journal of Corporate Law*, **33**, 789–818.
Drucker, Peter (1976), *The Unseen Revolution: How Pension Fund Socialism Came to America*, New York: Harper Collins.
Hansmann, H. and R. Kraakman (2001), 'The end of history for corporate law', *Georgetown Law Journal*, **89**, 439–68.
Hawley, James P. and Andrew T. Williams (2000), *The Rise of Fiduciary Capitalism: How Institutional Investors Can Make Corporate America More Democratic*, Philadelphia: University of Pennsylvania Press.
La Porta, R., R. Lopez-de-Silanes and A. Schleifer (2008), 'The economic consequences of legal origins', *Journal of Economic Literature*, **46** (2), 285–332.
McDonnell B. (2008), 'Two goals for executive compensation reform', *New York Law School Law Review*, **52**, 585–97.

Jurisprudence

Dodge v Ford Motor Co, 170 NW 668 (Mich 1919).
In re Citigroup Inc Shareholder Derivative Litigation, 964 A 2d 106 (Del Ch 2009).
Paramount Communications, Inc v Time, Inc, 571 A.2d 1140 (Del. 1989).
Peoples Department Stores, Inc (Trustee of) v Wise, 2004 SCC 68, [2004] 3 SCR 461.
Revlon, Inc v MacAndrews & Forbes Holdings, Inc, 506 A (2d) 173 (Del 1986).
Unocal Corp v Mesa Petroleum Co, 493 A (2d) 946 (Del 1985), available at http://www.nyls.edu/user_files/1/3/4/30/31/UnocalvMesa.pdf (accessed 21 April 2011).

Legislation and Regulations

Companies Act 2006 (UK), c. 46.
Dodd-Frank Wall Street Reform and Consumer Protection Act (Pub L 111-203, HR 4173).
Joint Stock Companies Act 1844 (UK), (7 & 8 Vict c.110).
NYSE Rules (2010), New York Stock Exchange Listing Rules, *NYSE Listed Company Manual*, section 303A, Corporate Governance Standards, available at http://nysemanual.nyse.com/LCMTools/PlatformViewer.asp?selectednode=chp%5F1%5F4&manual=%2Flcm%2Fsections%2Flcm%2Dsections%2F (accessed 27 May 2011).
SEC Rule 14a-11, 17 CFR §§ 200, 232, 240 and 249 [Release Nos 33-9136; 34-62764; IC-29384; File No S7-10-09] (25 August 2010).

Web Resources

Allen, T. (2010), 'The SEC puts proxy access rule on hold', 4 October 2010, available at http://blog.riskmetrics.com/gov/2010/10/the-sec-puts-proxy-access-on-hold.html (accessed 7 June 2011).
Glen, J. and A. Singh (2004) 'Corporate governance, competition and finance: re-thinking lessons from the Asian crisis', ESRC Centre for Business Research, University of Cambridge Working Paper No. 288, available at http://www.cbr.cam.ac.uk/pdf/wp288.pdf (accessed 16 June 2011).
Organisation for Economic Co-operation and Development (OECD) (2004), *OECD Principles of Corporate Governance,* available at http://www.oecd.org/dataoecd/32/18/31557724.pdf (accessed 17 June 2011).
Ryterbrand, D. (2010), 'Dodd-Frank: what it means for comp and governance', *Business Week*, 16 July 2010, available at http://www.businessweek.com/managing/content/jul2010/ca20100716_567635.htm (accessed 7 June 2011).

PART I

The 'Great Debate'

1. New thinking on 'shareholder primacy'

Lynn A. Stout

INTRODUCTION: THE RISE OF SHAREHOLDER PRIMACY THINKING

Of all the controversies in US corporate law, one has proven most fundamental and enduring. This is, of course, the debate over the proper purpose of the public corporation (Bratton and Wachter 2008, pp. 100–103).[1] Should a public company seek only to maximize the wealth of its shareholders (the so-called 'shareholder primacy' view)? Or should public corporations be run in a manner that considers the interests of other corporate 'stakeholders' as well, including employees, consumers, even the larger society?

The Great Debate, as it has been characterized by two sitting and one former member of the Delaware judiciary (Allen, Jacobs and Strine 2002, p. 1067), dates back at least to the initial emergence of the public corporation as a powerful business form in the early twentieth century.[2] For several decades afterwards, the two sides in the controversy seemed evenly matched. Neither the champions of shareholder primacy, nor the defenders of stakeholder interests, enjoyed the upper hand.

This changed in the 1970s with the rise of the 'Chicago School' of economists. Prominent members of the School argued that economic analysis could reveal the proper goal of corporate governance quite clearly and that goal was to make shareholders as wealthy as possible. Thus Nobel-prize winner Milton Friedman (1970) argued in the pages of the *New York Times* Sunday magazine that because shareholders 'own' the corporation, the only 'social responsibility of business is to increase its profits'. In more-academic writings, Michael Jensen and William Meckling (1976) published their influential paper on the theory of firm, describing shareholders in a corporation as principals who hire corporate officers and directors to act as their agents. According to this thesis, corporate managers' only job was to maximize the wealth of the shareholders (the firm's so-called 'residual claimants') by every means possible short of violating the law.

Directors and officers who pursued any other goal only reduced social wealth by increasing 'agency costs'.

Such arguments appealed to a number of groups for a number of reasons. To legal scholars, the application of economic theory lent an attractive patina of scientific rigor to the shareholder side of the longstanding 'shareholders versus stakeholders' dispute. To the popular press and business media, shareholder primacy offered an easy-to-explain soundbite description of what corporations are and what they are supposed to do. To businesspeople and reformers seeking a way to distinguish between good and bad governance practices, the shareholder-centric view promised a single, easily read measure of corporate performance in the form of share price.

The end result was that the Chicago economists significantly shifted the balance of opinion in the Great Debate. By the 1990s, most scholars and regulators, and even many business practitioners, had come to accept shareholder wealth maximization as the proper goal of corporate governance. Some commentators continued to argue valiantly for a more stakeholder-friendly view of the public corporation, but they were increasingly dismissed as sentimental sandals-wearing leftists whose hearts outweighed their heads. Shareholder primacy became widely viewed as the only intellectually respectable theory of corporate purpose.

My use of the past tense is not inadvertent. This chapter argues that the shareholder primacy view, as conventionally understood, has reached its zenith, and is poised for decline. Traditional shareholder primacy thinking is being rapidly undermined by new developments in economic and corporate theory; by striking changes in business practice; and by a flood of recent empirical studies. In its classic form, the shareholder-centered model of the corporation is on the brink of failure. To survive it will be forced to evolve into a new, more complex and far more subtle understanding of what, exactly, shareholders as a class want from corporations. In the process it will come to resemble its former rival, the stakeholder model, far more closely. Indeed in many cases the two may merge. Although the Great Debate may not be resolved entirely, the distance between the two sides in the debate seems destined to shrink dramatically.

SHAREHOLDER PRIMACY REACHES ITS APOGEE

The high-water mark for traditional shareholder primacy thinking can perhaps be set early in the year 2001, when Professors Henry Hansmann and Reinier Kraakman – leading corporate scholars from Harvard and Yale law school respectively – published an essay entitled 'The end of history for corporate law' (2001). Echoing the title of Francis Fukayama's (1992) book about the overwhelming triumph of capitalist democracy over communism, Hansmann and Kraakman argued that shareholder primacy thinking similarly had triumphed over other theories of corporate purpose. '[A]cademic, business, and governmental elites,' they wrote, shared a consensus 'that ultimate control over the corporation should rest with the shareholder class; the managers of the corporation should be charged with the obligation to manage the corporation in the interests of its shareholders; . . . and the market value of the publicly traded corporation's shares is the principal measure of the shareholders' interests' (Hansmann and Kraakman 2001, pp. 440–41). What's more, Hansmann and Kraakman asserted that this 'standard shareholder-oriented model' not only dominated US discussions of corporate purpose, but conversations abroad as well. In their words, 'the triumph of the shareholder-oriented model of the corporation is now assured' not only in the US, but in the rest of the civilized world (ibid., p. 468).

Hansmann and Kraakman were quite correct in observing that, as a descriptive matter, shareholder primacy thinking dominated academic discussions of corporate law in early 2000, and indeed still dominates many discussions in the media and among business leaders today. There were several ironic aspects, however, to their prediction that this state of affairs would prove permanent. For one thing, it was only a few months later that Enron's collapse provided a dramatic object lesson in the perils of management obsession with share price. But there were more subtle and important ironies in the timing of their announcement.

In particular, even as Hansmann and Kraakman were proclaiming that shareholder primacy had triumphed, three ironic realities of business law, practice and theory were becoming clear. First, it was becoming increasingly obvious to legal experts that US corporate law does not, in fact, follow the shareholder primacy model. Contrary to Hansmann and Kraakman's ideal, the 'shareholder class' does not in any realistic sense retain ultimate control over the public corporation, nor do corporate directors always seem to seek to maximize share price. Second, the corporate world in general, and equity investors in particular, gave every sign of preferring this state of affairs, at least when deciding how to structure new firms. Although the enabling and state-based nature of US corporate law allows corporate promoters a great deal of leeway to select corporate rules that come closer to the shareholder primacy ideal by giving shareholders greater power, in fact promoters generally chose to go in the opposite direction, choosing rules that weakened shareholder authority – and shareholders were enthusiastically endorsing this approach by opening their wallets and buying the promoted shares. Third, and perhaps most striking, it was becoming increasingly obvious from developments in the economic literature that the shareholder primacy model, in its standard form, rested on shaky theoretical foundations. Indeed, it might be incoherent.

The rest of this chapter examines each of these ironies in turn. In the process, it lays the foundation for several important lessons to be learned from the new thinking on shareholder primacy.

THE EMPIRICAL CASE AGAINST SHAREHOLDER PRIMACY

Even as shareholder primacy thinking gained traction among non-experts and in the business media in the 1980s and 1990s, it was becoming increasingly clear to legal specialists that US law did not, and does not, actually follow the 'standard' model. (Hansmann and Kraakman implicitly recognized this in their essay, where they suggested that shareholder primacy thinking would lead to the 'reform' of corporate law (Hansmann and Kraakman 2001, p. 439).) I have discussed this reality of corporate law in detail elsewhere (Blair and Stout 1999; Stout 2002; Stout 2007), as have many others (Allen et al. 2002; Blair 1995; Elhauge 2005), so I will not offer more than a brief survey here. The point is obvious enough. *Corporations are run by boards of directors, not by shareholders.* The US system of corporate governance is more accurately described as 'director primacy' than 'shareholder primacy' (Bainbridge 2006). This does not mean that corporate law does not grant shareholders certain rights. Indeed, they have three: the right to vote, the right to sue, and the right to sell their shares. But these rights are of remarkably little value to shareholders seeking to force managers of a public company to act as their 'agents' and serve only their interests.

Consider first shareholders' voting rights. As a matter of law these are severely limited in scope, principally to the right to elect and remove directors. Shareholders have no right to select the company's CEO; they cannot require the company to pay them a single penny in dividends; they cannot vote to change or preserve the company's line of business; they cannot stop directors from squandering revenues on employee raises, charitable contributions, or executive jets; and they cannot vote to sell the company's assets or the company itself (although they may in some cases vote to veto a sale or merger proposed by the board). The rules of voting procedure further limit exercise of the shareholder franchise. Delaware law, for example, presumes only directors have authority to call a special shareholders' meeting, and shareholders who wait for the regularly scheduled annual meeting to try to elect or remove directors usually must pay to solicit proxies.[3] Finally and perhaps most significantly, in a public firm with widely dispersed share ownership, shareholder activism is a public good, and shareholders' own 'rational apathy' raises an often-insurmountable obstacle to collective action. As Robert Clark has put it, a cynic could easily conclude that shareholder voting in a public company is 'a mere ceremony designed to give a veneer of legitimacy to managerial power' (Clark 1986, p. 95).

What about the shareholders' right to sue corporate officers and directors for breach of fiduciary duty if they fail to maximize shareholder wealth? Here too, shareholders' 'rights' turn out to be illusory. The fiduciary duty of loyalty precludes officers and directors from using their corporate positions to line their own pockets. They remain free, however, to pursue other, non-shareholder-related goals under the comforting mantle of the business judgment rule. As I have pointed out in writings with Margaret Blair, courts consistently permit directors 'to use corporate funds for charitable purposes; to reject business strategies that would increase profits at the expense of the local community; to avoid risky undertakings that would benefit shareholders at creditors' expense; and to fend off a hostile takeover at a premium price in order to protect employees or the community' (Blair and Stout 1999, p. 303). Contrary to the shareholder primacy thesis, shareholders cannot recover against directors or officers for breach of fiduciary duty simply because those directors and officers favor stakeholders' interests over the shareholders' own.

Finally, a shareholder's right to sell her shares sometimes can protect an individual investor who wants to express her unhappiness with a board by 'voting with her feet.' But disappointed shareholders cannot sell en masse without driving down the share price, making selling a Pyrrhic solution. An important exception to this rule arises when shareholders as a group have the opportunity to sell to a single buyer who, because he does not face collective action problems, can depose the incumbent board more readily. During the 1970s and early 1980s, as the Chicago economists' arguments began to gain steam and changes in the banking industry made hostile takeover bids more feasible, it appeared that just such a lively 'market for corporate control' might develop. A series of legal developments, however, soon brought most hostile takeovers to an effective halt. The list is legion, but prominent examples include the passage by almost every state of some form of antitakeover statute; the invention of the 'poison pill' defense by *über*-corporate lawyer Martin Lipton; and the effective reversal of the Delaware Supreme Court's 1986 *Revlon* ruling (which seemed to require boards facing a hostile offer to maximize shareholder wealth) by subsequent opinions issued only a few years later (Stout 2002, pp. 1203–4). Thus by the mid-1990s, US corporate law may have insulated incumbent directors from the pressures of the market for control even more effectively than it did in 1970, when Milton Friedman trumpeted shareholder primacy in the pages of the *New York Times*.

The irony does not stop there. Even as corporate law was stubbornly refusing to follow the dictates of shareholder primacy, common corporate practices were weakening shareholders' power still further in many firms. To understand this point it is important to understand that US corporate law is enabling, meaning that corporate promoters can to a great extent choose the rules that apply to their firms. They can do this in at least two ways. First, they can select a state of incorporation. (Under the 'internal affairs' doctrine, corporations are governed by the rules of the state in which the promoter chooses to incorporate.) Second, they can add customized provisions to the corporate charter that enhance or dilute either directors' or shareholders' power.

For the past two decades, promoters have been taking advantage of the enabling nature of US corporate law to select governance rules that insulate boards from shareholder influence. Studies have found for example, that states that offer directors strong protection against hostile takeovers seem more successful in attracting new incorporations and in retaining existing firms than states whose laws are more 'shareholder friendly' (Stout 2002, p. 1206, note 53). The trend away from shareholder primacy can also be observed when we look at charter provisions. In particular, many firms 'go public' with dual-class voting structures that disenfranchise public shareholders almost entirely. (Google offers one high-profile example (Stout and Anabtawi 2004).) In contrast, charter provisions that make it easier for shareholders to force directors to do their bidding 'are so rare as to be almost nonexistent' (Coates 2001, p. 1397).

Such empirical findings set the stage for the third irony associated with Hansmann and Kraakman's declaration that 'there is no longer any serious competitor to the view that corporate law should . . . strive to increase . . . shareholder value.'[4] Even as Hansmann and Kraakman were observing in their 2000 draft that the 'standard' model had achieved the status of received truth, corporate theorists were busily exploring new and alternative theories of corporate structure and shareholder interest that undermined it.

To use the phrase Thomas Kuhn made famous in his classic 1962 book *The Structure of Scientific Revolutions*, by 2001 the shareholder primacy model had indeed become the 'dominant paradigm' for understanding the purpose of the corporation. But it failed to explain at least two important empirical anomalies. First, the default rules of US corporate law simply refused to treat shareholders as 'owners,' 'principals,' or 'residual claimants.' Unlike owners, shareholders lacked the ability to control how the corporation used its assets and outputs. Unlike principals, shareholders lacked the power to command the board. And unlike residual claimants, shareholders were not entitled to demand to receive even a penny of the corporation's profits, assuming the company had 'profits' in the first place. (Although the point may be obvious, it is perhaps worth reminding readers that profit is an accounting concept that depends on expenses as well as revenues, with the result that the amount of profit earned by a company to a great degree is determined by its board.)

The second anomaly that could not be easily explained by the standard model was that corporate promoters bringing new firms to market often took advantage of the enabling nature of US law to weaken shareholders' already-weak position in the firm even further. This observation was especially puzzling because it suggested that *shareholders themselves* did not object to director primacy. After all, prospective investors who are thinking of buying shares in an initial public offering (IPO) can easily determine the company's state of incorporation and the nature of its charter. If they are troubled by governance structures that dilute shareholder rights, they should discount their willingness to pay accordingly. Corporate promoters cannot pull the wool over shareholders' eyes at the IPO stage. If they structure the firm in a fashion that harms investors, it is the promoters themselves who should pay the price, because they have devalued the very shares they are trying to sell.

As Kuhn famously observed, wherever one finds persistent empirical anomalies inconsistent with a dominant theory's predictions, one eventually finds at least a few free-thinking (or foolhardy) souls who want to understand and explain those anomalies. Eventually these free spirits may develop a new, alternative theory. When they do, the battle begins: many of the intellectual leaders who built their careers on the original paradigm can be expected to fight tooth and nail to kill off the newcomer. But if the new theory is sound – if it does a better job of explaining what we observe in the real world than the old theory does – it will win hearts and minds and ultimately prevail. Of course, the process may be slow. In science, it is said that intellectual progress is made 'one funeral at a time.'

There is reason to hope the pace in corporate theory may be more brisk. Even as Hansmann and Kraakman were announcing the triumph of the shareholder wealth maximization paradigm in 2000, scholars were at work exploring not just one, but several, alternative theoretical models of corporate purpose that could explain director primacy. Indeed in today's literature one can identify at least five recently developed lines of thought that challenge the traditional shareholder primacy paradigm while simultaneously offering to explain the twin anomalies of director primacy in the default rules of US law and promoter preference for even greater director primacy at the IPO stage.

THE THEORETICAL CASE AGAINST SHAREHOLDER PRIMACY: FIVE THEORIES OF DIRECTOR GOVERNANCE

The balance of this chapter is devoted to exploring those five emerging theories of director primacy. Given space constraints I cannot do them justice, and I urge interested readers to consult the primary sources that develop these arguments in detail. But even a cursory glimpse at economic and corporate law scholarship at the turn of the millennium offers a number of important observations.

Market Inefficiency and Director Primacy

Of all the weaknesses of the 'standard' model of shareholder primacy described by Hansmann and Kraakman, one in particular has captured the attention of the business community almost from the beginning of the model's ascendance. This weakness is the standard model's need to assume the stock market is 'fundamental value efficient.'

The literature on market efficiency is enormous. Nevertheless, the basic idea can be easily summarized. In brief, a stock market is deemed 'fundamental value efficient' to the extent the market price of a company's stock incorporates all the information relevant to its value so effectively that the market price reflects the best-possible estimate of the stock's fundamental or intrinsic economic value in terms of its likely future risks and returns. In such a market, there is no need for an investor to stay up late trying to figure out what a particular stock is really worth; an efficient market has already done her valuation homework for her. Nor is there any need to worry about whether today's stock price reflects the firm's long-run value. In a fundamental value market, the long run and the short run merge because there is only one accurate way to measure a stock's future risks and returns: by today's market price.

Even during the 1970s and 1980s – the heyday of efficient market theory and the period during which the shareholder primacy model came to dominate academic thinking about corporate law – many experienced business people believed stock prices often failed to reflect reasonable estimates of fundamental value. (Renowned corporate lawyer Marty Lipton advanced just this argument in an early and famous challenge to shareholder primacy thinking (Lipton 1979).) Since the Crash of 1987 and the bursting of the

1990s internet bubble, doubts have become even more widespread. This is true even among finance theorists, the original inventors of efficient market theory and, once upon a time, its most vocal supporters. Finance economists are now developing ideas and producing empirical studies that challenge the theoretical and empirical validity of efficient market theory, including heterogeneous expectations asset-pricing models; an emerging literature on the limits of arbitrage; and the behavioral finance literature (Stout 2003a).

If, as the growing 'New Finance' literature suggests, stock prices can depart dramatically from rational estimates of fundamental value, the possibility arises that business strategies that raise share prices in the short term can harm firm value and shareholder wealth over the long term. The result is a conflict of interest between short-term investors (for example, hedge funds and mutual funds) and investors who expect to hold shares for longer periods.

One possible solution to the conflict is for both groups to cede control to a board of directors that has the authority to pursue business strategies that preserve long-term value even if they don't produce immediate gains in share price (for example, investing in research and development, or in employee or community relations). This idea supports arguments raised over the years by a variety of governance experts who have suggested that director authority can sometimes benefit shareholders by protecting long-term value, even while the short-term share price languishes (see, for example, Kihlstrom and Wachter 2003; Kraakman 1988; Lipton 1979; Stout 1990).

Capital 'Lock-in' and Director Primacy

Corporations have traditionally been defined as entities with the standard attributes of limited shareholder liability, centralized management, perpetual life and freely transferable shares. In recent years, however, a variety of scholars, including Harold Demsetz, Margaret Blair and Hansmann and Kraakman themselves, have argued that corporate entities are also marked by a fifth essential attribute that Blair dubs capital lock-in (Blair 2003; Demsetz 1995, pp. 50–51 (discussing 'the absence of a repurchase condition') and Hansmann and Kraakman 2000 (discussing 'affirmative asset partitioning')). This phrase captures the notion that equity investors in a corporation, unlike investors in a partnership or proprietorship, lack the ability to unilaterally withdraw their capital from the firm.

Capital lock-in protects equity investors from the risk their fellow investors will want, or need, to withdraw their equity investment, triggering a dissolution or 'fire sale' of the firm. This encourages equity investors to participate in long-term projects that require large amounts of firm-specific assets (for example, a railroad, manufacturing plant or brand name) that cannot be easily liquidated or sold without harming their value. Hansmann and Kraakman (2000) have emphasized that it may also encourage creditors to lend to the firm by similarly protecting their interest in the firm from shareholder demands for a return of capital.

For a variety of reasons, explicit contracts often cannot lock in capital effectively. Incorporation offers an alternative means of achieving lock-in, because the corporate entity becomes the legal 'owner' of the firm's specific assets and control of the firm rests in the hands of a board. Thus lock-in supports the claim that director primacy can serve investor interests *ex ante* even as it weakens investor control *ex post*, by reassuring both creditors and other equity investors they can safely invest in or lend to the firm. In the process, it provides normative support for board decisions that benefit shareholders and creditors alike by protecting the firm's specific assets from *ex post* shareholder attempts to withdraw capital.

Team Production Theory and Director Primacy

Like lock-in theory, team production theory focuses on the economic importance of firm-specific investment (Blair and Stout 1999, p. 253). Team production theory recognizes, however, that equity investors are not the only group whose resources can be converted into firm-specific assets. Employees, for example, may make specific investments by putting in time and effort far beyond the minimum their contracts require, or by developing knowledge, skills and relationships of greater value to the firm than any other potential employer. Customers may invest time and effort becoming familiar with the firm's products. Local communities may build roads, schools and other specialized infrastructure to support the firm's manufacturing plant or headquarters.

It is often in shareholders' *ex ante* interest to encourage such specific stakeholder investments. However, once the investments have been made, shareholders also often stand to profit from opportunistic strategies that threaten to destroy their value (for example, from firing loyal employees, or closing a manufacturing plant originally built with tax breaks). Formal contracts often can provide only limited and inadequate protection against such shareholder opportunism. As an alternative, shareholders might reassure stakeholder investors and encourage their specific investment by ceding control to a board that cannot personally profit (as shareholders can) from business strategies that enhance shareholder wealth by destroying the value of other stakeholders' specific investments. Again, the team production approach supports a director-centric governance structure that serves shareholders' *ex ante* interests by giving boards *ex post* power to favor other constituencies.

Director Primacy and the Universal Shareholder

The standard shareholder primacy model assumes that shareholder wealth is best maximized by strategies that maximize the price of the company's own shares. Very often, however, directors and executives can increase the share price of Firm A by pursuing strategies that impose costs on Firm B. (For example, Oracle might pursue monopolistic acquisitions that allow it to charge its corporate customers higher prices.) Alternatively, they can raise Firm A's share price by harming the value of Firm B's bonds. (Consider Enron's decision to load up on risky energy derivatives, or BP's reported decision to cut safety corners in off-shore drilling.)

Such decisions increase the wealth of the non-diversified shareholders of Firm A. But they may reduce the aggregate wealth of the 'Universal Investor' – the highly diversified pension or mutual fund that owns stocks and bonds in many different firms. Moreover, Universal Investors are often fiduciaries for individual beneficiaries who are themselves customers and employees of firms and who are also biological organisms that depend on their environment. One can question whether such fiduciaries truly serve their individual beneficiaries' interests by supporting business strategies that raise share prices by harming employees or customers, or by creating an unhealthful environment.

Proponents of the Universal Investor idea – most notably, investor activist Bob Monks (2001) and professors James Hawley and Andrew Williams (2000) – have tended to focus on the idea that the best way to get corporations to serve the interests of the Universal Investor rather than the canonical undiversified shareholder is to increase the political power of diversified pension funds and mutual funds. Director-centric governance rules offer an alternative means toward this end, however. This is because directors have no innate interest in favoring the interests of the undiversified shareholder over the interests of the Universal Investor who is also a shareholder. As a result, directors who are free to pursue corporate goals other than maximizing share price are also free to pursue strategies that ultimately benefit the Universal Investor who is also a creditor, a shareholder in other firms, an employee, a customer and an organism dependent on its environment.

Director Primacy and the Concept of the Prosocial Shareholder

To be a Universal Investor, one must still be a shareholder, either directly or through a diversified pension or mutual fund. But what of the interests of employees and customers who do not also hold stock in a particular company? What of community and environmental concerns above and beyond those that affect the health and wealth of the moneyed 'investing class?'

Conventional shareholder primacy theory presumes that investors, Universal or not, care only about themselves. There is a substantial body of evidence from the social sciences, however, including extensive evidence from experiments with human subjects, that documents that most people are more altruistic and 'prosocial' (Stout 2011). Prosocial shareholders might prefer to sacrifice at least some corporate profits in order to benefit (or at least avoid harming) employees, consumers, society, or the environment. Direct evidence for this can be found in the significant and growing investor interest for 'social' investment funds (Williams 1999, p. 1287).

Einer Elhauge (2005) has employed the idea of prosociality as an interesting platform for yet another theory of director governance. This theory recognizes that, just as shareholders face obstacles bringing firms to heel to serve their economic interests, they face obstacles making firms serve their altruistic, prosocial desires. For a host of reasons – including lack of access, lack of time, lack of information and their own rational apathy – shareholders often find it difficult to determine whether and to what extent the corporations that they invest in are reaping profits from socially harmful behavior. Directors stand in a much better position to make such judgments. Also, anonymous shareholders are largely insulated from shaming or other 'social sanctions' that follow corporate misbehavior, where directors are not. The end result is that corporations run by directors who enjoy a range of authority to sacrifice profits in the public interest may end up serving investors' interests – including investors' altruistic, prosocial interests – better than corporations run according to the 'standard model' would.

CONCLUSION: SOME LESSONS FROM THE NEW THINKING

Until recently, it has been commonplace to conceptualize the Great Debate in corporate law as a duel between those who think that directors ought to run corporations only in the interests of shareholders, and those who think boards ought to consider the interests of others in society as well. The first group has been associated with economic theory, and the second with political agendas.

By the turn of the millennium, shareholder primacy thinking shows signs of becoming more subtle. Scholars increasingly argue that, for a variety of economic reasons, shareholders themselves might prefer more stakeholder-friendly director primacy governance rules. Such arguments offer to explain a number of otherwise-puzzling empirical realities of corporate law and practice. In the process, they also offer a number of interesting and potentially useful insights into the proper purpose of the business corporation.

Perhaps the first lesson is that shareholder primacy is no longer the only intellectually respectable game in town. Indeed, shareholder primacy theory suffers from a potentially fatal weakness. As Stephen Bainbridge (2002, p. 3) has pointed out, the chief criterion for any model of the corporation must be the model's ability to predict the separation of ownership and control that is the hallmark of the public firm. The 'standard shareholder-oriented model' described by Hansmann and Kraakman fails this basic criterion (Stout 2003b). In contrast, each of the five theories discussed below can explain the twin anomalies of substantial director autonomy under the default rules of corporate law, and promoter preference for enhancing director power in firms going public.

Second, each of these five models explains these anomalies by suggesting why investors purchasing stock in a public company might *prefer* that company to be governed by a board of directors largely insulated from shareholders' own command and control – not just despite, but in some cases because of, the fact that this makes it more difficult for shareholders to stop the board from pursuing strategies that benefit stakeholders at the expense of share price. In other words, each of the theories suggests that shareholders, like the mythic hero Ulysses, benefit from 'tying their own hands.' In the process they offer insights into such notions as the claim that a business strategy that decreases the share price nevertheless benefits shareholders 'in the long run,' or the idea that action that harms shareholders nevertheless helps 'the firm.' They also illustrate how conventional shareholder primacy thinking rests on a flawed, narrow, cartoonish and ultimately incoherent notion of shareholder 'interest.'

Third, while these theories suggest how director governance of public companies benefits investors as a whole, they also suggest how that director authority can cut against the interests of certain shareholders at certain times. Thus the theories predict – in accord with what we actually observe – that even while investors are happy to purchase shares in director-run public companies *ex ante*, at the IPO stage, certain shareholder groups are equally happy to protest, and even try to overturn, director governance rules *ex post* (Daines and Klausner 2001). Such protests and 'reform' proposals do not serve the interest of investors as a class. They may, however, serve the interests of particular subgroups of investors in particular situations (Anabtawi 2006).

A fourth and related point is that US regulators and policymakers should not reflexively respond to every business crisis or scandal *du jour* by trying to 'reform' corporate law to give shareholders greater power. The assumption often seems to be that anything that gives shareholders greater leverage necessarily serves investors' interests. The new scholarship severs this supposed linkage. While the elimination of staggered boards, shareholder rights to vote on executive compensation, etc. can all attract political support by promising an immediate windfall to certain types of shareholders, there is every reason to suspect such 'shareholder democracy' rules may ultimately work against the interests of the investing class as a whole.

Fifth, this analysis cautions even more strongly against attempts to export the 'standard shareholder-oriented model' abroad. During the 1970s, many experts argued that US corporations could learn from the example of highly successful, stakeholder-friendly German and Japanese firms. With the decline of the Japanese and German economies and the bubble-fueled ascendancy of the US stock market during the 1990s, however, the advice tended to flow the other way. Corporate governance experts trumpeted the success of the 'US model' and counseled other countries to follow the United States' lead by moving their corporate law rules closer to shareholder primacy. A few nations actually heeded this advice, sometimes with disastrous results (Black et al. 2000). The new literature suggests at least two reasons why governance experts who tout the 'US model' abroad may in fact be exporting damaged goods. First, as already noted, the 'standard' shareholder-oriented model does not actually describe US law, and this may be no accident: US law may not follow the 'standard' model because that model does not in fact serve investors' interests in publicly held companies. Second, the US's director-centric governance rules evolved to solve the problems of companies with widely dispersed share ownership, not 'private' companies with controlling shareholders. Accordingly, experts may do other nations whose companies tend to have controlling shareholders a grave disservice by urging them to adopt rules that are not designed for that share ownership pattern.

Finally, by suggesting how director primacy rules ultimately serve public shareholders' interests better than the 'standard' model of shareholder-focused governance would, the five theories of director primacy examined here may go a long way toward resolving the Great Debate. Each of the five theories suggests different and increasingly broad reasons why shareholders might not only want to grant boards the sort of authority that permits them to serve other stakeholders at shareholders' expense, but *actually prefer that boards in fact do this.* Because the five theories provide different accounts of exactly what range of stakeholder interests a firm's shareholders would like directors to consider – creditors? employees?

society as a whole? – the area of dispute that remains in the Great Debate will depend to some extent on exactly how many, and which, theories of director primacy one subscribes to. But to the observer who finds merit in all five – and as I have argued, all five have merit – the Great Debate, if not entirely resolved, is at least diminished in scope and importance.

NOTES

1. Before the emergence of the publicly held company the question of corporate purpose was far less salient. The reason is simple: one can safely assume that a corporation with a controlling shareholder will be managed, for good or for ill, in a fashion that is agreeable to that shareholder. See discussion of the importance of distinguishing publicly-held firms from firms with controlling shareholders, above.
2. In 1932, Adolph A. Berle engaged in a spirited debate in the pages of the *Harvard Law Review* with Harvard Professor E. Merrick Dodd over the proper purpose of the new business entity. According to Berle, 'all powers granted to a corporation or to the management of a corporation . . . [are] at all times exercisable only for the ratable benefit of all the shareholders . . .' (Berle 1932, p. 1049). Dodd disagreed, instead favoring 'a view of the business corporation as an economic institution which has a social service as well as a profit-making function' (Dodd 1932, p. 1148).
3. In 2010 the US Securities Exchange Commission voted to modify this rule to permit shareholders who had held 3 per cent or more of a company's stock for more than three years to access corporate funds to solicit proxies for director candidates (Behan 2010).
4. I have intentionally omitted from this quote two fundamental – indeed arguably capitulating – qualifications that appear in the original article, which reads 'there is no longer any serious competitor to the view that corporate law should *principally* strive to increase *long-term* shareholder value' (Hansmann and Kraakman 2001, p. 439 [emphasis added]). I have left out the qualifiers 'principally' and 'long-term' because the more one tries to rely on them, the more they undermine Hansmann and Kraakman's main thesis as they express it elsewhere: that managers should be directly accountable 'only' (not merely 'principally') to shareholders' interests, and that the 'market value of the publicly traded corporation's shares' – meaning, presumably, today's market value, not yesterday's or tomorrow's – 'is the principal measure of its shareholders' interests' (Hansmann and Kraakman 2001, pp. 440–41). With apologies to Professors Hansmann and Kraakman, I emphasize their more-unqualified expression of the shareholder primacy thesis here because I think it better represents the dominant form of shareholder primacy thinking today, and so offers the best foil for my arguments. I agree, however, with their highly qualified version, as the balance of this chapter attests.

REFERENCES

Allen, W., J. Jacobs and L. Strine, Jr. (2002), 'The great takeover debate: a meditation on bridging the conceptual divide', *University of Chicago Law Review*, **69** (3), 1067–100.

Anabtawi, I. (2006), 'Some skepticism about increasing shareholder power', *UCLA Law Review*, **53** (3), 561–600.

Bainbridge, S. (2002), 'The board of directors as a nexus of contracts', *Iowa Law Review*, **88** (1), 1–33.

Bainbridge, S. (2006), 'Director primacy and shareholder disempowerment', *Harvard Law Review*, **119** (6), 1735–58.
Behan, B. (2010), 'Proxy access: be sure your board is ready', BusinessWeek online, available at http://www.businessweek.com/managing/content/aug2010/ca20100831_192896.htm (accessed 17 February 2011).
Berle, A. (1932), 'Corporate powers as powers in trust', *Harvard Law Review*, **44** (7), 1049–74.
Black, B., R. Kraakman and A. Tarassova (2000), 'Russian privatization and corporate governance: what went wrong', *Stanford Law Review*, **52** (6), 1731–808.
Blair, Margaret (1995), *Ownership and Control*, Washington, DC: Brookings Institution Press.
Blair, M. (2003), 'Locking in capital: what corporate law achieved for business organizers in the nineteenth century', *UCLA Law Review*, **51** (2), 387–455.
Blair, M. and L. Stout (1999), 'A team production theory of corporate law', *Virginia Law Review*, **85** (2), 247–328.
Bratton, W. and M. Wachter (2008), 'Shareholder primacy's corporatist origins: Adolph Berle and the modern corporation', *Journal of Corporation Law*, **34** (1), 99–152.
Clark, Robert C. (1986), *Corporate Law*, New York, NY: Aspen Publishers.
Coates, J. (2001), 'Explaining variation in takeover defenses: blame the lawyers', *California Law Review*, **89** (5), 1301–421.
Daines, R. and M. Klausner (2001), 'Do IPO charters maximize firm value? Antitakeover protections in IPOs', *Journal of Law, Economics and Organization*, **17** (1), 83–120.
Demsetz, Harold (1995), *The Economics of the Business Firm*, Cambridge, UK and New York, NY: Cambridge University Press.
Dodd, E. (1932), 'For whom are our corporate managers trustees?', *Harvard Law Review*, **45** (7), 1145–63.
Elhauge, E. (2005), 'Sacrificing corporate profits in the public interest', *NYU Law Review*, **80** (3), 733–869.
Friedman, M. (1970), 'The social responsibility of business is to increase its profits', *New York Times Sunday Magazine*, 32–3.
Fukayama, Francis (1992), *The End of History and the Last Man*, New York, NY: Free Press.
Hansmann, H. and R. Kraakman (2000), 'The essential role of organizational law', *Yale Law Journal*, **110** (3), 387–440.
Hansmann, H. and R. Kraakman (2001), 'The end of history for corporate law', *Georgetown Law Journal*, **89** (2), 439–68.
Hawley, James P. and Andrew Williams (2000), *The Rise of Fiduciary Capitalism*, Philadelphia, PA: University of Pennsylvania Press.
Jensen, M. and W. Meckling (1976), 'Theory of the firm: managerial behavior, agency costs, and ownership structure', *Journal of Financial Economics* **3** (4), 305–60.
Kihlstrom, R. and M. Wachter (2003), 'Corporate policy and the coherence of Delaware takeover law', *University of Pennsylvania Law Review*, **152** (2), 523–75.
Kraakman, R. (1988), 'Taking discounts seriously: the implications of "discounted" share prices as an acquisition motive', *Columbia Law Review*, **88** (5), 891–941.
Kuhn, Thomas S. (1962), *The Structure of Scientific Revolutions*, Chicago, IL: University of Chicago Press.

Lipton, M. (1979), 'Takeover Bids in the Target's Boardroom', *Business Lawyer*, **35** (1), 101–34.
Monks, Robert A.G. (2001), *The New Global Investors*, Oxford, UK: Capstone Publishing.
Stout, L. (1990), 'Are takeover premiums really premiums? Market price, fair value, and corporate law', *Yale Law Journal*, **99** (6), 1235–96.
Stout, L. (2002), 'Bad and not-so-bad arguments for shareholder primacy', *Southern California Law Review*, **75** (5), 1189–209.
Stout, L. (2003a), 'The mechanisms of market inefficiency: an introduction to the new finance', *Journal of Corporation Law*, **28** (3), 635–69.
Stout, L. (2003b), 'The shareholder as Ulysses: some empirical evidence on why investors in public corporations tolerate board governance', *University of Pennsylvania Law Review*, **152** (2), 667–712.
Stout, L. (2007), 'The mythical benefits of shareholder control', *Virginia Law Review*, **93** (3), 789–809.
Stout, Lynn (2011), *Cultivating Conscience*, Princeton, NJ: Princeton University Press.
Stout, L. and I. Anabtawi (2004), 'Sometimes democracy isn't desirable', *Wall Street Journal*, 10 August 2004, B2.
Williams, C. (1999), 'The securities exchange commission and corporate social transparency', *Harvard Law Review*, **112** (6), 1197–311.

2. Shareholder primacy in corporate law – a response to Professor Stout

Peter Watts

SHAREHOLDER PRIMACY IN CORPORATE LAW

There is one key proposition in Professor Stout's chapter, which is directed to United States law, that I think is true of orthodox company law in the Commonwealth. This is that there is no legally enforceable duty on directors to maximize profits for shareholders. If, therefore, one identifies 'shareholder primacy' with 'profit-maximization', then one might agree with her that the attempt to promote shareholder primacy as a legal norm is both heterodox and unwise.

However, in New Zealand anyway, it is not usual to identify shareholder primacy with profit maximization. Rather the phrase is taken more literally. It imports that it is the interests of shareholders that directors are to pursue, if necessary above those of others. Those interests might embrace things other than short-term profits. In this part of the world, and in some others, the central debate in relation to shareholder primacy is not about profit maximization but about the broader issue of whether directors are legally obliged to have regard to the interests of 'stakeholders' other than shareholders. Although Professor Stout's analysis is directed to the narrow issue of profit maximization, I believe that some aspects of her argumentation do, misguidedly, give credence to the view that directors should be legally obliged to consider the interests of other stakeholders. Hence, in the very first paragraph of her chapter Professor Stout states:

> Of all the controversies in US corporate law, one has proven most fundamental and enduring. This is, of course, the debate over the proper purpose of the public corporation. Should a public company seek only to maximize the wealth of its shareholders (the so-called 'shareholder primacy' view)? Or should public corporations be run in a manner that considers the interests of other corporate 'stakeholders' as well, including employees, consumers, even the larger society?

The two questions found in this paragraph are posited as if they represented a dichotomy from which the law has to choose. In fact, the answer in Commonwealth company law to *both* questions is 'No'. So, as indicated already, the law makes no assumption that profit-maximization at all costs is what shareholders want. If shareholders want that, they have two choices; they can mandate it in the constitution (though laws outside of company law may restrain the profits that can be obtained), or they can band together to vote for directors whose manifesto *is* profit-maximization. Short of that, the courts simply refuse to get involved in judicially reviewing the decisions of directors. It is up to shareholders to hold directors to account if they think directors are falling short, not the courts.

Equally, while there is no *duty* on directors to maximize profit, there is also nothing to prevent them from doing so. Directors commit no actionable wrong if they thumb their noses at other stakeholders and seek short-term gain for shareholders. There is, for example, nothing that says long-term, and not short-term, profits are the legally enforceable endgame of company law.

In my view, Professor Stout is right to have attacked those who have argued that the law dictates profit-maximization, but she has attacked the lesser evil. For there is a whole academic industry out there, the more radical elements of which would attempt, even without legislation, to instil the interests of stakeholders as legally cognizable interests that directors *must* consider, at the peril of judicial review. Not only would that be socialism, but it would be a bad mistake to make the courts the arbiters of business decision taking, even on an 'unreasonableness' standard. These matters are not justiciable, though there are plenty of meddlers, even among the body of shareholders, who would delight in engaging in showcase litigation.

There are a number of other statements in Professor Stout's chapter that could, in other hands anyway, be taken as supporting a stakeholder view of company law. These statements seem to me false, or at least inapplicable, in relation to the generality of Commonwealth company law. So Professor Stout says: 'In its classic form, the shareholder-centered model of the corporation is on the brink of failure.' I regard this as a most misleading statement. The profit-maximization argument was never 'classic', but the shareholder-centered model of the corporation *is*, and it is nowhere near the brink of failure. Classic shareholder primacy does not need to evolve, and there is no call for it to merge with the stakeholder model of company law as the professor suggests in the same paragraph might happen.

Next let me take another two paragraphs (redacted here), which would be objectionable if treated as applicable to New Zealand company law, and for that matter many other Commonwealth jurisdictions:

> *Corporations are run by boards of directors, not by shareholders.* The US system of corporate governance is more accurately described as 'director primacy' than 'shareholder primacy. . .'.
>
> Consider first shareholders' voting rights. As a matter of law these are severely limited in scope, principally to the right to elect and remove directors. Shareholders have no right to select the company's CEO; they cannot require the company to pay them a single penny in dividends; they cannot vote to change or preserve the company's line of business; they cannot stop directors from squandering revenues on employee raises, charitable contributions or executive jets; and they cannot vote to sell the company's assets or the company itself (although they may in limited circumstances vote to veto a sale or merger proposed by the board).

I accept that much of what Professor Stout says in this may be true of the *practice* of corporate governance of larger corporations in the United States, and even in New Zealand and elsewhere in the Commonwealth, but it is certainly not an accurate representation of the *law*, at least in New Zealand, and it is the law to which she speaks, not the practice. Hence, there is nothing in underlying New Zealand company law, nor in the current listing rules of the New Zealand Stock Exchange (New Zealand Stock Exchange Listing Rules 2011), that prevents the following:

- All shareholders voting to appoint themselves directors. There is no upper limit on the number of directors that a company can have in New Zealand law. Stakeholders, in contrast, have no standing at all in appointing directors. And if those shareholders wish qua directors to engage in profit maximization there is nothing in company law that will stop them.
- Shareholders giving themselves the right to select the company's CEO. It would require a constitutional provision, but the content of the constitution is in general the fiefdom of shareholders, not that of directors, let alone stakeholders.
- Shareholders otherwise removing from directorial control the majority, if not all parts, of business decision making. While initially this would require a special resolution, there is nothing in law that prevents a constitutional provision from permitting a bare majority of shareholders to make business decisions for the company. They might become deemed directors by so doing, but we are presently concerned with powers, not duties. It follows that by these means shareholders *can* vote to change or preserve the company's lines of business, they *can* stop directors from squandering revenues on employee raises, charitable contributions and executive jets. They can also vote to sell the company's assets. One of the few exceptions to this is dividend policy, which our statute does reserve to direct-

ors, though even here the concern is the solvency of the corporation not any particular animus against shareholders. Anyway, as I say, shareholders can in law appoint themselves as directors.

It seems to me beside the point that in companies with widely dispersed shareholdings, a more common phenomenon I understand in the US than New Zealand, it is unlikely that there would be sufficient shareholder co-operation to achieve many of the things just listed. The critical question is *can* in law the shareholders do these things? Answer: 'Yes'. Securing the necessary consensus is an issue of practicalities, not law. The fact that shareholders might be less powerful in practice, or indeed even impotent (as to which I am skeptical), provides no mandate whatever for conferring rights on stakeholders. The powerlessness of shareholders, should it exist, creates no vacuum that can legitimately be filled by other stakeholders.

In short, in my view it is impossible to sustain a stakeholder view of New Zealand company law. Shareholder primacy is alive and well. It is not a post-1980s phenomenon, but a nineteenth-century one. It is only profit maximization that is a novice concept. It can safely be rejected, but that should not be done by encouraging a view that shareholder primacy itself is both a relatively new concept and one that has already had its day. It would be a major mistake to juridify the interests of stakeholders. By all means pass specific laws protecting employees and the environment, but let's not permit judges to engage in judicial review of decisions on the basis of a mixed constituency of interests. There has never been judicial review at the behest of *shareholders* (hence the absence of a legal duty to profit-maximize), so why would we contemplate it at the behest of other stakeholders?

There is one final response that needs to be made to Professor Stout's chapter. The chapter says that 'we may do other nations a grave disservice by urging them to adopt rules that give shareholders greater power'. If by this she means that we should not make shareholder involvement in day-to-day decision making *compulsory*, then I agree with her. But a model that gives shareholders the *choice* (that is, the power) to do so is in my view one that could safely be promoted abroad. Most shareholders would choose not to exercise it. The fact is that very many nations already have this model, and many adopted it without encouragement from the US, and indeed they had it long before the US had much global influence. If any trend in US law is to be deprecated, it is the one that is emerging from some state legislatures whereby individual shareholders are deprived of having a free decision as to when and to whom they should sell their shares. This is not to argue that minority shareholders should be protected against a majority that wishes to appoint directors as bargaining agents, but this should be based on shareholder choice, not legislative fiat.

REFERENCE

New Zealand Stock Exchange Listing Rules (2011), available at http://www.nzx.com/market-supervision/rules/nzsx-and-nzdx-listing-rules (accessed 15 June 2011).

3. Derivation of powers of boards of directors in UK companies

Susan Watson

STATUTORY SOURCE OF POWERS OF BOARDS

One of the major characteristics of the corporate form is and always has been the separation of ownership (in shareholders) from control (in boards of directors) (Berle and Means 1932). As Stephen Bainbridge says, 'Corporation statutes effectively separate ownership from control. Indeed this *de jure* separation of ownership and control is one of the chief features distinguishing the corporation from other forms of business organization' (Bainbridge 2009).

The default position in most jurisdictions is that the statute gives powers to the board of directors. In the US (with the exception of Missouri), boards derive their authority from the statute. The *Model Business Corporation Act* states that '[a]ll corporate powers shall be exercised by or under the authority of the board of directors of the corporation, and the business and affairs of the corporation shall be managed by or under the direction, and subject to the oversight, of its board of directors.'[1] The *Delaware General Corporation Law* states that the 'business and affairs of every corporation organized under this chapter shall be managed by or under the direction of the board of directors . . .' (§ 141). Section 128(1) and (2) of the *Companies Act 1993* (NZ) gives the function of the management, or direction or supervision, of the business and affairs of the company to the board of directors, as well as all the powers necessary to perform this function.[2] Similarly, section 198A of the *Corporations Act 2001* (Australia) is a replaceable rule that provides that 'the business of the company is to be managed by or under the direction of the directors' and the 'directors may exercise all the powers of the company except any powers that this Act or the company's constitution (if any) requires the company to exercise in general meeting'.[3]

Manson v Curtis (1918), a decision of the Court of Appeals of New York, contains an important and much cited discussion of the role of a board that derives its powers from a statute:

> In corporate bodies, the powers of the board of directors are, in a very important sense, original and undelegated. The stockholders do not confer, nor can they revoke those powers. They are derivative only in the sense of being received from the state in the act of incorporation. The directors convened as a board are the primary possessors of all the powers which the charter confers, and like private principals they may delegate to agents of their own appointment the performance of any acts which they themselves can perform. The recognition of this principle is absolutely necessary in the affairs of every corporation whose powers are vested in a board of directors. (*Hoyt v Thompson's Executor* 1859, p. 216)

The position remains less straightforward in the United Kingdom. The UK *Companies Act 2006* does not confer the powers to supervise the management of the company on the board of directors. Those incorporating the company must agree on articles of association (bylaws in North American terminology) to be adopted by the company (*Companies Act 2006,* section 18 (UK)). If articles are not registered, model articles are imposed on the company (ibid., section 19). The model but non-mandatory articles for public and private companies provide that: 'Subject to the articles, the directors are responsible for the management of the company's business, for which purpose they may exercise all the powers of the company.'[4] Thus it might appear that the source of the powers of boards in the UK companies is the shareholders through the articles of association. The leading text, *Gower and Davies' Principles of Modern Company Law*, states that: 'It is . . . a point of some theoretical (even ideological) importance: the directors' authority is derived from the shareholders through a process of delegation via the articles and not from a separate and free-standing grant of authority from the State. This helps to underline the shareholder-centred nature of British company law.'[5] The UK legislative approach thus differs from other comparable jurisdictions and, as pointed out by Davies 2008 (pp. 365–6), is at odds with the Financial Reporting Council Combined Code on Corporate Governance (Combined Code 2006).

This chapter questions the significance that should be attached to the fact that UK company boards derive their powers from the articles of association rather than the statute. The fact that the source of the powers of boards in UK companies is the constitution rather than the statute might support an argument that UK companies are akin to incorporated partnerships with the consequence that the directors are the agents of the shareholders. Boards of directors being given management powers might then be viewed as optional, with shareholders having ultimate management control in a company. If directors derived their powers from shareholders, it would seem to follow logically that directors would owe obligations primarily to the shareholders and that shareholders, as principals, would have the power at any time to control directors as their agents by the removal or restriction of those powers. Complete separation of ownership and control would not be possible. Conceptions of corporations that give shareholders ultimate authority would be unassailable in a legal sense.

The chapter attempts to discover the source of the legal idea that directors derive their powers from shareholders. The norm in most jurisdictions is that boards derive their powers from the statute. In those jurisdictions, arguments that the source of the powers of boards of directors is the shareholders and that directors are therefore the legal agents of the shareholders are not sustainable. Even in jurisdictions where the allocation of powers to boards is through a constitution rather than the statute itself, such as the UK, it is argued that the reality is that a board of directors being given management powers and the resulting separation of ownership and control is a core component of company law. The article demonstrates that the allocation of powers to boards through the constitution is most likely an anomaly brought about by the drafters of the original *Joint Stock Companies Act 1856* using as a precedent existing deeds of settlement. Accordingly, it is suggested that no significance at all should be attached to this point of difference in UK company law and no conclusions about the legal relationship between boards and shareholders should be drawn from the allocation of powers being in the constitution rather than the statute.

Despite the focus of the chapter being on the position in the UK, the question of the source of the powers of boards is of relevance elsewhere. It is only relatively recently that jurisdictions such as Australia and New Zealand moved to statutory allocation of powers. If the fact that boards derive their powers from the articles and therefore shareholders is, as Davies (2008) suggests, of fundamental importance, the change in approach in Australia and New Zealand would be significant. But in this chapter it is suggested that whether the powers are allocated in the articles or the statute is of secondary importance; what is truly significant is that a board of directors being given management powers is a core component of corporate law.

An acceptance that boards do not derive their powers from shareholders has wider implications for an understanding of corporate law and of the corporation itself. It calls the basic premises of both shareholder primacy and agency theory into question. Jensen and Meckling (1976) explain agency theory as involving a contract under which one or more persons (the shareholders) engage another person (the directors) to perform some service on their behalf which includes delegating some decision-making authority to the agent. Although agency theory has been refined somewhat from its initial iteration, the underlying assumption is that the source of the powers of directors is the shareholders collectively. Such an understanding sits oddly with the fact that the source of the powers of boards in US corporations has always been statutory for as long as incorporation statutes have existed in the US. A possible explanation may be the influence of UK company law on the principles of US corporate law (P.M. Vasudev 2010, citing Hohfeld 1909). The tendency in the US from the 1880s onward was to describe corporations as aggregations of shareholders with increasing references to and reliance on UK company law. The source of the powers of directors in UK company law therefore becomes of wider significance.

DEVELOPMENT OF UNINCORPORATED JOINT STOCK COMPANIES

The history of joint stock companies, perhaps the most widely acknowledged antecedent of the modern company, is well documented.[6] The reason that joint stock companies came into being was to allow private groups of entrepreneurs and investors to take advantage of the corporate form for private gain. The corporate form had existed for a considerable period of time in the corporation and had a body of law and principle surrounding it, famously summarized by Coke in 1612 in the *Case of Sutton's Hospital* (1612). But until the development of the joint stock company corporations, whether ecclesiastical or lay, were given grants of the privilege of incorporation by the sovereign only for a public purpose. They were 'instituted through a concession by the King to some of his subjects' rather than the corporation being a 'contractually, voluntarily-devised aggregate person' (Harris 2000, p. 18). The 'new idea' that arose in England at about the time of the Elizabethan privateering ventures was using the corporate form for the private gain of the members as a whole (Cooke 1950, p. 55).

From the second half of the sixteenth century on, joint stock companies were ventures given their powers by means of monopoly grants by the sovereign. At least ostensibly these ventures, chartered corporations, continued to have a public purpose (ibid., p. 47). At the same time, the application of the partnership form into general business use and the notion of the business as a separate accounting entity developed. In the eighteenth century the general law of the corporate form continued to be dominated, as Cooke puts it,

> by the concept of the corporation as a public body, an institution created by a specific act of parliament or the Crown for purposes approved as being in the national interest. There is already a body of law governing the life and acts of

> corporations which has its roots deep in the past. But there is also emerging in the eighteenth century a body of law governing the rights and duties which radiate from the joint stock funds of trading corporations. Here the law takes no heed of the reason for the existence of each particular joint stock company. The sole field of conflict in this body of law is the relationships of stock-holder and committee man [director] and the company and its external contractual links. (p. 55)

To the investors of the seventeenth century one of the attractions of the corporate form, as opposed to the partnership, must have been that the management control of the company would be allocated to the board, and the stock-holders (of which there were sometimes hundreds or even thousands) would share in the profits. Separation of ownership and control was from the earliest period a key aspect of the corporate form. In his seminal text, Davis (1905) outlined the phenomenon of corporate shrinkage, where power tended to become focused in such a governing group.[7] Gevurtz (2005) tracks a history of boards running parallel with the history of corporations. The vesting of control in a board or equivalent has been a defining characteristic of corporations since their inception.

The development of common law principles of joint stock company law was diverted in the early part of the eighteenth century by the passage of the *Bubble Act* in 1720, which prohibited the formation of new joint stock companies without legislative charters. Incorporation could only legally be achieved by charters granted by the Crown or by private Acts of Parliament, which became difficult to obtain (Du Bois 1938, p. 15). But the development of company law did not cease because of the passage of the *Bubble Act*. Legal ingenuity led to the devising of an unincorporated form; the deed of settlement joint stock companies linked to the two equitable forms of group association – the partnership and the trust. Such companies thus came within the bounds of the equitable jurisdiction. Despite the prohibition of the *Bubble Act*, corporations were created 'without troubling King or Parliament, though perhaps we said we were doing nothing of the kind' (Maitland (1911), cited in Cooke 1950, p. 283).

In the deed of settlement, mutual covenants were signed between the shareholders as partners and the trustees selected by them. The trustees covenanted to observe all the terms of the deed and to apply the funds settled on them for the specified purposes (Cooke 1950, p. 88). The office of director was a separate office from the office of trustee with the first directors appointed in the deed of settlement and granted their powers in the deed. A typical deed of settlement made it clear that the board of directors had responsibility for the 'entire management and superintendence over the affairs and concerns of the company' with the obligation to act in conformity with the laws and regulations in the deed of settlement.[8]

Adam Smith described joint stock companies as 'always managed by a court of directors' (Smith [1776] 1789, vol. 3, p. 123). Whereas previously the source of powers of the joint stock company had been the grant of the charter by the Crown, the source of powers of the directors was the deed signed by all the 'partners'.

The deed of settlement joint stock company form was upheld by the Chancery courts as a form of corporation, with a body of law developing around the form and with the form being widely adopted for the conduct of business. Rather than the *Bubble Act* leading to a halt in the development of UK company law, it is becoming more widely accepted that the exigencies of the restrictions in the *Bubble Act* in fact forced the development of an alternative to the partnership and the chartered corporation that was available to all rather than being a privilege granted by the state to a few. Despite Lord Eldon in *Kinder v Taylor* (1825) stating that acting as a corporation without being one was illegal at common law, the unincorporated form flourished.

There were limitations to the form. Even after the repeal of the *Bubble Act* in 1825, at common law these unincorporated joint stock companies were treated as partnerships, with the directors on the board being regarded as the agents of the shareholders, with the source of the powers of the board being treated as the shareholders, and with the shareholders having overriding authority over the board. But these companies were not true partnerships. As Cooke (1950) describes them, '[i]n the large unincorporated company, the shareholders were not partners in the sense that they could bind each other, nor were they partners in the sense that they combined the ownership of capital with its direction and management' (p. 95). The clear expectation in deed of settlement joint stock companies, and indeed a reason for choosing to adopt this form, continued to be that management control would reside with the directors. Shareholders were excluded from management. A typical clause in a deed of settlement vested management power in the directors of the company.[9] The corollary of this allocation of management control to the board, and the reason it was desirable for stockholders that this allocation of power to boards take place, was that stock-holders would only be liable to pay their share of the joint stock. Indeed the provision that distinguished an unincorporated company from a partnership was the provision in a deed of settlement that each shareholder was liable only to the extent of his own share in the capital stock. Also, those setting up the companies, the promoters, who were often also the first directors, had no desire to cede management control to investing shareholders.

In *Burnes v Pennell* (1849), the House of Lords, considering a deed of settlement unincorporated joint stock company, opined:

> [O]n the principle which regulates the liability of common parties, a distinction must be made between a member of a common mercantile partnership and a shareholder in a joint stock company. No one will contend that a joint stock company would be liable on a bill of exchange, drawn, accepted, or indorsed by any one shareholder. Why? Because it is known that the power of carrying on the business of the company, and of drawing, accepting, and indorsing bills of exchange, is vested exclusively in the directors. This shews that, although a joint stock company is a partnership, it is a partnership of a different description and attended with different incidents and liabilities from a partnership constituted between a few individuals who carry on business jointly, with equal powers and without transferable shares. All who have dealings with a joint stock company know that the authority to manage the business is conferred upon the directors, and that a shareholder, as such, has no power to contract for the company. For this purpose, it is wholly immaterial whether the company is incorporated or unincorporated. (p. 521)

So in summary, owing to the *Bubble Act*, deed of settlement joint stock companies were not incorporated and were not recognized at common law. As Farrar (2008) points out, '[t]he deed of settlement company was built on a foundation of trust and partnership and was at best an inchoate corporation' (p. 9). Certainly the purpose in creating a deed of settlement joint stock company was to attempt to create a corporation by conferring management powers on the board. No legitimizing statute existed so this had to be done in the deed of settlement document itself. The allocation of management power to the board was recognized in the Chancery courts, and the unincorporated joint stock company was a widely accepted business form.

Once incorporation by registration became possible, the attempts to allocate management power to boards in deeds of settlement were legalized and legitimized by registration of existing unincorporated joint stock companies pursuant to the statute. The next section examines the early companies statutes that permitted incorporation by registration.

INCORPORATION BY REGISTRATION STATUTES

The context of the enactment of the *Joint Stock Companies Act 1844* (UK), the first Companies Act allowing incorporation by registration, was one where companies and those who operated them were viewed with suspicion. William Gladstone, that towering figure of the Victorian age, was brought in to head a select committee on joint stock companies that was established to identify measures to prevent fraud. The subsequent Gladstone Committee Report catalogued the various modes of deception adopted by unincorporated companies and argued for government legislation to tackle such practices. It was considered that only a limited number of enterprises, such as banking, insurance, canals and water supply that required large amounts of capital, high risk and long amortization periods, were suited to the corporate form (McQueen 2009, pp. 43–4). The principle of incorporation as of right if certain requirements were met was nevertheless enshrined in the 1844 statute. Hurdles such as minimum capitalization requirements, a two-stage registration process, publicity requirements and enforcement difficulties, however, meant that 76 per cent of companies were abandoned before completing registration in the period between 1844 and 1856. The legislation was regarded as harsh and restrictive (ibid., pp. 49–51).

How very different the legislative environment ten years later with the shift from the early Victorian period to the more optimistic and expansionary mid-Victorian period. In 1850 a Select Committee on Investments for the Savings of the Middle and Working Classes had argued that the benefits of investing in companies would be acceptable to 'Middle and Working Classes, and would tend to satisfy them that they are not excluded from fair competition by laws throwing obstacles in the way of men with small capitals' (Select Committee 1850, p. iv). Despite a Royal Commission established to consider limited liability coming out six for/two against limited liability, the *Limited Liability Act* was pushed through Parliament in 1855. The *Joint Stock Companies Act*, eventually passed in 1856, was introduced by the Vice-President of the Board of Trade, Robert Lowe, who was described recently as the 'father of modern company law' (Micklethwait and Wooldridge 2003, p. 51). Lowe was a trenchant opponent of the trade unions – he favored the progress of the working man being through investment in companies.

Lowe was somewhat scornful of the existing *Joint Stock Companies Act 1844*, describing Gladstone's committee as appearing to

> have conducted its deliberations in a state of mental perturbation . . . for when I look at their Report, I find the headings of the different sections of what one would generally expect to be a very demure and quiet sort of document running thus: – 'Form and Destination of the Plunder', 'Circumstances of the Victims', 'Impunity of the Offenders', and the like; so that a hurried glance at the contents might make a man fancy he was reading a novel instead of a blue Book.[10]

In Lowe's view, such suspicion of corporate form was not necessary: 'Fraudulent people will never form a limited liability company,' he stated confidently.[11]

The internal management rules of the modern companies incorporated by registration pursuant to the 1856 Act were not set out in the statute itself but rather in the articles of association appended to the statute. These rules included the clause empowering boards.

Other models for provisions empowering boards existed and could have been adopted. Separation of ownership and control was mandated in the 1844 Act, with section 27 of the statute granting management powers to the board and making it clear that shareholders could not take part in the management of companies 'otherwise than by means of directors'. No standard form articles of association were included in that statute; rather the rule on directors' powers was included in the statute.

The *Companies Clauses Consolidation Act 1845* brought together a model set of rules applicable to public utility companies created by statute. Section 90 of the *Act* made the exercise of management powers by the board of directors subject to the power of shareholders in general meeting. Not only could shareholders alter or remove the powers of management of the board in the constitution, shareholders could in general meeting over-ride decisions by the board. The exact wording of the section was:

> The directors shall have the management and superintendence of the affairs of the company, and they may lawfully exercise all the powers of the company, except as to such matters as are directed by this or the special Act to be transacted by a general meeting of the company; but all the powers so to be exercised shall be exercised in accordance with and subject to the provisions of this and the special Act; and *the exercise of all such powers shall be subject also to the control and regulation of any general meeting specially convened for the purpose,* but not so as to render invalid any act done by the directors prior to any resolution passed by such general meeting. (emphasis added)

Wordsworth, on joint stock companies (1851), refers to the general rule in relation to statutory corporations being that directors were subject to the powers of the shareholders exercised in general meeting. This continued to be the position for statutory corporations and for those registered under the *Companies Clauses Consolidation Act 1845* (ibid., p. 1185).

A provision equivalent in wording to section 90 of the *Companies Clauses Consolidation Act* was not included in the *Joint Stock Companies Act 1856* or the *Companies Act 1862* or in Table B of the 1856 Act or Table A of the 1862 Act. This non-inclusion permits at least an inference to be drawn that, with the new corporate form created by registration, the default position was intended to be that directors would have the power to manage. But a section equivalent to section 27 of the *Joint Stock Companies Act 1844* bestowing management powers on the board was not included in the statute itself. Rather, it was inserted in the non-mandatory articles of association.

The central question therefore remains the significance that should be attached to the allocation of management powers to directors in the non-mandatory articles of association rather than in the statute itself in the 1856 and 1862 Acts. The issue is not one of merely historical interest. Powers are still allocated to boards in the articles of association rather than the statute in the UK *Companies Act 2006*, marking the point of some theoretical (even ideological) importance in UK company law highlighted in Gower (Davies 2008, p. 366).

Certainly, an acceptance that the allocation of powers occurs in the non-mandatory articles rather than the statute means that the legislative intention is that boards derive their powers from shareholders. This would support a shareholder primacy model of company law. It could be assumed that the intention of the legislature was that shareholders would have both the right and power to remove through the constitution some or all of the powers of the board. Conceptualized in this way, incorporated companies would be seen to resemble unincorporated deed of settlement joint stock companies at common law. There, as we have seen, the shareholders were partners and the directors were the agents of the shareholders. At common law, therefore, the directors were subject to the instructions of the shareholders as principal. The shareholders were also the source of the powers of the directors. Contrast this with the position at equity where it was accepted that unincorporated deed of settlement companies were a form of corporation with directors deriving their powers from the deed of settlement itself. In other words, were registered companies to be treated as akin to incorporated partnerships or as corporations? Two completely different conceptions of the company underpin the common law and the equitable form – which form prevailed for companies formed by registration under an enabling statute has important consequences for our understanding of the modern corporate form.

Little external guidance about the intention of the architects of the 1856 and 1862 Acts exists. A commentator of the time, discussing the *Joint Stock Companies Act 1856* in the *Law Quarterly Review*, said 'Our legislature . . . delivered itself on the Companies Acts in its usual oracular style, leaving the Courts the interpretation of its mystical utterances' (cited in Farrar 1998, p. 146). The debate over the 1855 and 1856 Acts recorded in Hansard was extensive but mostly did not extend beyond the discussions about the merits of incorporation by registration to discussion in any depth about the nature of the new legal form.

The incorporation statutes could be viewed as a statutory adoption of the deed of settlement form. The existing deed of settlement companies were widely recognized by the Chancery courts and more significantly by business as a form of corporation. Lord Eldon's statements in *Kinder v Taylor* (1825) questioning the legitimacy of the unincorporated form were widely derided by business commentators of the day. Lowe and others, fiercely pro-business, were fully aware of this criticism (see Sealy 1996, pp. 11–13). In fact the driving motivation behind the legislation was legitimizing the limited liability company.

It is clear that, unlike the 1844 Act, the 1856 Act was not intended to restrict incorporations but rather to encourage them. All that was required to form a company pursuant to the *Joint Stock Companies Act 1856* or the subsequent *Companies Act 1862* was seven or more persons associating together and subscribing to a memorandum of association, a name and a registered office. In the same way as currently in the US, competition between states for incorporations and potential corporate mobility determines to some extent the content of corporate legislation; it was considered that other jurisdictions such as France, with the *commandite* form, were winning the battle to attract capital into trade (McQueen, pp. 43–4). Legislators of the day obviously knew that a simple procedure for incorporation by registration would encourage the investment of capital using this legal form. The driving purpose behind the legislation was to make incorporation by registration as simple as possible. The purpose of incorporation for many enterprises was to raise capital. Shareholders were expected to provide that capital.

At least at the outset it was intended that shareholders would have a more extensive monitoring role than subsequently eventuated. But that does not mean it was contemplated that companies would operate like partnerships to the extent that they would not have boards of directors, even though the non-mandatory nature of the articles of association made this theoretically possible. No evidence exists of shareholders altering articles of association to remove the management powers of boards.[12] It is suggested that such removal would have been seen to negate the purpose of incorporation. Even though Lowe regarded incorporated companies as akin to 'little republics' rather than partnerships, the mechanisms that were intended to operate to constrain management abuses were constitutional – through the general meeting and through disclosure of information by management to shareholders rather than through informal action by a few controlling shareholders (McQueen, p. 43). It was possible to form a company with seven incorporators but it was always intended that the corporate form would be used as a mechanism to raise capital from multiple investor-shareholders. Small closely held private companies were not envisaged (Harris 2000).

It was only in the latter part of the nineteenth century that the private company developed and convergence of ownership and control took place. Various editions of texts by Francis Beaufort Palmer, including one with a set of precedents that modified Table A, and one entitled *Private Companies, or How to Convert Your Business into a Private Company, and the Benefit of So Doing*, contributed to and perhaps even caused the adoption of the corporate form for small businesses. As Palmer (1881) himself pointed out, not immodestly but probably accurately:

> During the last ten years the conversion, under the Companies Act, 1862, of business concerns into private companies, i.e., companies started without any appeal to the public for capital, has made extensive progress, and, as the writer has good reason to know, in a very large number of cases the conversion has made extensive progress, and, as the writer has good reason to know, in a very large number of cases the conversion has resulted from a perusal of this little book. (ibid., preface to the tenth edition)

Palmer (1881) also said that all companies registered under the *Companies Act 1862* were in contemplation of law public companies; that is, companies intended to be carried on with capital obtained from the public (ibid., p. 1). The use of the private company was novel not just within the UK but internationally. It was not contemplated by the legislature in 1862. The fact that articles of association could be amended, and thus permitted the creation of the private company, was a happy (or some might say, not so happy) chance. The 1862 legislation showed an intention that companies would have boards with management powers. Enabling incorporation by registration was a legitimization of the equitable form of the corporation; in a legislative environment which preferred to facilitate rather than prevent incorporation, the statute would have had no purpose otherwise.

It is suggested that the clause empowering boards was included in the articles of association rather than the statute simply because the articles of association were an adoption by the legislature of the drafting method used in the deed of settlement form, developed and refined over the period when incorporation was generally not possible. The empowering clause had been included in deeds of settlement simply because no incorporation statute existed and this practice was continued by the legislature with the articles of association.

The default articles in Table B of the *Joint Stock Companies Act 1856* (later Table A in the *Companies Act 1862*) were in content direct descendants of the deeds of settlement drafted by lawyers in the eighteenth century (Cooke 1950, p. 88). The form of words used to empower the board or equivalent were remarkably similar and consistent. Article 46 of Table B of the *Joint Stock Companies Act 1856* read: 'The Business of the Company shall be managed by the Directors, who may exercise all such Powers of the Company as are not by this Act, or by the Articles of Association, if any, declared to be exercisable by the Company in General Meeting . . .'. Article 55 of Table A of the *Companies Act 1862* was almost identical. A typical clause in a deed of settlement, the Deed of Settlement of the Nottingham and Nottinghamshire Banking Company (1834), reads as follows:

> That the business, affairs, and concerns of the Company shall, from time to time, and at all times, be under the control of five Shareholders (as Directors), who shall have the entire ordering, managing and conducting of the Company, and of the capital, stock, estate, revenue, effects, affairs, and other concerns thereof;

The clauses in deeds of settlement were drafted to be as similar as possible to the clause empowering boards in the charters that had been granted earlier. For example, in The Charter of the Company of Clothworkers of London (1648) the empowering clause stated that: 'The Freemen . . . may chuse and make themselves three Wardens to support the business of the same Mistery or Art, and Comminalty and Fraternity or Gild aforesaid, to oversee, Rule and Governe the Mistery or Art and Comminality aforesaid.' The Charter of the Corporation of the Amicable Society for a Perpetual Assurance-Office (1710) stated: 'And it shall and may be lawful to and for the Directors of the said Amicable Society, or the major Part of them, from time to time assembled in Court as aforesaid, to order, manage and direct the Affairs and Business of the said Corporation, . . .'.

Where did the idea of articles of association come from? The answer to this question may lie across the Atlantic. In some US charters of the period, the clause empowering directors was included in the bylaws rather than in the statutory instrument itself. For example, Article 2 of the Bylaws of the Maine Atlantic Granite Company (1836) stated that: 'The business of the Company shall be conducted by seven Directors who shall be annually elected by the Stockholders.'[13] The fact that for a period some boards obtained their powers from the bylaws rather than the statutory instrument was clearly not considered to be significant in the US. In almost all US States, statutes provide that a corporation shall be managed by or under the direction of its board of directors (Gevurtz 2005, p. 92), and this model is the norm in most other jurisdictions as well.[14] In numerous decisions it has been made clear that the power of management control is original and un-delegated and derived directly from the Act itself.[15]

CONCLUSION

Prior to its latest statutory incarnation as the *Companies Act 1993*, New Zealand, in common with other former English colonies, had Companies Acts that were based on the UK Companies Acts of the period. In those Acts powers were conferred on the board of directors through the articles of association of the company.[16] In its report on company law reform leading up to the enactment of the *Companies Act 1993*, the New Zealand Law Commission commented that section 34 of the *Companies Act 1955*

(NZ), which stated that the memorandum and articles of association bound the company and the members as if it were a deed, was enigmatic:

> As the statutory platform for identification of allocation of responsibility and duties within the company, it is entirely unsatisfactory . . . It creates the fiction of a contractual regime which is then overlaid by statutory provisions which impose obligations and powers outside the 'contract', including the power to alter the contract without the consent of all. (NZ Law Commission 1989, paragraph 155)

Pointing out that the section was descended from the *Joint Stock Companies Act 1856*, the Law Commission further commented that the section marked the transition between the old deed of settlement constitution and the statutory constitution and that it was an anachronism. The Law Commission recommended that the current Table A standard provision found in the schedule to the *Companies Act 1955* should be adopted as a statutory presumption. 'Director management would therefore be conferred by statute directly, except where the constitution makes express provision for another arrangement' (ibid., paragraph 156).

The conferring of powers on boards through the articles of association rather than by means of the statutory instrument remains the position in the UK today. It originated in the *Joint Stock Companies Act 1856*. Certainly the source of the powers of boards was original and undelegated in other earlier forms of the corporation. Prior to the *Joint Stock Companies Act 1856*, boards of corporations derived their powers from the statutory instrument or equivalent. Corporations created by charter have existed in the UK at least since medieval times. The source of the powers of chartered corporations was the Crown through the charter.[17] Statutory power bestowed on boards was one of the incidences of incorporation given to companies by registration under the *Joint Stock Companies Act 1844*, the earliest UK Act permitting incorporation by registration. Section 27 of the 1844 Act, noted earlier, stated that the directors would have the powers to 'conduct and manage the affairs of the company'. Shareholders could not take part in the management of companies 'otherwise than by means of directors'.

In the *Joint Stock Companies Act 1856*, no power of management control was bestowed on the board by the Act nor was there a requirement that directors be appointed. Table B in the Schedule to the 1856 Act, and subsequently Table A in the Schedule to the 1862 *Companies Act*, contained articles of association that bestowed management powers on directors. But the adoption of the Tables in the forms set out in the Acts was not mandatory.[18] Section 14 of the *Companies Act 1862* stated that all or any of the provisions included in Table A could be adopted but that subscribers to the memorandum of association could prescribe such regulations for the company as deemed expedient. It was thus theoretically possible to register a company under the *Joint Stock Companies Act 1856* or the subsequent *Companies Act 1862* without a board of directors or without those directors having the power to manage the company.

This chapter suggests that the original conferment of powers through the articles of association may not have been due to a philosophical policy-driven desire to ensure that boards derive their powers from shareholders rather than the state. Rather, this was brought about by the adoption of the pre-existing deed of settlement form as a precedent for the articles of association introduced under the statute. Accordingly, minimal or no significance should be attached to the source of the powers of boards in UK companies.

Works that focus on historical material risk getting a 'so what' reaction. The analysis presented here might be regarded as being of historical interest with its relevance to current law and practice questioned. But the source of the powers of UK companies remains unchanged from 1856; powers are still allocated in the articles of association. In some jurisdictions, particularly the US, powers have been statutorily allocated for a long time. In other jurisdictions, such as Australia and New Zealand, allocation of management powers to boards is now statutory. Increasingly the UK stands alone. The difference is described in Davies and Gower as a point of some theoretical (even ideological) importance and the authors derive principle from the apparent allocation by shareholders (Davies 2008, p. 366). Shareholders in an agency theory sense are thus perceived to be in a somewhat special position compared with other stakeholders such a debt investors or employees. In short, the apparent source of the powers of boards can be used as a plank in an argument for shareholder primacy.

The notion that in a conceptual sense the corporate structure allows shareholders to exercise ultimate authority in a company is seen as a constraint on the powers of boards of directors of UK companies. The statement in a 1909 text on investment cited by Brian Cheffins is typical: 'The shareholder, therefore, although he surrenders the control of his capital to his directors, is still in a position to exercise a very effective control over his directors . . .' (Lowenfeld 1908, cited in Cheffins 2008, p. 30). In jurisdictions where the source of the powers of boards is statutory such arguments are no longer sustainable. In fact, this chapter suggests these arguments never were sustainable and that the difference for UK companies is more illusory than real. The default position in all jurisdictions is that power is allocated to the board of directors, either through the statute or the articles of association.[19] Statutory provisions allowing shareholders to reduce or remove the powers of boards through the constitution of the company exist in most jurisdictions, except the UK where a clause will be found in the articles of association. The logical enquiry therefore becomes the extent to which the powers of boards are in fact restricted. Unless evidence can be produced that shows that the practice in the UK has been to restrict the powers of boards to a greater extent than in comparable jurisdictions where board powers are statutorily allocated, the difference is of little or no practical significance.

The inclusion in the model articles of association for public and private companies of a clause allowing shareholders to make management decisions is of more practical significance. Clause 4 of the model articles for both private and public companies states that the shareholders may, by special resolution, direct the directors to take, or refrain from taking, specified action. Article 70 of Table A of the UK *Companies Act 1985* stated that the powers of the board were subject to any directions given by special resolution. Such a clause, if widely adopted in the articles of association of public companies, would merge ownership with control and entrench shareholder primacy in a manner not yet achieved. Such an entity, with its board powers neutered, would be closer in form to an incorporated partnership than a corporation. The previous incarnation of the clause was however rarely adopted by public companies – a position unlikely to change (Pennington 2001, p. 699).

Of more significance is the decision by the UK legislature to in essence codify the duties of directors in the *Companies Act 2006*. This codification, like the statutory statement of powers in other jurisdictions such as Australia and New Zealand, and in the *Model Business Corporations Act* in the US, confirms the statutory basis of the modern UK company.

An acceptance that the powers of boards of directors are original and un-delegated in the UK as well as in other jurisdictions has several consequences. First, the acceptance negates, at least to some extent, shareholder primacy conceptions of the company. Shareholder primacy is given some weight by an underlying assumption that, in a legal sense, directors as managers are agents of the shareholders as owners and that they derive their powers from shareholders. That assumption has several legal consequences. First, it is expected that shareholders as 'principals' can control management – in fact it may be their obligation to do so. If shareholders do not control management it may be because they are not trying hard enough. The solution is considered to be mechanisms that boost the powers of shareholders. Secondly, at least in jurisdictions dominated by UK company law, it is believed that powers of directors to manage the company are derived from the shareholders. Finally, and perhaps most significantly, it is difficult to see a significant role for a board of directors distinct from other managers if in fact directors are no more than agents of shareholders. Directors have either fiduciary or fiduciary-law derived statutory obligations to the company, conceived in an agency framework as the shareholders collectively. But fiduciary obligations are owed by agents to their principals. If in fact directors are the agents of the shareholders, then there seems to be little point or need to distinguish the obligations of directors from other corporate agents.

An acceptance that directors are not in fact legal agents of the shareholders but perform a distinct role separate from management as part of the board of directors calls into question the role of the board of directors. If shareholders do not in fact control management, then it becomes the role of boards to monitor and control management. The extent to which they are willing or able to exercise control over management may be compromised by the dual role of executive directors as corporate managers and directors, and by the lack of truly independent non-executive directors. The 'blow out' in executive remuneration may be a reflection of the actual inability of shareholders to control management excess and the unwillingness or inability of boards of executive and non-executive directors to control management excess and to act as guardians for the interests of the company broadly conceived. If boards are unable or unwilling to so act, alternatives such as supervisory boards found in Germany or independent auditors might be considered. What is clear is that the structure of corporations has evolved to a point where, like charters, total control is given to the governing group, the board of directors.

In many ways, Robert Lowe, the architect of the *Joint Stock Companies Act 1856*, the antecedent of the UK *Companies Act 2006,* was a visionary. Stripping away the florid mid-Victorian language, his idea of registered companies as 'little republics' where 'men of little capital' could invest and participate in the fruits of the enterprise was admirable. But the idea that those investors could control those who controlled the funds, the board of directors, proved to be flawed (McQueen 2009). Allocation of management powers to boards of directors is a core component of company law. It is of no actual significance whether that allocation is in the constitution or statute. With control comes power. Pretending otherwise is failing to understand exactly what a modern company is.

NOTES

1. *Model Bus Corp Act* Ann § 8.01. This power is subject to any limitations in the articles of incorporation or a shareholders' agreement of a close corporation pursuant to § 7.32.
2. *Companies Act 1993* (NZ), section 128(3). These default rules are subject to the provisions in the constitution of the company.
3. In the *Uniform Companies Act 1961* (Commonwealth) (Australia), which was based on

the *Companies Act 1948* (UK), the provision empowering the board was found in the articles of association (Schedule 4, Table A, regulation 73). Subsequently the empowering regulation was found in regulation 66 of the *Corporations Act 2001*.

4. Model articles for public companies, article 3; Model articles for private companies limited by shares, article 3.
5. Davies 2008, p. 366. See also Pennington 2001, p. 696 ('Unlike American law and the laws of most European countries, English law does not regard certain functions and powers as managerial or executive and therefore as inherently exercisable by the board and inalienable by it.'), and Cheffins (2008) ('UK company law, in contrast, has never dictated who will have managerial authority in a company or the method by which managers are selected. This has instead been left to the internal governance rules of companies, most typically the articles of association, the contents of which the shareholders determine.')
6. See generally Davies (1997) and also earlier editions of Gower's commentary on company law. Sadly the history was omitted from the seventh edition of Gower. See also C.A. Cooke (1950) and A.B. Du Bois (1938).
7. 'In the political, eleemosynary, educational and religious corporations, the process is almost complete; what is regarded as the corporation, both in law and in popular estimation, is the governing body, the council, board of trustees or board of managers' (Davis 1905, vol. 2, p. 277).
8. The excerpt is from a clause in the deed of settlement for the London Ale Brewing Company found in the appendix to J. Collyer (1832), p. 731.
9. A typical example is found in the deed of settlement of the Halifax Joint Stock Banking Company dated 1831. It states, 'That the entire management of the business, concerns and affairs of the Company shall be, and is hereby vested, and reposed in the several persons, parties, hereto of the first part, as the first Directors of the Company, and in all future Directors, to be nominated at the times and in manner hereinafter expressed; and the present and all future Directors shall have the sole and exclusive control, management, and disposal of the Capital Stock, funds, estate property, revenue, affairs and concerns of this Company; and shall and may regulate and determine the mode and means of carrying on and transacting the business of the said Company, and all other matters and things whatsoever connected with or relating to the business and affairs of this Company.'
10. UK, HC, *Parliamentary Debates* (Hansard), 3d ser, vol. 139, col. 110 (7 February 1856) (Robert Lowe).
11. Ibid.
12. It is unlikely however that many companies were registered without directors. Palmer's *Company Precedents*, which was widely utilized in the nineteenth century, does not recommend the exclusion of articles relating to the appointment and proceedings of directors (Palmer 1881).
13. See also the charter and bylaws of The Great Western Iron Company (1836, State of Pennsylvania). Article V states that 'The affairs of the said corporation shall be managed by directors, to be chosen annually from the stockholders.' The practice of including the clause empowering directors in the articles rather than the charter was by no means universal. In a number of charters of the period, it was included in the charter itself.
14. Germany is an exception with a dual board structure. A supervisory board appoints and oversees a managing board that operates the company.
15. In Canada, see *Peoples Department Stores, Inc v Wise* (2004). The Supreme Court of Canada pointed out: 'For the directors of [Canada Business Corporations Act] corporations, this power originates in s 102 of the Act' (Paragraph 34).
16. The New Zealand *Companies Act 1955* was based on the *Companies Act 1948* (UK). Article 80 of Table A of the Third Schedule to the New Zealand *Companies Act 1955* gave authority to the directors.
17. For example, the provision from the Charter of the Company of Clothworkers of

London (1648) stated that the overseeing wardens would 'oversee, rule and governe the mistery or art and comminality aforesaid'. The Charter of the Corporation of the Amicable Society for a Perpetual Assurance-Office (1710) states that the Court of Directors are 'to order, manage and direct the Affairs and Business of the said Corporation'.

18. *Joint Stock Companies Act 1856*, Table B, Article 44, 'The Number of the Directors and the Names of the First Directors, shall be determined by the Subscribers of the memorandum of Association.' Article 46, 'The Business of the Company shall be managed by the Directors, who may exercise all such Powers of the Company as are not by this Act, or by the Articles of Association, if any, declared to be exercisable by the Company in General Meeting . . .'. Article 55 of Table A of the *Companies Act 1862* was almost identical.
19. The decision to include in the model articles of association for public and private companies a provision allowing shareholders to make management decisions may, if widely adopted, prove to be of more practical significance.

REFERENCES

Articles, Books, Reports and Press Releases

Bainbridge, Stephen M. (2009), *The New Corporate Governance in Theory and Practice*, New York, NY: Oxford University Press.

Berle, Adolph A. and Gardiner C. Means (1932), *The Modern Corporation and Private Property*, New York, NY: The Macmillan Company.

Cheffins, Brian R. (2008), *Corporate Ownership and Control: British Business Transformed*, Oxford, UK: Oxford University Press.

Collyer, John (1832), *A Practical Treatise on the Law of Partnership: with an Appendix of Forms*, London, UK: S. Sweet.

Cooke, Colin A. (1950), *Corporation, Trust and Company: an Essay in Legal History*, Manchester, UK: University Press.

Davies, Paul L. (1997), *Gower's Principles of Modern Company Law*, London, UK: Sweet and Maxwell.

Davies, Paul L. (2008), *Gower and Davies' Principles of Modern Company Law*, London, UK: Sweet and Maxwell.

Davis, John P. (1905), *Corporations: a Study of the Origin and Development of Great Business Combinations and of Their Relation to the Authority of the State*, New York, NY: G.P. Putnam's Sons.

Du Bois, Armand B. (1938), *The English Business Company after the Bubble Act 1720–1800*, New York, NY: The Commonwealth Fund.

Farrar, J.H. (1998), 'Frankenstein incorporated or fools' parliament? Revisiting the concept of corporation in corporate governance', *Bond Law Review*, **10**, 142–64.

Farrar, John H. (2008), *Corporate Governance: Theories, Principles and Practice*, South Melbourne, Australia: Oxford University Press.

Gevurtz, F.A. (2005), 'The historical and political origins of the corporate board of directors', *Hofstra Law Review*, **33** (1), 89–174.

Harris, Ron (2000), *Industrializing English Law: Entrepreneurship and Business Organisation 1720–1844*, Cambridge, UK: Cambridge University Press.

Hohfeld, W.N. (1909), 'Nature of stockholders' individual liability for corporation debts', *Columbia Law Review*, **9** (4), 285–320.

Jensen, M.C. and W.H. Meckling (1976), 'Theory of the firm: managerial behaviour, agency costs and ownership structure', *Journal of Financial Economics*, **3**, 305–60.

Lowenfeld, Henry (1908), 'Investment practically considered', in Brian R. Cheffins (2008), *Corporate Ownership and Control: British Business Transformed*, London, UK: Oxford University Press.

Maitland, F.W. (1911), 'Collected Papers III', in Colin A. Cooke (1950), *Corporation, Trust and Company: an Essay in Legal History*, Manchester, UK: University Press.

McQueen, Rob (2009), *A Social History of Company Law: Great Britain and the Australian Colonies 1854–1920*, Farnham, UK: Ashgate Publishing Ltd.

Micklethwait, John and Adrian Wooldridge (2003), *The Company: a Short History of a Revolutionary Idea*, New York, NY: The Modern Library Chronicles.

NZ Law Commission (1989), *Company Law Reform and Restatement*, New Zealand Law Commission Report 9, Wellington, New Zealand.

Palmer, Francis B. (1881), *Company Precedents for Use in Relation to Companies Subject to the Companies Acts 1862 to 1880: with Copious Notes*, London, UK: Stevens.

Pennington, Robert R. (2001), *Pennington's Company Law*, London, UK: Butterworths.

Sealy, L. (1996), 'Perception and policy in modern company law', in David Feldman and Frank Meisel (eds), *Corporate and Commercial Law: Modern Developments*, London, UK: Lloyds of London Press.

Smith, Adam (1789), *An Inquiry into the Nature and Causes of the Wealth of Nations*, London, UK: A. Strahan and T. Cadell.

UK, HC, *Parliamentary Debates* (Hansard), 3d ser, vol 139 (7 February 1856).

Vasudev, P.M. (2010), 'Corporate law and its efficiency: a review of history', *American Journal of Legal History*, **50** (3), 237–83.

Wordsworth, Charles F.F. (1851), *The Law of Railway, Canal, Water, Dock, Gas, and Other Companies, Requiring Express Authority of Parliament*, London, UK: Benning.

Jurisprudence

Burnes v Pennell, [1849] 2 HL Cas 497.
Case of Sutton's Hospital (1612), 10 Coke Rep 22b, 77 ER 960.
Hoyt v Thompson's Executor, 19 NY 207 (1859).
Kinder v Taylor, [1825] 3 L J Ch 68.
Manson v Curtis, 223 NY 313, 119 NE 559 (1918).
Peoples Department Stores v Wise, 2004 SCC 68, [2004] 3 SCR 461.

Statutes and Regulations

Bubble Act 1720 (UK), 6 Geo I, c 18.
Charter and bylaws of The Maine Atlantic Granite Company (1836) (US).
Charter of the Company of Clothworkers of London (1648) (UK).

Charter of the Corporation of the Amicable Society for a Perpetual Assurance-Office (1710) (UK).
Companies Act 1862 (UK), 25 & 26 Vict, c 89.
Companies Act 1948 (UK), 11 & 12 Geo VI, c 38.
Companies Act 1955 (New Zealand).
Companies Act 1985 (UK), c 6.
Companies Act 1993 (New Zealand), 1993/105.
Companies Act 2006 (UK), c 46.
Companies Clauses Consolidation Act 1845 (UK), 8 & 9 Vict, c 16.
Corporations Act 2001 (Cth) (Australia).
Delaware General Corporation Law, Del Code Ann tit 8 (US).
Joint Stock Companies Act 1844 (UK), 7 & 8 Vict, c 110.
Joint Stock Companies Act 1856 (UK), 19 & 20 Vict, c 47.
Limited Liability Act 1855 (UK), 18 & 19 Vict, c 133.
Model Business Corporation Act (2003) (US).
Uniform Companies Act 1961 (Cth) (Australia).

Web Resources

Combined Code (2006), Financial Reporting Council, 'The combined code on corporate governance', available at http://www.frc.org.uk/documents/pagemanager/frc/combined%20code%20june%202006.pdf (accessed 26 June 2011).
Select Committee (1850), 'Investments for the savings of the middle and working classes', available at http://books.google.co.nz/books?id=6NYJAAAAIAAJ&printsec=frontcover&dq=Select+Committee+on+Investments+for+the+Savings+of+the+Middle+and+Working+Classes+1850&source=bl&ots=ox3KNFMJt4&sig=IOp2b02G4BXaspgprb7VnCdZtB0&hl=en&ei=-fd2TJuvBIOgsQPz-bijDw&sa=X&oi=book_result&ct=result&resnum=1&ved=0CBQQ6AEwAA#v=onepage&q&f=false (accessed 27 August 2010).

4. Enlightened shareholder value, social responsibility and the redefinition of corporate purpose without law

David Millon

INTRODUCTION

Enlightened shareholder value (ESV) is the idea that corporations should pursue shareholder wealth with a long-run orientation that seeks sustainable growth and profits based on responsible attention to the full range of relevant stakeholder interests. This approach to management contrasts with a short-term focus on current share price even when that objective entails immediate or longer-term negative effects on non-shareholders. Enlightened shareholder value still recognizes the priority of shareholder interests and therefore differs from a pluralist management model based on balancing all stakeholder interests. Nevertheless, because ESV recognizes that long-term business success depends on having regard for the interests of all who contribute to and are affected by corporate activity, it represents an alternative to a narrow conception of shareholder primacy. The combination of a long-range, sustainable conception of value coupled with acknowledgement of the importance of stakeholder considerations for achievement of that goal thus resonates with notions of corporate social responsibility (CSR).

This chapter considers the prospects for acceptance of an ESV approach to management by US transnational corporations. It begins by explaining management practice, looking first for legal determinants and then at the non-legal causes that actually shape current behavior. US corporate law provides ample space for express recognition of non-shareholder interests and a long-run approach to management. The law does not mandate short-term shareholder primacy. Neither, however, does it require commitment to social responsibility. US law, in other words, is surprisingly agnostic on the important question of management's primary duty. And, by disclaiming a clear definition of the constituencies that management is supposed to serve, the law also declines to address the question of corporate purpose. Despite the emergence in recent years of 'soft law' norms that encourage responsibility for human rights and environmental values, international law also does not provide a basis for holding transnational corporations accountable to non-shareholders except in the most egregious cases. Within this legal vacuum, the current practice in the US – shaped by extra-legal factors such as shareholder expectations and management compensation – is to prioritize short-term, quarter-to-quarter share price. Stakeholder or sustainability considerations typically are ignored unless they bear on that objective.

The ESV approach to management responsibility and corporate purpose was endorsed in the UK *Companies Act 2006* (s 172). Under that statute, management's ultimate responsibility is to the shareholders, but it is required to pursue that objective with regard to long-term consequences; employee interests; relations with suppliers, customers and others; impact on the community and the environment; and impact on the company's ethical reputation. This, in other words, is an explicit repudiation of an exclusive focus on shareholder wealth defined in terms of short-term share price. It is not, however, a requirement that management balance the interests of all of the corporation's stakeholders, non-shareholders as well as shareholders. Thus, ESV has been seen as a possible 'third way,' an alternative to strict shareholder primacy on the one hand, and also on the other to a pluralist vision of CSR that elevates non-shareholders to the same plane as shareholders.

Beyond the specific mandate of section 172, ESV can be seen as a general approach to management that differs from current US business practice. There are two dimensions to this difference. A 'longitudinal' or temporal dimension refers to the appropriate time frame for achievement of corporate goals. Under ESV, a long-run horizon replaces short-termism. There is also a 'latitudinal' dimension that defines the breadth of management's perspective. Enlightened shareholder value rejects a sole focus on shareholder interests and instead embraces a broader approach that includes the corporation's other stakeholders as well.

My aim in this chapter is to consider whether market pressures might generate a version of ESV that could have the effect of shifting US transnational corporations away from narrowly focused shareholder primacy. The model I explore here is based on corporate risk management practices. Activities that reduce operating expenses in the short term – such as labor and environmental policies – may present litigation and reputational risks because of the threat of public exposure, especially by non-governmental organizations (NGOs) and the media. The result may be significant litigation and settlements costs, as well as negative reputational effects in product, labor and capital markets. Consumers may stop buying, employee morale may suffer, recruitment may become more difficult, and investors may move their money to companies that are more attentive to the potential costs of human rights and environmental violations. In these various ways, members of the public acting as critics and responding to corporate misbehavior can exert pressure on corporations to behave in more socially responsible ways. Conceived of in terms of risk management, attention to stakeholder interests under pressure from public scrutiny may result in better outcomes for affected constituencies.

The market-driven version of ESV discussed here may have limited effects in the longitudinal or temporal dimension. A shift to a long-run approach requires more than just avoidance of human rights or environmental wrongdoing. US corporations also need to discard their preoccupation with short-term, quarter-to-quarter financial results in favor of long-term, sustainable growth and profits. Avoiding litigation or reputational costs does not necessarily imply a reorientation of focus toward the long run. That is likely to require investments – for example, in improved working conditions or environmental facilities – that are costly in the near term and offer only long-run payoffs. Shareholder pressures for short-term results and compensation packages that reward management for delivering them will presumably continue to encourage a myopic outlook. Competition in product markets – especially from firms that already enjoy cost advantages – may also cause reluctance. In short, even if market-based considerations based on risk management can expand management's outlook latitudinally, it is hard to see how they might have that effect in the longitudinal dimension. Law might be necessary to bring about a longitudinal reorientation.[1]

Although the market-driven model of ESV may not be sufficient to lengthen management's time horizon, there is reason to expect that it could have beneficial latitudinal effects. Risk management concerns driven by externally generated transparency and accountability pressures are leading transnational corporations to pay closer attention to potential human rights and environmental problems. By broadening the range of interests attended to by management to include important stakeholder considerations, ESV therefore does have the potential to produce CSR benefits. This is the sense in which ESV might realistically be characterized as a third way, an alternative to short-term shareholder primacy as well as to an approach to management based on stakeholder balancing. Accordingly, this chapter focuses on that aspect of ESV.

This approach to change appears to hold significant promise. Rather than relying on new legal mandates to redefine management responsibility and corporate purpose, extra-legal pressures can have that effect instead. And, because concerned private actors apply the pressure, public opinion about socially acceptable behavior drives management's rethinking of its role. The result may be a richer, more socially-oriented notion of the corporate objective, shaped by public opinion, and this would occur without public intervention through law.

Despite the promise of a public redefinition of corporate purpose without law, some caveats are in order. As mentioned above, it seems unlikely that market-driven ESV will itself be sufficient to produce a commitment to long-run sustainability. There are also some serious questions as to the capacity of ESV to broaden management's focus to include important non-shareholder considerations even in the short term. For public pressure to be effective, transparency is necessary so that corporate activity can be subjected to scrutiny. As explained below, there is no reason to think that private actors alone can generate the amount of information needed to hold transnational corporations fully accountable for their behavior. And, even when misdeeds are exposed and pressure brought to bear, it is not clear that corporations necessarily deal fully with the problems they have created. Public relations and reputational recovery may be the real objective. Finally, and most importantly, this approach to CSR is driven by bottom-line considerations. Enlightened shareholder value is still about shareholder value after all, and this objective imposes a limit on how far corporations are likely to be willing to go. Certainly this approach to management will not necessarily result in corporations 'doing the right thing' where that would be costly to shareholders. To the extent that this is true, critics of transnational corporations should not expect that a commitment to shareholder value, even if enlightened, will necessarily generate the measure of socially responsible behavior that they believe to be appropriate. There may still be a role for law.

CORPORATE PURPOSE IN US LAW AND PRACTICE

Delaware

Under the US federal system, most business corporations are formed pursuant to a state's corporation statute. Because a business need not be headquartered or even do business in the state in which it is incorporated, corporations are free to choose the legal regime that their managers prefer. For most of the largest corporations, the jurisdiction of choice is Delaware. This state's corporation statute and common law therefore govern questions of internal affairs – including the structures and procedures of governance authority – and corporate purpose. US securities law, though complex and intricate, is primarily concerned with disclosure requirements and other mechanisms designed to facilitate shareholders' exercise of substantive rights – such as voting and trading rights – defined by state law regimes. Federal law does not play an important role in the definition of corporate purpose.

It is often assumed that Delaware corporate law mandates a shareholder primacy conception of management's responsibility.[2] This means that the company is supposed to be managed with the financial interests of shareholders primarily in mind. The shareholders' assumed interest in wealth maximization is not to be sacrificed for non-shareholder considerations, such as human rights or environmental concerns. This notion of management's duty in turn implies a particular conception of corporate purpose, which is to generate profits for shareholders.[3]

The assumption that Delaware law requires shareholder primacy is wrong. It has long been clear that management owes its fiduciary duties of care and loyalty not simply to the shareholders but to the corporation as well (*Guth v Loft* 1939). This formulation recognizes the shareholders' special status as residual claimants – they are traditionally referred to as the firm's owners – but at the same time also emphasizes that management is not simply the agent of the shareholders charged with maximizing their wealth. Instead, management is also responsible for the well-being of the corporation as an entity. As such, management must attend to the full range of considerations that determine its well-being. So, for example, in responding to the threat of a hostile takeover, management is supposed to evaluate 'its effect on the corporate enterprise' (*Unocal v Mesa* 1985, p. 955). In addition to possible harms to shareholders, relevant considerations may include 'the impact on "constituencies" other than shareholders (that is, creditors, customers, employees and perhaps even the community generally) . . .' (ibid.). Only in special cases – when management has chosen to cede its managerial discretion to chart the corporation's future by agreeing to a transfer of control or to the corporation's break-up and dissolution – does its duty change from a responsibility for the well-being of the entity as a whole to one of obtaining the best deal possible for the shareholders alone (see, for example, *Revlon v MacAndrews* 1986; *Paramount v QVC* 1994).

Shareholders lack the ability to mount legal challenges to management's exercise of its authority. Under the well-known 'business judgment rule,' the judiciary will not second-guess strategic and operational decisions as long as they are based on sufficient information, are not subject to conflict of interest, and are made in good faith. Of special importance is the courts' willingness to defer to managerial judgment about the corporation's long-run best interests. A broad range of decisions that seemingly sacrifice short-term shareholder profits for the sake of non-shareholder considerations can be justified by reference to the corporation's long-run well-being. So, for example, employment policies that seem costly in the short term can be said to improve worker morale and productivity over a longer time horizon. Charitable expenditures or decisions to forgo profitable but unsavory business opportunities may enhance the corporation's 'good will' among consumers despite immediate impact on profits. When management appeals to long-run corporate benefit, courts do not require a demonstration of actual gains (*Shlensky v Wrigley* 1968, upholding the directors' refusal to play night-time baseball games because of concerns about common well-being).

The *Dodge v Ford* case, decided by the Michigan Supreme Court in 1919, is often cited for the proposition that corporate management may not subordinate shareholder financial interests to non-shareholder considerations. In that case, Henry Ford refused to cause the corporation to declare a special dividend despite a huge holding of cash and a massive accounting surplus because he preferred to pursue policies designed to benefit employees and consumers. In an oft-quoted passage, the court declared that '[a] business corporation is organized and carried on primarily for the profit of the stockholders. The powers of the directors are to be employed for that end. The discretion of directors is to be exercised in the choice of means to attain that end, and does not extend . . . to other purposes' (*Dodge v Ford* 1919, p. 664). Despite its strong language, the opinion has had little influence on US corporate law. As Professor Stout notes, Delaware courts have cited the decision only once in the last 30 years, and for an altogether different proposition (that is, concerning oppression of minority shareholders by a controlling shareholder) (Stout 2008, p. 4).

More significant is the adoption by 41 states of so-called constituency or stakeholder statutes (Millon 1991; Mitchell 1992). These statutes expressly authorize the board of directors to consider non-shareholder interests, which are typically expressed in terms of a list including employees, customers, suppliers, creditors and local communities. They also typically include a provision allowing the board to prioritize the shareholders' long-term financial interests over enhancement of share price in the short term. While some statutes are limited to the hostile takeover context, most are not. These statutes are important because they represent deliberate rejection of the shareholder primacy conception of corporate purpose and managerial responsibility. Delaware has not enacted one of these statutes but, as we have seen, Delaware's common law of fiduciary duty embraces an essentially similar approach, at least outside the narrow case of management decisions to enter into change of control or entity break-up transactions.

Other legal mechanisms are no more effective than fiduciary duty law at rendering management directly accountable to shareholders. It is highly unusual for shareholders to replace an incumbent board of directors via the annual election. Even with ownership of shares of the largest companies increasingly concentrated in the hands of large institutional investors, collective action costs remain extremely high and the presumption in favor of the status quo remains extremely difficult to overcome. The threat of a hostile takeover via tender offer is also of limited effect because the Delaware courts have allowed target company managers generous leeway in deploying effective defensive measures. The important *Paramont/Time* decision in particular endorses the authority of management to determine the corporation's future where its existing business strategy would not accommodate an unwelcome change of control (*Paramount v Time* 1989). The Delaware Supreme Court stated:

> The fiduciary duty to manage a corporate enterprise includes the selection of a time frame for achievement of corporate goals. That duty may not be delegated to the stockholders . . . Directors are not obliged to abandon a deliberately conceived corporate plan for a short-term shareholder profit unless there is no clear basis to sustain the corporate strategy. (p. 1155)

Under US corporate law, transnational companies have broad freedom to pursue policies that temper the quest for profits with other considerations, such as human rights or environmental concerns. Nothing in current law *mandates* such behavior, but management's authority to cultivate the corporation's long-range well-being provides ample space for more than mere profit maximization. Shareholders who might object face formidable doctrinal and practical obstacles.

International Law, 'Hard' and 'Soft'

Traditionally, the focus of international human rights law has been on state actors as the most likely source of abuse. Non-state actors generally have not been subject to its requirements, except in extreme cases of egregious conduct. No multilateral human rights treaties exist that require states to police the activities of corporations within their borders or to regulate their own corporations extraterritorially. The International Covenant on Civil and Political Rights (ICCPR) specifies a number of 'negative' rights of individuals against the state (UN Human Rights 1966a). States that are parties to the ICCPR are obligated to ensure that their citizens enjoy its guarantees and the preamble affirms that individuals too are subject to the treaty's prohibitions. However, because the treaty's focus is on civil and political rights, it does not deal with corporate responsibility for a broad range of human rights and environmental issues.

In contrast, the International Covenant on Economic, Social and Cultural Rights (ICESCR) does contain a range of substantive pronouncements on 'positive' entitlements to basic human needs, including provisions dealing with labor, health, food, housing and education (UN Human Rights 1966b). These quality of life issues are fundamentally important adjuncts to the civil and political rights specified in the ICCPR and, because of frequent lack of host state regulation, are subject to serious infringements by transnational corporations (Nolan and Taylor 2009). However, the ICESCR itself does not impose substantive obligations on state governments as the ICCPR does; instead, the parties undertake to operationalize the benefits of the ICESCR's provisions over time, by enacting legislation or otherwise. This is necessarily a gradual, state-by-state process and progress so far has been sporadic even among the parties to the treaty. Meanwhile, the US has signed but has yet to ratify the ICESCR.

Customary international norms are limited in scope as to economic, social and cultural human rights. The relatively narrow ambit of customary international law governing human rights has had the effect of significantly restricting the scope of one potentially important remedy for abusive conduct. The US *Alien Tort Claims Act* provides a cause of action for aliens seeking to bring tort claims based on a 'violation of the law of nations or a treaty of the United States.' This statute could provide a basis for claims against US transnational corporations that commit human rights violations abroad, but the US Supreme Court has held that the norm on which the plaintiff relies must be a clearly established principle of customary international law (*Sosa v Alvarez-Macain* 2004).[4] Customary law is an evolving corpus but at the moment proscribes only the most heinous forms of human rights violation, such as genocide, slavery or war crimes (Williams 2002).

While currently neither treaty nor customary law specifies corporations' human rights and environmental obligations or the responsibility of states to protect citizens against violations committed by transnational corporations, 'soft law' developments indicate movement in the direction of a set of substantive standards governing the activities of transnational companies. The UN Universal Declaration of Human Rights specifies a number of basic human rights, including rights to equal protection of the law, freedom of expression, personal security, food and housing, work, an adequate standard of living, and education and cultural opportunities

(Human Rights 1948). The Declaration states expressly that no '[s]tate, group or person' may violate any of the rights contained in it and thus is potentially applicable to corporations and other private actors (ibid., Article 30). However, the Declaration is simply a declaration, and as such is hortatory and inspirational rather than legally binding.

Other 'soft law' initiatives are similarly noteworthy. Perhaps best known is the UN Global Compact. Launched in 2000, the compact is a set of ten principles defining 'corporate citizenship in the world economy' in the areas of human rights, labor, the environment and anti-corruption (UN Global Compact 2000). Although participation is voluntary, this project currently includes over 5200 businesses in 130 countries. Annual reporting is required, with reports being publicly available, and companies are 'de-listed' for failure to comply.

Other statements of voluntary standards of good conduct include the International Labor Organization's Declaration on Fundamental Principles and Rights at Work (ILO 1998) and the Rio Declaration on Environment and Development (Rio Declaration 1992). In a similar vein, the World Economic Forum, a non-profit Swiss foundation, is working with business leaders, government representatives, civil society organizations and others to develop the concept of 'corporate global citizenship' (WEF 2011).

Especially important for transnational corporations is the UN's project on business and human rights. Pursuant to an appointment by the UN Human Rights Commission, Dr John Ruggie has served as Special Representative to the Secretary-General since 2005, charged with clarifying the role and responsibilities of business with respect to human rights. Following extensive consultations with government officials, business people and representatives of the NGO community, Dr Ruggie issued a report in 2008 proposing a policy framework consisting of three elements: the state duty to protect against human rights abuses by third parties, including business; the corporate responsibility to respect human rights; and greater access to remedy, judicial and non-judicial, for victims (Ruggie 2008). This document endorses corporate responsibility to avoid infringement of human rights and recommends due diligence systems aimed at clarifying human rights responsibilities and monitoring business activities for potential violations.[5]

The Organisation for Economic Co-operation and Development (OECD), which currently includes 30 member countries (including the US), has published 'Guidelines for Multinational Enterprises' (OECD 2008). These Guidelines provide a code of conduct covering a wide range of topics, including human rights, the environment, labor relations, consumer interests and corruption. They are not binding on corporations but

OECD countries have agreed to promote their implementation. As such, the Guidelines are an important instance of governmental endorsement of important human rights principles.

These 'soft law' developments do not as yet provide a legal means for holding transnational corporations accountable for human rights or environmental violations. Nevertheless, they do constitute an emerging body of substantive norms specifying standards for appropriate corporate behavior. They therefore have the potential to shape corporate management's own sense of responsibility. For example, some of these norms may be incorporated in companies' voluntarily adopted codes of conduct. These norms also provide criteria against which corporate activities can be assessed and evaluated by external critics. As yet, however, as explained below, US corporations tend to define their purpose in terms of shareholder wealth maximization. As a result, it seems clear that emerging 'soft law' norms have so far had limited impact.

Corporate Purpose in the US Today

While observers of worldwide business practice conclude that CSR is now 'mainstream' (see, for example, *The Economist* 2008), managers of US corporations tend to conceive of their duties in terms of shareholder primacy. Institutional shareholders share this view. As a matter of practice, this approach to management means attention to short-term, quarter-to-quarter share price maximization at the expense of longer-term considerations. A group of concerned business leaders, investment professionals and academics states, 'in recent years, boards, managers, shareholders with varying agendas, and regulators, all, to one degree or another, have allowed short-term considerations to overwhelm the desirable long-term growth and sustainable profit objectives of the corporation' (The Aspen Institute 2009, p. 2).

The general acceptance of the view that short-term share price maximization is the appropriate objective for managers and shareholders is reflected in current law reform initiatives in the US that would strengthen shareholders' ability to hold management responsible for inadequate financial performance. These initiatives take for granted that accountability to shareholders is the primary objective of corporate law. Strangely, some reformers claim that the excessive risk-taking and abuse of leverage that were major causes of the current financial crisis were due at least in part to insufficient managerial accountability to shareholders. In fact, however, this reckless behavior was a response to investor demands for immediate profits and high stock prices (Strine 2009). In this respect, much of the irresponsible activity that led to the financial crisis reflected dominant views about the legitimacy of a short-term focus on shareholder value.

As discussed above, this shareholder primacy approach to corporate purpose and management responsibility is not the result of legal requirements. Instead, several non-legal factors seem to be at work. Equity-based executive compensation arrangements align management's financial incentives with those of shareholders (Walker 2009). To the extent they reward short-term results rather than longer-term performance these practices encourage management to disregard considerations – including stakeholder considerations – that would benefit the corporation only over the long haul.

Management seems to be increasingly wary of institutional shareholder activism. Many of these investors – particularly public pension funds – are under extreme pressure to generate high returns on a regular basis (Walsh 2010). From their point of view, management therefore needs to constantly focus on enhancement of share prices. Even though voting majorities continue to be very hard to assemble, major institutional investors are succeeding in making their presence felt. Proxy advisory firms – Institutional Shareholder Services is especially influential – have been effective in mitigating collection action problems. These firms evaluate companies according to shareholder accountability criteria and advise large institutional investors about how to vote their shares. Recommendations to vote contrary to management can result in large negative blocks (Belinfanti 2009). In recent years, a number of US corporations have dismantled poison pills and eliminated staggered boards of directors in response to shareholder objections. Some have also voluntarily adopted shareholder access to management's proxy solicitation materials and non-binding 'say on pay' shareholder referenda, initiatives currently under consideration by Congress and the Securities and Exchange Commission (SEC). These developments reflect a climate in which corporate managers seem increasingly attentive to the preferences of institutional shareholders.

Cultural factors also appear to be at work. It seems to be widely assumed in US business circles that management's primary loyalty should be to shareholders. Business schools encourage this outlook, generally taking for granted that this is the relevant benchmark (Khurana 2007). The business press and law reformers likewise speak of shareholder value as the appropriate goal for corporate management. Calls for a reorientation toward the long term have gained urgency in the wake of the financial crisis, but still seem to run counter to dominant views. US norms and practices emphasizing short-term shareholder value are thus out of sync with notions of CSR widely accepted elsewhere in the world.

ENLIGHTENED SHAREHOLDER VALUE AND CORPORATE SOCIAL RESPONSIBILITY

As we have seen, US law is flexible enough to accommodate corporate policies that reject short-term shareholder wealth maximization in favor of an approach that takes a fuller range of stakeholder values and long-term sustainability into account. It does not mandate that approach, but neither does it mandate shareholder primacy. US law, in other words, is agnostic on the question of corporate purpose. While 'soft law' developments and different social and political value systems around the world seem to be pushing companies in the direction of heightened regard for human rights and other non-shareholder values, US business practice currently is to focus on short-term share prices without express regard to social responsibility or sustainability concerns. I now turn to the question of whether we can expect US transnational corporations to reorient their approach to management and their conception of corporate purpose. In particular, I explore the possibility of reorientation without legal intervention.

Enlightened Shareholder Value

Scholars have suggested that there may be an emerging 'third way' between US shareholder primacy and the CSR approach to management – emphasizing stakeholder balancing – that is increasingly influential in much of the rest of the world (Williams and Conley 2005a; Ho 2010). The ESV model was developed in the UK and is expressed in section 172 of the *Companies Act 2006*. That provision provides that directors are supposed to promote the interests of the corporation for the benefit of the shareholders but then goes on also to require regard for long-term consequences; employee interests; relations with suppliers, customers and others; impact on the community and environment; and the company's reputation for 'high standards of business conduct.'[6] Rather than embracing stakeholderism over shareholder primacy, the approach taken by section 172 rejects an emphasis on short-term share price in favor of an approach to management that seeks to promote the long-term sustainability of the firm. A long-term perspective requires attention to the full range of stakeholder concerns that have the capacity to affect the corporation's business success. Sustainability values are thus seen to rest on recognition of the legitimacy of non-shareholder as well as shareholder interests. In this respect, a long-term orientation depends on recognition of the corporation's responsibility to its various internal and external constituencies.

Enlightened shareholder value's more expansive time frame and richer sense of the factors that contribute to long-run business success resonate with elements of existing US law, particularly the non-shareholder constituency statutes discussed above. As noted, these statutes authorize management to take an enlightened approach to shareholder value that is based on the long-run well-being of the corporation as a whole. The business judgment rule shields from shareholder challenge and judicial review management's discretion to approach its responsibilities in this way if it so chooses. The Delaware Supreme Court has been clear in its endorsement of management's authority to chart the future of the 'corporate enterprise' without interference from shareholders' preferences for immediate returns. Nevertheless, however, current US law differs from the UK's recently enacted section 172 in an important respect. While UK law appears to mandate an ESV philosophy, US law merely allows management to exercise its authority in that way if it chooses to do so.

The question, then, is whether in the absence of legal mandate US corporations might be persuaded to reorient their priorities. Internal pressures – compensation practices, social norms, and pressure from institutional shareholders – currently drive the shareholder primacy focus, which is understood to require an obsession with short-term share value. Countervailing external pressures therefore appear to be needed. In the discussion that follows, I explore one possible source of such pressures: management concerns about risk. Corporations are increasingly augmenting existing approaches to risk monitoring and loss prevention with more sophisticated strategies that recognize the potential costs to the corporation of activities that cause human rights abuses or environmental damage. Such costs can take the form of litigation risk and also the risk of harm to a corporation's reputation. Management has a natural incentive to minimize these risks because they can result in significant expense. Economic self-interest therefore seems to have the potential to generate heightened attention to human rights and environmental considerations.

The dynamic that might produce such outcomes is fairly straightforward. Exposure of human rights or environmental wrongdoing can lead to losses in the form of litigation and settlement costs and also of harm to the corporation's reputation, which in concrete terms can mean lost sales, disinvestment by shareholders and employee morale problems. Accordingly, prudential considerations – independent of any moral ones – should lead transnational corporations to pay more attention to the human rights and environmental impacts of their activities. While this model seems simple enough and good outcomes seem plausibly predictable, each element deserves close scrutiny. The analysis that follows below attempts to do this, focusing in turn on the built-in limits of risk management – a cost–benefit exercise – as a device for discouraging bad behavior; on the limited ability of consumers and shareholders to bring pressure to bear on corporate management; and on the limited abilities of private parties such as NGOs or the media to expose corporate misbehavior to public scrutiny. Finally, and perhaps most important, it should be kept in mind that even if the dynamic sketched here leads corporations to avoid some human rights or environmental abuses, that does not necessarily translate into a shift in management outlook from a reactive strategy that aims to prevent losses to a proactive one that seeks long-run sustainability by cultivating productive relations with all of the corporation's stakeholders. This seems to be the vision behind section 172's concept of ESV. Even though US corporations approaching human rights and environmental issues from a risk management perspective may improve their behavior in important ways, that would not necessarily indicate embrace of ESV in section 172's more robust sense.

Risk Management

Liability risk

Risk management is part of any responsible corporate management's efforts to meet its financial targets. Management must typically attend to a range of standard financial risks. These include liquidity and cash flow considerations, credit risks involving customer or other counterparty obligations, the reliability of supply chains, possible changes in consumer demand, pressure from competitors, workforce disruptions and market risks relating to the value of a company's financial assets. Management must also be aware of governmental and regulatory risks posed by the prospect of new laws or regulations and the possibility of political instability and natural disasters.

Litigation risk is part of this mix. US companies operating abroad increasingly must be wary of civil or criminal prosecutions based on activities that have negative human rights or environmental effects. Local law of host states may in many situations have little to say about such matters and, even if it does, governments may be reluctant to confront businesses whose presence is thought to be valuable for a number of reasons. Nevertheless, there are numerous instances of high-profile judicial proceedings that have resulted in costly judgments or settlements.

The Bhopal disaster may be the best-known example. In 1984, a toxic gas leak at a Union Carbide facility in India resulted in over 20 000 deaths and an additional 100 000 people suffering various adverse health effects. A settlement was reached in 1989 committing the corporation to pay US$470 million for the benefit of the victims. Criminal prosecutions brought in India against the corporation and its senior officers are ongoing.

In 2005, Unocal Corporation agreed to settle several lawsuits filed in

California arising out of its complicity with the Burmese government in forced labor, rape, torture and murder of villagers in connection with a natural gas pipeline project (Eviatar 2005). The amount of the cash settlement was confidential but compensation for the victims is said to be significant. In addition, Unocal also undertook to provide funds to improve living conditions, health care and education for residents of the pipeline region.

Another notable example is the settlement in 2009 of charges brought against Royal Dutch Shell PLC and its Nigerian subsidiary for its involvement in the torture and execution by the military government of non-violent Nigerian activists protesting Shell's destruction of local communities and the environment. The US$15.5 million settlement represents compensation for the victims and also provides for a range of social programs for the people of the affected region. Meanwhile, US federal court cases are underway against Chevron for human rights abuses in Nigeria and against Occidental Petroleum for environmental and public health violations in the Amazon region.[7]

High-profile cases like these cannot be ignored by corporate management. Aside from the costs of bad publicity, they are expensive to defend and to settle. Because it is clearly in their self-interest to limit litigation exposure, transnational corporations are increasingly including human rights and environmental impact in their routine risk management protocols. This requires clear statements of company policy – often in the form of codes of conduct – and careful monitoring of the activities of a company's various subsidiaries.

It should be noted, however, that there is a limit to the extent to which concerns about litigation can affect corporate behavior. Lawsuits like the ones referred to here are likely to occur only as a result of especially egregious human rights or environmental abuses that are serious enough to draw the attention of NGOs and other activists. As noted above, because the statute has been interpreted as proscribing only behavior that amounts to clear violation of customary international law, the *Alien Tort Claims Act* gives US courts jurisdiction only over especially serious wrongs like genocide, slavery or war crimes. Prosecution by home state authorities for less grievous offenses is still possible, but local governments are sometimes themselves implicated in corporate wrongdoing – as in the Unocal/Burma case, for example – and even if they are not they may be reluctant to bring cases against companies whose presence provides economic benefits. Developing countries compete for foreign investment capital as a way to promote economic growth and prosperity. They therefore have an incentive to provide hospitable legal environments for transnational corporations doing business within their borders

(Anderson 2009). Litigation risk thus may not deter behavior that does not rise to the level of a serious human rights or environmental violation. Further, litigation risk does not appear to be a lever for encouraging corporations to reorient their direction from short-term share price maximization to a longer-term approach based on sustainability principles. This requires affirmative initiatives – such as improved working conditions and attention to environmental impacts – as well as avoidance of policies that inflict serious harms. Failure to move forward proactively typically is not by itself a basis for litigation.

Reputational risk

The costs of major human rights or environmental litigation are greater than just the massive expenditures required for defense and resolution. They also present major public relations challenges. This is evident in the fact that settlements often involve more than just payment of compensation to the victims of the wrongs at issue. Corporations also typically undertake to assume additional obligations that have nothing directly to do with compensation. These can include contributions designed to improve the quality of life for local residents. Companies will also, if they haven't already, adopt new codes of conduct designed to prevent recurrence of the kind of activities at issue. Nike, discussed below, is an example of this phenomenon. The point is that these initiatives amount to recognition that corporations that have been implicated in these kinds of wrongdoing must take affirmative steps to demonstrate that they disapprove of such conduct and will not engage in it in the future. The motivation is to remove the reputational stain that high-profile litigation leaves on the company's reputation.

Transnational corporations also face reputational risk even where conduct does not generate litigation. If a corporation is shown to be engaged in human rights or environmental abuses, the harm to its reputation can cost it money. Sales may suffer if consumers are sufficiently concerned. Further, the cost of capital could increase if investors perceive the possibility of future legal difficulties or simply object to the conduct in question. Avoidance of these kinds of reputational costs is simply the flip side of affirmative efforts to burnish the company's public image by expensive advertising of its activities as a 'good citizen.' Thus, risk management extends beyond avoidance of litigation to the broader challenge of avoiding behavior that is likely to be condemned in the court of public opinion.

Transnational corporations increasingly are attempting to formalize attention to these kinds of issues. General Motors Corporation, for example, has not one but two high-level committees charged with monitoring reputational considerations (Williams and Conley 2005b). Many of the largest corporations now have board of directors committees dedicated to social responsibility (Fairfax 2006).

While avoidance of reputational costs can certainly create incentives to avoid bad behavior, here as with litigation risk it should be kept in mind that this dynamic is subject to built-in limitations. Relatively minor activities are unlikely to trigger significant reputational backlash because they may not receive significant public attention. Further, the desire to avoid bad publicity would not necessarily lead corporations to adopt affirmative measures necessary to shift from a short-term, share price focus to a longer-term, sustainability management philosophy.

Accountability

Shareholders

Litigation and reputational risk are matters of financial concern to corporate management because increasingly shareholders are factoring these costs into their decisions about whether to invest in particular companies. This is true not just of 'socially responsible' investment funds, for which human rights and environmental issues have always been highly relevant. Mainstream institutional shareholders, concerned primarily about investment return, are also taking an increasingly broad view of risk and are now routinely including so-called 'environmental, social, and governance' (ESG) metrics into their investment decisions.

Most notable in this regard is the UN Principles for Responsible Investment (UNPRI). In 2005, at the invitation of the UN Secretary-General, 20 institutional investors from 12 countries consulted with 70 representatives of the investment industry, government, civil society and academia. Under the coordination of the UN Global Compact and the UN Environment Programme Finance Initiative, this process resulted in a set of six core principles. Most importantly, signatories commit to 'incorporate ESG issues into investment analysis and decision-making processes, . . . be active owners and incorporate ESG issues into our ownership policies and practices, . . . [and] seek appropriate disclosure on ESG issues by the entities in which we invest' (UN Responsible Investment 2005). They also agree to promote the acceptance of the principles, to work together to implement them, and to report on progress. By agreeing to these principles, large institutional shareholders and other investors undertake to evaluate their investment decisions according to long-term criteria that expressly recognize the relevance of a range of stakeholder concerns for the financial success of their portfolio companies. In other words, they purport to eschew an approach to investment management that focuses primarily on short-term share prices rather than sustainability over time. To date 201 asset owners, 375 investment managers and 137 professional service providers have signed on. US institutions include the AFL-CIO; CalPERS; CalSTRS; the Connecticut, Illinois, Los Angeles County, Maryland, New York State and City pension funds; and TIAA-CREF.

It remains to be seen how far this development will spread. Mutual funds are notably absent from the current list, but Vanguard recently decided to include portfolio company human rights practices in its investment decisions (Ho 2010). It is also unclear how rigorously these investors will evaluate ESG criteria or how much weight they will accord to them. As discussed below, disclosure on such issues is often superficial or even lacking altogether. Nevertheless, wealthy, activist institutions like CalPERS certainly have the clout to influence the corporations in which they invest. Their endorsement of the financial relevance of ESG criteria cannot easily be dismissed, as one might disregard a proponent of CSR whose shareholding is small and who is more concerned with human rights or environmental issues than with investment return.

Public opinion

So far, at least, institutional investors are not the primary constituencies pressuring corporate management to pay more attention to possible costs of human rights and environmental misbehavior. Consumers too can put effective pressure on companies to behave in a socially responsible manner. For example, when it came to light in the early 1990s that Nike relied on child labor to manufacture many of its products, NGO- and student-organized boycotts and demonstrations targeted its retail outlets. As a result of this major public relations disaster, in 1992 Nike adopted a code of conduct for its suppliers that mandates observance of basic labor, health and safety standards. Although monitoring of compliance has proved to be difficult, it is clear that Nike is very concerned about its public image and devotes substantial resources to its enhancement.

Other examples of transnational corporations responding to public pressure are abundant. Starbucks' introduction of Fair Trade coffee in 2000 was a response to public criticism of its global expansion strategy. Major drug companies, initially unwilling to reduce prices of anti-HIV/AIDS drugs sold in South Africa, eventually backed down in the face of widespread pressure from consumer groups and others (Dickerson 2002). It is also common for corporations to adopt socially responsible policies because of employee recruitment and retention concerns. For example, a Goldman Sachs executive said, 'people want to be part of a company that stands for something' (Fairfax 2006).

It is a fair question whether highly publicized corporate responses to criticism from consumers, activists and employees are driven primarily by genuine motivation to solve problems or are instead aimed mostly at improvement of the company's public image. For example, critics of Nike point out that wages at its contract factories remain very low even as it tries to eliminate child labor. Fair Trade represents only a small fraction of Starbucks' coffee sales. Goldman Sachs' announcement in 2009 of a plan to distribute capital to small businesses was seen by some as a scheme to deflect public outrage over its historic profits facilitated in part by the largesse of the US government. The very existence of emerging CSR standards may ironically make it easier for corporations to create the appearance of responsible behavior by endorsing CSR precepts and adopting CSR rhetoric but without necessarily making significant changes to their business policies (Williams and Conley 2005c). For example, a high-profile initiative designed to confer laudable benefits on a local population may actually involve only a small part of a transnational corporation's global activities.

There is no doubt that public relations considerations are a major element of many CSR initiatives. Nevertheless, in at least some cases there is a sincere effort to respond in a meaningful way to legitimate public criticism of corporate behavior. One study of 14 pulp and paper manufacturing mills located in Australia, Canada, New Zealand and the United States found significant improvements in the reduction of environmentally harmful emissions (Kagan et al. 2003). Some had done better than others, but differences in legal regulation did not explain these discrepancies. Instead, 'social pressures' – such as local communities, activists, NGOs and the media – seem to have been a key variable, along with differences in attitude among corporate managers, in determining the extent to which companies exceeded legally mandated minimum standards. A highly visible, worldwide campaign by Greenpeace targeting use of chlorine as a bleaching agent was apparently especially influential. In some cases, consumer demands have also played an important role. This study demonstrates that corporations pay attention not only to legal mandates – the 'regulatory license' to operate – but also to extra-legal public pressure, the 'social license.' In this way, public values can shape corporate behavior independently of law and regulation.

Transparency

In order for external pressure to be effective in compelling corporate management to take into account the potential costs of human rights or environmental abuses, mechanisms must first exist that are capable of bringing such behavior to light. Mandatory and voluntary disclosure can play a role here, but even more important are the concerted efforts of NGOs like Amnesty International, EarthRights International, Human Rights Watch, Greenpeace, World Wildlife Federation and many others.

Disclosure

US law does not specifically mandate social or environmental reporting beyond required disclosure of the costs of compliance with new environmental regulations or information about pending environmental litigation (17 CFR §§ 229.101 and 229.103 (2010)). In this respect, the US differs from a number of European countries. Several require broader environmental disclosure, and France goes further and requires companies whose shares are traded on the Bourse 'to provide extremely detailed environmental, labor, community involvement, health, and safety information in its annual reports to shareholders' (Williams and Conley 2005a). The EU now requires reporting on social and environmental as well as financial matters (ibid., p. 509).

Even so, US securities laws do require disclosure of 'material' information, including 'any known trends or uncertainties' that the reporting corporation expects will have an unfavorable impact on financial performance' (17 CFR § 229.303 (2010)). This provision is general enough to impose a duty to disclose information about any social or environmental risk that has potentially significant financial implications. As yet the SEC has not interpreted the materiality requirement in terms of a general obligation to report on sustainability or social responsibility issues. However, because the operative criterion is whether a reasonable shareholder would consider the information in question to be important, evolving expectations within the investment community about the relevance of social and environmental risk factors are likely to result in more expansive disclosure requirements.

By relying on a general 'materiality' requirement defined in terms of investor expectations, US law essentially adopts a market-driven approach to disclosure. This is in contrast to a command-driven approach that would be based on governmental mandate of specific ESG disclosures. It also contrasts with an ethics-based approach that would rely simply on the good will of the corporations themselves, on their desire 'to do the right thing.'[8] Assigning responsibility to the investment community to shape corporate disclosure according to its own needs has the advantage of placing power in the hands of actors to whom corporations must pay attention. Perhaps this is preferable to government mandates, which generate concerns in the business community about over-regulation and would not necessarily respond accurately to investor needs. Nevertheless, this approach has built-in limits because it is driven solely by investors' concerns about the need for information relevant to pricing decisions. Disclosure that might have other social value but that cannot be linked to investment return therefore is not likely to emerge from this process.

In the US, the SEC defines its mission solely in terms of investor interests. It has not attempted to mandate ESG disclosure but, speaking on behalf of shareholders, it nevertheless is able to influence disclosure practices. An important recent development in this regard is an SEC interpretive release on climate change disclosure (SEC 2010). The release offers guidance with reference to four potential issues that could trigger reporting obligations, including the potential impact of pending US legislative and regulatory initiatives and international treaties and accords, and also indirect risks such as decreased demand for existing products that produce greenhouse gas emissions. The release also refers expressly to reputational considerations: 'Depending on the nature of a [reporting company's] business and its sensitivity to public opinion, [it] may have to consider whether the public's perception of any publicly available data relating to its greenhouse gas emissions could expose it to potential adverse consequences to its business operations or financial condition resulting from reputational damage' (ibid., p. 26). Although the SEC disclaims any intention to impose any new disclosure obligations, it is nevertheless likely that corporations for whom these issues are potentially relevant will focus more closely on these issues than they have in the past. This will be a significant improvement over recent practice, which according to one report has produced very little disclosure of climate risk, even in sectors for which carbon reduction is likely to be quite costly (The Corporate Library 2009).

In a related development, the SEC late last year reversed a Bush administration policy that had allowed corporations to refuse to include shareholder proposals in their proxy solicitation materials where the proposals were requests for information regarding financial risks associated with environmental, human rights and other social issues (SEC 2009a). Now, where the underlying subject matter of the proposal raises a 'significant policy issue,' shareholders will be able to submit their proposed requests for information to a shareholder vote. Here too the SEC appears to be sympathetic to shareholders' interest in obtaining disclosure of risk information that goes beyond traditional financial metrics.

Although as yet mandated disclosure of human rights and environmental matters is still limited, a number of US companies voluntarily exceed the minimum requirements. As of 2002, 36 per cent of the largest US corporations published social reports (Williams and Conley 2005a), a number that is very likely higher today. Among major companies issuing sustainability reports today are Anheuser-Busch, AT&T, General Motors, Intel, Johnson & Johnson, McDonald's, Nike and PepsiCo (SEC

2009b). Companies that publish separate documents often refer to them as 'corporate citizenship' or 'corporate responsibility' reports (Fairfax 2006). These focus on the company's good relations with customers, employees and the broader community. Even if they do not produce a separate document, most Fortune 500 companies now include discussion of stakeholder issues in their annual reports, often quite prominently.

It is important to distinguish between disclosure that candidly and thoughtfully explains potential human rights or environmental problems that might arise out of the company's operations on the one hand, and less concrete pronouncements about the company's asserted commitment to social and environmental values on the other. The latter is more likely to reflect public relations considerations than it is rigorous self-examination. Nevertheless, all of this voluntary disclosure does indicate increasing acknowledgement by corporate management that more is expected of business activity than simply the enhancement of share prices.

US developments in the area of voluntary reporting are part of a larger worldwide movement in the direction of expanded corporate disclosure. The Global Reporting Initiative has developed the GRI Sustainability Reporting Framework (GRI 2006). The purpose is to provide a standardized template for economic, environmental and social disclosure, facilitating thorough treatment of the full range of stakeholder interests and allowing comparisons among companies. According to a GRI press release dated 15 July 2009, over 1000 organizations are now using GRI guidelines for their social reporting, including 13 per cent of the S&P 500 in the US.

External scrutiny

The developments discussed above are important and indicate movement in the direction of routine inclusion of social and environmental considerations in corporate reporting. Nevertheless, most US transnational companies do not do this or do so incompletely. And in many cases disclosure seems to be motivated as much by public relations considerations as it is by genuine desire to present a full picture of the human rights or environmental challenges confronting a particular business. For example, one study concludes that, even among companies that chose to publish sustainability reports in 2009, human rights reporting 'still falls far short when measured in relation to certain key principles and elements of good human rights reporting' (GRI 2009). In particular, reporting companies tended to emphasize implementation of policies and positive impacts while underplaying potential negative human rights effects arising from their operations.

For the moment at least, a more promising source of transparency is the work of NGOs and other activists who are committed to the investigation and exposure of human rights and environmental problems. NGOs like Amnesty International, EarthRights International, Human Rights Watch, Greenpeace, World Wildlife Federation and others have played important roles in uncovering and publicizing activities that otherwise might not receive the notice of anyone other than the people immediately affected. The mainstream media can also play a role by publicizing the results of NGO investigations. For example, the *New York Times* reported prominently on a small Indian NGO's discovery of pesticide in Coca-Cola and Pepsi soft drinks (Gentleman 2006).

Amnesty International, for example, states:

> Our mission is to conduct research and generate action to prevent and end grave abuses of human rights and to demand justice for those whose rights have been violated. Our members and supporters exert influence on governments, political bodies, companies and intergovernmental groups. Activists take up human rights issues by mobilizing public pressure through mass demonstrations, vigils and direct lobbying as well as online and offline campaigning. (Amnesty 2009)

Despite its historic focus on state-sponsored human rights violations, Amnesty International recognizes that transnational corporations can also be responsible for abuses, especially where local governments fail to protect their citizens, and is publicizing corporate human rights violations and campaigning for global standards on business and human rights.

EarthRights International (2011) documents and publicizes human rights and environmental abuses, with a particular focus on the activities of transnational corporations. For example, a series of reports exposes the complicity of Chevron and the French oil company Total in murder, forced labor and high-level government corruption in connection with the construction of a natural gas pipeline in Burma. EarthRights International also supports litigation in US courts, including the *Doe v Unocal* case on behalf of Burmese villagers.

Greenpeace continues its non-violent confrontations with businesses and other actors who engage in environmental destruction. The aim is to shed light on such activities 'in order to raise the level and quality of public debate' (Greenpeace 2011). It also tries to influence corporate behavior in other ways. Currently underway is a campaign to persuade major information technology firms to take leadership roles in developing technological solutions to climate change problems and in advocating for energy use regulations. Greenpeace seeks to apply the pressures of public opinion by grading CEOs of leading companies according to a set of criteria and publishing the results. Google, Microsoft, and IBM are criticized for failing to stand up against the US Chamber of Commerce's opposition to climate change legislation, while Apple is praised for its high-profile decision to withdraw its membership.

Through investigation and publicity, NGOs have the potential to expose corporate behavior and policies to a far broader audience than might otherwise learn of them. Certainly for egregious human rights or environmental abuses, this is likely to provide far greater transparency than would reliance on voluntary disclosure alone. Publicity can also be effective for less dramatic but no less important activities like greenhouse gas emissions that companies also would not necessarily disclose voluntarily.

Greater transparency resulting from NGO activity facilitates public scrutiny and pressure. NGOs are mission-driven, but because they must rely so heavily on private donations, they must necessarily pursue agendas that resonate with public opinion and values. In this way, they act as conduits for the views of a larger public constituency. Likewise, once the light of publicity has been directed at particular behavior, those members of the public who care can use their resources to bring pressure to bear. As we have seen, this pressure can come from consumers or investors. It may result in litigation but it need not in order to be effective. Ultimately publicity can also result in governmental action, as occurred in India when several states enacted partial bans on sales of Coca-Cola products in the wake of the pesticide controversy mentioned above.

Technology may also make it possible for activists with very limited resources to make a difference. The example of a Californian named Amit Srivastava is instructive (Stecklow 2005). Working alone, he has created a website for the collection of information about Coca-Cola's public health and environmental offenses in India and which serves as a resource for activists around the world. His site also provides a coordination point for otherwise dispersed and disconnected local protesters in India. His speeches to college students in the US and Europe have resulted in a number of colleges banning Coke products. He has organized a 'fax action' campaign that resulted in over 9000 faxes being sent to Coca-Cola headquarters. Even a determined individual apparently can have an impact on public opinion.

Powerful as this process of transparency and pressure can be, it should still be recalled that NGOs and individual activists inevitably have limited resources and areas of interest. There is no reason to think that all of the kinds of problematic corporate behavior that society might legitimately be worried about will be brought to light in this way. Technology allows anyone with a camera phone and a computer link to YouTube to expose bad behavior, and there is evidently a sympathetic audience for these messages, consisting of numerous concerned people around the world who are deeply sceptical about the good will of transnational corporations. Even so, it would be a mistake to conclude that the threat of exposure by private actors can be sufficient to deter the full range of human rights and environmental abuses that businesses are likely to cause. Moreover, to the extent that corporations are concerned solely with 'damage control,' there is no reason to assume that risk management policies themselves can be powerful enough to produce a shift from short-term shareholder wealth concerns to longer-term sustainability values.

CORPORATE SOCIAL RESPONSIBILITY WITHOUT LAW?

Because it is market-driven rather than legislatively or judicially mandated, the version of ESV presented in this chapter relies on management's evaluation of the corporation's self-interest as the driving force behind expanded attention to human rights, environmental and other CSR values. As explained above, US law does not require the emphasis on short-term share price that currently preoccupies corporate management; various extra-legal factors account for that. The question therefore is whether – or rather to what extent – financial considerations might spur management to embrace a broader conception of its responsibilities. The prospect of reform without legal intervention is surely intriguing. Even so, there is reason to think this process may disappoint the ambitions of CSR advocates.

According to the model presented above, ESV would emerge naturally from business practice. Transnational corporations that have committed serious human rights or environmental violations have been subjected to lawsuits in the US and elsewhere resulting in substantial litigation and settlement costs. In addition to paying compensation, corporations have also agreed to significant changes in their behavior, including efforts to prevent future violations and also measures to improve living conditions for affected populations. Companies have also sustained significant reputational costs, measured most concretely in lost sales but probably also including less quantifiable but still substantial damage to corporate 'brands.' They have therefore found themselves compelled to adopt well-publicized policies designed to improve their public image as 'good corporate citizens.' *Ex ante*, anticipating and avoiding material litigation and reputational costs is now an accepted part of risk management. Companies thus acknowledge an incentive to take proactive steps to avoid activities that could expose them to lawsuits or negative publicity. Attention to human rights and environmental considerations, motivated by financial self-interest, thus can lead corporations to behave in ways that are in many respects consistent with the objectives of CSR advocates.

Importantly, under this model, progress can be achieved without resort to legal mandates that redefine management's responsibility and corporate purpose in terms of CSR. Although the legal regimes of some western European states include elements that reflect appreciation of stakeholder and sustainability values, for the most part states around the world have been very reluctant to enact legislation mandating CSR for corporations organized under their laws or operating within their borders. Certainly there has been no significant movement in that direction in the US. Typically such legislation is viewed as a trade-off between the interests of investors and non-shareholder stakeholders. Developed countries fear loss of investment and higher costs disadvantaging firms in product markets. Developing countries, often competing with each other for foreign investment, are concerned about regulations that might deter entry. Multilateral initiatives, if widely adopted, could address concerns about jurisdictional competition by leveling the playing field but as yet consensus on such matters has proved to be exceedingly difficult to realize. The dynamic sketched here, in contrast, presents the prospect of progress without law, by relying on the financial self-interest of transnational corporations.

Instead of legal mandate, extra-legal pressures reshape management attitudes and behavior. Importantly, these pressures come from private actors, whose influence over corporate behavior causes it to change, in the process in effect redefining corporate purpose. NGOs, community activists and the media in particular devote substantial resources to the investigation and public exposure of human rights and environmental problems. Consumers can punish companies whose activities they disapprove of by refusing to buy and discouraging others from doing so. Employees' morale may depend in part on a sense that the companies they work for behave in acceptable ways, and this may also be a factor in employee recruitment as well. Institutional shareholders, motivated by concerns about investment return rather than CSR as such, nevertheless must evaluate risk, and pension funds in particular need also to worry about the long-term performance of their portfolios. Corporations seeking investors therefore must increasingly acknowledge that their human rights and environmental policies are relevant to valuation metrics. As part of this process, evolving understandings of materiality in turn encourage disclosure of social and environmental information. In all these ways, segments of the public impose their own notions of appropriate corporate behavior on management. The public rather than the law thus has the potential to redefine corporate purpose.

To be sure, law is not entirely irrelevant to this story. NGOs, activists, consumers and the media often express their critique of corporate behavior with explicit or implicit reference to western legal rules and principles. Tort law, environmental regulations or international human rights norms can result in lawsuits. Investors concerned about litigation and reputational risk likewise evaluate corporate policies against a backdrop of law that can result in expensive litigation or provide the basis for negative publicity. Nevertheless, the point is that pressure to change corporate behavior under the model discussed here comes from a range of private, non-state actors rather than from government acting under color of law and according to a redefined concept of management responsibility and corporate purpose. Sometimes there is an actual or implied threat of resort to legal process, but not necessarily. Sometimes the threatened harm may simply be lost business.

Promising as it might be, the process described here, by which the public influences and reshapes corporate purpose, still raises some important questions. First, the process of change based on external pressure depends on exposure of problematic behavior by private actors. Unless human rights or environmental violations are revealed somehow, public opinion cannot bring its power to bear. NGOs, other activists and the media have limited resources. These actors also have a built-in interest in investigating and documenting especially egregious violations. These are the kinds of wrongdoing that will draw the most attention to the crusaders who expose them; favorable, high-profile publicity will garner donations or sell copy. This means that less newsworthy kinds of wrongdoing are less likely to attract attention. Some – perhaps a great deal – of problematic corporate activity inevitably will escape discovery.

Increased corporate disclosure in response to pressure from institutional shareholders likewise is an incomplete source of information on potentially important human rights and environmental matters. Because their concern is investment return, shareholders are typically only interested in such matters to the extent it might affect the corporation's financial performance. Information that is not material in that sense is irrelevant and need not be disclosed, even though it might be important for other, non-financial, reasons. Moreover, a commitment to sustainability may express itself in many small, seemingly routine policies and decisions. Failures to adopt measures are likely not material in themselves, even though together they might signal lack of commitment to sustainability values. Again, this class of private actors may lack the incentives to cause corporations to disclose the full range of information that might be of interest to CSR advocates.

If the first set of concerns centers on whether the optimal amount of information will come to light, a second set considers the efficacy of public pressure when information actually is made available. In the gravest cases of abuse, those most likely to be exposed and arouse public outrage, corporations are likely to respond appropriately, by paying compensation, attempting to fix the problem and, often, investing in improvements for the affected community. They may also embrace general policies that go beyond the particular incident in question and seek to prevent recurrences in other places. In some cases, however, responses may be more symbolic than genuinely transformative. A corporation might announce a high-profile initiative that sounds promising but in fact has a limited impact on the firm's business. This is to be expected. If public opinion is the source of external pressure for change, a response designed to placate the public and deal effectively with the company's reputational concerns may be all that is forthcoming. NGOs or activists may try to expose this fact, but even despite widespread misgivings about corporate good will, a wealthy corporation with a well-respected brand may have an advantage in the public relations contest.

A third caveat is particularly important. At the end of the day, even if there is sufficient transparency and public pressure generates genuine accountability, it must be kept in mind that any social benefits depend ultimately and entirely on the corporation's own voluntary choices. The bottom line in most cases will be the bottom line – namely, the impact of the available alternatives on the corporation's finances. All businesses must earn profits in order to survive and prosper. This is just as true for corporations that pay attention to non-shareholder interests as it is for those that pursue short-term shareholder primacy. Confronted with human rights or environmental problems, corporations must engage in cost-benefit analysis just as they do with other business decisions. This perspective imposes a limit to how far a company will be willing to go. Even if its perspective is broader than short-term shareholder value alone, there will be cases where management will not go as far as a robust conception of social responsibility might seem to demand.

This is the key difference between social responsibility mandated by law and socially responsible behavior that is the voluntary response to external pressures based on financial considerations. Even if 'enlightened' by a broader sense of corporate purpose, voluntary corporate behavior may not attain the breadth of social responsibility that legal mandate could achieve. This is because law has the power to demand behavior based on a range of criteria. Corporate financial considerations may be one, but so too might human rights or environmental values that are deemed to be right even if they are not profitable. The law thus has the ability to require behavior that would not otherwise be chosen willingly. Those who are committed to human rights and environmental values that cannot be justified in cost-benefit terms may therefore find themselves disappointed by an approach to CSR that is based on shareholder value, however enlightened it might be by the pressures of public opinion.

CONCLUSION

The promise of the model of ESV analyzed in this chapter is the possibility of social responsibility being embraced voluntarily by US transnational corporations. This would make up for the absence of legal mandate in this area. Instead, corporations concerned about litigation and reputational risk find it to be in their self-interest to pay attention to human rights and environmental norms of good behavior. Corporate purpose, currently thought of in the US in terms of short-term shareholder value, can thus be redefined more broadly to encompass non-shareholder interests as well – and the engines of change can be NGOs, community activists, consumers, the media and even investors, rather than government regulators. We should hesitate, though, before concluding that all is well or soon will be. For one thing, there is little reason to think that market-based pressures will cause corporate management to discard short-termism in favor of a long-run perspective. There are also reasons to doubt the efficacy of this process as a vehicle for expanding the breadth of management's perspective. Before the public can bring pressure to bear on corporate management, it must have information about what corporations are doing. NGOs, other activists and the media have had some notable successes exposing cases of egregious corporate behavior, and institutional shareholders are encouraging corporations to expand disclosure beyond traditional financial metrics. Still, it would be a mistake to think that these processes will be sufficient to expose the full range of activities that can have negative human rights or environmental impacts. Absent such information, accountability will necessarily be limited. Even where the public is made aware of corporate misdeeds and brings pressure to bear, there is reason to doubt that corporate responses are fully attentive to the affected stakeholder interests. Because management is concerned about reputational costs, it may be motivated by public relations considerations as much as by genuine desire to fix problems and prevent their recurrence. Ultimately, corporate management is and will continue to be driven by cost-benefit concerns, which means that certain problems will not be addressed or prevented if it is not cost-effective to do so. There is, in other words, no reason to think that corporations will voluntarily move in the direction that CSR advocates might think they should go. From this point of view, then, there is a responsibility gap – a disjunction between actual and ideal behavior – that seems inevitable. How large that gap is and will continue to be is an open question. So too is the question as to whether we should tolerate it.

NOTES

1. See for example, the reforms proposed by The Aspen Institute (2009). The proposals would address both managerial and shareholder incentives.
2. I use the term 'management' to refer to the corporation's board of directors and senior officers.
3. Notice that shareholder primacy here refers to the relative weight to be accorded to shareholder versus non-shareholder interests but does not imply primacy as to governance authority. As between managers, shareholders, or other corporate constituencies, management has responsibility for governance, with shareholders exercising only very limited powers of control. The recent 'shareholder empowerment' movement in the US aims to redefine that balance.
4. See also *Flores v Southern Peru Copper Corp* (2003); *Beanal v Freeport-McMoRan* (1997).
5. In 2003, the UN Sub-Commission on the Protection and Promotion of Human Rights produced a draft document called 'Norms on the Responsibilities of Transnational Corporations and Other Business Enterprises with Regard to Human Rights'. This document was based on the inadequacy of a purely state-centric approach to the problem of human rights. The Human Rights Commission, in 2004, chose to do nothing further with it, however, and instead appointed Dr Ruggie to conduct further investigation of the problem. The Norms are thus considered to be 'defunct'. See Nolan and Taylor (2009).
6. The statute also requires, in section 417, disclosure regarding environmental, employee, social, and community issues to the extent 'necessary for an understanding of . . . the company's business.' As Ho (2010) notes, this is 'a much watered-down version of the mandatory social reporting requirements that were initially introduced . . . in 2005' (p. 78, note 94), but later abandoned.
7. For discussion of recent litigation in a number of countries, see Altschuller and Lehr (2009).
8. I draw the distinction among market, command and ethics-based disclosure regimes from Clark and Knight (2008).

REFERENCES

Articles, Books, Reports and Press Releases

Altschuller, S.A. and A. Lehr (2009), 'Corporate social responsibility', *The International Lawyer*, **43**, 577–88.

Anderson, R.J. (2009), 'Toward global corporate citizenship: reframing foreign direct investment', *Michigan State University Journal of International Law*, **18**, 131.

Belinfanti, T. (2009), 'The proxy advisory and corporate governance industry: the case for increased oversight and control', *Stanford Journal of Law, Business and Finance*, **14**, 384–439.

Clark, G.L. and E.R. Knight (2008), 'Institutional investors, the political economy of corporate disclosure, and the market for corporate social responsibility:

implications from the UK Companies Act (2006)', Alfred P. Sloan Foundation Industry Studies, Massachusetts Institute of Technology.
Dickerson, C.M. (2002), 'Human rights: the emerging norm of corporate social responsibility', *Tulane Law Review*, **76**, 1431–60.
Eviatar, D. (2005), 'A big win for human rights: Unocal's settlement with Burmese villagers may spur better corporate conduct', *The Nation*, 9 May 2005.
Fairfax, L.M. (2006), 'The rhetoric of corporate law: the impact of stakeholder rhetoric on corporate norms', *Journal of Corporation Law*, **31**, 675–718.
Gentleman, A. (2006), 'For 2 giants of soft drinks, a crisis in a crucial market', *New York Times*, 23 August 2006.
Ho, V.H. (2010), '"Enlightened shareholder value": corporate governance beyond the shareholder–stakeholder divide', *Journal of Corporation Law*, **36**, 59–112.
Kagan, R.A., N. Gunningham and D. Thornton (2003), 'Explaining corporate environmental performance: how does regulation matter?', *Law & Society Review*, **37**, 51–90.
Khurana, Rakesh (2007), *From Higher Aims to Hired Hands: the Social Transformation of American Business Schools and the Unfulfilled Promise of Management as a Profession*, Princeton, NJ: Princeton University Press.
Millon, D. (1991), 'Redefining corporate law', *Indiana Law Review*, **24**, 223–77.
Mitchell, L.E. (1992), 'A theoretical and practical framework for enforcing corporate constituency statutes', *Texas Law Review*, **70**, 579–643.
Nolan, J. and L. Taylor (2009), 'Corporate responsibility for economic, social and cultural rights: rights in search of a remedy?', *Journal of Business Ethics*, **87**, 433–51.
SEC (2009a), Securities and Exchange Commission, Division of Corporate Finance, Staff Legal Bulletin No. 14E (CF) (27 October 2009).
SEC (2009b), Securities and Exchange Commission, Investor Advisory Committee Briefing Paper No. 1, 'Possible Refinements to the Disclosure Regime' (27 July 2009), p. 7.
SEC (2010), Securities and Exchange Commission, Guidance Regarding Disclosure Related to Climate Change, Releases Nos. 33-9106, 34-61469, FR-82 (2 February 2010).
Stecklow, S. (2005), 'How a global web of activists gives Coke problems in India', *Wall Street Journal*, 7 June 2005.
Stout, L. (2008), 'Why we should stop teaching *Dodge v. Ford*', in Jonathan R. Macey (ed.), *The Iconic Cases in Corporate Law*, St Paul, MN: Thomson/West, pp. 1–10.
Strine, L.E. Jr. (2009), 'Why excessive risk-taking is not unexpected', *New York Times*, 5 October 2009.
Walsh, M.W. (2010), 'Public pension funds are adding risk to raise returns', *New York Times*, 8 March 2010.
Williams, C.A. (2002), 'Corporate social responsibility in an era of economic globalization', *UC Davis Law Review*, **35**, 705–77.
Williams, C.A. and J.M. Conley (2005a), 'An emerging third way? The erosion of the Anglo-American shareholder value construct', *Cornell International Law Journal*, **38**, 493–551.
Williams, C.A. and J.M. Conley (2005b), 'Corporate social responsibility in the international context: is there an emerging fiduciary duty to consider human rights?', *University of Cincinnati Law Review*, **74**, 75–103.
Williams, C.A. and J.M. Conley (2005c), 'Engage, embed, and embellish: theory

versus practice in the corporate social responsibility movement', *Journal of Corporation Law*, **31**, 1–38.

Jurisprudence

Beanal v Freeport-McMoRan, Inc, 969 F Supp 362 (ED La 1997).
Dodge v Ford Motor Co, 170 NW 668 (Mich 1919).
Doe v Unocal, 248 F (3d) 915 (9th Cir 2011).
Flores v Southern Peru Copper Corp, 343 F (3d) 140 (2d Cir 2003).
Loft, Inc v Guth, 2 A (2d) 225 (Del Ch 1938), aff'd (*sub nom Guth v Loft, Inc*) 5 A (2d) 503 (Del 1939).
Paramount Communications, Inc v QVC Network, Inc, 637 A (2d) 34 (Del 1994).
Paramount Communications, Inc v Time Inc, 571 A (2d) 1140 (Del 1989).
Revlon, Inc v MacAndrews & Forbes Holdings, Inc, 506 A (2d) 173 (Del 1986).
Shlensky v Wrigley, 237 NE (2d) 776 (Ill App Ct 1968).
Sosa v Alvarez-Machain, 542 US 692 (2004).
Unocal Corp v Mesa Petroleum Co, 493 A (2d) 946 (Del 1985).

Statutes and Regulations

Alien Tort Claims Act, 28 USC § 1350 (2009).
Companies Act 2006 (UK), c 46, s 172.
17 CFR §§ 229.101 and 229.103 (2010).
17 CFR § 229.303 (2010).

Web Resources

Amnesty International (2009), 'Amnesty International Report 2009: state of the world's human rights', available at http://report2009.amnesty.org/en/about-amnesty-international (accessed 2 June 2011).
Aspen Institute, The (2009), 'Overcoming short-termism: a call for a more responsible approach to investment and business management', available at http://www.aspeninstitute.org/sites/default/files/content/docs/pubs/overcome_short_state0909_0.pdf (accessed 2 June 2011).
Corporate Library, The (2009), 'Climate risk disclosure in SEC filings: an analysis of 10-K reporting by oil and gas, insurance, coal, transportation and electric power companies', available at http://www.edf.org/documents/9903_sec_12_web.pdf (accessed 2 June 2011).
EarthRights International (2011), 'What we do', available at http://www.earthrights.org/about (accessed 2 June 2011).
Economist, The (2008), Special report on corporate social responsibility, 'Just good business', 17 January 2008, available at http://www.economist.com/node/10491077 (accessed 2 June 2011).
Greenpeace (2011), 'About Greenpeace', available at http://www.greenpeace.org/international/en/about/ (accessed 2 June 2011).
GRI (2006), UN Global Compact, Global Reporting Initiative and Realizing Rights, 'Sustainability reporting framework', available at http://www.globalreporting.org/ReportingFramework/ (accessed 2 June 2011).

GRI (2009), UN Global Compact, Global Reporting Initiative and Realizing Rights, 'Corporate human rights reporting: an analysis of current trends', available at http://www.globalreporting.org/NR/rdonlyres/4C5DB4C6-5084-4A84-BE51-0D134B3B5A2E/3605/Human_Rights_analysis_trends.pdf (accessed 2 June 2011).
Human Rights (1948), United Nations Organization, 'Universal Declaration of Human Rights', available at www.un.org/en/documents/udhr/ (accessed 2 June 2011).
ILO (1998), International Labor Organization, 'Declaration of fundamental principles and rights at work', available at http://www.ilo.org/declaration/lang--en/index.htm (accessed 2 June 2011).
OECD (2008), Organisation for Economic Co-operation and Development, 'Guidelines for multinational enterprises', available at http://www.oecd.org/dataoecd/56/36/1922428.pdf (accessed 2 June 2011).
Rio Declaration (1992), United Nations General Assembly, 'Rio Declaration on Environment and Development', available at http://www.un.org/documents/ga/conf151/aconf15126-1annex1.htm (accessed 2 June 2011).
Ruggie, J. (2008), 'Protect, respect and remedy: a framework for business and human rights', available at http://www.reports-and-materials.org/Ruggie-report-7-Apr-2008.pdf (accessed 2 June 2011).
UN Global Compact (2000), 'Overview of the UN Global Compact', available at http://www.unglobalcompact.org/AboutTheGC/index.html (accessed 2 June 2011).
UN Human Rights (1966a), 'International Covenant on Civil and Political Rights', available at http://www2.ohchr.org/english/law/ccpr.htm (accessed 2 June 2011).
UN Human Rights (1966b), 'International Covenant on Economic, Social and Cultural Rights', available at http://www2.ohchr.org/english/law/cescr.htm (accessed 2 June 2011).
UN Responsible Investment (2005), 'United Nations Principles for Responsible Investment', available at www.unpri.org (accessed 2 June 2011).
Walker, D. (2009), 'Evolving executive equity compensation and the limits of optimal contracting', available at http://papers.ssrn.com/sol3/papers.cfm?abstract_id=1443170 (accessed 2 June 2011).
WEF (2011), World Economic Forum, 'Global corporate citizenship', available at http://www.weforum.org/s?s=global+corporate+citizenship (accessed 2 June 2011).

5. Re-evaluating the basis of corporate governance in the post, post-Enron era

Leonard I. Rotman

INTRODUCTION

The Enron scandal of 2001 shook the foundation of modern corporate governance in many ways. It resulted in the collapse of one of the giants of corporate America, taking with it numerous jobs, investment dollars and confidence in the securities marketplace. However, it also brought into question the manner in which corporations were governed and how they ought to be governed.

Curiously, Enron's collapse coincided with the publication of Henry Hansmann and Reinier Kraakman's article 'The End of History for Corporate Law' (2001), which sought to end discussions of how modern corporations were to be governed by asserting the triumph of the shareholder primacy norm over competing progressive theories of the corporation. Hansmann and Kraakman claimed that worldwide convergence in corporate theory had led toward a unitary vision of corporate purpose founded on shareholder primacy. This in turn resulted in their claim of the 'end of history for corporate law,' in which the struggle for dominance between the shareholder primacy and stakeholder theories of corporate governance rooted in the famous Berle–Dodd debate of the 1930s had ended.

It will be argued that the reality of corporate governance in the post, post-Enron era is entirely inconsistent with the vision articulated by Hansmann and Kraakman. This chapter sets out Hansmann and Kraakman's 'end of history' thesis and assesses whether it can be justified on grounds traditionally used to corroborate their vision of corporate governance. The chapter considers the strength of Hansmann and Kraakman's claim by examining two of the cases most often used to demonstrate the validity of the shareholder primacy model: *Dodge v Ford Motor Co* (1919) (*Dodge v Ford*) and *Revlon Inc v MacAndrews & Forbes Holdings Inc* (1986) (*Revlon*).

The chapter concludes that Hansmann and Kraakman's claim of the 'end of history' for corporate law is factually incorrect. Analysis of the *Dodge v Ford* (1919) and *Revlon* (1986) cases demonstrates the untenable grounds on which Hansmann and Kraakman's argument rests. Close scrutiny of *Dodge v Ford* and *Revlon* demonstrates that neither is actually supportive of the shareholder primacy model. Rather, those cases are shown to be far more consistent with a broader, stakeholder-oriented model of corporate governance that is generally associated with the progressive corporate law movement and the entity theory of corporate law than with the shareholder primacy norm.

THE 'END OF HISTORY' CLAIM

Hansmann and Kraakman contended in 2001 that it was pointless to continue debating the merits of progressive models of corporate governance in which corporate management must be mindful of a variety of stakeholder interests beyond those of corporate shareholders. Based upon mounting pressures imposed by the 'business, government and legal elites in key commercial jurisdictions' they contended that '[t]here is no longer any serious competitor to the view that corporate law should principally strive to increase long-term shareholder value' (Hansmann and Kraakman 2001, p. 439). They claimed that that vision had already 'profoundly affected corporate governance practices throughout the world' (ibid.) and that it was only a matter of time until those same pressures were also brought to bear upon corporate law. For this reason, they concluded that '[t]he triumph of the shareholder-oriented model of the corporation over its principal competitors is now assured' (ibid., p. 468).

Hansmann and Kraakman recognize the existence of alternative theories of corporate purpose throughout the twentieth century in their article, but insist that these other theories had failed to provide a serious threat to the shareholder primacy model. In support of this assertion, they identify five basic characteristics of the corporate form – '(1) full legal personality, including well-defined authority to bind the firm to contracts and to bond those contracts with assets that are the property of the firm, as distinct from the firm's owners; (2) limited liability for owners and managers; (3) shared ownership by investors of capital; (4) delegated management under a board structure and; (5) transferable shares' (ibid., pp. 439–40) – which, they maintain, 'provide, by their nature, for a firm that is strongly responsive to shareholder interests' (ibid., p. 440).

These 'core' characteristics of corporations were said to create particular efficiencies in organizing corporations, though especially corporations with multiple shareholders and which dominated developed market economies. Tellingly, these same five characteristics, according to Hansmann and Kraakman's views, do not necessarily dictate how the interests of other participants in the firm – such as employees, creditors, other suppliers, customers, or society at large – will be accommodated, nor do they address how conflicts of interest between shareholders, specifically those between controlling and non-controlling shareholders, are to be resolved (ibid.).

According to Hansmann and Kraakman (2001), these characteristics have existed in corporations created in every major corporate law jurisdiction since 1900.[1] Thus they claim that the very convergence that led to the triumph of the shareholder primacy model can be traced to that time. If, as they contend, only the 'more detailed structure of corporate law' has been altered since then (Hansmann and Kraakman 2001, p. 440), why did the supposed triumph of the shareholder primacy model not happen until quite some time later? In fact Hansmann and Kraakman (2001) admit that their assertion that '[t]he triumph of the shareholder-oriented model of the corporation over its principal competitors is now assured,' is not an undisputed claim, but 'was problematic as recently as twenty-five years ago' (p. 468). If alternative theories of corporate governance could legitimately compete with shareholder primacy theory, what caused the former's inability to compete after that time? This is particularly deserving of discussion if, as Hansmann and Kraakman claim, the triumph of the shareholder primacy model was premised on events established by 1900 and corporate law has seen changes only to the 'more detailed structure of corporate law' since that time. Further bringing their conclusion about the 'end of history' into question is their contention that shareholder primacy earned its stripes as the dominant theory of corporate governance by defeating alternative theories of the corporation in competitions during the period following World War II without providing substantive evidence to demonstrate or justify their claim.

Hansmann and Kraakman (2001) identify three principal factors which, they assert, drove a consensus on the shareholder primacy model: (1) the failure of alternative models including manager-oriented, labor-oriented, state-oriented and stakeholder models; (2) the competitive pressure of global commerce created by the forces of logic (that is, shareholder primacy results in greater efficiencies than other models), example (as seen by observing the economic performances of jurisdictions in which shareholder primacy predominates) and competition (shareholder primacy-based corporations have competitive advantages, compared to other firms organized according to different theories, as a result of (a) access to equity capital at lower cost; (b) more aggressive development of new product markets and (c) more rapid advancement of inefficient investments); and (3) the shift of interest groups' influence in favor of an emerging shareholder class. Logically, these factors took some time to have their claimed effect. Perhaps this accounts for the 75-year gap between the convergence of corporate law statutes and the triumph of shareholder primacy theory. They make no such claim, though.

While Hansmann and Kraakman (2001) claim that corporations ought not be run in the interests of shareholders alone,[2] they nonetheless assert 'as a consequence of both logic and experience,' that the best means to obtain widespread social welfare is 'to make corporate managers strongly accountable to shareholder interests and, at least in direct terms, only to those interests' (p. 441). Thus they believe that benefiting shareholders is the best way for corporations to benefit society. Precisely why this is so is not substantially addressed in their paper. Rather, it is merely asserted as fact. Prioritizing shareholders necessarily comes at the expense of the other claimants to corporate profits, such as employees or creditors. Hansmann and Kraakman (2001) support their conclusion by asserting that those other stakeholders (other than creditors) are beneficiaries of alternative forms of protection that exist outside the bounds of corporate law – such as labor law, tort law or antitrust – from which shareholders do not benefit.

Questions over the timing of shareholder primacy theory's alleged dominance of corporate governance or the enhanced protection of non-shareholder stakeholder interests aside, Hansmann and Kraakman (2001) were not the only commentators articulating the shareholder primacy vision of corporate governance. Few others were as bold or provocative in their assertions, though. One notable exception was Bainbridge (1997), who made the claim that '[o]ver the last few decades, law and economics scholars have mounted a largely successful hostile takeover of the corporate legal academy' (p. 857).

Why, one might ask, were these authors so brash about their extravagant claims? Were they simply articulating their shared vision of the status quo or did other motivations underlie their grandiose claims? In later years, Hansmann (2006) conceded that the 'end of history' paper 'was written to capture, a bit provocatively, a particular perspective in a debate on convergence in corporate law that was just then gathering steam' (p. 745). He further accepted that '[t]here will probably never be perfect homogeneity in the approaches taken to these issues,' with the result that 'it might be said that this leaves most of the important and interesting debates within corporate law today untouched by our thesis [in the 'end of history' paper]. And, admittedly, that's not an unreasonable thing to say' (ibid., p. 750). Hansmann's recognition of the hyperbole surrounding the 'end of history' claim is another step towards debunking it as being appropriately representative of the state of corporate law jurisprudence in the post, post-Enron era.

What is truly ironic about Hansmann and Kraakman's assertion of the 'end of history' for corporate law is that it was published in the same year that witnessed the collapse of Enron and the onset of the corporate scandals that erupted in its wake. The Enron debacle is often regarded as a turning point in American corporate law for its illustration of both the limitations and failures of the shareholder primacy model. The desire to keep share prices high in order to satisfy, inter alia, the short-term profit motivation underlying the shareholder primacy model is largely responsible for the downfall of Enron, one of the darlings of post-1980s American corporate law. In retrospect, Hansmann and Kraakman (2001) could not have chosen a worse time to claim that shareholder primacy had won the battle for corporate governance theory supremacy than when Enron, a poster child for the shareholder primacy model, was collapsing under the weight of scandal and allegations of impropriety and corruption. The fact that they articulated their thesis without substantive evidence or argument indicating the triumph of the shareholder primacy model over competing progressive visions of corporate activity further undermines the legitimacy of their claim.

Perhaps most importantly, however, Hansmann and Kraakman (2001) ignore the very real conclusion that, in 2001, many of the issues that plagued corporate law were the same as those that had hampered it decades before. These very same problems of widespread corruption and abuses of managerial power were the foundations of progressive critiques of the undue emphasis on shareholder interests by corporate management so many years before.

In 1934, then-Yale law professor and future US Supreme Court Justice William O. Douglas wrote a scathing attack on corporate management's improper use of corporate powers:

> [T]he criticism [leveled at corporate practices] has been symptomatic of indignation and disapproval of many different abuses and malpractices disclosed in recent years . . . secret loans to officers and directors, undisclosed profit-sharing plans, timely contracts unduly favorable to affiliated interests, dividend policies based on false estimates, manipulations of credit resources and capital structures to the detriment of minority interests, pool operations, and trading in securities of the company by virtue of inside information, to mention only a few. These are not peculiar to recent times. They are forms of business activity long known to the law. But lately they have increased in intensity and frequency in spite of a more articulate statement of the law governing them and in the face of a growing recognition of the broad bases of an equitable jurisdiction for their regulation and control. All of which means that

> business, and its legal advisors, have shown great ineptitude in appreciating and appraising the social importance and significance of many of their activities. Also, it means that considerable refashioning of codes of conduct – in business as well as in law – must be effected if the next cyclical trend is not to produce as many malpractices and abuses as has the current one. (Douglas 1934, p. 1306)

In the post, post-Enron era, similar descriptions have become commonplace. However, Douglas's decades-old critique pointedly illustrates that some of the most pressing of contemporary corporate law issues are merely the most recent incarnations of long-disputed matters (see, e.g., Freund 1897; Hohfeld 1909). These matters have remained contentious specifically as a result of the ongoing debate over the appropriate characterization of corporate governance, a matter incorrectly dismissed out of hand by Hansmann and Kraakman in 'The End of History for Corporate Law' (2001) (paraphrasing Fukuyama 1992).

As strenuously as Hansmann and Kraakman (2001) extolled the complete dominance of the shareholder primacy model over stakeholder and other, alternative, theories of the corporation, other equally prominent commentators opposed it with the same exuberance. These latter commentators have continued to do so following the publication of 'The End of History for Corporate Law.' In the face of claims of shareholder primacy, they and others have held fast to a broader vision of the duties of corporate management that extends beyond shareholders to include other important corporate stakeholders.

While shareholder primacy may have held a dominant position among corporate law scholars at the time of Hansmann and Kraakman's 'end of history' paper, particularly in the United States, what they were articulating was a rather different proposition, namely the complete eradication of alternative theories of corporate governance. These statements were particularly damning to scholars who viewed the fulfillment of corporate duties as extending beyond shareholder interests to other corporate stakeholders.

Although progressive corporate law ideas may have held a minority position in corporate law scholarship in 2001, to suggest that the progressive corporate law movement was either moribund or its ideas unworthy of consideration or debate on the merits required more evidence than either Hansmann and Kraakman (or Bainbridge) adduce in their papers. Indeed, progressive corporate law scholars have been around as long as corporate law scholarship has existed (Millon 1990; Wells 2002). While progressive corporate law scholars may have been fewer in number than their shareholder primacy counterparts, to have them or their contentions be written off as completely as they were by Hansmann and Kraakman's 'end of history' thesis is neither historically accurate nor factually supportable.

To scholars who considered themselves progressives or stakeholder theorists, Hansmann and Kraakman (2001) were effectively throwing down the gauntlet in their 'end of history' paper with their claims about the eradication of meaningful progressive corporate law theory. Progressives were, directly or indirectly, being challenged by Hansmann and Kraakman to demonstrate that their work was still relevant and meaningful to corporate law and retained an important place within corporate law scholarship. Many progressives responded to that challenge. Today, progressive corporate law scholarship, both in the United States and elsewhere, is more plentiful than it has been in years and includes contributions from an increasing number of scholars. It remains to be seen how significant the impact of the most recent financial crisis will be on corporate law scholarship in the ensuing years and how that will reflect on the continuing debate between shareholder primacy and stakeholder theory.

The very debate that Hansmann and Kraakman contended was undoubtedly over by 2001 is still being waged (see, e.g. Friedman 1970; Elhauge 2005; Bratton and Wachter 2008). Indeed, a recently published téte-â-téte between progressive scholar Kent Greenfield (2008) and shareholder primacy advocate Gordon Smith (2008) intentionally harkens back to the Berle–Dodd debate of the 1930s (Berle 1931, 1932; Dodd 1932, 1935). How then could the 'end of history' thesis for corporate law have been reached in 2001 as Hansmann and Kraakman (2001) claimed? As a result of events unfolding in the post, post-Enron era, its achievement looks even less convincing.

The Enron collapse significantly wounded Hansmann and Kraakman's 'end of history' claim by illustrating some of the harmful consequences of adhering to the shareholder primacy model. The recent worldwide financial collapses have raised even further questions about the legitimacy of their claim of the triumph of shareholder primacy (particularly since Hansmann and Kraakman insisted that their 'end of history' thesis was part of a worldwide convergence of thought about corporate purpose). At least part of the blame for these collapses must be attributed to the pursuit of short-term profit at the expense of long-term fiscal responsibility that has been a fundamental part of the shareholder primacy model.

Enron and other corporate scandals demonstrate that market pressures and managerial incentivism sometimes influence directors to take risks where they are either not warranted or for the sole purpose of increasing share value. Such actions please shareholders (at least in the short term), and often have a direct benefit upon the directors' own compensation as a result of stock options and other benefits conferred upon them, but do little to address the concerns of other stakeholders. In some circumstances, as with Enron, these actions may lead to the financial collapse of the corporation, which ultimately removes the value provided to shareholders as their shares become worthless, but leaves directors' benefits untouched.

The publicity generated from the trials of corporate executives such as Jeffrey Skilling has brought greater awareness of these occurrences. With this increased awareness comes a considerable degree of cynicism. Post, post-Enron there is far less support for incentive-based payment systems like stock options for directors than may have previously existed. The notion that corporate directors might benefit from actions they take on behalf of their corporations is now more likely to be characterized as running afoul of their fiduciary obligations than being regarded as sound corporate practice or applauded as paralleling the best interests of corporations. While the immediate post-Enron era drastically altered previously held conceptions of what constitutes appropriate business practice for corporate directors, the recent financial crisis and the slow recovery that has characterized its aftermath have further shifted academic and public opinion away from the shareholder primacy model.

While shareholders do have clear and legitimate interests in corporate activities, that does not entail that they are the only corporate stakeholders deserving of attention, or even the majority of attention, from corporate directors and officers. By emphasizing shareholder interests at the expense of those belonging to other stakeholders, shareholder primacy inappropriately skews the focus of corporate directors and officers in discharging their duties and allocating benefits (Blair and Stout 2001). Blair and Stout (2001) further contend that arguments in favor of shareholder primacy ignore a variety of economic arguments that suggest that it could be inefficient. These include options theory, firm-specific investment, team production analysis (Blair and Stout 1999) and the efficient capital markets hypothesis (ECMH) (Stout 2000).

Thus, while shareholder interests are definitely accounted for in the grand scheme of directors' and officers' decisions made on behalf of corporations, those interests are not the only determinants for the actions taken. Rather, they are merely considerations (albeit important ones) existing alongside others, such as the interests of other stakeholders and the broader communities that are economically or physically affected by the corporation's actions. As Greenfield (2005) stated, '[f]or most people honestly wrestling with issues of corporate governance . . . shareholder primacy is not the foundational assumption but rather one of the potential conclusions. . . . [O]ther potential conclusions exist as well' (p. 89).

A meaningful separation between the corporation and its shareholders – and, for that matter, its other stakeholders – is necessary since the recognition of the corporation as a legal entity distinct from its shareholders is, as Farrar (1998) states, 'not simply a matter of form and fiction,' but, rather, 'the way in which law defines and regulates economic reality' (p. 142). The corporation, by definition, is not the same as its stakeholders – whether they be shareholders or others – and may legitimately have different interests to some, or perhaps all, of its shareholders (*Shlensky v Wrigley* 1968). Recognizing this basic characteristic of the corporate form is fundamentally inconsistent with the notion of shareholder primacy. This fact ought to prove fatal to the continued existence of the shareholder primacy norm as a legitimate basis for corporate governance without the need for further argument.

If the financial casualties observed in the post, post-Enron era do not warrant questioning the future role of shareholder primacy theory in corporate law, one wonders what will. When the even more varying, and legitimate, interests of other corporate stakeholders are factored in alongside those of shareholders, reconciling the range of divergent interests becomes even more difficult, if not impossible, to accomplish if the interests of corporations are viewed as entirely synonymous with the interests of its shareholders.

THE JURISPRUDENTIAL COUNTERCLAIM

An often-neglected element of shareholder primacy scholarship is a consideration of the impact of corporate personality on assertions that corporations exist to make money for shareholders and that corporate management is obliged to further that end. As discussed above, shareholder primacy advocates assume that corporations exist to make money for their shareholders, but they provide scant evidence in support of this proposition. In the absence of substantive reasoning supporting the shareholder primacy model, the jurisprudential understanding of corporate personality may not mesh as well with Hansmann and Kraakman's 'end of history' thesis as many shareholder primacy theorists have imagined.

Corporations, as legal entities, have interests that may or may not mesh well with the interests of its shareholders, such as long-term corporate sustainability. If a corporation possesses such interests, what justifies subordinating them in favor of maximizing shareholder value, particularly in the short term? Certainly, entity theory dictates that where a corporation's interests are inconsistent with the maximization of profit for distribution to shareholders, then engaging in shareholder profit maximization is not a legitimate corporate purpose. It stands to reason then that shareholder wealth maximization, on its own, cannot be a universal basis for ascertaining corporate purpose.

This reasoning brings into question the long-standing reliance of shareholder primacy theorists on the *Dodge v Ford* (1919) and *Revlon* (1986) cases and their apparent endorsement of the shareholder primacy model. However, a closer examination of these cases indicates that they do not support the shareholder primacy model. Rather, the findings therein are far more consistent with progressive analyses of corporate purpose and corporate entity theory than with the shareholder primacy norm.

Dodge v Ford Motor Co (1919)

The facts of *Dodge v Ford* (1919) are generally well known, but their full implications are not always recognized. The Dodge brothers held 10 per cent of the shares in Ford Motor Co (FMC) and had grown accustomed to earning large dividends on their investment. In addition to the $1.2 million that FMC paid annually in regular dividends, FMC had paid some $41 million in special dividends to its shareholders between December 1911 and October 1915. However, following the declaration of a special dividend of $2 million in November 1916, FMC's board of directors decided to cease paying such large special dividends, opting instead to invest its profits to improve its infrastructure and further reduce the price of its vehicles.

In response to this change in corporate policy, the Dodge brothers commenced a lawsuit against FMC's management for failing to distribute an appropriate amount of FMC's earnings to its shareholders. They sought a special dividend of not less than 75 per cent of FMC's accumulated cash surplus, as well as injunctions to prevent the planned infrastructure improvements and vehicle price reductions.

At trial, the Dodge brothers were largely successful in their claim. The trial court ordered the declaration of a dividend in excess of $19 million and granted an injunction to halt construction of FMC's planned new manufacturing and smelting facilities. The trial court did not, however, prevent the reduction in the price of Ford vehicles. The judgment was appealed and the Michigan Supreme Court was not as favorable toward the Dodge brothers as the trial court had been, despite the Supreme Court's use of rhetoric that has long been used to support the shareholder primacy model.

The Michigan Supreme Court determined that FMC's decisions to stop paying large special dividends, to invest in infrastructure improvements and to reduce the price of its vehicles:

> does not call for and is not intended to produce immediately a more profitable business but a less profitable one; not only less profitable than formerly but less

> profitable than it is admitted it might be made. The apparent immediate effect will be to diminish the value of shares and the returns to shareholders. (p. 683)

The court also expressed its understanding of the purpose of for-profit corporations in the following famous quote:

> A business corporation is organized and carried on primarily for the profit of the stockholders. The powers of the directors are to be employed for that end. The discretion of directors is to be exercised in the choice of means to attain that end, and does not extend to a change in the end itself, to the reduction of profits, or to the non-distribution of profits among stockholders in order to devote them to other purposes. (ibid.)

The Michigan Supreme Court held that it could interfere with business decisions where profit maximization was not the primary motivation of directors.[3] Accordingly, the court ordered the payment of significant dividends to FMC's shareholders, which was what the court determined 'the circumstances required to be done' (ibid.). However, in apparent opposition to the ordered payment of dividends, the court vacated the injunction imposed by the trial court on the construction of FMC's new manufacturing and smelting facilities. Further, it did not enjoin the corporation's plan to lower the price of its vehicles from $440 to $360, even though that price reduction would have lowered FMC's sales figures by at least $48 million in the first year of the reduction.

By allowing FMC's board to invest in infrastructure improvement and to reduce its vehicle price, the court expressly 'recognized that plans must often be made for a long future, for expected competition, for a continuing as well as immediately profitable venture' (*Dodge v Ford* 1919, p. 683). This is inconsistent with the short-term emphasis on maximizing shareholder profits under the shareholder primacy model. Further, as I have argued elsewhere, FMC's decision to invest in its infrastructure and reduce the price of its vehicles cannot be appropriately assessed in the absence of the context in which those decisions were made (Rotman 2010).

At the time of the judgment in *Dodge v Ford*, FMC was the most efficient and profitable automobile manufacturer in the world. However, it was also facing increasing competition for market share in the crowded automobile sector. The Dodge brothers had started to manufacture their own vehicles in 1914. General Motors Corp, which had been formed in 1908 by the merging of Buick and Oldsmobile and expanded in 1909 by adding the Oakland Motor Company (later called Pontiac) and Cadillac, merged with the Chevrolet Motor Company in 1916 to create serious competition for FMC's formerly unchallenged position of market dominance (General Motors 2011). As a result of these developments, FMC had to be legitimately concerned about maintaining its market position in the increasingly competitive automotive manufacturing industry. These realities justified FMC's board taking the action it did in order to protect the corporation's short- and long-term interests.

The infrastructure improvements that facilitated the vehicle price reductions brought more potential customers for Ford vehicles than had existed previously. Further, combining these price reductions with increased wages for FMC employees – notably by way of the famous '$5 day' – may have initially appeared to be antithetical to FMC's profit-making mission, but ultimately created a new class of people who could afford to purchase Ford vehicles. The $5 a day wage more than doubled the previous wage when the one-hour reduction in the length of the work day is factored into the equation (Michigan Department of Natural Resources 2010).

Consequently, while FMC may have earned less profit per vehicle sold following the price reduction, that did not invariably translate into a reduced corporate profit. Moreover, the price decrease was consistent with fostering longer term profitability by increasing the volume of FMC vehicles sold and maintaining its position as the leading automobile manufacturer in the world.

Dodge v Ford (1919) is, therefore, more consistent with a broader, stakeholder-oriented vision of corporate purpose and with entity theory than it is with the pro-shareholder primacy manner in which it is typically understood. FMC did not ignore the making of profit through its actions, but its decisions were measured against the changing realities of the automobile industry and the necessity of maintaining the corporation's long-term viability. Properly understood, *Dodge v Ford* does not support the idea of shareholder wealth maximization but indicates that the pursuit of corporate profits does not exist in a vacuum. A number of considerations that are primarily oriented towards the sustainability of corporate interests and long-term viability must be accounted for. Since FMC's board properly accounted for these key issues to corporate sustainability, its exercise of business judgment went largely unchallenged by the Michigan Supreme Court in *Dodge v Ford* (1919).

***Revlon Inc v MacAndrews & Forbes Holdings Inc* (1986)**

Like *Dodge v Ford* (1919), the more recent *Revlon Inc v MacAndrews & Forbes Holdings Inc* (1986) is generally considered to be a case affirming the shareholder primacy model. Yet, upon closer inspection, the logical implications of the case reveal that it cannot be properly understood to support shareholder primacy as the normative basis of corporate governance.

The directors of Revlon, faced with a hostile takeover bid for the company, engaged in defensive tactics in an attempt to quash the bid. They negotiated the purchase of the company with a friendly buyer at a lower price than under the hostile bid, but one which protected the interests of certain creditors and allowed management to continue to operate the company if it agreed to sell off certain divisions and remained capable of servicing its debts. In overturning the directors' decision to sell to the friendly buyer, the Delaware Supreme Court held that the directors' actions were improper, insofar as 'obtaining the highest price for the benefit of the stockholders should have been the central theme guiding director action' (p. 182).

The court determined that Revlon's directors had a duty, once the breakup of the company was inevitable, to shift focus from 'the preservation of Revlon as a corporate entity to the maximization of the company's value at a sale for the stockholders' benefit' (ibid.). Since the directors' role had changed from 'defenders of the corporate bastion to auctioneers charged with getting the best price for the stockholders,' their agreement to sell to a lower bidder was held to be in breach of their duty of care owed to the company's shareholders (ibid.).

The shift in the directors' duties, as laid down in the *Revlon* case, known as '*Revlon* duties,' requires directors to shift their duties from the best interests of the corporation to maximizing shareholder value when the breakup of the company is inevitable. This aspect of the *Revlon* judgment was subsequently affirmed and clarified in *Paramount Communications Inc v Time Inc* (1989), where the Delaware Supreme Court determined that there were generally two circumstances that resulted in *Revlon*-type duties, both of which focused on the breakup of the target: when 'a corporation initiates an active bidding process seeking to sell itself or to effect a business reorganization involving a clear breakup of the company' or when 'in response to a bidder's offer, a target abandons its long-term strategy and seeks an alternative transaction involving the breakup of the company' (*Paramount v Time* 1989, p. 1150). It was also affirmed in *Paramount Communications v QVC Network* (1994), where the Delaware Supreme Court stated that it was not necessary for an inevitable breakup of the corporation to occur before *Revlon*-type duties were triggered. Rather, the court held that the key to the application of those duties was the pending sale of corporate control. Thus, the court concluded that directors owed shareholders a duty of loyalty to maximize shareholder value where a corporation engaged in a transaction that either caused a change in corporate control or resulted in the breakup of the corporation.

What may be understood from the application of these *Revlon* duties is that in circumstances where a corporation is not under threat of a hostile takeover involving either the inevitable breakup of the company or the sale of corporate control, its directors' duties are not restricted to an exclusive focus on shareholders' interests.

If directors' duties to shareholders under the shareholder primacy model are to facilitate the best interests of shareholders, logic dictates that where a shift in those duties is mandated by the imposition of *Revlon* duties, such a shift would require a shift *away from* the shareholders' interests. The Delaware Supreme Court is clear in stating that *Revlon* duties are of a different type than those which directors normally owe to shareholders. Thus, if the end result of imposing *Revlon* duties is to maximize shareholder value, then the duty owed before the *Revlon* shift must be something *other than* maximizing shareholder value. This conclusion is consistent with the court's finding in *Revlon* (1986) that the directors' duties existing prior to the shift necessitated by the inevitable breakup of the company was 'the preservation of Revlon as a corporate entity' (p. 182). This finding is also consistent with the entity theory of the corporation, not the shareholder primacy model.

While the existence of *Revlon* duties may have been weakened by subsequent jurisprudential developments, this does not affect the impact of *Revlon*'s shifting duties on Hansmann and Kraakman's assertion of the triumph of the shareholder primacy model. It could be argued that the *Revlon* shift in directors' duties is merely a shift to a more immediate shareholder benefit and, therefore, remains consistent with the shareholder primacy model. Yet if such a characterization is accurate, the court in *Revlon* would not have described the shift as being *toward* shareholder benefit, which implies that those duties did not point in that direction previously.

Consequently, it may be seen that the *Revlon* judgment is properly regarded as inconsistent with the triumph of the shareholder primacy norm and Hansmann and Kraakman's assertion of the 'end of history' for corporate law. While Lynn Stout (2002) has found that '*Revlon* . . . defines the one context in which Delaware law mandates shareholder primacy' (p. 1204), it is clear that *Revlon* mandates shareholder primacy only where a shift in directors' ordinary duties to shareholders is required by a transaction either causing a change in corporate control or resulting in the inevitable breakup of the company.

CONCLUDING THOUGHTS

So where does the foregoing analysis leave our understanding of the theoretical basis of corporate governance? If Hansmann and Kraakman's 'end of history' thesis no longer holds water, as this chapter asserts, what ought our understanding of corporate purpose be in the post, post-Enron era? Stephen Bainbridge, formerly a shareholder primacy advocate, has recently advocated a shift to director primacy as a more accurate representation of the true basis of corporate power, but his analysis remains predicated upon shareholder wealth maximization (Bainbridge 2003). The team production model conceived by Blair and Stout (1999) also places significant emphasis on the role of directors as 'mediating hierarchs' within the corporate structure. Certainly, directors hold considerable power within the corporate vehicle. As a result, there are significant limitations imposed upon their exercise of power. These limits are tempered, however, by the business judgment rule.

The business judgment rule states that corporate directors will not be held responsible for errors in judgment while acting in their directorial capacities if they can demonstrate that they exercised their judgment in good faith, with due care and using sound business judgment. Under the business judgment rule, courts will defer to the judgment exercised by directors and will not substitute their analysis for directors' decisions made or actions taken that may have been less than ideal but that may nonetheless be justified under the circumstances as a proper exercise of business judgment. Yet if we are to view directors or corporate management more generally, as holding the seat of power within the corporate form, that tells us only who possesses the power to make corporate decisions; it does not tell us what their duties in facilitating the best interests of the corporation are, or what the purpose of the corporation is.

This broader issue of corporate purpose has been addressed by the Supreme Court of Canada in *Peoples Department Stores Inc v Wise* (2004) (*Peoples*), where the court unanimously clarified that corporate management is responsible to act in the best interests of the corporation as an entity. The court further held that, in determining what those interests are, management may account for the interests of 'shareholders, employees, suppliers, creditors, consumers, governments and the environment' (*Peoples* 2004, para 42). This key aspect of the *Peoples* decision was subsequently affirmed in *BCE Inc v 1976 Debentureholders* (*BCE Inc*) (2008). These decisions have a profound impact on the appropriate characterization of corporate governance and Hansmann and Kraakman's 'end of history' claim in the post, post-Enron era.

In Canadian corporate jurisprudence, not only has the shareholder primacy model been clearly and thoroughly discredited in favor of the entity theory, the categories of stakeholders whose interests may be relevant in assessing a corporation's best interests are not restricted to shareholders but also include a host of others, including natural persons, artificial persons, government and the environment. However, the extent to which those stakeholders' interests are considered ultimately rests with corporate management and those interests are not to supersede the corporation's own independent interests.

Are there such significant distinctions between Canadian corporate law and the regimes existing in other countries that render the resolution of these matters by the Supreme Court of Canada inappropriate for use elsewhere? Canadian corporate statutes do create some unique formulations that either do not exist in other countries or do not operate in quite the same way as they do elsewhere. This may be seen, for example, in the more extensive derivative action and oppression remedy provisions in Canadian division of powers corporation statutes (referring to the statutory division of corporate powers between management and various stakeholders) – such as the *Canada Business Corporations Act* – than may exist in other jurisdictions. However, the corporate purpose aspect of the *Peoples* (2004) and *BCE Inc* (2008) judgments is not at all dependent upon these formulations. Consequently, the corporate purpose thesis advanced in *Peoples* and *BCE Inc* is an appropriate point of reference for other countries.

Interest in foundational corporate law issues has lately appeared to be on the upswing. The *Citizens United* (2010) case has further moved the question of corporate purpose to the forefront of deliberations in American corporate law, at least among corporate law commentators. This case, which concerns corporate political speech, not corporate purpose, raises serious questions about the implications of corporate personality that are quite pertinent to the shareholder primacy–stakeholder theory debate. While the US Supreme Court did not concern itself with the issue of corporate purpose in that case, if corporations may now access general revenues for political speech purposes, the extent to which that use of corporate funds is consistent or inconsistent with the issue of corporate purpose is an important and relevant matter.

While the fundamental questions of corporate identity and corporate purpose are as old as the corporate form, they have never truly been resolved. Indeed, the questions raised in the Berle–Dodd debate still resonate with contemporary corporate law scholars. Further, these issues are not restricted to any particular jurisdiction but are equally important wherever corporations exist. Hansmann and Kraakman (2001) may have sought to end this debate with their 'end of history' thesis, but the history they viewed as being at an end is still unfolding in the post, post-Enron era.

NOTES

1. Hansmann and Kraakman (2001) observed, '[b]y around 1900, however, every major commercial jurisdiction appears to have provided for at least one standard-form legal entity with the five characteristics listed above as the default rules, and this has remained the case ever since' (p. 440).
2. 'All thoughtful people believe that corporate enterprise should be organized and operated to serve the interests of society as a whole and that the interests of shareholders deserve no greater weight in this social calculus than do the interests of any other members of society' (*ibid*, p. 441).
3. Significantly in *Dodge v Ford Motor Co* (1919), the court also observed that 'it is not within the lawful powers of a board of directors to shape and conduct the affairs of a corporation for the merely incidental benefit of shareholders and for the primary purpose of benefiting others, and no one will contend that if the avowed purpose of the defendant directors was to sacrifice the interests of shareholders it would not be the duty of the courts to interfere' (p. 683).

REFERENCES

Books and Articles

Bainbridge, S.M. (1997), 'Community and statism: a conservative contractarian critique of progressive corporate law scholarship', *Cornell Law Review*, **82**, 856–904.

Bainbridge, S.M. (2003), 'Director primacy: the means and ends of corporate governance', *Northwestern University Law Review*, **97**, 547–606.

Berle, A.A. Jr. (1931), 'Corporate powers as powers in trust', *Harvard Law Review*, **44**, 1049–74.

Berle, A.A. Jr. (1932), 'For whom corporate managers are trustees: a note', *Harvard Law Review*, **45**, 1365–72.

Blair, M.M. and L.A. Stout (1999), 'A team production theory of corporate law', *Virginia Law Review*, **85,** 247–328.

Blair, M.M. and L.A. Stout (2001), 'Director accountability and the mediating role of the corporate board', *Washington University Law Quarterly*, **79**, 403–47.

Bratton, W.W. and M.L. Wachter (2008), 'Shareholder primacy's corporatist origins: Adolf Berle and "The Modern Corporation"', *Journal of Corporation Law*, **34**, 99–152.

Dodd, E.M. Jr. (1932), 'For whom are corporate managers trustees?', *Harvard Law Review*, **45**, 1145–63.

Dodd, E.M. Jr. (1935), 'Is effective enforcement of the fiduciary duties of corporate managers practicable?', *University of Chicago Law Review*, **2,** 194–207.

Douglas, W.O. (1934), 'Directors who do not direct', *Harvard Law Review*, **47**, 1305–34.

Elhauge, E. (2005), 'Sacrificing corporate profits in the public interest', *New York University Law Review*, **80**, 733–869.

Farrar, J.H. (1998), 'Frankenstein incorporated or fools' parliament? Revisiting

the concept of the corporation in corporate governance', *Bond Law Review*, **10**, 142–64.
Freund, Ernst (1897), *The Legal Nature of Corporations*, Chicago: University of Chicago Press.
Fukuyama, Francis (1992), *The End of History and the Last Man*, New York: Free Press.
Greenfield, K. (2005), 'New principles for corporate law', *Hastings Business Law Journal*, **1**, 87–118.
Greenfield, K. (2008), 'Proposition: saving the world with corporate law', *Emory Law Journal*, **57**, 947–84.
Hansmann, H. (2006), 'How close is the end of history?', *Journal of Corporation Law*, **31**, 745–51.
Hansmann, H. and R. Kraakman (2001), 'The end of history for corporate law', *Georgetown Law Journal*, **89**, 439–68.
Hohfeld, W.N. (1909), 'The nature of stockholders' individual liability for corporation debts', *Columbia Law Review*, **9**, 285–320.
Millon, D. (1990), 'Theories of the corporation', *Duke Law Journal*, **39**, 201–62.
Rotman, L.I. (2010), 'Debunking the "end of history" thesis for corporate law', *Boston College International and Comparative Law Journal*, **33**, 219–72.
Smith, D.G. (2008), 'Response: the dystopian potential of corporate law', *Emory Law Journal*, **57**, 985–1010.
Stout, L.A. (2002), 'Bad and not-so-bad arguments for shareholder primacy', *Southern California Law Review*, **75**, 1189–209.
Wells, C.A.H. (2002), 'The cycles of corporate social responsibility: an historical retrospective for the twenty-first century', *University of Kansas Law Review*, **51**, 77–140.

Legislation

Canada Business Corporations Act, RSC 1985, c C. 44, section 42.

Jurisprudence

BCE Inc v 1976 Debentureholders, 2008 SCC 69, [2008] 3 SCR 560.
Citizens United v Federal Election Commission (2010), 558 US 50, 130 SCt 876.
Dodge v Ford Motor Co (1919), 170 NW 668 (Mich).
Paramount Communications Inc v QVC Network Inc (1994), 637 A (2d) 34 (Del SC).
Paramount Communications Inc v Time Inc (1989), 571 A (2d) 1140 (Del SC).
Peoples Department Stores Inc (Trustee of) v Wise, 2004 SCC 68, [2004] 3 SCR 461.
Revlon Inc v MacAndrews & Forbes Holdings Inc (1986), 506 A (2d) 173 (Del SC).
Shlensky v Wrigley (1968), 237 NE (2d) 776 (Ill App Ct).

Web Resources

Friedman, M. (1970), 'The social responsibility of business is to increase its profits', *New York Times Magazine*, available at http://www.colorado.edu/studentgroups/libertarians/issues/friedman-soc-resp-business.html (accessed 17 May 2011).

General Motors (2011), 'Generations of GM history', available at http://www.gm.com/company/history-heritage (accessed 17 May 2011).

Michigan Department of Natural Resources (2010), 'The assembly line and the $5 day – background reading', State of Michigan, available at http://www.michigan.gov/dnr/0,1607,7-153-54463_18670_18793-53441--,00.html (accessed 17 May 2011).

Stout, L.A. (2000), 'Stock prices and social wealth', Harvard Law and Economics Discussion Paper No. 301, available at http://www.law.harvard.edu/programs/olin_center/papers/pdf/301.pdf (accessed 17 May 2011).

6. Corporate stakeholders in New Zealand – the present, and possibilities for the future

P.M. Vasudev

The interaction between global economic growth and global social challenge has led to changes in the character and behaviour of corporations and in public expectations about the role and responsibility of corporations within society.

(James Post et al. 2002)

1 INTRODUCTION

The stakeholder principle has gained significant recognition in corporate governance in recent times. It represents a refinement of the more limited conception of business corporations as vehicles designed to promote the economic interests of their shareholders. The stakeholder vision articulated in recent times is more expansive and proactive. It covers a large number of non-shareholder groups – employees, suppliers, communities and so on – and advocates greater corporate engagement in protecting their interests and enhancing their welfare.

This chapter presents the results of a survey of the companies listed on the New Zealand Stock Exchange (NZSX) to determine how far they reflect the stakeholder idea in their governance policies. The results of the survey, summarized below, point towards rising acceptance of the stakeholder vision in New Zealand.

- Out of the 130 companies that have listed their shares on the NZSX, 91 recognize stakeholders in some form. The references are found in different documents – namely, governance charters, annual reports, mission statements and so on (herein collectively termed 'governance documents').
- Among these 130 listed companies, 20 are incorporated overseas. Three-fourths or 15 of the companies incorporated outside New

Zealand acknowledge non-shareholder interests in their governance documents.

- The remaining 110 companies are incorporated in New Zealand. Of these, 76, or about 70 per cent, recognize non-shareholder interests.

Reviewing company law in New Zealand, the chapter finds that the current statute, the *Companies Act 1993*, does not explicitly recognize the stakeholder idea. Yet it has a mechanism that potentially enables companies to name any individual or group as an 'entitled person' for invoking the oppression remedy and certain other purposes. Companies can include employees, suppliers or any other stakeholder as entitled persons. This device available in the New Zealand *Companies Act* can be interpreted as a combination of the public and the private in promoting the stakeholder ideal in corporate governance. Legislation facilitates stakeholder engagement through the 'entitled person' device. Individual companies must then act to include non-shareholder groups in their framework through appropriate provisions in their constitutions.

The survey found that no company in New Zealand has included any provisions on stakeholders in its constitutions. This is not surprising because the 'entitled person' mechanism was not originally crafted for the purpose, as the chapter explains. Yet it *can* help companies which swear by the stakeholder principle to institutionalize it by recognizing non-shareholder groups as 'entitled persons.'

The chapter is divided into five sections. Section 2 provides an overview of the stakeholder idea and Section 3 discusses the results from the survey of the companies listed on the NZSX. Section 4 discusses company law and the increasing recognition it accords the stakeholder principle. Section 5 concludes with a plea for the adoption of a robust stakeholder vision in corporate theory in New Zealand.

2 THE STAKEHOLDER PRINCIPLE – AN EXPOSITION IN BUSINESS MANAGEMENT AND LAW

The traditional shareholder model treats companies as the property of the shareholders and understands the corporate goal as maximizing their benefit. The stakeholder model, in contrast, recognizes a number of constituencies – shareholders, employees, suppliers, communities and so on – all of which have an interest or a stake in the organization and are entitled to consideration. These groups are not necessarily viewed in hierarchical terms, nor do any of them have automatic preference over the others.

Several New Zealand companies accept the broad stakeholder vision, outlined above, as a management principle. The New Zealand Refining Company (NZRC) presents a good example. Its 2009 annual report makes, in all, 19 references to stakeholders. The NZRC is a mid-sized company. In 2008 it had sales of NZ$397 million and had 3179 shareholders and 384 employees. The references to stakeholders appear in various contexts:

- in its Vision Statement ('we aim to delight our customers, shareholders, staff and other stakeholders')
- in the Statement of Directors' and Management Commitment (providing 'shareholders and other stakeholders with the assurance that the Company delivers on its promises')
- in its statement on Ethical and Responsible Decision Making (reference to 'the highest standards of corporate behaviour towards our stakeholders'), and
- in its statement on Capital Risk Management ('safeguard[ing] the Group's ability to continue as a going concern in order to provide returns for shareholders and benefit for other stakeholders').

The trend to bracket stakeholders and shareholders together is evidently quite strong. It indicates a weakening of notions about the differences between shareholders and other constituencies. The understanding of the stakeholder principle in management theory is general – as a broad principle that informs governance. This understanding is apparent in corporate documents, such as the one cited above, and the works of management scholars. R. Edward Freeman, a leading proponent of the stakeholder principle in the US in the 1980s, defined stakeholders as including 'any group or individual who can affect or is affected by the achievement of the firm's objectives' (Freeman 1984, p. 25). Recently James Post et al. defined the corporate objective as 'creat[ing] wealth and other benefits (and not to intentionally destroy wealth, increase risk, or cause harm) for its multiple stakeholders' (Post et al. 2002, p. 17). These are broad-brush statements of principle which reflect typical management thinking on the subject.

In the legal setting, there can be difficulties with the breadth and lack of specificity in the stakeholder model envisioned in management theory. The legal system is ill at ease with 'interests,' which are the focus in management theory. Rather, legal theory is built around 'rights,' and remedies for breach of rights. A lawyer will likely find the discussion of stakeholder 'interests' in management theory obscure. He or she will be surprised that no efforts are made to define these interests with greater precision and prioritize the positions of the various groups in companies.

In law, the problem is compounded by the adversarial system of litigation in which judges usually make a choice between the litigants. Adjudication in courts is not usually about balancing and reconciling different interests that are in conflict with one another. The task is to select a winner among them. For the legal system to deal with conflicts among constituencies, a broad principle of commonality of interests would be inadequate. The stakeholder principle would be of little use even if there were no basic disagreement with it; the conventional world of legal adjudication is about making choices. These are some of the complexities in developing a *legal* model of the stakeholder corporation, as distinct from a management concept.

The shadow cast by these difficulties is apparent in the stakeholder idea stated in the OECD *Principles of Corporate Governance*, which recommend:

> The corporate governance framework should recognize the rights of stakeholders established by law or through mutual agreements and encourage active co-operation between corporations and stakeholders in creating wealth, jobs, and the sustainability of financially sound enterprises. (2004, p. 21)

This formulation is clearly legalistic. The OECD Principles only recognize stakeholders with 'rights' that are 'established by law or through mutual agreements.' In effect, stakeholders are only those who have legal or contractual rights against companies. The contrast between the generalist expositions by management scholars and the legalistic version in the OECD Principles is quite clear. It is proof of the tension inherent in the stakeholder idea as a management concept and in legal practice. The former tends to be inclusive and open, but the latter is restrictive and specific. The NZRC discussed earlier proves this point. Despite the several references to stakeholders in the governance documents, the company's annual report is clear about the scope of the accountability of the board and the corporate goal. It is mostly about the shareholders. The annual NZRC report states:

> The Board is ultimately responsible for setting the strategic direction of the Company, oversight of the management of the Company and direction of its business strategy, with the ultimate aim being to increase shareholder value while sustaining and ensuring the obligations of the Company are properly met. The Board is accountable to shareholders for the performance of the Company. (2009, p. 21)

'Increas[ing] shareholder value' is presented as the 'ultimate aim' of the company. That there could be difficulties in increasing 'shareholder value while sustaining and ensuring the obligations of the Company are properly met' (ibid.) is a different matter. Experience has shown that the shareholder value maxim can aggravate conflicts between the shareholders and other groups. The takeover battles fought in the US in the 1980s, often waged in the idiom of shareholder value, led to plant closings and mass redundancies with serious consequences for the employees and the communities in which the plants were located. Considering these realities, there would be significant challenges in applying the stakeholder principle to conflicts among the groups in business corporations and resolving them in that spirit. A legal version of the stakeholder model must, therefore, be sensitive to these issues.

3 STAKEHOLDERS IN NEW ZEALAND – A SURVEY OF LISTED COMPANIES

Evidence is unambiguous that companies listed on the NZSX are increasingly adopting the stakeholder vision. This is the conclusion from a survey of the companies' governance documents. The survey consisted of two parts, namely (1) a review of companies' governance documents to identify the recognition of stakeholder interests, and (2) an examination of individual constitutions to determine whether the companies had included non-shareholder groups as 'entitled persons' as provided under the *Companies Act 1993*. The second part of the survey was restricted to companies incorporated in New Zealand. Overseas companies listed on the NZSX, mainly Australian and UK companies, are not governed by New Zealand statutes so they are not relevant for this purpose.

This section has two subsections. The first explains the dataset used in the survey and the exclusions made from the complete list of issuers trading on the NZSX. The second subsection presents the data gathered in the survey and an analysis of the results from a study of the governance documents of the companies.

3.1 The Survey – Determination of the Dataset

Securities listed on the NZSX numbered 170 at the end of 2009. The actual number of issuers was smaller because some issuers, such as Allied Farmers Ltd, ASB and Barramundi, had more than one listed security. The complete list of issuers also included non-company entities such as income funds and trusts, which would not be relevant for the survey about corporate enterprises and their adoption of the stakeholder vision. The survey was carried out between December 2009 and January 2010, and covered the companies

Table 6.1 Sample considered in survey

Number of securities listed on NZX	170
Total number of issuers	160
Non-company issuers – namely, income funds, property funds, trusts, and the like	40
Company issuers	130
New Zealand companies	110
Overseas companies	20

listed on the NZSX only. It did not cover companies listed on the New Zealand Debt Exchange (NZDX) or the Alternative Exchange (NZAX).

The stakeholder principle is valid for companies in any sector – manufacturing, trading, service or banking and finance. These enterprises usually have sizable numbers of employees, vendors and customers and a significant presence in the community. In other words, these companies have 'stakeholders' with a real and substantial stake in the enterprise. This is not the case with non-company issuers such as income funds, unit trusts or property trusts engaged in financial investment. This was the reason for excluding them from the survey.

The process of elimination left a balance of 130 companies for the survey. Among these, there were two classes: companies incorporated in New Zealand (110) and those formed in other jurisdictions (20). The survey of governance documents for identifying recognition of stakeholder interests covered all the 130 companies listed on the NZSX, including those incorporated overseas. But the review of constitutions was restricted to the New Zealand companies as explained earlier. The numbers are set out in Table 6.1.

3.2 Stakeholder Survey – A Review of Governance Documents

This part of the survey covered the 130 companies incorporated in New Zealand or overseas. Their documents were examined to find out whether they acknowledged any concerns for non-shareholder groups. Corporate governance charters, board charters, codes of ethics and conduct, best practices codes, annual reports and other similar material available online were used for the survey. Annual reports were, by far, most commonly used by the companies to state their concerns for non-shareholder constituencies. Other documents which frequently reflected stakeholder interests were corporate governance charters (for example, Abano Healthcare, Austral Pacific Energy and Fletcher Building) and board charters (for example, ANZ Banking Group, Team Talk and Tower).

Table 6.2 Stakeholder interests – a survey of NZX listed companies

	Total number of companies	Companies recognizing stakeholder interests		Companies not recognizing stakeholder interests	
		Number	%	Number	%
Overall	130	91	70	39	30
New Zealand companies	110	76	69	34	31
Overseas companies	20	15	75	5	25

As noted, 91 companies out of the 130 included in the survey acknowledged non-shareholder groups and their interests in one or more governance documents. This is about 70 per cent of the total. There is a marginal, yet significant, difference in the percentage when we compare companies incorporated in New Zealand with the overseas companies listed on the NZSX. A slightly higher ratio of overseas companies (75 per cent) recorded stakeholder concerns in their governance documents versus 69 per cent for New Zealand companies. The results of the survey for all the companies listed on the NZSX and the breakdown of New Zealand and overseas companies are presented in Table 6.2.

Evidence of adoption of the stakeholder vision is quite impressive. At over two-thirds, it is apparent that the companies treat the issue with seriousness. It can be viewed as an emerging trend, which will probably become even stronger in the future.

There was also a practice for companies to report on the special features of their business. Most companies considered the environment to be an important stakeholder and exhibited concern for environmental issues. Sanford Limited, a company incorporated in New Zealand, is an example of this trend. It has published a Sustainable Development Report, which is apparently a regular annual feature. The report is inspired by the nature of the company's business, namely seafood, which is increasingly considered a scarce resource. The report addresses different dimensions of the sustainability issue – environmental, social and economic – and displays keen sensitivity for the interests of non-shareholder groups and the externalities of corporate business.

There is an interesting issue about the nature or character of the documents in which the companies have acknowledged their concern for stakeholder groups: not all of these documents are legal in character in the sense that a company's constitution or filings under securities regulations such as prospectuses are requirements under the law. It is also true that companies use governance documents for purposes such as building their brand image and reputation for quality of governance. This raises a question about how seriously we can treat the statements about stakeholders made in these documents, which lack substance in a strict legal sense. This question is especially important from the perspective of the division between the disciplines of management and law in their respective understandings of the stakeholder concept discussed earlier. Management, as noted, approaches the subject in a broad and generalist fashion while law tends to be narrow and specific.

However, there are a number of reasons why the validity of representations made by companies in their governance documents should not be underrated. For one, many of the documents reviewed in the survey can be traced to company legislation or securities regulation – either directly or through the listing rules of the stock exchange which are quasi-legislative in character. To illustrate, annual reports are a requirement under the *Companies Act*. The NZSX (2010) Listing Rules require companies to disclose in their annual reports 'any corporate governance policies, practices and processes, adopted or followed' by them. The corporate governance charters of the companies can be traced to this rule.

It would therefore be difficult to argue that the governance documents examined in the survey and their contents have no legal backing or effect. Considering their origin in legal regulation, it is possible to treat them as disclosures made under regulatory requirements. In any event, the statements in these documents would be 'representations' in common law and reliance on such representations can give rise to legal consequences. The reasoning proposed here could be a tool to strengthen the legal effect of the stakeholder principle which companies increasingly acknowledge in diverse circumstances and documents.

4 STAKEHOLDER PRINCIPLE UNDER THE *COMPANIES ACT 1993* – A SURVEY OF NEW ZEALAND COMPANIES

The stakeholder vision adopted by the companies discussed above is recorded in various governance documents prepared by them. The concept of 'entitled persons' in the New Zealand *Companies Act* offers a path to carry the idea further and empower non-shareholder groups. It can provide stakeholder groups with a better-defined position in the legal framework of companies. The definition of an 'entitled person' in the *Companies Act* (section 2) reads:

> *entitled person*, in relation to a company, means –
> (a) a shareholder; and
> (b) a person upon whom the constitution confers any of the rights and powers of a shareholder.

Thus a provision in the *Companies Act* enables companies to name any person or group as 'entitled persons' in their constitutions. This can enable the entitled persons to invoke the remedy against oppression, unfair prejudice or unfair discrimination (section 174), or seek injunctive relief (section 164) against companies. By recognizing non-shareholder groups as entitled persons, companies can strengthen the position of these groups.

There are no apparent limitations on the groups that can be named as entitled persons. By including non-shareholder groups in this category through a provision in the constitution, companies could institutionalize the stakeholder principle. This would be a step forward from their current practice of acknowledging or accepting the stakeholder vision in governance documents. Companies can actually empower non-shareholder constituencies. Considering the broad nature of the 'oppression' remedy in company law in the British Commonwealth jurisdictions, this could be effective in enabling non-shareholder groups to question actions or policies that harm their interests unreasonably. This is a potential stakeholder perspective in the New Zealand *Companies Act.*

The survey carried out for this chapter, however, revealed that no company has made use of the option available in the *Companies Act* to empower non-shareholder groups. To be clear, the 'entitled person' mechanism conceived by the New Zealand Law Commission (1990) which prepared the *Companies Act* was quite different. It was not exactly designed to promote stakeholder vision in corporate governance. Concerning the definition of 'entitled persons' in the *Companies Act*, the Law Commission stated that the definition was added to take care of companies in which some significant power or entitlement, such as the right to residue when a solvent company is liquidated, is in someone other than a shareholder. The definition was meant to protect the right of that person and his/her interest.

Clearly, the provision was meant to include persons having rights similar to those of the shareholders – possibly persons claiming under the shareholders. The Law Commission did not seriously consider including non-shareholders in the framework of the companies' statute. Indeed, it considered 'social purposes' to be outside the scope of company law, inspired by the American scholar who advocated libertarian corporate law, H.W. Ballantine.

While launching the company law review exercise in the 1980s, the Law Commission 'indicated that it was not attracted to the view that wider social purposes should be imposed upon companies through the *Companies Act* (p. 66) and believed that the task was better left to other legislation. Describing the response to its proposal to eschew social considerations in the company statute, the New Zealand Law Commission stated:

> The responses we received agreed. In particular, the inclusion of a provision such as is found in section 4 of the State-Owned Enterprises Act 1986 (which requires state-owned enterprises to act in a socially responsible manner) was opposed by a number of respondents and none supported the inclusion in the Companies Act of the imposition of a system of worker participation in management. (1989, p. 66)

It is not clear which persons or agencies submitted these responses, and whether they represented a broad cross-section of society and the spectrum of interest groups. In any event, this view prevailed and as a result the *Companies Act* avoids a broader conception of corporate enterprise (Fitzsimons 1996). It avoids any 'social' considerations clouding company law. This is perhaps natural considering that the *Companies Act* was conceived in the 1980s – a time when ideas about market efficiency were quite strong.

The Law Commission made a reference to the need to develop 'appropriate regulation to prevent abuse' of the corporate form, but its overriding concern was providing a 'simple and cheap method of incorporation' that did not 'frustrate the economic and social benefits of the company form' (New Zealand Law Commission 1989, pp. 4–5) The reference to 'social' benefits is curious, considering the Commission's statements on the social dimension cited earlier. Obviously, the Law Commission treated simple and cheap incorporation itself as a social benefit.

In any event, the Law Commission was not oblivious to the stakeholder issue or the groups to whom corporate directors must be accountable. Following Canadian and Australian precedents, it decided to codify the fiduciary duties of the directors and officers of companies. Indeed, the New Zealand Law Commission included additional standards for directors. These include exercise of powers for a proper purpose, not trading when insolvent and not using corporate information for personal benefit.

In discussing the scope of the fiduciary duties of directors and the 'best interests of the company,' the New Zealand Law Commission referred to the distinction between a company understood as its shareholders in the collective and the 'enterprise' (1989, p. 45). It stated that the 'identification of the company with the enterprise may have been largely achieved in law' (ibid.). In other words, the Law Commission implied that the statutory duty of the directors to act in the best interests of the company directed them to act in the interests of the enterprise. In discussing the enterprise, the concern of the Law Commission was apparently more about future shareholders rather than non-shareholder groups. This mode of thinking is also seen in the Commission's discussion on the remedies provided in the statute. These again focus on the shareholders.

To be fair, the Law Commission suggested that the 'best interests of the company' were not to be equated with the interests of the shareholders and made references to the 'enterprise' as something distinct from the shareholders. But it did not plan to include non-shareholder groups in the framework of the enterprise. This is clear from the statements about the difficulties in giving directors 'competing responsibilities' which can result in situations where 'one interest can be played off against another' (New Zealand Law Commission 1989, p. 47). The Law Commission also suggested that the interests of other groups, such as employees, must be the concern of employment legislation rather than company law.

As a result, the company statute in New Zealand retains more or less the traditional principle of shareholder primacy. An improvement is that it places directors under codified duties and provides various remedies such as derivative actions, injunctions and a remedy against oppression. There is a case for revisiting the rather narrow conception of companies in the current New Zealand statute. Issues about the theoretical underpinning of business corporations have become more urgent in the present times – in the post-Enron, post-AIG world in which we live. Within New Zealand, the string of finance company failures in recent years and the serious consequences for the investors who had deposited their savings in them provide a wake-up call. They highlight the broader character of corporate enterprises and the need for promoting a greater sense of responsibility in their governance.

It may be time to look for other, more expansive frameworks for the corporate form of business enterprise. The current model relies predominantly on private contracts and market processes for producing ideal outcomes – mostly understood as immediate economic gain. The stakeholder principle offers a handle for developing a richer and more nuanced theory for the companies of the future – one that can equip companies to better handle their responsibilities to various stakeholder groups and promote the increasingly important agenda of sustainability. The stakeholder principle has made considerable progress in other common law countries – namely the US, UK and Canada, and an option for New Zealand is to look to these other jurisdictions in the quest for a new model of company law.

4.1 The Stakeholder Regime and Its Variants

At present, two major variants can be seen in the legislative approach towards non-shareholder groups. One is the directors' duty version adopted in the UK and the US and the other is a remedy-based version prevailing in Canada. A potential third approach – namely, providing representation to non-shareholder groups on corporate boards, was considered in the UK and Canada, but was dropped. This subsection examines the prevailing stakeholder models.

4.2 The Directors' Duty Model – UK and US

Owen Young, chairman of General Electric Company, was among the earliest to articulate the stakeholder vision in corporate governance. Young viewed the matter through the lens of directors' duties and argued in 1929 that their duties must not be restricted to serving the shareholders (Dodd 1932). This approach took the principle of 'central command' in business corporations, or the vesting of very substantial corporate powers in the directors, as a given. Starting from here, the effort was to promote a broader vision for the directors and greater accountability in the exercise of their powers. The approach advocated by Owen Young drew enthusiastic support from E. Merrick Dodd (1932). A broader set of fiduciary duties, it was argued, promoted accountability overall and greater harmony in corporate functioning.

Adolf Berle, a leading corporate scholar of the time, was opposed to the idea of broadening the scope of directors' powers and loyalty (Berle 1932). His opposition was on the ground of practicability rather than principle. Berle argued that widening the responsibilities of corporate directors diluted accountability. This was similar to the approach of the New Zealand Law Commission which, almost five decades later in 1989, stated that 'competing responsibilities' created a situation in which 'one interest can be played off against another' (New Zealand Law Commission 1989, p. 47). However, Berle later veered around to the view of Merrick Dodd and expressed support for broad-basing the duties of corporate directors (see Wells 2002).

In the directors' duty version of the stakeholder corporation, directors are expressly authorized by the statutes to consider non-shareholder interests. By permitting a wider range of considerations to govern policy and decision making, legislation modifies, to some extent, the common law which limits directors' loyalty to the shareholders and constrains them from taking into account any other factors. The directors' duty model has been adopted in legislative reforms in Britain and America since the 1980s.

In Britain, the first step in this direction was taken in 1980 when directors were placed under a general duty to consider the interests of employees also. In the same decade – the 1980s – several American states introduced stakeholder provisions in their statutes. These provisions had their origin in the fierce battles for corporate control waged at the time.

The stakeholder provisions introduced in the American jurisdictions were a direct result of the takeover phenomenon of the 1980s, which led to widespread changes in corporate control, plant closings and employee layoffs. In many cases, the takeovers were justified in terms of the benefit they conferred on the shareholders through potential cost savings and resulting increases in share prices. The shareholder primacy rule, which appeared to confer legitimacy on these practices, cast its shadow on takeovers. In response to complaints about plant closings and disruption in the lives of the affected employees and communities, it was argued that directors' hands were tied by the shareholder primacy rule in corporate law.

Against this background, amendments were made to the corporate statutes to empower directors to consider a wide range of interests. The new schema, incidentally, operated in favor of incumbent managements, as it improved their ability to protect themselves against hostile takeover bids. To be clear, managements often actively lobbied for stakeholder legislation. They had mixed motives in doing so, as it helped protect their position; it was not entirely about ensuring the continuity of business operations (see Orts 1993; Branson 2001).

By 1991 a total of 28 states had included stakeholder concerns in their corporate statutes in varying forms. The following extract from the Georgia statute is representative of the stakeholder provisions adopted in several jurisdictions:

> A provision that, in discharging the duties of their respective positions and in determining what is believed to be in the best interests of the corporation, the board of directors, committees of the board of directors, and individual directors, in addition to considering the effects of any action on the corporation or its shareholders, may consider the interests of the employees, customers, suppliers, and creditors of the corporation and its subsidiaries, the communities in which offices or other establishments of the corporation are located, and all other factors such directors consider pertinent; however, that any such provision shall be deemed solely to grant discretionary authority to the directors and shall not be deemed to provide any constituency any right to be considered. (*Georgia Business Corporation*, Ga Code Ann tit 14, § 14-2-202(b)(5))

Most states permit directors to consider non-shareholder interests only in dealing with attempts at takeover or change of control. The stakeholder principle does not have uniform or ongoing application. The only exceptions are the states of Arizona, Idaho and New Mexico, which have adopted a more expansive version. They have made the stakeholder principle mandatory, with continuing application to all aspects of corporate governance. Despite this difference among the states, the inclusion of stakeholder concerns in the statutes marks the formal entry of the principle in corporate legislation. It is a different matter that most states have done so in a tentative manner and have provided limited scope to the idea.

Delaware, which is home to the largest number of public corporations, is not among the states that have included the stakeholder principle in their statutes. This is, however, not to suggest that the idea does not find a place in Delaware corporate law. More than once the Delaware court has recognized the stakeholder principle. In *Unocal Corp v Mesa Petroleum Co* (1985), the Delaware court upheld the defensive tactics adopted by the board of Unocal against a hostile takeover bid launched by Mesa. In doing so, the court referred to the directors' 'fundamental duty and obligation to protect the corporate enterprise, which includes stockholders' (paragraph 2). The observation affirmed a more institutional vision of the corporation. It showed a perception that business corporations were more than just aggregations of their shareholders, and stressed the duty of the boards towards the enterprise as a whole.

The trend was further strengthened in 1989 in *Paramount Communications, Inc v Time, Inc.* In this case the court upheld the action taken by the directors of Time, Inc to protect the company's corporate culture and journalistic integrity, subordinating shareholder interests in the process. *Credit Lyonnais Bank Nederland, NV v Pathe Communications Corp* (1991) was another important milestone in the Delaware court's journey on the stakeholder path. Ruling that the fiduciary duties of the directors could extend to the creditors of corporations 'operating in the vicinity of insolvency,' Chancellor Allen defined the scope of their duties:

> [The board has] an obligation to the community of interests that sustained the corporation to exercise judgment in an informed, good faith effort to maximize the corporation's long-term wealth creating capacity. (p. 38 (**1156))

An important contribution to stakeholder theory came from Margaret Blair and Lynn Stout (1999), who articulated their team production model of business corporations. Blair and Stout conceived directors as being the 'mediating hierarchs' who must ensure equity in the distribution of the corporate surplus among the different constituencies. The model developed by Blair and Stout has proved to be quite influential, as evident from its citation in the minority dissenting opinion of the US Supreme Court in *Citizens United v Federal Election Commission* (2010).

There are, however, also other strands in Delaware corporate law. In

Revlon, Inc v MacAndrews & Forbes Holdings, Inc (1986) the court had to deal with a takeover and the breakup of a corporation after the takeover. In that setting, the court treated the board of directors as auctioneers for the shareholders and charged them with a duty to procure the highest possible price for the shares. There was little room for non-shareholder groups in that framework. The role of directors as auctioneers for the shareholders, which has come to be known as the *Revlon* principle, was recently applied *In re Netsmart Technologies, Inc* (2007).

It would be difficult to reconcile the shareholder-centric outcomes in *Revlon* and *Netsmart* with cases such as *Unocal* and *Paramount Communications*. The latter group was based on a broader vision of corporate enterprises. The dichotomy is understandable considering the different fact situations with which the court had to deal in these sets of cases. It illustrates the perils in relying entirely on judicial decisions in developing corporate theory and the importance of statements of public policy on the subject. Further deliberation is needed to facilitate the development of a more wholesome theory to underpin corporate enterprises – which must ideally be stated in legislation. The proposals made in this chapter are based on this notion.

The UK recently expanded and strengthened the stakeholder principle in its corporate statute. The British stakeholder model is also, as noted earlier, based on the directors' duty concept. An expansive stakeholder version is included in the *Companies Act 2006* (UK). The statutory provision in section 172, extracted below, is comprehensive and sets out the principle with considerable clarity:

> A director of a company must act in the way he considers, in good faith, would be most likely to promote the success of the company for the benefit of its members as a whole, and in doing so have regard (amongst other matters) to –
>
> (a) the likely consequences of any decision in the long term,
> (b) the interests of the company's employees,
> (c) the need to foster the company's business relationships with suppliers, customers and others,
> (d) the impact of the company's operations on the community and the environment,
> (e) the desirability of the company maintaining a reputation for high standards of business conduct, and
> (f) the need to act fairly as between members of the company.

The stakeholder regime included in the current UK *Companies Act* is mandatory and applies to company directors on an ongoing basis. If we look carefully, it is clear that the statutory stakeholder model introduced in the UK is not radical although it looks so at first glance. It recognizes the 'success of the company for the benefit' of the shareholders as the overriding objective and subordinates other considerations. To be fair, no one can deny that a company must be profitable for it to take care of stakeholders. We cannot lose sight of the fact that companies are commercial enterprises operating in competitive markets and their business must be successful for them to be able to address other concerns. This is more so in the globalized markets of the present times when competitive pressures are greater than they were before.

In any case, in the UK a black-letter law now puts forth the stakeholder model as a principle of governance and broadens the fiduciary duties of directors. It moves away from the restrictive approach traditionally applied in common law and the tendency to emphasize shareholder primacy. Directors are now under a duty to consider a variety of interests in promoting company success. As pointed out, there can be little dispute with the proposition that a company must be successful for it to take proper care of its various stakeholders – including shareholders.

4.3 The Stakeholder Remedy Model – Canada

Among the common law jurisdictions, Canada was in fact the earliest to recognize the stakeholder principle in legislation. It did so by including non-shareholder groups in the remedies available under the *Canada Business Corporations Act (CBCA)* – namely, derivative actions for wrongs done to corporations and the oppression remedy for the wrongs done to specific individuals or groups in corporations. Traditionally, these remedies were available only to the shareholders of companies. The Robert Dickerson Committee (1971), which produced the *CBCA*, recommended extending the statutory remedies against managements to all the constituencies in business corporations. In doing so, it clearly adopted a stakeholder approach and stated:

> [The remedy] is made applicable to all cases of conduct that are 'oppressive or unfairly prejudicial to or in disregard of the interests of' any security holder, creditor, director or officer and not just to the narrow case where a shareholder is oppressed in his capacity as a shareholder. (Dickerson Committee 1971, p. 163)

The Dickerson Committee bracketed all stakeholders together, including shareholders. This approach is derived from the committee's understanding of the role of the shareholders. The Dickerson Committee adopted the Berle–Means paradigm of passive shareholders who play no meaningful role in corporations – at any rate, a role commensurate with the proprietary position attributed to them in corporate theory. This is evident from the committee's rejection of notions about corporate democracy and the voting rights of shareholders:

> We have also rejected the argument made by some that 'corporate democracy' should be improved by investing corporate shareholders with some of the powers now commonly exercised by directors. In our view, this idea is quite misconceived, not least because the analogy between democracy in a political context and the relationships between the shareholders and directors of a corporation is tortured and misleading. (Dickerson Committee 1971, p. 3)

As a result, the Dickerson Committee treated shareholders as little more than 'security holders' several years before this position was formally proclaimed for shareholders in economic theory (see Easterbrook and Fischel 1989). This framework had little place for attributing proprietary rights to shareholders or the idea that directors were their elected surrogates. Shareholders had no special position or rights and they were, in substance, little different from other groups such as employees, suppliers and creditors who also had interests in the corporations.

The Canadian Parliament accepted the recommendation of the Dickerson Committee and, as a result, the two remedies in the *CBCA* – derivative action and relief against oppression – are available to a generic class of 'complainants.' The term 'complainant' is defined in section 238 of the *CBCA* as follows:

> 'Complainant' means
>
> (a) a registered holder or beneficial owner, and a former registered holder or beneficial owner, of a security of a corporation or any of its affiliates,
> (b) a director or an officer or a former director or officer of a corporation or any of its affiliates,
> (c) the Director, or
> (d) any other person who, in the discretion of a court, is a proper person to make an application under this Part.

Reflecting the approach of the Dickerson Committee outlined earlier, the term 'shareholders' is not used in the definition of 'complainant.' Rather, shareholders are included under 'security holders,' which covers both shareholders and creditors who lend money under bonds or debentures. This is clear from the definition of 'security,' which means 'a share of any class or series of shares or a debt obligation of a corporation and includes a certificate evidencing such a share or debt obligation' (*CBCA*, section 2).

Other than security holders, the definition of complainants in the *CBCA* quoted earlier includes directors and officers, current or former.

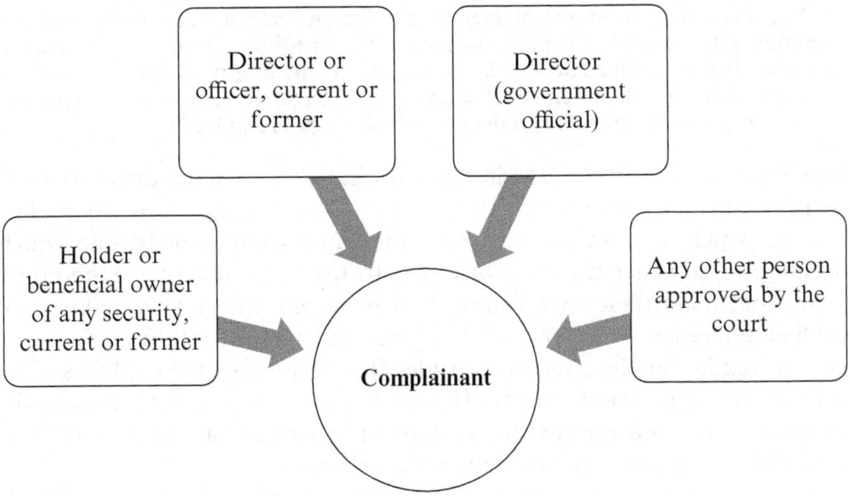

Figure 6.1 The concept of 'Complainant' in the Canada Business Corporations Act

The Director of Corporations, a government official, is also empowered to take action, presumably in the public interest. Finally, the court is given discretion – a carte blanche – to determine any other person as being 'proper' to invoke the remedies provided in the statute. Thus the *CBCA*'s conception of the groups that may be entitled to complain against business corporations is broad. The figure below explains the extended concept of complainants in the *CBCA*.

Thus the remedy in the *CBCA* is, in theory, available to a wide range of constituencies. Referring to this feature of the statute, Stephanie Ben-Ishai (2006) developed the 'team production' model of Canadian corporate law. Ben-Ishai argued that corporate law in Canada accords primacy to the directors and, considering the broad and inclusive character of the remedies provided in the statute, directors of Canadian corporations must be assimilated to the position of 'mediating hierarchs' conceived in the team production theory of Margaret Blair and Lynn Stout (1999).

It is, however, an open question as to how far the broad stakeholder remedy provided in the *CBCA* has been effective. The results in recent stakeholder cases – *Peoples Department Stores v Wise* (2004) and *BCE, Inc v 1976 Debenture holders* (2008) – went against the creditors. The outcome favored the directors in *Peoples* and the shareholders in *BCE, Inc.* This is despite an affirmation by the Supreme Court of Canada about the stakeholder vision in corporate governance. In *Peoples* (2004), the court observed:

> We accept as an accurate statement of law that in determining whether they are acting with a view to the best interests of the corporation it may be legitimate, given all the circumstances of a given case, for the board of directors to consider, inter alia, the interests of shareholders, employees, suppliers, creditors, consumers, governments and the environment. (paragraph 42)

The Supreme Court of Canada ruled in that case that the directors of a corporation did not owe fiduciary duties to the creditors. In *BCE, Inc* (2008), which was an action under the oppression remedy, the court declined to consider the issue of injury to the 'interests' of the creditors as distinct from their legal rights. This is despite the statute making an explicit reference to 'interests.' The reference in the statute could have been a handle for the court to consider the interests of the creditors who invoked the oppression remedy. However, the court restricted its analysis to legal rights, and rejected the case of the creditors on the ground that their rights had not been violated by the company.

In *Air Canada Pilots Association v ACE* (2007), the Ontario court refused to recognize the Pilots Association of Air Canada as a 'proper person' to bring an action questioning a proposal of the corporation to distribute assets to the shareholders. Case law is yet to develop on who would qualify as a proper person to bring complaints against business corporations under the derivative action remedy or the oppression remedy.

In stakeholder conflicts, the issue is often about 'interests' which may not have crystallized into clear 'rights' with which the legal system is familiar. The adversarial system of the courts and technical rules of form, procedure and evidence are other impediments for the courts to effectively respond to stakeholder disputes. These are some of the issues with the remedy-based approach to the stakeholder principle. They reinforce the need for developing a clear policy on stakeholders in corporate legislation.

4.4 The Third Alternative – Representation and Empowerment

The discussion on stakeholder variants would be incomplete without a brief reference to the third option, namely, representation of non-shareholder groups on boards and empowering them to participate in governance. Germany is the most-cited example here. In Germany, public corporations must have a broad cross-section of people on their boards, including employee representatives, and the principle is termed 'codetermination.' The participatory arrangement is intended to promote a broad stakeholder approach to corporate governance.

The 'representation and empowerment' model could have been expected to be popular in English-speaking countries considering their political history and longstanding ideas about representative democracy. However, it has not been so. The subject of stakeholder representation, in particular employee representation on boards, has been discussed but the idea was abandoned. Significantly, resistance to the idea came from labor unions in Britain and Canada. In the UK in the wake of recurrent labor unrest in the 1970s, a committee, grandiloquently termed the 'Committee on Industrial Democracy,' was constituted under the chairmanship of Lord Bullock to enquire into labor participation on corporate boards. The Bullock Committee reported in 1977 that labor unions were reluctant to sit on company boards.

Earlier in Canada the Dickerson Committee (1971) examined the representation and empowerment approach. Acknowledging the emerging notions about non-shareholder groups and their importance, the committee observed:

> Suggestions have been made from time to time that corporation law focuses too narrowly on shareholders, and ignores the reality that others, especially the corporation's employees and creditors, are affected by and concerned with what corporations do. It follows from this, so the argument goes, that these groups should have some voice in the choice of corporate directors. Moreover, it is said, there is a broad public interest in corporations and this interest should also be represented in corporate boardrooms. (Dickerson Committee 1971, p. 9)

The original idea was thus about empowering non-shareholder groups by permitting them to have representative directors. The Dickerson Committee had no quarrel with the validity of the argument about stakeholders, but it had reservations about enlarging the electorate. It stated: '[B]ut we do not see any practical way, in the context of a corporations act, in which it can be implemented. 'The problem is one of establishing the electorate' (Dickerson Committee 1971, p. 10).

After stating this difficulty, the Dickerson Committee rejected the representation model as an option of dealing with stakeholder interests. Pointing out that few legal impediments existed for including a wider section of stakeholders on boards if corporations wanted to do so, the committee concluded that a regulatory model based on representation was unworkable. In doing so, it referred to the fact that 'trade unions ha[d] not shown much interest in having representation on the boards of corporations' (Dickerson Committee 1971). This was an important reason for the Dickerson Committee to explore other means of fostering the interests of non-shareholder groups. Finally, it settled in favor of the remedy model discussed earlier.

In the US, the idea of stakeholder representation does not appear to have been considered with any degree of seriousness. A possible explanation is the heightened adversarial culture that has traditionally informed union–management relationships and the consequent inability to conceive of other possibilities. Alfred Conard (1991) pointed out that the milieu in the United States has not encouraged the representation model.

It is apparent that there are (or at least were, a few decades ago) significant cultural impediments in English-speaking countries to the principle of codetermination adopted in Germany. In common law countries, the trend appears to be more in favor of continuing with centralized powers in the boards elected by shareholders but providing the shareholders with a broader mandate in decision making. The top-down structure in corporate organizations is retained, and this is supplemented with efforts to enlighten the leadership through rules considering stakeholder interests.

There has been little effort at diffusing corporate power or empowering people at the middle or bottom levels. Clearly, such efforts would undermine the economic efficiency of the corporate form of enterprise in which central command is one of the chief advantages. Central command promotes greater efficiency in planning and execution and discourages a bureaucratic approach to management, which can be a serious issue in the highly competitive globalized markets of the present age.

In any event, lack of formal representation for stakeholders may not be a major issue in the emerging milieu. Ideas about director independence and board committees have gained significant traction in recent years, and they have the potential to promote a broader vision in public corporations. Board committees and independent directors are not, in theory, identified with any particular group in corporations, either shareholders or managements. They are given specific responsibilities. These emerging trends promote greater balance and wider perspectives on company boards, even if there is no formal representation for specific stakeholder groups.

5 A STAKEHOLDER MODEL FOR NEW ZEALAND – A MODEST PROPOSAL

The stakeholder vision in corporate governance is an important current trend. This much is beyond doubt, as I have tried to explain in this chapter. Efforts have been made to institutionalize the stakeholder model both through legislative recognition and in judicial lawmaking. Equally important, there have been significant changes in the political economy since the 1980s and the trend towards deregulation. Scandals at the turn of the century in companies such as Enron and WorldCom and more recently the Financial Crisis of 2008–09 have demonstrated the limitations of markets and their self-correcting ability. It has been found necessary to respond to these developments with elaborate regulation – the *Sarbanes-Oxley Act* of 2002 and now the *Dodd-Frank Act* of 2010.

In any case, regulation has re-emerged as a potential economic tool. This is not, however, to suggest the re-imposition of the static models of regulation that were tried in the past, such as price controls, wage controls or bureaucratic oversight. These have been attempted and their limitations have been proven. The need in the new age is for more institutional engineering. In recognizing companies as socioeconomic institutions and avoiding mono-dimensional approaches, public policy can rise to the challenge of engineering companies to suit the needs of the present times. In doing so, it will be necessary to strike a fine balance between the age-old values of liberty and business freedom and the imperatives of responsible governance and corporate accountability.

New Zealand, as noted earlier, has had its share of corporate woes. The string of finance company failures witnessed in recent years has had serious consequences for everyone – shareholders and non-shareholders. The shareholders of these companies lost their investments, employees their jobs and persons who had made deposits with them their savings. This experience underscores the need for a more vigorous response from public policy.

In corporate governance, evidence points towards widespread adoption of the stakeholder principle by New Zealand listed companies. This is clear from the survey presented here. A potential next step is for law and public policy to reflect on the trend and consider developing appropriate follow-up measures. Emerging legal theory, termed 'new legal realism,' is more sensitive to the limitations of the mono-dimensional approaches of the past and advocates greater engagement of the law and the legal system with socio-economic and political issues (Nourse and Shaffer 2009).

The New Zealand *Companies Act 1993*, as pointed out earlier, is a modern statute that includes a number of devices designed to promote responsible governance. For instance, the duty of directors not to trade recklessly is an important tool in ensuring that the use of the corporate form does not prejudice creditors, and it also provides a remedy for creditors in the case of breach by directors. As I have pointed out, the 'entitled persons' concept in the New Zealand *Companies Act* can be applied by companies to empower non-shareholder groups to make use of the statutory remedies even now. It is interesting that the 'entitled persons' mechanism in New Zealand appears to reflect the principle of the *Canada Business Corporations Act*, which extends the statutory remedies to non-shareholder groups.

The New Zealand *Companies Act* took shape in the late 1980s and early 1990s and it reflects, understandably, the market ideology which was dominant at the time. An example of this mode of thinking can be seen in David Henderson (2001), who referred to notions of corporate social responsibility as 'misguided virtue.' Recent events and corporate failures reveal the limitations of this approach and stress the importance of promoting a more responsible culture of governance. They present an opportunity to revisit the theory underlying companies, which are arguably a key economic institution. The stakeholder principle can be a useful tool in the efforts to develop a richer, more inclusive and nuanced theory that reflects the lessons of the past and avoids dogmatic or doctrinaire approaches.

A new theory of companies must reflect the unique features of the corporate landscape in New Zealand. The experience with the stakeholder model in other jurisdictions can provide some guidance in developing a version to suit the New Zealand climate. Towards this effort, empirical studies of companies in New Zealand and the experience with the *Companies Act* would be valuable. Some key issues for inquiry are shareholding and control patterns; data on employment provided by the companies; revenues and income; and any specific advantages/disadvantages from the use of the corporate form. These are areas for future research.

In any event, it is worth reiterating that companies can institutionalize the stakeholder model even within the existing framework. They need not wait for regulatory or legislative developments. The 'entitled persons' mechanism in the New Zealand *Companies Act* can be beneficially used for empowering non-shareholder groups and providing them with a better-defined position in the corporate framework. The statutory provision in its current form is broad enough to facilitate companies, in particular those already espousing the stakeholder principle, to explicitly recognize it.

REFERENCES

Articles, Books, Reports and Press Releases

Ballantine, Henry W. (1946), *Ballantine on Corporations*, Chicago, IL: Callahan.

Ben-Ishai, S. (2006), 'A team production theory of Canadian corporate law', *Alberta Law Review*, **44**, 299–322.

Berle, A. (1932), 'For whom corporate managers *are* trustees', *Harvard Law Review*, **45**, 1365–72.

Blair, M. and L. Stout (1999), 'A team production theory of corporate law', *Virginia Law Review*, **85**, 247–328.

Branson, D. (2001), 'Corporate governance "reform" and the new corporate social responsibility', *University of Pittsburgh Law Review*, **62**, 605–48.

Bullock Committee (1977), UK Department of Trade, *Report of the Committee of Inquiry on Industrial Democracy*, London, UK: Her Majesty's Stationery Office.

Conard, A. (1991), 'Corporate constituencies in western Europe', *Stetson Law Review*, **21**, 73–95.

Dickerson Committee (1971), *Proposals for a New Business Corporations Law*, Ottawa, Canada: Information Canada.
Dodd, E.M. (1932), 'For whom are corporate managers trustees?', *Harvard Law Review*, **45**, 1145–63.
Easterbrook, F.H. and D.R. Fischel (1989), 'The corporate contract', *Columbia Law Review*, **89**, 1416–48.
Fitzsimons, P. (1996), 'Australia and New Zealand: on different corporate paths', *Otago Law Review*, **8**, 267–93.
Freeman, Edward R. (1984), *Strategic Management: a Stakeholder Approach*, Marshfield, MA: Pitman Publishing.
Henderson, David (2001), *Misguided Virtue: False Notions of Corporate Social Responsibility*, Wellington, NZ: New Zealand Business Round Table.
New Zealand Law Commission (1989), *Company Law: Reform and Restatement* (NZ Law Commission Report 9), Wellington, NZ: Law Commission.
New Zealand Law Commission (1990), *Company Law Reform: Transition and Revision* (NZ Law Commission Report 16), Wellington, NZ: Law Commission.
Nourse, V. and G. Shaffer (2009), 'Varieties of new legal realism: can a new world order prompt a new legal theory?', *Cornell Law Review*, **95**, 61–138.
Orts, E.W. (1993), 'Beyond shareholders: interpreting corporate constituency statutes', *George Washington Law Review*, **61**, 14–135.
Post, James E., Lee E. Preston and Sybille Sauter-Sachs (2002), *Redefining the Corporation: Stakeholder Management and Organizational Wealth*, Stanford, CA: Stanford Business Books.
Wells, H. (2002), 'The cycles of corporate social responsibility: an historical perspective for the twenty-first century', *University of Kansas Law Review*, **51**, 77–140.

Jurisprudence

Air Canada Pilots Association v ACE, [2007] OJ No 89 (QL), 2007 CanLII 337 (Ont Sup Ct).
BCE, Inc v 1976 Debenture holders, 2008 SCC 69, [2008] 3 SCR 560.
Citizens United v Federal Election Commission, 130 S Ct 876 (US 2010).
Credit Lyonnais Bank Nederland, NV v Pathe Communications Corp, [1991] WL 277613 (Del Ch).
In re Netsmart Technologies, Inc Shareholders Litigation, 924 A (2d) 171 (Del Ch 2007).
Paramount Communications, Inc v Time, Inc, 571 A (2d) 1140 (Del 1989).
Peoples Department Stores, Inc (Trustee of) v Wise, 2004 SCC 68, [2004] 3 SCR 461.
Revlon, Inc v MacAndrews & Forbes Holdings, Inc, 506 A (2d) 173 (Del 1986).
Unocal Corp v Mesa Petroleum Co, 493 A (2d) 946 (Del 1985).

Statutes and Regulation

Canada Business Corporations Act, RSC 1985, c C-44.
Companies Act 1993 (NZ), 1993/105.
Companies Act 2006 (UK), c 46.
Dodd-Frank Act, Pub L 111-203, 124 Stat. 1376 (2010).

Georgia Business Corporations, Ga Code Ann tit 14 (2010).
Sarbanes-Oxley Act (SOX), Pub L No 107-204, 116 Stat 745 (2002).

Web Resources

NZRC (2008), The New Zealand Refining Company Limited, 'Annual report for 2008', available at http://www.nzrc.co.nz/investor-centre/reports--releases/annual-reports.aspx (accessed 9 March 2010).

NZRC (2009), The New Zealand Refining Company Limited, 'Annual report 2009', available at http://www.nzrc.co.nz/investor-centre/reports--releases/annual-reports.aspx (accessed 9 March 2010).

NZSX (2010), New Zealand Stock Exchange 'NZSX/NSDX listing rules', available at http://www.nzx.com/market-supervision/rules/nzsx-and-nzdx-listing-rules (accessed 4 July 2011).

OECD (2004), Organisation for Economic Co-operation and Development, 'OECD principles of corporate governance', available at: http://www.oecd.org/dataoecd/32/18/31557724.pdf (accessed 25 February 2010).

Sanford Limited (2009), 'Sustainable development report 2009', available at http://live.isitesoftware.co.nz/sanford/documents/sdr/Sustainable_Development_Report_-_published_16_December_2009.pdf (accessed 9 March 2010).

7. Institutional investors as blockholders

Aviv Pichhadze

1 INTRODUCTION

In describing the rise to prominence of the shareholder-oriented model of the corporate form, Hansmann and Kraakman (2004) noted, inter alia, that this process involved the diffusion of public firm ownership and the rise to prominence of the institutional investors (IIs). In the context of IIs, Hansmann and Kraakman (2004) noted that the interests of this shareholder group coincide 'with those of public shareholders and . . . [IIs] are prepared to articulate and defend those interests' (p. 49). In addition, they noted that '[t]hese institutions not only give effective voice to shareholder interests, but promote in particular the interests of dispersed public shareholders rather than those of controlling shareholders or corporate insiders' (ibid.). Finally, in this context, they note that 'the new activist shareholder-oriented institutions [i.e., IIs] are today acting increasingly on an international scale . . . We now have not only a common ideology supporting shareholder-oriented corporate law, but also an organized interest group . . . that is broad, diverse, and increasingly international . . .' (ibid.).

Accordingly, IIs seem to (i) have interests that coincide with the interests of the shareholder body in general in the public firm, (ii) promote dispersed ownership, and (iii) crusade for shareholder interests internationally. Hence, they play an important role in corporate governance both domestically in the US and internationally. In this chapter, I examine these three propositions. I do this against the background of Pichhadze's Market Oriented Blockholder Model (MOBM) that shows that the new blockholder in the American public equity markets is the II (Pichhadze 2010a).[1]

This assessment is both timely and important as policymakers around the world are looking to fundamentally reform the global financial system and its various components (see, e.g., OECD 2009). These reform initiatives are pursued with the view to correcting, in a coordinated and harmonized manner, the failures that led to the recent economic crisis.

The initiatives cover various levels and aspects of the financial system and include such things as transparency, risk management, supervision, regulation, and corporate governance (ibid.). This chapter is concerned with the last area of proposed reforms – namely, corporate governance. It is in this area that IIs play a significant role – a role that needs to be assessed for the purpose of promoting a stable and efficient global financial system.

The chapter is organized around three themes. First, in Section 2, I show that the fact that IIs promote diffused ownership is a paradox given that they are the emerging blockholder in the equity markets, in general, and in large firms, in particular. Second, in Section 3, I examine the extent to which II interests are aligned with those of other shareholders. More specifically, the chapter seeks to examine whether IIs behave in a manner that is not dissimilar to that of non-financial (e.g. retail or family) blockholders or controlling shareholders. Finally, in Section 4, the chapter will address some regulatory implications, both domestically in the US and internationally, of the fact that IIs are the emergent blockholder. Section 5 provides some concluding remarks.

2 INSTITUTIONAL INVESTORS AND THE PROMOTION OF DIFFUSED OWNERSHIP – THE PARADOX

As can be seen from the above, IIs are said to shepherd the interests of dispersed owners and, in so doing, promote dispersed ownership as the appropriate form of public firm ownership in the equity markets. Yet, IIs are the emergent blockholder in the American equity markets holding over 66 per cent of the equity in these markets (Hawley and Williams 2007; Brancato and Rabimov 2008).[2] Thus, we have a paradox between the stated purpose or objective of IIs in promoting dispersed ownership, on the one hand, and the reality of IIs as a blockholder, on the other. To understand how we arrived at this paradox, we need to examine the ownership trend in the American equity markets over the course of the twentieth century.

Institutional investors in the US developed during the early years of the capital markets in that country and increased their exposure to equity investments during the 1950s. By the end of the 1950s the observed pattern in share ownership 'was that individuals were shifting their capital from direct share ownership to institutional investments and bank deposits' (Pichhadze 2010a, p. 68). By the end of the 1960s, interested observers were talking about the institutionalization of the

American capital markets (Pichhadze 2010a), a process that continues to this present day and sees the re-concentration of public corporate equity into the hands of IIs.

The process of the institutionalization of the American capital markets and the associated re-concentration of corporate ownership into the hands of institutional investors were an integral part of the trend towards MOBM, as market forces were driving ownership patterns in the publicly listed firm towards the blockholder levels of ownership. Yet, since the early years of the American capital markets, IIs were treated as vehicles for diffusion, rather than concentration of ownership (see generally, Pichhadze 2010a). In addition, some went as far as to proclaim that IIs 'are the trustees for all shareholders. They establish the moral tone in Wall Street' (Livingston 1963, p. 216), a point of view that is both contradictory and forms the basis for the paradox.

MOBM is a hybrid ownership structure that features a blockholder pattern of ownership that works with market mechanisms for the promotion of maintaining stability in the pattern of ownership (i.e., the maintenance of ownership equilibrium at the blockholder levels). The emergent blockholder in the US, as already noted, is the II. The synthesis of the blockholder mode of ownership with market mechanisms, such as takeovers, allows for the transformation of what Coffee (1999, p. 648) described as the trade-offs between the monitoring of corporate managers and the promotion of efficient and liquid markets resulting from the choice of the two polar ownership structures (i.e., concentrated and diffused, respectively) into complements (Pichhadze 2010a, p. 83).

MOBM is created through the need of market forces to arrive at an ownership equilibrium that affords both liquidity in the capital markets and monitoring of corporate management. MOBM is facilitated by market mechanisms that assist in the promotion of such an equilibrium and its maintenance over time. Maintenance is required because the ownership equilibrium, once achieved, does not remain static, rather it is a dynamic process that exhibits deviations from, and restoration to, the state. In this dynamic process, market mechanisms such as corporate control transactions (including private equity) have an important role in restoring the equilibrium state, when disturbances occur or there are deviations from the state of equilibrium.

Pound (1992) observed in the context of leveraged buyout transactions, '[o]versight by entrepreneurial insurgent investors has been generated by two central (and related) features of U.S. capital markets: their fragmentation and their openness to innovation' (p. 8). According to this view, when the ownership of a public firm becomes too fragmented such that (i) the firm experiences a reduction in the effective monitoring of the firm's management, and (ii) such reduced monitoring results in the introduction of inefficiencies to the firm, then (iii) market mechanisms such as takeover activity introduce into the firm improved monitoring and enhanced efficiency by, inter alia, concentrating, at least temporarily, the ownership of the firm.

Thus, advancement of MOBM required two principal realizations by market forces. First, as industrial blockholders were diminishing from the large public corporation landscape during the early part of the twentieth century, market forces, in looking to fill the ownership gap, were re-concentrating ownership in the hands of fiduciaries who could take up the role of blockholders in these firms.[3] Second, to achieve/maintain stability in this form of ownership, IIs, qua blockholders, realized that (in order to protect their investment, ensure increased returns on such investment, and ensure liquidity for such investments) they needed to participate in the market for corporate control, as they have done since the 1980s.

In order to facilitate their fuller participation in this type of activity, IIs successfully lobbied for amendments to legal rules, such as the proxy rules which prevented their fuller participation in the takeover arena (see, e.g., Pichhadze 2010a, p. 79). This was complemented by active investors who, as gap fillers in the corporate governance vacuum created as a result of fragmented ownership, realized the dual role and importance of institutional investors both as providers of capital and as blockholders in the execution of deals.

Thus, the paradox in the American capital markets vis-à-vis IIs is that while they are viewed as promoting diffused ownership in both the US and elsewhere, they are in fact blockholders in these markets. While paradoxical in the context of IIs, in the context of the MOBM, however, the fact that the MOBM is the emerging ownership pattern in the US shows us that market forces in that country are driving ownership patterns towards what can be said to be an optimal ownership structure that is also socially optimal.

Social optimality in the context of the corporation refers to the notion that the shareholders' representatives serve the shareholders' interest (Grossman and Hart 1980). One way of ensuring that this social welfare is met in the context of the corporation is through the monitoring of managers. The problem is that, absent anyone owning sufficient stakes in the corporation, monitoring is left to market mechanisms such as takeovers (Grossman and Hart 1980). Market forces and socio-economic realities, however, created a venue for the promotion of social optimality in the corporation. They have paved the way for the re-concentration of equity ownership into the hands of IIs, who have sufficient stake in the corporation and, therefore, an interest in monitoring corporate managers.

IIs, as blockholders, and takeovers are also two key features in MOBM. They promote efficiency and liquidity in the capital markets while enabling the increased monitoring of corporate managers. In addition, given that a feature of MOBM is the presence of a blockholder (whether an II or not), it points to the observation that market forces, in gravitating towards MOBM, are attempting to reduce the sub-optimality created by the diffused ownership pattern of corporate ownership (Bebchuk and Zingales 2000, p. 57).[4]

Care, however, should be exercised in reading the above. While MOBM may be structurally and, probably, socially optimal as an ownership structure, it does require a shift in regulatory thinking and approaches to corporate governance. This shift, and its nature, are not immediately available in the standard literature on corporate governance and, as such, there is no immediate 'off-the-shelf' solution.

This is because the literature generally provides analysis of, and solutions to, cases involving the two polar extremes of corporate ownership (i.e., dispersed and concentrated). Whereas under the dispersed mode of ownership, the literature seeks to protect shareholders from managers, under the concentrated mode of ownership, the literature seeks to protect the shareholder class from the controlling shareholder (Bebchuk and Hamdani 2009). There are no solutions contemplated (or, indeed, discussed) to cases such as MOBM.[5]

3 INSTITUTIONAL INVESTORS AS BLOCKHOLDERS

IIs are not a homogeneous group. They include pension funds, insurance companies, banks, and mutual funds to name a few. Despite this, they have generally come under criticism as owners of equity (in monitoring portfolio firms) and for failing to function as fiduciaries (on behalf of the investors that entrust them with their savings). For example, it was commented that '[h]istorically, millions of investors have acted like renters of corporate shareholdings rather than fractional owners of actual companies. Even worse, so do many of the mutual funds, retirement systems, and other fiduciaries to which citizen investors have entrusted their assets' (Davis et al. 2006, p. 66).

In this subsection of the chapter, I examine the behavior of IIs qua shareholders, using a number of examples, to see whether they behave in a manner that is distinct from other non-financial blockholders. Prior to this, however, let us briefly look at the arguments claiming that IIs fail in their function as fiduciaries.

3.1 Institutional Investors as Blockholders – Some Industry Shortcomings

Davis et al. (2006) provide a number of reasons for IIs' failure in their role as fiduciaries. These criticisms relate to the fund industry in general and include: (i) the manner in which fund managers are given compensation; (ii) lack of economic incentive to monitor portfolio firms; (iii) the investment horizon of fund managers; and (iv) lack of member input and/or representation on corporate pension funds.

The first criticism results from the manner in which fund managers' compensation is calculated. In this context the authors note that because fund managers are paid on a percentage-of-assets basis (i.e., fees are based on the quantum of assets under management), fund managers have little (economic) incentive to monitor the assets under their care (see generally, ibid., Chapter 4).

Another reason is the investment horizon adopted by fund managers. The authors note that the fund industry rates fund managers' performance based on their relative performance over short time frames. These ratings translate themselves into bonuses for individual managers and analysts. 'The natural result is that they [i.e., fund managers and analysts] focus on lucrative short-term trading rather than on vigilant long-term owning' (ibid., p. 72).

A related reason for the failure of fiduciaries to act like owners according to the authors is the fact that the economic cost of monitoring does not result in a corresponding financial benefit to the individual fiduciary as all investors will share in the benefits resulting from the monitoring activities by the particular II. As such, fund managers prefer to beat market benchmarks (i.e., exhibit improved relative performance) (ibid.).

A final criticism of IIs relates to pension funds. In this context Davis et al. (2006) noted that 'many pension funds around the world operate with no representation at all from the very members they are supposed to benefit. Almost all corporate pension funds in the United States and Japan . . . are run exclusively by company officials, with no such thing as a trustee board with seats for current or retired employees' (p. 75). In addition, the authors note that this practice allows corporate managers to hire fund managers that will not oppose management for fear of losing the company's fund business – i.e., fund managers do not exercise the ownership rights on behalf of the pension funds' beneficiaries.

3.2 Institutional Investors as Owners

Despite some of the shortcomings of IIs at the industry level, IIs do perform and act as equity owners. It is worth examining their actions as shareholders in light of the fact that they are the emerging blockholders in the capital markets and the fact that they can potentially perform a valuable corporate governance function at both the domestic and international levels. In this subsection, IIs are treated as a homogeneous group for the sake of simplifying the discussion. While IIs, generally, are treated in the discussion below as a homogeneous group, shareholders are not. This is because shareholders have interests that are not common with other shareholders (Anabtawi 2005).

The literature on corporate governance identifies several potential areas where a dominant shareholder can negatively impact the corporation and, as such, other shareholders. While a complete catalogue is beyond the scope of this chapter, I examine some of these areas to see if IIs have the capacity of behaving in a like manner. This will enable us to assess whether, on balance, IIs act as a dominant shareholder or a blockholder for the purposes of impacting corporate performance. This is important because the two types of shareholders (i.e., IIs, on the one hand, and blockholders, on the other) are generally treated differentially in the literature. In particular, I focus on (i) corporate boards and management catering to shareholder interests, (ii) ability to exercise formal power, and (iii) rent seeking and opportunism.

Board catering to shareholder interests

In firms with a controlling shareholder there is the risk that management and the board of directors will follow the direction of the blockholder(s) while ignoring the interests of minority shareholders. 'The agency problem here is the possible conflict of interest between the dominant shareholder (supported by the officers and directors who are under the dominant shareholder's control) and other shareholders' (Daniels and Morck 1995, p. 12).

In the context of IIs, this raises the question of whether IIs receive (whether actual or perceived) special treatment from managements of boards. Recent developments in the capital markets point to the growing recognition by boards and managements of leading corporations of the important power of IIs qua blockholders. This has recently been observed by the American Bar Association Section of Business Law (ABA Task Force 2009):

> Boards also are more actively engaging in discussions with shareholders on a variety of governance related topics outside of the proxy proposal context, including nomination of directors, compensation matters, social and environmental issues, and the range of matters raised by shareholders during proxy season. Pfizer, UnitedHealth, and Home Depot, for example, initiated meetings with *large institutional investors* to discuss issues ranging from executive compensation to board composition. (p. 107, emphasis added)

Does this mean that Pfizer and other corporations are serving the interests of large IIs at the expense of the remaining shareholder body? Not necessarily. But it does create a risk. First, such activity by corporations appears to signal that corporations are listening to IIs in a manner that is not too dissimilar to listening to a non-financial blockholder (i.e., providing a preferential treatment to IIs over other shareholders). Similarly, Anabtawi and Stout (2008, pp. 1285–6) noted that IIs can, in some instances and contrary to conventional understanding, act in a manner similar to that of a controlling shareholder in influencing corporate conduct. Second, as Friday and Crum have cautioned, '[d]irectors should . . . be wary . . . Activist shareholders are often motivated by their own economic, social or political agendas and do not necessarily speak for the silent majority of investors' (2008, p. 12).

Ability to exercise formal power

It is generally accepted that dominant shareholders are likely to use formal powers to maximize the value of the share they own (see, e.g., Bebchuk and Hamdani 2009).[6] In a widely held firm the probability for this type of activity is less likely because 'collective action and free-rider problems . . . often prevent outside shareholders from effectively using whatever formal powers that they have to constrain and influence management' (ibid., p. 1282).

These assertions may be true in the polar cases of ownership structures (i.e., diffused and concentrated). Pichhadze (2010a), in his MOBM analysis, noted that IIs are using legal tools to influence corporations. For example, IIs are successfully using the proxy system and other shareholder rights mechanisms as well as lobbying with the SEC to introduce changes for the removal of barriers to enable fuller II participation in corporate affairs.

Rent seeking and opportunism

Shareholders are a group. As such, this allows them to benefit from the cooperative actions of group members.[7] Such gains, however, are balanced against the negative impact of activities such as rent seeking and opportunism carried out by some group members at the expense of others. This is because shareholders, as a heterogeneous group, have their own interests in addition to the common interests.

Rent seeking is 'the socially costly attempt to obtain wealth transfers' (Anabtawi 2005, p. 575). In firms with dominant shareholders, for example, Bebchuk and Hamdani (2009) noted that the dominant shareholders can use self-dealing transactions to extract value. Anabtawi and Stout (2008) observed that this situation can also arise with IIs in countries such as the US (i.e., where ownership is assumed to be diffused), as in the case where IIs represent and promote their own interests. This relates to the risks associated with interplay between interest group politics and diffused ownership. The risk was highlighted as far back as 1925 where it was cautioned that interest groups (whether left- or right-wing), in advancing their interests, might use diffused ownership to their advantage (Lindsay 1925, pp. 2–3).

A related type of rent seeking is the political rent seeking. Here, public choice theory provides that larger groups will be 'more inclined to produce pressure in the pursuit of group-specific public goods' (Winden 2003, p. 120). An example of this can be found in the efforts of IIs to influence the composition of corporate boards. Recently SEC proposed a rule (SEC 2009) that is couched in language which embraces all shareholders and allows them to participate in the process of nominating directors, but the threshold requirements are such that only a select group of shareholders can meet them (Pichhadze 2010a). This group is composed mainly of IIs, who are able to meet these threshold requirements as a consequence of the size of their holdings.

This type of rent seeking (i.e., influencing the representatives) also manifests itself at the level of the corporation and may provide another example of the conflict of interests between IIs and other shareholders. For example, where an II has cross-ownership in both the target and the bidding firms in cases of takeover transactions, the II can limit losses associated typically with the holdings of the bidding firm (Anabtawi and Stout 2008; Matvos and Ostrovsky 2008). Such crossholdings also translate to the reduction in the wealth of non-crossholding shareholders. This is because while the crossholding II seeks to optimize its return resulting from a transaction, it does so at the expense of the non-crossholding shareholder (or even a crossholding II with the 'wrong' weight of stockholdings in either of the companies). The attempted takeover of Yahoo! by Microsoft in 2008 provides an illustration of this.

In the proposed transaction, Microsoft made a $44.6 billion bid for Yahoo! It was reported that nearly 90 per cent of Yahoo's IIs had crossholdings in Microsoft, and most of Yahoo's top 20 IIs were also significant holders in Microsoft. Ray (2008), discussing a report prepared by Institutional Shareholder Services (ISS), observed, '[w]hat's the implication? Any concession by Yahoo! to Microsoft's $44.6 billion buyout has to benefit both holdings in order to be a net benefit to shareholders.' Ray (2008) quoted from the ISS report that 'in theory an institutional shareholder may be likely to support a transaction, even one that is a poor deal for one side, provided the other side reaps a greater reward'. Ray (2008) concluded that '[w]ith most of Yahoo!'s top investors having greater dollar exposure to Microsoft stock than Yahoo! shares in their portfolio . . . the most likely scenario is that "we can expect shareholders who own both companies to pressure Yahoo directors to extract a material sweetener from Microsoft . . ."'.

Summary

The above discussion and examples point to the shortcomings in Hansmann and Kraakman's observations cited at the outset of this chapter vis-à-vis IIs. More specifically, the discussion showed that IIs interests do not coincide with those of other shareholders and, indeed, are often in conflict with those of the shareholder body as a whole. Moreover, the discussion points to the fact that IIs may behave in a manner akin to that of a dominant shareholder under the traditional analysis of diffused versus concentrated ownership structures in corporate scholarship. Finally, the observations raise doubts on the extent to which IIs provide voice to all shareholders.

4 REGULATORY IMPLICATIONS OF INSTITUTIONAL INVESTORS AS BLOCKHOLDERS

The thrust of this chapter is that ownership patterns within a given economy matter from a regulatory standpoint for corporate governance initiatives. Observing changes in the landscape subject to this regulation is paramount if such initiatives are to have a positive impact (and, therefore, social utility) rather than negative or neutral impact. This is the case whether we approach corporate governance from a domestic or international perspective (Wymeersch 2002; Claessens 2003). I will explore the significance of these statements in the context of the subject of this chapter – institutional investors.

It has been noted that '[i]n its broadest sense, corporate governance is concerned with holding the balance between economic and social goals and between individuals and communal goals . . . The aim is to align as nearly as possible the interests of individuals, of corporations, and of society' (Cadbury 2003, p. iii). One way of achieving these goals is through the promotion of international corporate governance standards – standards that started as national codes and later became international guidelines (ibid.). Key players identified in the promotion of these standards are IIs (Cadbury 2003, pp. v–vi).

IIs are instrumental in the introduction of codes of corporate governance. They produce their own codes of best corporate governance practices, which they encourage their portfolio firms to adopt. IIs are also relied upon by governmental agencies to get their portfolio firms to adopt the codes recommended by IIs (Mallin 2007). As Peer Zumbansen observed, corporate governance regulation can be seen as 'transnational and hybrid in nature' (Zumbansen 2010, p. 21).

The reliance on IIs poses a challenge to policymaking. As noted at the outset of this chapter, American IIs are credited for the promotion of a shareholder-oriented model of corporate law around the world, which, inter alia, includes the promotion of dispersed ownership as the optimal model for corporate ownership. In addition, institutional investors are also credited with the reduction of public distrust in large firms (see, e.g., Stimson 1925; UNEP 2009). Yet, as we have seen in Section 2 of this chapter, IIs are the emerging blockholder in the American equity markets. This paradox presents a potential challenge to policymaking. The potential challenge stems from the treatment of IIs in the corporate governance literature. This challenge also represents the point where economic analysis and legal analysis yield different results and, as such, depart from one another.

From an economic analysis perspective, whether we view them as blockholders or as agents for the diffusion of ownership, IIs are a powerful actor in the capital markets. They hold out significant potential as instruments for bringing about improvements in corporate governance practices. That is, IIs, as blockholders and transnational agents, possess the power to introduce the requisite change at both the national and international levels. Yet this change poses a potential conflict due to the legal treatment accorded to IIs.

The conflict may be due to IIs being the source of the change in corporate governance policies or practices. If the proposed change originates with IIs, it does not automatically mean that it is for the benefit of all the shareholders of the corporation. II's interests are not necessarily identical to those of other shareholders. If, on the other hand, the change originates from the state, the state may need to rely on IIs to promote compliance by portfolio firms with the proposed change. When the state does this, it does so based on the notion that institutional investors are powerful and influential blockholders in the markets.

While there may not be conflict per se in this process, it does lead us to question the fundamentals of corporate laws in countries such as the US, where the notion of dispersed ownership as being characteristic of the ownership pattern is still upheld. In result, a distortion is introduced into the legal system which views the American capital markets as characterized by fragmented shareholding. Therefore, the regulatory framework in the US needs to be updated in order to give recognition to the fact that the ownership pattern in the US is MOBM and that the blockholder in these markets is the II.

We can take this a little further. By failing to recognize that MOBM represents the appropriate ownership pattern in the US and by continuing to promote policy initiatives that are premised on the assumption that the ownership pattern in the US is diffused, policymakers are likely introducing a distortion into the regulatory system. This is because the two ownership patterns (i.e., diffused, on the one hand, and MOBM, on the other) give rise to different results and, as such, require different regulatory treatment. Moreover, there is an equal possibility that this failure leads policymakers to introduce systemic risk into both the national and international financial systems (Pichhadze 2010b).

5 CONCLUSION

US markets have gravitated towards a corporate ownership model represented by MOBM. This affords liquidity in the capital markets, on the one hand, and enhanced monitoring of corporate managers, on the other. Market forces facilitated the concentration of ownership in the hands of a class of shareholders, namely, the institutional investor, thereby transforming the American equity markets into a variant of the blockholder model.

From a policy perspective this trend and the resulting ownership model – MOBM – are significant. Failure to recognize it and adjust policy thinking in order to accommodate it (via changing regulatory attitudes and policies) may result in the introduction of systemic risk into the financial structure. This is because of the major impact that ownership structures have on corporate and securities laws and regulation.

The urgency of this accommodation is for two fundamental reasons. First given that IIs, as blockholders, do not behave in the manner that is predicted in the scholarship (i.e., representing and advancing shareholder interests), policymakers need to update the fundamentals of corporate and securities regulations to reflect fully the realities created by IIs as blockholders. Second, the important role of IIs in the international arena also mandates such an update in order to reduce the introduction of systemic risk into the financial system, global and domestic, resulting from reliance on IIs for the promotion of improved corporate governance. Such regulatory rethinking is important for developed nations, and imperative for developing nations that rely on the leadership of developed nations to improve their corporate sectors and overall financial and economic viability and stability.

NOTES

1. Given that the literature on corporate ownership structures does not make an explicit differentiation between the concentrated and the blockholder modes of ownership (and they are generally used interchangeably), for the sake of clarity, I divide the spectrum of public-firm ownership into three clusters: concentrated ownership represents ownership levels in excess of 50.1 per cent of the firm's outstanding shares;

blockholder ownership represents ownership levels between 5 per cent and 50 per cent; and dispersed ownership represents ownership levels below the 5 per cent level. The choice of the 5 per cent threshold is based on the requirements under s. 13(d), *Securities Exchange Act of 1934*, for disclosure of beneficial ownership of 5 per cent or more by any person of the outstanding shares of a firm's securities subject to the *Securities Exchange Act of 1934*. One should note, however, that while the above are used as a general guide, these lines of demarcation are fluid, subject to change from one firm to another based on factors such as the size of the firm and shareholdings of individual investors.

2. Hawley and Williams (2007) pointed out that ownership is further concentrated within the class of IIs, '. . . most importantly, while there are many institutional investors, holdings are, in fact, concentrated in the hands of a relatively small number of the very largest institutional investors. For example, in the USA, the 100 largest fiduciary institutions hold fully 52 per cent of *all* publicly held equity' (p. 415) (emphasis in the original).
3. According to Livingston (1963) IIs are as important as non-financial blockholders for the purpose of monitoring corporate managers (pp. 57 and 210).
4. The assumption in the analysis of Bebchuk and Zingales (2000) appears to be that going public translates into the assumption of diffused ownership structure for the corporation (i.e., atomistic share ownership).
5. For example, Bebchuk and Hamdani (2009), in an analysis of corporate governance evaluation systems, noted, '[a]t the outset, we should acknowledge that some public companies lie in the gray area between those pure types because they have a dominant shareholder with substantial influence but not a compete lock on control. We leave it for another day the refinement of our analysis necessary for extending it to such companies' (p. 1271). The omission from their analysis of those companies that fall in the 'gray area' is unfortunate given that they form the bulk (as opposed to 'some' as argued by Bebchuk and Hamdani) of the companies found in the US equity markets (see, e.g., Pichhadze 2010a, p. 71 and the references cited therein). In addition, the discussion in Bebchuk and Hamdani (2009) is premised on the notion that blockholder ownership patterns are not conducive to market mechanisms such as takeovers.
6. However, it has also been observed that '[d]ominant shareholders are perhaps less likely deliberately to push the firm toward non-value-maximizing activities . . . After all, the dominant shareholder pays a high percentage of the cost himself' (Daniels and Morck 1995, p. 13).
7. In corporate law, efforts by IIs during the 1990s to reduce restrictions on shareholder communications may be thought of as an example of such efforts (Pichhadze 2010a, p. 81). Yet, even this example is subject to a qualification. IIs were arguing in support of the proposed changes claiming that they were long-term investors whereas the evidence was to the contrary (*ibid*).

REFERENCES

Articles, Books and Reports

ABA Task Force (2009), 'Report of the task force of the ABA section of business law corporate governance committee on delineation of governance roles and responsibilities', *Business Lawyer*, **65** (1), 107–52.

Anabtawi, I. (2005), 'Some skepticism about increasing shareholder power', *UCLA Law Review*, **53**, 561–99.

Anabtawi, I. and L. Stout (2008), 'Fiduciary duties for activist shareholders', *Stanford Law Review*, **60** (5), 1255–308.

Bebchuk, L.A. and A. Hamdani (2009), 'The elusive quest for global governance standards', *University of Pennsylvania Law Review*, **157** (5), 1263–317.
Bebchuk, L.A. and L. Zingales (2000), 'Ownership structures and the decision to go public: private versus social optimality', in Randall Morck (ed.), *Concentrated Corporate Ownership*, Chicago and London: University of Chicago Press.
Brancato, C.K. and S. Rabimov (2008), *The 2008 Institutional Investment Report: Trends in Institutional Investor Assets and Equity Ownership of US Corporations*, New York: The Conference Board.
Cadbury, A. (2003), 'Foreword to Stijn Claessens, "Corporate governance and development"', *Focus* **1**.
Claessens, S. (2003), 'Corporate governance and development', *Focus* **1**.
Coffee, J. (1999), 'The future as history: the prospects for global convergence in corporate governance and its implications', *Northwestern University Law Review*, **93,** 641–707.
Daniels, R.J. and R. Morck (1995), 'Canadian corporate governance: the challenge', in Ronald J. Daniels and Randall Morck (eds), *Corporate Decision-Making in Canada*, Calgary, Canada: University of Calgary Press.
Davis, Stephen, John Lukomnik and David Pitt-Watson (2006), *The New Capitalists: How Citizen Investors Are Reshaping the Corporate Agenda*, Boston: Harvard Business School Press.
Friday, N.K. and T. Crum (2008), 'Top 10 Topics for Directors in 2008', *Corporate Governance Advisor*, **16** (3), 11–21.
Grossman, S.J. and O.D. Hart (1980), 'Takeover bids, the free-rider problem, and the theory of the corporation', *The Bell Journal of Economics*, **11** (1), 42–64.
Hansmann, H. and R. Kraakman (2004), 'The end of history for corporate law', in Jeffrey N. Gordon and Mark Roe (eds), *Convergence and Persistence in Corporate Governance*, Cambridge: Cambridge University Press, pp. 33–68.
Hawley, James and Andrew Williams (2007), 'Universal owners: challenges and opportunities', *Corporate Governance: An International Review*, **15** (3), 415–20.
Lindsay, S.M. (1925), 'The economic revolution in the ownership of property in the United States', *Proceedings of the Academy of Political Science in the City of New York*, **11** (3), 1–5.
Livingston, J.A. (1963), *The American Stockholder*, New York: Collier Books.
Mallin, Christine A. (2007), *Corporate Governance*, Oxford: Oxford University Press.
Matvos, G. and M. Ostrovsky (2008), 'Cross-ownership, returns, and voting in mergers', *Journal of Financial Economics*, **89** (3), 391–403.
Pichhadze, A. (2010a), 'The nature of corporate ownership in the USA: the trend towards the Market Oriented Blockholder Model', *Capital Markets Law Journal*, **5** (1), 63–88.
Pichhadze, A. (2010b), 'Private equity, ownership, and regulation', *Journal of Private Equity*, **14** (1), 17–24.
Pound, J. (1992), 'Raiders, targets, and politics: the history and future of American corporate control', *Journal of Applied Corporate Finance*, **5** (3), 6–18.
Stimson, H.L. (1925), 'The effects of popular ownership on public opinion', *Proceedings of the Academy of Political Science in the City of New York*, **11** (3), 134–6.
Winden, F. (2003), 'Interest group behavior and influence', in Charles K. Rowley and Friedrich Schneider (eds), *The Encyclopedia of Public Choice*, New York: Springer, pp. 118–29.

Wymeersch, E. (2002), 'Convergence or divergence in corporate governance patterns in Western Europe', in Joseph A. McCahery, Piet Moerland, Theo Raaijmakers and Luc Renneboog (eds), *Corporate Governance Regimes: Convergence and Diversity*, Oxford and New York: Oxford University Press, pp. 230–49.

Statutes and Regulations

Securities Exchange Act of 1934, 15 USC § 78a et seq. (US).

Web Resources

OECD (2009), 'Policy framework for effective and efficient financial regulation – OECD recommendations and principles', available at http://www.oecd.org/dataoecd/18/53/44187223.pdf (accessed 19 May 2011).

Ray, T. (2008), 'Report: Yahoo–Microsoft investor overlap supports a deal', *Barron's*, available at http://blogs.barrons.com/techtraderdaily/2008/02/15/report-yahoo-microsoft-investor-overlap-supports-a-deal/ (accessed 19 May 2011).

SEC (2009), 'Facilitating shareholder director nominations', 17 CFR Parts 200, 232, 240, 249 and 274 [Release Nos. 33-904660089; IC-28765; File No. S7-10-09], available at http://www.sec.gov/rules/proposed/2009/33-9046.pdf (accessed 19 May 2011).

UNEP (2009), *Fiduciary responsibility – legal and practical aspects of integrating environmental, social and governance issues into institutional investment*, Geneva, Switzerland: UNEP Finance Initiative, available at http://www.unepfi.org/fileadmin/documents/fiduciaryII.pdf (accessed 19 May 2011).

Zumbansen, P. (2010). 'Transnational Legal Pluralism', CLPE Research Paper; v. 6, no. 1 (2010); RPS-01, available at http://papers.ssrn.com/sol3/papers.cfm?abstract_id=1542907 (accessed 19 May 2011).

PART II

Private remedy in corporate law and its limits

8. The role of corporate law in preventing a financial crisis – reflections on *In re Citigroup Inc Shareholder Derivative Litigation*

Franklin A. Gevurtz

1 INTRODUCTION

As we survey the wreck of the economy left in the wake of the recent financial crisis, the question inevitably becomes what to do in order to prevent another such meltdown. This question, in turn, divides into two subsidiary inquiries: (1) What substantive rules are necessary to prevent another crisis; and (2) Who should impose such rules? This chapter looks at one aspect of the latter question.

The debates over who should impose rules to prevent another financial crisis tend to focus on agencies that regulate financial institutions (for example, bank regulators) and agencies that regulate financial markets (for example, securities regulators) (Paletta 2009). Commentators have given less attention to the role of government bodies that create and enforce corporate law more generally. The lack of attention given to those responsible for enforcing corporate laws in preventing a future financial crisis seems surprising. After all, one would not assume a priori that corporate law is irrelevant to preventing a crisis involving the collapse or bailout of major corporations. Indeed, among the potentially more significant legal actions to date from the recent crisis has been a shareholder derivative lawsuit seeking to hold the directors of the mega financial firm, Citigroup, liable under Delaware corporate law for the massive losses suffered by the firm (*In re Citigroup* 2009).

This chapter seeks to fill the gap. Specifically, it looks at the role of state legislatures and courts – such as those of the State of Delaware – which are the governmental bodies primarily responsible for creating and enforcing corporate law in the United States. The question is whether these organs of state government are institutionally capable of deploying corporate laws – the laws governing the internal affairs of business corporations – to reduce the possibility of a replay of the recent financial crisis.

The discussion will proceed through a blending of the particular and the general. Specifically, Section 2 of this chapter will use a review of the activities within Citigroup as a case study in excessive risk-taking by financial institutions that led to the recent financial crisis. Section 3 will outline generally the tools available to the law to limit the sort of excessive risk-taking that occurred at Citigroup and other financial institutions. It will then divide these tools into those addressed by banking law and those for which state corporate law may play a role. We will see that tools given in whole or in part to corporate law constitute potentially important mechanisms in the toolbox available to the law to curb excessive risk-taking by financial institutions. Section 4 will use the results in the *Citigroup* litigation as a case study in the limited willingness of state legislatures and courts to use the tools allocated to corporate law to curb excessive risk-taking by financial institutions. It will explain why the results in *Citigroup* are inherent in the structural underpinnings of state-created and enforced corporate law. The normative implication of this analysis is that, regrettably, one cannot look to state-created and enforced corporate law – as opposed to aggressive use of all available tools by banking authorities – to limit excessive risk-taking by financial institutions.

2 CITIGROUP AS A CASE STUDY IN EXCESSIVE RISK-TAKING

The financial crisis climaxing in late 2008 had a number of causes – ranging from macro-economic conditions of excessive liquidity stemming from low interest rates and saving imbalances between the United States and Asia, which, in turn, fueled a bubble in housing prices in the United States (Scott 2010); to micro-economic factors of risky borrowing against residential real estate through subprime loans (Hilsenrath and Di Leo 2010);[1] to conflicts of interest afflicting key gatekeepers, especially credit rating agencies (Calomiris 2009); to legal factors flowing from a pervasive deregulatory philosophy (Levitin 2009). No doubt the relative significance of each of these and other factors will be debated for some time. For the purposes of a chapter focused on the role of corporate law in preventing a financial crisis, however, the factor of concern is excessive risk-taking within financial corporations.[2] Rather than discuss such risk-taking in the abstract, it may be useful to describe briefly the events at one company. Citigroup provides a convenient example.

Citigroup is a bank-holding company that operates, through its subsidiaries, both banking and non-banking financial services businesses – at one time being the world's largest bank (Martin and Morgenson 2009). In late 2007 and 2008, Citigroup suffered more than $65 billion worth of losses (Dash and Creswell 2008), which, coupled with the fear of further losses, threatened Citigroup's survival. Concerned with damage to the broader economy from the collapse of such a massive financial institution, the United States federal government agreed to a bailout plan in November 2008 (Dash 2008b). Under the plan, the federal government invested $20 billion in Citigroup, and also agreed to absorb 90 per cent of the losses beyond the first $29 billion, if Citigroup suffered further losses in its portfolio of approximately $306 billion in residential and commercial real estate loans, as well as other assets. To cover these losses, if necessary, the United States Treasury Department would use $5 billion of its bailout fund, the Federal Deposit Insurance Corporation (FDIC) would cover the next $10 billion, and the Federal Reserve would guarantee the rest. In exchange, the federal government received preferred stock.

While Citigroup's losses flowed from a number of sources, for present purposes it is enough to focus on the largest source: mortgage-related securities involved with Citigroup's operations in collateralized debt obligations. Collateralized debt obligations (often referred to as CDOs) are created by packaging together various secured obligations, such as home loans secured by mortgages, and then selling rights to the cash flows from the pooled secured obligations in classes, or tranches. Some of these tranches possess a senior right to be paid (thereby having less risk of default), while the subordinated tranches receive a greater interest rate in exchange for taking the greater risk of non-payment. The prevailing view was that one could create tranches which, because of their senior position, justifiably could claim even extremely low investment-grade (such as AAA) levels of risk despite the underlying assets in the pool being more risky home loans, including subprime loans (Sjostrom 2009).

Citigroup engaged in packaging and selling CDOs using not only home loans it originated, but also home loans it purchased from other lenders, as well as other secured obligations. Following Charles Prince (who later became Citigroup's CEO) taking charge of Citigroup's corporate and investment bank in 2002, Citigroup ramped up its CDO operation so that by the middle of the decade it became one of the biggest players in generating and selling CDOs. This produced considerable income for Citigroup, which charged fees for managing the CDOs (Dash and Creswell 2008).

This operation not only increased Citigroup's earnings, it also increased its risks. In part, this was because Citigroup itself invested in CDOs. In part, however, Citigroup was creating an inventory risk; in other words, the risk that, if the market for CDOs dried up, Citigroup would be stuck with not only the CDOs it was creating for sale but also with the various secured obligations, such as mortgage-backed home loans, that it was generating or buying to package into CDOs (ibid.).[3] Moreover, among the secured obligations Citigroup purchased for packaging into CDOs, which consequently added to its inventory risk, were CDOs Citigroup issued earlier (Martin and Morgenson 2009).[4] Compounding the inventory risk to an even greater degree, Citigroup included a 'liquidity put' – an option allowing purchasers of the CDOs to sell them back to Citigroup at original value – along with the CDOs it created (ibid., p. 113).[5]

The risk Citigroup faced from holding an inventory of CDOs and securities for packaging into CDOs, as well as from the obligation to repurchase CDOs sold with liquidity puts, came home to roost in 2007 and 2008 when the housing price bubble, which peaked in 2006, burst completely; whereupon subprime home loan defaults accelerated and the market prices for CDOs collapsed. In stages, Citigroup was forced to recognize losses by writing down the value of its one-time $50 billion plus inventory of CDOs and subprime mortgage-backed home loans, in many cases to between 21 and 41 cents in the dollar (Dash and Creswell 2008)

While Citigroup's losses came from risks taken on the assets side (CDOs and subprime loans), liabilities incurred to finance the CDOs and subprime loans also created risks which came back to bite Citigroup. Specifically, Citigroup established so-called Special Investment Vehicles (SIVs), which issued commercial paper – very short-term notes – the proceeds of which were used to fund subprime loans and CDOs. The risk thereby created was that very short-term borrowing was funding long-term investments, which was acceptable so long as the investments were safe and liquid. When these investments became devalued and illiquid, the SIVs could not repay the commercial paper. While Citigroup claimed it was not legally obligated to do so, it nevertheless made emergency transfers of funds into the SIVs and ultimately assumed the assets and liabilities of the SIVs (*Citigroup* 2009, p. 113).

The fact that Citigroup took business risks in search of profits, and that those business risks led to losses, would be unexceptional – except perhaps for the magnitude of the misadventure. What is important is whether there are facts to suggest that persons within Citigroup acted unreasonably, even without the benefit of 20/20 hindsight, in incurring these risks. If so, then it becomes useful to discuss how the law might seek to prevent persons from taking unreasonable risks.

Based upon reports of investigative journalists and review by regulators, there are grounds to believe that Citigroup's misfortune was not simply the result of bad luck following the pursuit of reasonable business risks. Specifically, Citigroup had risk management systems in place designed to prevent its executives – including the executives who allowed the dangerous buildup in its inventory of CDOs and subprime loans to occur – from taking unreasonably dangerous risks. However, a serious flaw apparently in Citigroup's risk management systems was a lack of independence of the risk managers from the executives whom the risk managers were supposed to monitor, both because of long-standing personal connections[6] and because of lines of authority under which risk managers reported to the person with an interest in promoting the activities they were monitoring.[7] Further, as discussed above, Citigroup's biggest risk came not so much from individual risky transactions as it did from a buildup in its overall inventory of CDOs and subprime securities; these became particularly dangerous the minute there were signs of a slowdown in the real estate market. Citigroup officials do not seem to have accompanied this dangerous buildup with any independent assessment of the risk it entailed, but simply relied blindly on favorable credit ratings given to CDOs.[8] Potentially embarrassing along this line, reports surfaced that the most senior officers and directors at Citigroup may not have been sufficiently well informed to be aware of the magnitude of the risk Citigroup was running in its CDO operations.[9] Regulatory actions give credibility to the press reports of Citigroup's risk management failings. Complaints by foreign regulators that Citigroup's risk management practices were dangerously lax led the Federal Reserve to bar Citigroup from making any acquisitions of other financial companies for 12 months between the spring of 2005 and 2006 (Martin and Morgenson 2009). In 2008, Federal Reserve examiners apparently gave Citigroup a scathing confidential review of its risk management practices (Dash and Creswell 2008).

Citigroup's losses seem to have resulted not only from a lack of brakes (as in a well-functioning risk management system) but also from too much steam in the engine (as in the focus on profits and bonuses). This ran from former Clinton Administration Treasury Secretary Robert Rubin, who, as Chairman of the Citigroup Board of Directors' Executive Committee, urged engagement in greater risks for greater profits; to Charles Prince, who pushed the expansion of the CDO operation to gain increased profits; to the persons running Citigroup's CDO trading operations, who because of bonuses geared to profits became among Citigroup's highest-paid employees. According to some at Citigroup, this created a culture in which those worried about the buildup of risk kept quiet (ibid.).

3 TOOLS FOR CURBING EXCESSIVE RISK-TAKING AND THE ROLE OF CORPORATE LAW

The Tools for Curbing Excessive Risk-Taking

To explore the potential role for corporate law in curbing excessive risk-taking such as occurred at Citigroup it is useful to step back and take an inventory of the key mechanisms available to the law to address the problem. There are at least five basic approaches:

Regulation of business activities
The most obvious approach for the law to take to limit excessive risk-taking by financial institutions is to enact and enforce rules regulating the activities whereby a financial company incurs risk. For example, to limit the risk that the failure of one borrower would ruin a bank, banking law prohibits a bank from lending more than a certain percentage of its assets to a single borrower (Felsenfeld 2006, pp. 77–8). For many years, concerns about the risks banks would face if engaged in securities transactions led Congress, in the *Glass-Steagall Act*, to limit the ability of banks to engage in the securities business.[10] This limit on potential risk substantially departed the scene in a much-noted symptom of increasing deregulation.[11] An obvious lesson from the role of 'no-doc loans' in the recent financial crisis is the need to enforce rules requiring adequate documentation of the borrower's earnings capability before making a home loan (Litan 2009). A more controversial lesson from the recent crisis could be the need to limit the use of certain derivative contracts, such as credit default swaps (Kulpa 2009). Regulation of business activities to curb excessive risk-taking can preclude a firm from engaging in certain risky activities; it can alternatively leave decisions to the firm but mandate certain processes, such as the establishment of risk management committees, designed to avoid ill-considered risks (Lipton 2009).[12]

Since the purpose of this chapter is to look at the role of corporate law in preventing a financial crisis, it is not necessary to go beyond these few examples and delve into extensive details on the regulation of business activities of financial firms. Such regulation, however, raises a couple of broad questions that are important to answer in order to consider the role of corporate law in this realm.

To begin with, it is useful to ask what justifies the regulation of the business activities of banks and other financial firms so as to limit their risk. After all, in seeking to prevent the sort of excessive risk-taking that might cause the failure of regulated financial institutions, these regulations seem quite different than most regulations the government imposes on business entities. Specifically, when dealing with worker health and safety, consumer protection, environmental regulations, and the like, it is easy to imagine that if left unregulated business entities would happily sacrifice the interests of their employees, customers and the environment to make extra profit for the owners. By contrast, when the law acts to prevent a financial institution from taking excessive risk, it seeks to prevent actions that could wipe out the owners' interests in the firm. Of course, the law is not trying to protect the owners. Rather it is trying to protect depositors, or the taxpayers in the case of deposit insurance, or the broader economy from the injury resulting from the collapse of financial institutions (Cassidy 2009). Yet, this does not answer the question of why the self-interest of the owners in avoiding failure does not provide adequate protection.

There are a couple of answers to this question. To begin with, the owners (the shareholders in a corporation) are not commonly the persons making the decisions regarding risk-taking. Particularly in the widely held company, managers, over whom shareholders may have limited practical influence, will be making the decisions.[13] Concededly, managers may have strong incentives to avoid business failure – depending particularly on their prospects for alternative employment and how much of their personal wealth is tied up in the company's stock (Bebchuk and Spamann 2010). Nevertheless, there is no reason to assume that the managers' precise calculus of costs and gains from risk-taking matches either the shareholders' or those of the broader society (ibid., pp. 265–7).

More fundamentally, there are very strong reasons to question whether the shareholders' views of acceptable risk match what is socially optimal. In fact, an examination of the stock market performance of shares in financial companies in the years leading up to the recent financial crisis shows that the stock market rewarded the shares of banks and financial firms, including Citigroup, that took what turned out to be excessive risks, while punishing the shares of more prudent institutions (Bratton and Wachter 2010). The existence of bank regulation is based upon the recognition of the moral hazard that afflicts a business whose essence is making money by risking other peoples' (depositors') money. While bank shareholders do not want their firms to fail, taking a risk in search of higher profits can make sense for the shareholders even when the risk no longer makes economic sense once one factors in the greater amount of depositors' money potentially lost (Bebchuk and Spamann 2010, pp. 256–73). Moreover, a highly significant (as illustrated by recent events) externality, presumably ignored by shareholders, is the systemic damage caused to the broader economy by the failure of large banks (Posner 2009b).[14]

Moving beyond the question of whether regulation is necessary, we must ask whether regulation of business activities by financial institutions is a sufficient legal tool to curb excessive risk-taking by financial institutions. If so, there is little need for corporate law to play a role in seeking to avoid a financial crisis. Noted economist Joseph Stiglitz has provided insights into the limits of regulation as a tool to control negative corporate impacts on society (Stiglitz 2007). He begins by asking why governments, including the United States' government, are concerned about sovereign investment funds (funds investing on behalf of foreign governments) acquiring controlling interests in corporations operating businesses in sensitive fields. If regulation of corporations is sufficient to ensure companies refrain from actions that create negative impacts, then corporate ownership and control, including by other countries, should not matter. The answer, Stiglitz concludes, is that governments recognize that ownership and control matter despite regulation. This is because regulation can never be complete. Those in charge of the corporation invariably have some freedom of action due to inevitable gaps in the regulations, or because the regulator cannot be present at all times. This means those in control of corporations can take actions that create negative consequences despite the best regulation.

Capital requirements

A second type of law aimed at curbing excessive risk imposes capital requirements on financial institutions. In this context,[15] and simplifying a great deal, the law defines a basket of items – such as the amount received for common and preferred stock, certain retained earnings and reserves, as well as the amount received for some types of debt instruments – as capital. The law then demands that capital constitute a percentage – which depends upon the nature of the capital and of the firm's assets – of the financial firm's total assets (Pollard and Daly 2009, § 11.02).

Capital requirements provide a cushion to help insure that a financial institution can still meet its obligation to depositors despite losses in its investment and lending portfolio (Norton 1989).[16] This effect of capital, however, mitigates the consequences of excessive risk-taking; it does not curb it. The way in which capital serves to curb excessive risk-taking is by addressing the moral hazard that results if shareholders can make money by risking the depositors' money without suffering the consequences of any losses (Allen et al. 2009).[17] By ensuring shareholders have some 'skin in the game,' capital serves to alleviate the moral hazard.

As with regulation of business activities, the question arises whether capital requirements in banking law can be sufficient in themselves to curb excessive risk-taking, thereby precluding the need for corporate law to play a role. There are several reasons to conclude capital requirements are not sufficient. To begin with, capital requirements work on the incentives of shareholders, but, as discussed above, managers make decisions regarding risk-taking.

More fundamentally, capital requirements have had limited success in forcing the shareholders to focus on excessive risk to a socially optimal level – as illustrated in the earlier discussion of the stock performance of banking and financial companies in the years leading up to the recent panic. Several factors may account for this.

For one, capital rules involve an inherent complexity which undercuts their effectiveness. A key purpose of the capital requirement is to deal with the prospect that bad loans and investments will mean that the institution's assets are not worth what was thought; yet central to applying the capital requirement is the value of the institution's assets (Scott 2010, p. 28). The effort to square this circle – for instance, by making the required capital depend upon the riskiness of the assets held by the bank (Malloy 2009, § 5.3.3.4.2) – may lead to gaming and unintended consequences (Bebchuk and Spamann 2010, pp. 286–7). For example, the presumably lower risk entailed with AAA-rated securitized investments, as opposed to individual mortgage-backed home loans, has meant a lower capital requirement for banks that hold more of their assets in AAA-rated securitized investments than that required for banks holding more of their assets in the form of individual home loans (Scott 2010, p. 28). This, in turn, may have led banks to place a premium on holding AAA-rated senior tranches of CDOs rather than individual home loans (Friedman 2009). As discussed earlier, these CDOs turned out to be a major source of Citigroup's multi-billion dollar losses; indeed, the added complexities of valuing and dealing with these securitized instruments in a collapsing housing market may have added a significant element of unexpected riskiness over individual mortgage-backed home loans (Scott 2010, pp. 24–5).

Capital requirements may also create a perverse effect. Since the shareholders have a greater investment, return on the investment will go down unless loans and other investments give a greater return. This may produce an incentive to take greater risks (Norton 1989, p. 1313; Mülbert 2009, p. 14).[18]

Finally, the effectiveness of the shareholders' capital investment in curbing the shareholders' appetite for excessive risk depends upon forcing the shareholders to internalize the societal cost of the financial institution's failure. One problem here is that this depends upon the shareholders' planning horizons. Despite capital requirements, shareholders with only a short-term planning horizon – in other words, shareholders only focused on near-term corporate profit performance – may be favorably disposed toward excessively risky behavior by financial firms when the likely positive result is near term and the possible negative consequences are of sufficiently small probability that they are unlikely to occur within the planning horizon (the so-called black swan event). Such short-term planning horizons exist among many institutional investors (for example, mutual funds) in substantial part because the actual decision-makers in such investors are managers whose compensation may depend more on the short-term performance of individual portfolio companies than on the long-term performance (Heineman 2009). Beyond the timing issue, there is the inherently large difference in the magnitude of what shareholders have to lose and the losses faced by depositors despite any reasonable capital requirement. The mathematics of banking are such that, unless one makes the capital requirement so large as to undercut the banking function altogether, investments that are not in the interests of depositors still could make sense for the shareholders despite the risk to their capital (Bebchuk and Spamann 2010, pp. 256–63). Compounding this problem, the cost of a bank's collapse may be the systemic damage caused to the broader economy, which could even exceed the depositors' losses (Macey and O'Hara 2003; Posner 2009b; Bebchuk and Spamann 2010, pp. 266–7).

Compensation rules

Sources from politicians to academic commentators have given considerable attention to the possible role of executive compensation in encouraging excessive risk-taking by financial institutions (Ebrahimi 2009; Bhagat and Romano 2009). The large size of executive compensation at financial firms has caught the public's attention (Puzzanghera and Zimmerman 2009) but this, in itself, is not the concern when it comes to excessive risk. The fact that executives who brought their firms to collapse nevertheless received such compensation begins to get to the problem, but we need to be more precise. The question is: what incentives does compensation create for executives as they make decisions through which the financial institution incurs risks as it seeks profits?

The very fact that executives who so miserably failed nevertheless received rewards presumably has some effect on incentives. Yet while such a no-fault system provides little carrot for good performance, it would not seem, at least on its own, to promote the pursuit of excessive risk. One possible exception would be when the laxity, potentially encouraged by such a compensation scheme, applies to persons (say members of the risk management department or of the board of directors) whose essential role lies in monitoring risk-taking by others. Still, this has not been the central focus of concern.

Much of the expressed concern has focused on the skewed incentives created by the timing structure common to executive compensation schemes, which grant rewards based upon earnings performance during a relatively short time, such as a year or a quarter (Bhagat and Romano 2009; Posner 2009c). The simple bonus based on earnings during a given accounting period creates the incentive to increase earnings during this period. Stock option plans add to the bonus incentive – to the extent the amount of the option grant depends on reported earnings – the additional incentive to increase earnings during current accounting periods because the market price of stock upon which the value of the option depends is highly responsive to near-term reported earnings (Bratton and Wachter 2010). The corporate scandals of 2001–02 involving accounting fraud at Enron, WorldCom and the like illustrated the incentives this system creates for gaming reported earnings during a given accounting period (Gordon 2002). The financial panic of 2008 may illustrate the incentive this system creates for improving earnings during a given accounting period by way of decisions involving unreasonably high levels of risk.

The problem is not simply that executives have the firm incur risk in order to achieve earnings – this is what such schemes hope to achieve (Walker 2010).[19] Rather, the problem is that such schemes create asymmetric incentives under which the executives take unreasonable risk because they gain benefit from increased reported earnings during the given accounting period yet do not suffer equal consequences from losses (Mülbert 2009; Posner 2009c, p. 1026).[20] The asymmetry results from the fact that there is no negative bonus or stock option under which the executive must pay the company for accounting periods in which there are losses. This 'heads-I-win, tails-who-cares' approach makes it rational to place a bet even if the odds of winning, or the payoff if one wins, would not make this a worthwhile bet with one's own money. This becomes even worse if the loss event has very low probability – a black swan event – in which case the executive might figure that the odds of such an event occurring within the period of time the executive cares about (say, before he or she moves on to another position) is so small as to be ignored (Stiglitz 2007, pp. 49–50). Yet as recent events show, even the risk of a black swan event can be excessive if the magnitude of harm is great enough.

While most attention has focused on this timing issue, Professors Lucian Bebchuk and Holger Spamann (2010) have noted an additional incentive problem regarding the encouragement of excessive risk that may arise from the compensation of financial firm executives (pp. 264–5). As discussed above, shareholders of financial firms have an incentive to take excessive risks insofar as most of the loss falls on depositors. Hence, executive compensation schemes – such as ones that pay in part with stock or stock options – designed to align executive interests with those of the shareholders may contribute to the incentives of executives taking excessive risks. Indeed, to the extent stock options allow executives to enjoy the upside potential of gains for the stockholders without the downside risks of holding stock, they further skew the incentives of executives toward excessive risk.

There are those who have challenged the thesis that incentives based upon executive compensation increased the danger to financial firms (Friedman 2009). Correlation studies comparing forms of compensation and how financial firms fared in the crisis have provided ammunition for both sides.[21] Resolving who has the better of the argument, however, is well beyond the scope of this chapter.

If in fact certain forms of executive compensation have encouraged excessive risk-taking, rules limiting the use of these forms of executive compensation become a useful tool in curbing excessive risk-taking. However, as conceded by the advocates of such rules (Bebchuk and Spamann 2010), this approach is unlikely to be sufficient, standing alone, to curb excessive risk-taking.

Liability for unreasonable risks

Imposing liability to pay the damages resulting from unreasonable risks is a conventional tool in the law to deter creating such risks. Indeed, this concept is a pillar of tort law. While one goal of tort recovery for negligence (taking unreasonable risks) is compensation for injured parties, another goal is to deter negligent conduct (Dobbs 2000, § 11).

Interestingly, there do not appear to be many empirical studies on the degree to which fear of liability for unreasonable risk has changed the conduct of corporate directors and executives. Nevertheless, those in the field operate on the assumption that such an impact exists. Indeed, as expressed in *Citigroup*, as well as numerous other court opinions (*Joy v North* 1982) and academic commentary (Philips 1984), the fear is that legal liability may overly deter risk-taking by directors and executives.

Of course, by definition, imposition of liability for taking unreasonable risks should not create liability for those who only create reasonable risks; therefore, as a first approximation, liability should not deter reasonable risk.[22] Hence, the concern about over-deterrence is based on either a supposition that there will be erroneous determinations of liability or the hypothesis that executives will avoid even reasonable risk for fear of erroneous determination of liability, or just to avoid the burden of being sued (Eisenberg 1990). It is useful to note, however, that this over-deterrence concern raises a challenge to the wisdom of much of tort law, and not just to liability for risk-taking by financial firm executives (Gevurtz 1994). Still, as discussed later, in reaction to the concern of over-deterring business risk-taking, corporate law commonly requires greater culpability than simply unreasonable conduct before finding liability – a doctrine referred to as the business judgment rule.

In any event, the impact of monetary liability is to some extent the flip side of the impact of compensation schemes that reward profit creation. If compensation based on company profits may encourage excessive risk, then paying damages in the event of losses from unreasonable actions should discourage excessive risk-taking. The degree to which the possible imposition of liability deters risk depends upon well-established factors: the magnitude of liability and the probability of its imposition (Vitiello 1997). These in turn depend upon both the substantive standards for imposing liability and the procedural rules that may facilitate or hinder prosecution of the claim. So, for example, procedural rules that facilitate private actions may increase deterrence by increasing the probability of sanction (*JI Case Co v Borak* 1964).[23] Finally, it should be noted that liability for unreasonable risks may fall both on those who unreasonably decided to take the risk and upon those whose job it was to prevent engagement in unreasonable risks but unreasonably allowed the risk to be taken. The events at Citigroup discussed above seemingly illustrate both types of conduct.

Selection of management (rules of corporate governance)

Rules impacting selection of corporate management may also provide a means to curb excessive risk-taking. Here, we are concerned with rules affecting the selection of those who decide whether the financial company will incur risks, the selection of those who supervise those who decide whether the financial company will incur risks, and even the selection of those who choose those who have these other roles. Such rules may help if they are able to address a couple of ways selection can either limit or foster excessive risk-taking.

Selection can influence excessive risk-taking to the extent such risk-taking results from incompetence (as opposed to rational responses to bad incentives). In fact, there is some reason to believe that lack of financial competence played a role in the financial crisis. A study of German state-owned banks by Professor Harald Hau found a statistically significant inverse correlation between the financial sophistication possessed by members of the bank supervisory boards and how poorly the banks did during the recent financial crisis; in other words, the less financial sophistication (as measured by various criteria) members of the board possessed, the worse the bank generally fared (Hau and Thum 2009).[24] On a more anecdotal level, references to the lack of knowledge in the field of CDOs possessed by Charles Prince, the Citigroup senior executive and then CEO who pushed Citigroup's unfortunate lunge into such investments,[25] raise the question as to what role lack of competence may have played in Citigroup's problems.

The other impact of selection on risk-taking involves incentives. Desire for advancement or fear of firing can discourage excessive risk-taking if executives perceive that those controlling appointments and removal will hold losses against the executives. On the other hand, desire for advancement or fear of firing can encourage excessive risk-taking if executives perceive that those controlling appointments and removal are more concerned with earnings than risk. This prospect in turn ties into the discussion of the incentives of bank shareholders, who elect the directors.[26] As explained above, shareholders have incentives to favor excessive risk-taking.

This discussion suggests that rules setting qualifications of financial competence for election to the board or appointment as an executive, or allowing removal and a bar from future service in case of incompetence, might limit excessive risk-taking. Rules mandating disclosure of financial qualifications of candidates to the board might also promote competence – assuming disclosure actually affects either voting or nominations. More controversially, the discussion above suggests that rules limiting the effectiveness of the shareholder electoral franchise might reduce excessive risk-taking. For example, as a radical thought, one might consider giving other stakeholders in the bank – those possessing a greater interest in prudence than the shareholders – some portion of the right to elect directors.

Dividing the Tools between Banking and Corporate Law

Having taken an inventory of basic approaches to curb excessive risk-taking, we now must ask which approaches lie entirely within the domain of banking law, and in which approaches corporate law might play a role. An initial problem with this task is that banking law and corporate law are loose concepts rather than precisely defined terms. After admitting that the term is amorphous, one treatise describes banking law as covering the corporate operation and establishment of banks as well as the regulation of the financial and related services provided by them (Pollard and Daly 2009, § 1.01). A basic working definition of corporate law would be the law governing the internal affairs of corporations. This includes the powers and duties of directors and officers and the rights and liabilities of shareholders.[27] Just from these definitions alone one sees an immediate overlap between banking and corporate law when it comes to financial firms: Specifically, since banks are organized as corporations, is the law governing the internal affairs of banks banking law or corporate law?[28]

Rather than answer this question in the abstract, we can take a more pragmatic approach. As stated in the introduction, this chapter fits within the broader inquiry of who should impose the rules necessary to prevent another financial crisis. More precisely, the question is whether state legislatures and state courts, when creating and enforcing laws for all business corporations (rather than just for banks), are up to the task of employing such laws in a way to prevent another financial crisis. Using this as a guidepost, banking law then becomes laws enacted as part of legislation (be it state or, increasingly, federal) as well as the actions of regulatory agencies which focus on banks or financial companies rather than business corporations more generally.

We can also use the Citigroup example to help sort things out. Citigroup is a bank holding company; it has subsidiaries organized under banking laws rather than incorporated under general state corporate laws (Citigroup Inc 2009). Citigroup itself is incorporated under the General Business Corporation Law of Delaware (ibid.). As such, Citigroup illustrates the interplay of banking law and corporate law with respect to the various tools available to curb excessive risk-taking by financial firms.

The two tools which are easy to categorize are regulation of business activities and capital requirements. Both clearly fall within banking law as they come from legislation directed at banks and are enforced by regulatory agencies concerned with banks rather than corporations generally. Indeed, regulation of a firm's business activities is not the sort of thing one considers to be internal affairs, even if one were dealing with general corporations rather than firms incorporated under banking laws (*McDermott v Lewis* 1987, p. 215). Admittedly, general corporate laws address capital requirements; but, especially in the United States,[29] capital rules found in general corporate laws have become little more than a minimal prohibition on those distributions to shareholders that would leave insufficient assets to cover debts and liquidation preferences.[30] Looking at Citigroup, agencies concerned with banking regulate the banking activities Citigroup conducts through its banking subsidiaries, the Federal Reserve having approved Citigroup's acquisition of these subsidiaries.[31] The mix of agencies regulating the subsidiaries depends upon whether they are national or state banks (Felsenfeld 2006, pp. 5–9), ignoring any overseas banking subsidiaries. The fact that the FDIC insures deposits in the banking subsidiaries, however, means there will be extensive federal regulation over both the subsidiaries and Citigroup in any event.[32] Citigroup's banking subsidiaries and Citigroup are also subject to capital requirements imposed by federal banking regulators.[33]

Things become more complicated concerning the regulation of compensation, the imposition of liability for taking excessive risks, and the supervision of management selection. As a Delaware corporation, Citigroup is subject to the corporate law of that state when it comes to rules governing compensation of Citigroup directors and officers; imposing liability on Citigroup directors and officers for damages incurred due to unreasonable risk-taking; and regulating the election and appointment of Citigroup directors and officers – as these are each normally a matter of internal affairs and state general corporate law.[34] This explains why Citigroup shareholders brought a derivative lawsuit against directors and officers of Citigroup in the Delaware Chancery Court to recover losses the company sustained from its dealings in CDOs, as well as the compensation it paid its ex-CEO,[35] and why the court resolved this suit through the application of Delaware corporate law. Given the widespread use of bank holding companies,[36] this shows the potential significance of state general corporate law with respect to the tools for curbing excessive risk-taking by financial firms.

On the other hand, what about Citigroup's banking subsidiaries? Because these companies are organized under banking statutes the issues of compensation, liability for excessive risks and management selection would all seem to be banking law, even if they are the internal affairs of the banking subsidiaries. Yet this does not mean that state general corporate law would necessarily be inapplicable. This is because provisions in the banking statute, judicial decisions or actions by the banking regulatory agency might call for the application of the state's general corporate law on the issue.[37]

This is best seen regarding liability for excessive risks. For decades, state and federal courts have held that bank directors are subject to common law fiduciary duties – including a duty of care to avoid damage to the company – the parameters of which courts often find in general corporate law (Malloy 2004, § 3.2.6.1). For state banks, courts presumably look to the common law of the bank's state,[38] while prior to *Erie Railroad Co v Tompkins* (1938), federal courts applied a federal common law to national banks (*Briggs v Spaulding* 1891). In 1997, however, the United States Supreme Court held that, even as to national banks, state corporate law (presumably of the state in which the national bank has its headquarters) dictates the contents of this duty (*Atherton v FDIC* 1997).

With the background of the savings and loan crisis, and dissatisfied with the developments in state law that made it more difficult to bring claims for breach of the duty of care (ibid., p. 228),[39] Congress intervened. In the *Financial Institutions Reform, Recovery, and Enforcement Act* (FIRREA), Congress added section 1821(k) to Title 12 of the United States Code. Section 1821(k) allows the FDIC to pursue claims against directors and officers of insured banks in receivership (or that accept FDIC assistance to avoid receivership). The section establishes the federal standard to impose liability as gross negligence or worse; albeit, it leaves open the possibility of recovery under state law in respect of standards that would impose liability for conduct not as culpable as gross negligence (ibid., p. 227), such as ordinary negligence.

An obvious gap in section 1821(k) is that it only kicks in upon the bank's failure (or the use of FDIC funds to avoid failure). To deter misconduct short of bank failure, the FIRREA also added a three-tier set of monetary penalties for, among others, officers and directors of banks with deposits insured by the FDIC,[40] as well as officers and directors of their holding companies.[41] The application of these penalties to unreasonable risks, however, is not entirely clear. The section penalizes engaging in unsafe or unsound practices, which would seem to include execution of unreasonable risks (Schooner 1995). However, this only encompasses reckless or knowing acts.[42] While the section also reaches breach of fiduciary duties, it is unclear if this encompasses negligence or gross negligence, or whether it requires some greater degree of culpability (Lapine et al. 2008, vol. 2, § 45.08).

All told, legal liability upon bank directors and officers for excessive risk involves a blending of rules specifically directed at banks, together with general corporate law applied by analogy. With executive compensation, too, use of general corporate law fiduciary duty rules applied by analogy (Comizio and Swartz 2000) mix with explicit banking law rules. Indeed, in the *FDIC Improvement Act* of 1991, Congress specifically identified compensation as one of the areas for banking agencies to address in regulations creating standards for safety and soundness of insured banks and their holding companies.[43] In October 2009, responding to concerns about the incentives for excessive risk-taking resulting from some forms of compensation, the Federal Reserve proposed incentive compensation policies for all banking organizations subject to its supervision, including member banks and bank holding companies (Morphy 2009). The policies are designed to prevent incentive compensation from encouraging excessive risk-taking.

Finally, a blended system also exists with respect to management selection. Banking statutes codify general corporate law principles under which the shareholders elect the directors and the directors appoint the officers for banks.[44] Moving beyond common norms of general corporate law, banking statutes grant regulatory agencies the power to remove directors, officers and other affiliated parties of insured banks – and even of bank holding companies[45] – for various misdeeds, and to prevent their further employment by any financial institution.[46] The impact of the removal power on excessive risk-taking is somewhat muted, however. Among conduct that can produce removal is participation in unsafe or unsound banking practices or breach of fiduciary duty.[47] Yet the conduct must demonstrate willful or continuing disregard for the institution's safety (or else personal dishonesty) in order to warrant removal.[48]

Banking law can also curb the effectiveness of the shareholder voting franchise. Specifically, as stated above, acquisition by one corporation of sufficient shares in a banking corporation to make the acquiring corporation a bank holding company requires approval by the Federal Reserve. Acquisition of a controlling amount of shares in an FDIC insured bank or a bank holding company by any person, whether or not the acquirer is a corporation, is subject to disapproval by banking authorities under the *Change in Bank Control Act*.[49] The significance of this veto over bank acquisitions should not be underestimated since the significance of the shareholder voting franchise in a widely held corporation often lies primarily in the prospect of a hostile tender offer (Manne 1965). Still, the impact of these provisions on the pressure to increase reported earnings because of the market for corporate control is attenuated by the fact that the acquisition of a bank with lower earnings by an institution with higher earnings, in and of itself, would not seem to be grounds for disapproval (Williams 2009).

4 WHY IT MATTERS: *CITIGROUP* AS AN ILLUSTRATION OF THE LIMITATIONS OF STATE CORPORATE LAW

In many instances, disputes over whether a particular tool of regulation belongs to one field of law or another seem to involve little more than tacky turf wars – whether that is between agencies and their legislative oversight committees or between professors carving up the law school curriculum. When asking whether the tools for limiting risk involve banking law or corporate law, however, something more important is at stake. This is because the two laws involve fundamentally different structural and philosophical underpinnings, which impact their effectiveness in employing the tools they possess to limit excessive risk-taking.

At its core, banking regulation is largely national and mandatory. Of course, this is an oversimplification. For example, the United States has a dual banking system with national banks chartered and regulated by the federal government through the Comptroller of the Currency and state banks chartered and regulated by state banking agencies (*Atherton v FDIC* 1997, pp. 220–21). This has allowed a certain degree of regulatory arbitrage as banks jump between federal and state charters to gain some advantage under the system (Felsenfeld 2006, pp. 28–9). Moreover, the narrative of the last couple of decades in banking law has been one of deregulation, as banks have been allowed to engage in practices (such as the securities business) previously barred to them.[50] Yet it is important not to let the details obscure the central core. Despite the existence of state chartered banks, banking law has essentially become national. This is because virtually all state chartered banks have opted for FDIC insurance, and in doing so they become subject to extensive federal regulation.[51] Also, despite liberalization, banking law is essentially mandatory. By and large, banking regulations are not default rules which the owners of the business can contract around.[52] This is because, as discussed earlier, the essence of banking is the effort by the business owners (shareholders), or managers working on the owners' behalf, to make money by risking the money of other persons – depositors, or the taxpayers in the case of deposit insurance – who are not in a position to contractually limit risk-taking by owners or managers. Under these circumstances, even before the most recent misadventure in finance, policy makers recognized the inherent temptation (or moral hazard) to engage in unreasonably dangerous risk-taking, as well as the externalities produced when the owners or managers succumb to this temptation. Accordingly, the law imposes mandatory limits on risky activities by banks.

By contrast, at its core, corporate law is state law and permissive. This difference in the source and underlying philosophy of corporate law limits its ability to utilize the tools available to it as an effective control on excessive risk-taking by financial institutions. To illustrate the point, we look to the *Citigroup* decision.

Citigroup as a Case Study in Weak Corporate Law

Overview

In *Citigroup*, shareholders of the company brought a derivative lawsuit against current and former directors and officers of Citigroup, alleging that the directors and officers breached their fiduciary duties by failing to properly monitor and manage the risks Citigroup faced in its dealings in CDOs and the subprime mortgage lending market. A derivative lawsuit is a procedural mechanism for enforcing fiduciary duties owed to the corporation by allowing a shareholder of the company to bring a suit seeking recovery for the company rather than for the shareholder (Gevurtz 2000, § 4.3). Because such a suit removes the board's normal control over corporate decisions – in this instance, whether to bring a lawsuit on behalf of the company – derivative suits face a special pleading requirement designed to establish that the board is not the appropriate body to decide whether to bring the lawsuit in question (*Aronson v Lewis* 1984). Specifically, the plaintiff must plead with particularity either that the plaintiff has made a demand for action upon the board and a reason why the court should ignore the board's rejection of the plaintiff's demand, or a good excuse for not making such a demand.[53] In most jurisdictions, including Delaware, a good excuse for not making a demand is that the demand would be futile because we know, even before the demand is made, that the court will ignore the directors' rejection of the demand (*Brehm v Eisner* 2000). The plaintiff can establish this by pleading with particularity that most of the board members breached their duty and should be sued by the corporation, meaning that most of the board members are not the parties who should decide whether the company should sue (*Beam v Stewart* 2004).

The *Citigroup* opinion arose from a motion to dismiss the complaint for failure to make such a demand or plead an adequate excuse. In response, the Delaware Chancery (trial) Court had to assess whether the plaintiffs had successfully pled, with particularity, the excuse that most of Citigroup's current directors had breached their fiduciary duty. With one exception, the court in *Citigroup* concluded that the plaintiffs had not succeeded in this task. In particular, the court rejected the plaintiffs' allegations that the directors had breached their duty by ignoring so-called red flags warning of trouble with the company's CDO business; as well as allegations that the directors breached their duty in failing to adequately disclose the situation to the shareholders, or by virtue of the decisions the directors made that exposed Citigroup to risks in the subprime market and that had the company repurchasing its stock when the price was high. The only claim which survived the court's scrutiny was the allegation that the compensation awarded to the fired CEO constituted waste.

Of course, the Chancery Court's dismissal of the excessive risk-taking claims, in itself, does not establish that either Delaware corporate law liability rules or their application are necessarily weaker than one might expect from rules or application under a different regime. Instead, we must examine more carefully the basis for the Delaware court's decision and compare the critical steps with the closest analogy arising under banking or other regulatory statutes. In this discussion, it is important to keep in mind that the goal is not to criticize the *Citigroup* decision from a doctrinal standpoint, or even, at this point, from a policy standpoint. Rather, the point is simply comparative: *Citigroup* illustrates that corporate law is weaker (in the sense of being less likely to produce liability) than banking law or other regulatory regimes are likely to be. In turn, as discussed earlier, there is less deterrence of excessive risk-taking.

The standard

We begin with the standard for imposing liability applied by the court. The court's opinion in *Citigroup* is littered with references to the business judgment rule; so much so that a casual reading might lead one to assume that this rule provided the standard against which the court assessed liability. The business judgment rule means different things to different courts, all of which center on the notion that courts should be reticent to impose liability based upon, or otherwise second guess, decisions by corporate directors (Gevurtz 1994, pp. 295–303). In Delaware, the rule requires the plaintiff to establish that disinterested directors are guilty of gross, rather than just ordinary, negligence in order to prove a breach of the directors' duty of care in making a decision (*Smith v Van Gorkom* 1985). The business judgment rule, however, did not provide the relevant standard in *Citigroup*. This is because Citigroup, as is typical of Delaware corporations, has a provision in its certificate of incorporation permitted by section 102(b)(7) of the *Delaware General Corporation Law*. Section 102(b)(7) allows a certificate of incorporation to contain a provision waiving damage claims against directors for breach of fiduciary duty unless the breach involves certain categories of conduct; for example, the section prohibits waiver of damages for acts not in good faith. Hence, to prevail, the plaintiffs in *Citigroup* had to establish that the directors failed to act in good faith.

Looking at the matter from scratch, one might be perplexed on how to apply the test of good faith to a case claiming that directors were not paying attention while corporate managers incurred excessive risk. After all, traditionally one thinks of good faith as meaning that the directors subjectively thought their action was in the best interest of the corporation (*Aronson v Lewis* 1984, p. 812). This works for a board decision – which is why courts commonly mention good faith in the context of the business judgment rule (*Brehm v Eisner* 2000, p. 263, note 66) – but seems less relevant in the context of an inattention case where, presumably, directors did not notice the danger to the corporation and the question is whether there was a reason for them to do so. Nevertheless, beginning with dicta in the landmark *In re Caremark Int'l Inc* (1996) opinion and culminating in a holding by the Delaware Supreme Court in *Stone v Ritter* (2006), Delaware courts have applied good faith to inattention claims. Specifically, Delaware courts have explained that if the plaintiff showed not only that the directors breached their duty of care due to inattention, but also showed the directors knew they were breaching their duty, the directors would not be acting in good faith (*Stone v Ritter* 2006). The problem, however, is to prove the directors actually knew they were breaching their duty when they failed to act. Instead of demanding direct proof of subjective knowledge, Delaware courts appear to allow a sort of indirect proof by a showing of a sufficiently egregious case of inattention. Specifically, a sustained or systematic failure to exercise oversight, such as utterly failing to implement any reporting system or consciously failing to monitor the operation of such a system, will establish a lack of good faith (ibid.). It was this standard of good faith that the court applied in *Citigroup*.

How does this good faith standard compare to a standard for imposing liability that we might expect to find in a national banking law? We need not guess, because we know. Recall the earlier discussion of 12 USC section 1821(k), enacted as part of the FIRREA. As explained earlier, this section allows the FDIC to pursue claims against directors and officers of insured banks in receivership. Section 1821(k) establishes gross negligence as the standard for finding liability. Is this the same as a lack of good faith, as Delaware courts have interpreted the terms? The answer, as the Delaware Supreme Court pointed out in its *In re Walt Disney Co* (2006) decision, is no. After all, equating gross negligence with a lack of good faith would render section 102(b)(7) illusory in the context it was meant to address since, as stated above, without gross negligence there is no liability to waive under Delaware's version of the business judgment rule. Indeed, it was a decision finding liability based upon gross negligence in making a business decision (*Smith v Van Gorkom*) which provoked the enactment of section 102(b)(7) (Hanks 1988). Hence by allowing directors to escape liability unless plaintiffs can demonstrate the directors' lack of good faith, the section 102(b)(7) waiver raises the barrier for imposing liability from the gross negligence standard called for in the case of an FDIC action on behalf of a failed bank under section 1821(k).[54]

Application

Ultimately, the significance of a standard for imposing liability comes in its application. Looking at the application of the standard in *Citigroup*, it is helpful to note that there are two types of inattention cases. There are the cases in which senior officers or directors ignore warning signs of employee misdeeds or other problems within the corporation.[55] Such warning signs are often, as in *Citigroup*, referred to as 'red flags.' Other cases, by contrast, involve claims that the directors failed to implement adequate systems to discover misdeeds or other problems without waiting for warning signs of particular trouble (*Graham v Allis-Chalmers Mfg Co* 1963). To use a metaphor, the first sort of case involves situations in which the directors smelled smoke but did not investigate to see if there was a fire; while the second sort of case involves situations in which the claim is that the directors failed either to install or maintain smoke detectors.

The Citigroup complaint seems to have given limited attention to possible claims based upon the inadequacy of Citigroup's monitoring systems (smoke detectors), in this case to monitor for excessive risk. Indeed, while the complaint quotes some newspaper stories that speak of poor risk management, and the plaintiffs' reply brief in opposition to the motion to dismiss introduces the more detailed news reports concerning the flaws in Citigroup's risk management, the Chancery Court treats the complaint as virtually conceding the monitoring systems issue by making reference to the Audit and Risk Management Committee of Citigroup's board, which was charged with oversight of the firm's risk management system and met 11 or 12 times a year in the years most relevant. The plaintiffs' failure to make more out of the structural problems in Citigroup's risk management systems that were discussed earlier seems perplexing. Of immediate relevance to the comparison between banking law and state corporate law standards, neither the plaintiffs nor the court seem concerned that federal regulatory officials had condemned Citigroup's risk management practices. Perhaps this simply reflects the competence of the plaintiffs' attorneys. Yet it probably did not matter. Given the Delaware Supreme Court's 2006 *Stone v Ritter* decision, so long as there is some system in place, complaints about the inadequacies of the system would not meet Delaware corporate law standards for imposing liability even when inadequacy in the system is documented by federal regulatory findings.

In fact *Stone v Ritter* (2006) provides a telling example of the disparity between banking standards and the standards for imposing liability under Delaware corporate law. In *Stone v Ritter*, the plaintiff shareholders alleged that the directors of a bank breached their duty by failing to ensure that the bank's employees complied with federal law requiring the filing of suspicious activity reports, which, in turn, resulted in federal banking authorities imposing $50 million in fines and penalties on the bank. Notably, in assessing these fines, federal banking officials found that the *Bank Secrecy Act* compliance program at the bank lacked adequate board and management oversight. However, the Delaware Supreme Court in *Stone v Ritter* affirmed the dismissal of the shareholders' complaint against the directors. How could the court do so in the face of federal regulatory findings of inadequate oversight by the bank's board? The answer is that the bank's certificate of incorporation contained a waiver of liability under section 102(b)(7). Since the plaintiffs' allegations in *Stone v Ritter* admitted that the board had instituted an extensive reporting system on employee regulatory compliance – even though one that the federal banking authorities ultimately found to be seriously inadequate – the plaintiffs' allegations were insufficient to establish the sort of sustained or systematic failure to monitor necessary to establish a lack of good faith.

Having eschewed much of a claim based upon inadequate monitoring systems, the *Citigroup* plaintiffs alleged that the directors ignored various published warnings of a housing bubble and publicly known events showing weakness in the subprime mortgage market, which the plaintiffs claimed constituted red flags of the dangerous risk stemming from Citigroup's huge positions in subprime mortgages and subprime mortgage-based securities (CDOs). To the court, however, such public red flags established nothing since they did not warn of wrongdoing at Citigroup.

There are a couple of different ways one could interpret the court's reaction in this regard. In part, this could be harkening back to a discussion in the court's opinion in which the court suggested that claims in Delaware based on inattention (so-called *Caremark* claims) might be limited to the failure to detect illegal actions or other specific wrongdoing by employees in the corporation – as in *Caremark Int'l Inc* (1996)[56] and *Stone v Ritter* (2006) – rather than the failure to detect and prevent excessive, but legal, business risks by company employees. Invoking the policies underlying the business judgment rule, the court expressed concern that a duty to monitor for business risk, as opposed to misconduct, could discourage the sort of risk-taking which is necessary in business. The court also used this distinction to explain the success of a recent derivative lawsuit against directors of AIG (*In re Am Int'l Group Inc* 2009) – noting that in the *Am Int'l Group* case (2009) the complaint alleged that directors failed to exercise oversight to prevent pervasive fraudulent and criminal conduct, rather than prevent excessive business risk-taking.

One could argue about whether the Chancery Court's views in regard to monitoring for business risk are an accurate reflection of Delaware corporate law.[57] The critical point for present purposes, however, is that there seems little basis, if one were applying banking law, for a possible rejection of a duty to monitor for business risks. Rather, it seems evident that bank directors are supposed to monitor for business risks and not just against wrongdoing (*Hoye v Meek* 1986; BIS 2006).

Alternatively, perhaps the Chancery Court could not accept the idea that public information ever constitutes a red flag. After all, by the very nature of the fact that the 'red flags' were public, we know that Citigroup's directors were hardly alone in missing the warnings about the existence of a housing bubble and the early signs of demise in the subprime market. Again we must ask whether those enforcing a banking law or another regulatory regime would see things differently. Here there is an informative comparison to be found in a decision applying federal securities law.

One of the lawsuits resulting from the spectacular collapse of WorldCom Inc in 2002 was a securities fraud class action brought by purchasers of bonds, which WorldCom sold to the public in 2000 and 2001 (*In re WorldCom Inc* 2004). Among the purchasers' causes of action was a claim under section 11 of the 1933 *Securities Act* against the underwriters in these bond offerings. Section 11 of the Act grants persons purchasing securities sold under a registration statement containing a misrepresentation a claim for damages against a number of parties, including the underwriter. The section creates a defense, however, for underwriters with respect to misrepresentations in portions of the registration statement prepared on the authority of an expert (such as audited financial statements) if the underwriters can establish they did not believe, and had no reasonable grounds to believe, the representations were false. This in turn raised the issue in *WorldCom Inc* (2004) as to whether there were any 'red flags' that gave the underwriters reasonable grounds to believe that the WorldCom audited financial statements contained misrepresentations understating WorldCom's costs. The underwriters argued there were not any such red flags, because the red flags argued by the plaintiffs consisted of comparisons of WorldCom's publicly reported cost margins with the publicly reported margins of WorldCom's competitors. The court, however, rejected the argument that, because everyone else missed the significance of a publicly known fact, such a fact cannot constitute a red flag the defendant should have noticed. The moral is that the answer to the question of what is a red flag may vary depending upon whether we are dealing with a regulatory regime imposing rigorous gate-keeping responsibilities, such as securities law imposes upon underwriters in a public offering, or whether we are dealing with the willingness of those enforcing ordinary corporate law to impose liability upon directors.

Finally, putting aside the questions of whether either public warnings, or warning of general business risk rather than misconduct, can constitute red flags, the court in *Citigroup* faulted gaps in the plaintiffs' pleading on the claim that the directors ignored the red flags. Specifically, the complaint left unanswered such questions as what exactly the directors did upon learning of the so-called red flags, and what exactly the plaintiffs claimed the directors should have done. Had the rules of ordinary notice pleading applied, such gaps probably would not have mattered.[58] However, the plaintiffs faced the requirement that, in order to excuse demand, they must plead 'with particularity' their claim against most of the current board. The problem the plaintiffs faced in pleading such detail was that they had not had the opportunity to take discovery during which they might investigate exactly what the directors' reactions were to the alleged red flags.

Once again, the question arises: Would the situation have been different in an action to enforce banking law or another regulatory scheme? Because the heightened pleading standard facing the plaintiffs in *Citigroup* is a product of the derivative suit mechanism used to enforce fiduciary duties owed to the corporation under corporate law, it would not have applied had there been an action, for instance, by the FDIC under section 1821(k) of the FIRREA on behalf of a financial firm in receivership.[59]

The waste claim

The Citigroup opinion showed much greater sympathy toward the plaintiffs' claim challenging the compensation awarded to Citigroup's outgoing CEO, Charles Prince. Here the plaintiffs' complaint incorporated a letter agreement entered into between Citigroup and Prince upon Prince's removal, under which Prince received $68 million – including bonus, salary and accumulated stockholdings.

Since the directors approving this agreement were not parties to it, the plaintiffs could only prevail in challenging the merits of this decision if, at the very least, they established that the agreement constituted 'waste.'[60] Waste is a transaction so unbalanced that no reasonable person would conclude the corporation received the equivalent to what it gave up in the deal (*Michelson v Duncan* 1979). In this instance, the court decided to allow the case to proceed because it could not tell, without more facts, whether the letter agreement was sufficiently one-sided to constitute waste.

The court's analysis of the 'compensation equals waste' claim seems inconsistent with the approach of the rest of the opinion. To begin with, what happened to the good faith standard resulting from the section 102(b)(7) provision in Citigroup's certificate of incorporation – that is, why is the court now applying a waste, rather than a good faith, standard? The answer must be that the court is treating waste as establishing a lack of good faith.

The greater inconsistency in the court's opinion comes in its attitude toward unanswered questions left after reading the plaintiffs' complaint. Addressing the compensation claim, the court resolved the uncertainties in what Citigroup received under the letter agreement in the plaintiffs' favor by making those the grounds for denying the motion to dismiss the complaint. In contrast, as discussed above regarding the red flags claim, when dealing with other claims in the complaint, the court pointed to critical gaps in its knowledge left by the plaintiffs' complaint as reasons why the complaint failed to meet the pleading standard for excusing demand.

In fact, the *Citigroup* court's liberality in dealing with the plaintiffs' pleadings when it came to the compensation claim appears to be inconsistent with other Delaware cases dealing with claims of waste in decisions to pay compensation. For example, in the leading *Aronson v Lewis* (1984) decision, the Delaware Supreme Court followed a more typical approach in dismissing a complaint about executive compensation because it contained insufficient details in alleging waste.

Still, one should not assume that the *Citigroup* opinion marks a significant stiffening of the Delaware courts' collective spine when it comes to compensation challenges. In fact, we have been down this road in Delaware before with complaints challenging compensation packages whose magnitude and circumstances have caught media attention. Most notably, in the *Disney Co* litigation, the Delaware courts faced a challenge to a compensation package under which Michael Ovitz received roughly $140 million upon his termination after an unsuccessful year as the number two senior executive at Disney. This inspired considerable media attention and shareholder litigation.

Initially in the *Disney Co* litigation (2003) the Delaware Chancery Court dismissed the plaintiffs' complaint, viewing the situation as an unremarkable exercise of business judgment. On appeal, however, the Delaware Supreme Court, cognizant of the case's notoriety, showed more concern (*Brehm v Eisner,* pp. 265–7). While the Supreme Court affirmed the dismissal of the plaintiffs' complaint due to its 'deficient pleading,' in an important post-script, the Supreme Court instructed the Chancery Court to grant the plaintiffs leave to amend. The plaintiffs' amended complaint turned out to be enough for the Chancery Court, whose attitude toward the case seemed to have undergone a shift. Still, the net upshot of the Chancery Court's new decision was simply to postpone the day of reckoning for the *Disney* plaintiffs. After several years and a long trial the Chancery Court, while remaining critical of the Disney directors, nevertheless gave judgment for the defendants, concluding that the directors' conduct was not so bad as to fall outside the protections of the business judgment rule. On appeal, the Delaware Supreme Court affirmed (*Disney Co* 2006). Whether a similar fate awaits the claim regarding Prince's compensation in *Citigroup* remains to be seen.

In fact, judging from the track record of Delaware cases dealing with waste, the odds are extraordinarily slim that the *Citigroup* plaintiffs will ultimately succeed at trial in their claim based on Prince's compensation. As put by a highly regarded Delaware Chancery Court judge, Delaware cases in which courts, after a trial, actually concluded there was waste might be as difficult to find as the Loch Ness monster (*Steiner v Myerson* 1995). Hence, this part of the *Citigroup* opinion may be bluff and bluster.

In any event, neither the waste standard itself nor the application of this standard when dealing with Prince's termination package suggests much focus on the possible effect of compensation in encouraging excessive risk-taking. The inquiry is a crude one of whether the corporation received so little in exchange for the compensation that no reasonable business person would say the corporation got anything equal to what it paid. Consistent with this, the unanswered questions about the letter agreement in *Citigroup* simply measured the value of what Citigroup received for the

$68 million (such as Prince's agreement not to compete with Citigroup and to waive stock option rights). The court does not engage in the more subtle inquiry of whether Prince's compensation package, by cushioning the impact of his dismissal, may encourage excessive risk-taking by other Citigroup executives in the future. Indeed, in the *Disney* litigation, arguments that the Ovitz contract constituted waste because of its incentive impact received little sympathy.[61]

The Structural Underpinnings of Weak Corporate Law

Citigroup illustrates that results under Delaware corporate law are weaker in imposing liability upon directors and officers who take unreasonable risks than what we might expect from banking or other regulatory law. This leads one to ask what produces this outcome. Specifically, is there something structural acting upon the legislatures and courts which create and enforce corporate law that leads it to be inherently weaker than banking or other regulatory law?

Who picked the Delaware legislature and courts to make the rules for Citigroup?

As previously stated, whereas banking law has become essentially federal, corporate law in the United States is, for the most part,[62] state law. Yet this sentence understates the difference in a key way: it ignores the degree to which the state law regime in corporate law consists of a supermarket where those operating corporations can shop for the law they desire.

Corporate law in the United States follows what is known as the incorporation doctrine, under which persons can form corporations in states (such as the state of Delaware) other than one in which the company will conduct operations.[63] What makes this significant is another doctrine generally followed in the United States, known as the internal affairs rule. Under the internal affairs rule courts, for the most part, apply the law of the state of incorporation when it comes to issues of corporate law.[64] The combination of the incorporation doctrine and the internal affairs rule means that parties forming a corporation can select which state's corporate law they wish to govern their corporation largely unencumbered by concerns about where the company actually intends to conduct business.

The result of parties' ability to choose their state of incorporation for its law has resulted in what Justice Brandeis famously labeled, a 'race . . . not of diligence but of laxity' (*Louis K Liggett Co v Lee* 1933, pp. 548–65). Specifically, he noted how a number of smaller states had enacted less restrictive corporate laws in order to gain revenues from incorporation fees and franchise taxes. New Jersey was a pioneer in this endeavor, but after it retrenched under the reform leadership of then-governor Woodrow Wilson, Delaware became the leading state in attracting incorporation through so-called liberal corporation laws (Seligman 1976).

Of course, persons might choose to set up their banks in jurisdictions with less regulation. Indeed this has become a concern with national, as opposed to international, bank regulation in an era of increasing global finance (Posner 2009b). Moreover, to the extent that moving bank operations to avoid regulation has a significant impact on jobs and the like, jurisdictions may be more susceptible to engage in a race to the bottom than in corporate law, where the impact is largely limited to franchise fees and the like. This said, however, there presumably are much greater constraints on a firm's willingness to attempt regulatory arbitrage when it must move actual banking operations to a potentially less desirable business location.

The focus of Justice Brandeis's famous quote was on the demise of corporate size and activity limits, a subject which is now the concern of antitrust rather than corporate law. In more recent decades, the concern about Delaware and the race to the bottom has focused instead on the notion that the Delaware legislature and courts have sought to appeal to those who plan to be directors or controlling shareholders – who normally choose where to incorporate – by watering down regulation on such persons (Cary 1974). One example relevant to this chapter is to reduce the prospects that directors will be held liable for breaching their duty of care to the corporation.[65]

Commentators point to a number of constraints on Delaware's ability to attract corporations by watering down regulations on corporate directors and controlling shareholders to an undesirable degree. One cynical theory postulates that Delaware has an interest in providing minority shareholder protections because the resulting litigation and extra planning creates work for the state's corporate bar (Macey and Miller 1987).

Another theory holds that the Delaware legislature and courts are limited in their protection of corporate directors and controlling shareholders by their concern that a backlash could provoke Congress to adopt federal standards (Roe 2003). Under this view, it is no coincidence that the 2003 Chancery Court decision in *Disney Co* – which allowed continuation of the highly publicized litigation – followed both the corporate scandals at Enron, WorldCom and other companies in 2001 and 2002 and the Congressional reaction to those scandals with the enactment of the *Sarbanes-Oxley Act* in 2002. Indeed, as previously suggested, the one partial victory for the plaintiffs in *Citigroup* may be understood in this light. Specifically, this decision coincides with widespread public disgust at the large pay packages awarded to managers like Charles Prince whose actions led to bailouts at financial institutions (Puzzanghera and Zimmerman 2009).

The most important constraint from a normative standpoint, however, lies in the theory that the reticence of shareholders to invest in corporations formed under state laws that provide inadequate protection of their interest will deter companies from incorporating in states with suboptimal corporate laws (Winter 1977). This theory is not without its critics (Bebchuk 1992). What is also important for the purposes of this chapter is that this theory largely focuses on protecting minority shareholders, rather than other parties who may be injured by management decisions (ibid.). This in turn brings us to the ability of corporate law to protect non-shareholder interests injured by directors, including by the directors' failure to prevent excessive risk-taking.

Shareholder primacy

Debates over whether the purpose of a business corporation is to maximize shareholder wealth (within the limits of the law), or to advance the interests of all stakeholders in the firm (including creditors, employees and the broader community), often occur at such a level of abstraction as to make one wonder if there is any real legal impact. Even when the debate turns to the concrete question of whether directors breach their duty toward shareholders by acting to advance the interest of other stakeholders – the issue in the classic *Dodge v Ford Motor Co* case (1919) – the board's vast discretion under the business judgment rule removes much of the practical importance of the question (Gevurtz 2002). Nevertheless, the role of shareholder interests is so central to the structural and philosophical underpinnings of corporate law that it has a real impact on the ability of corporate law to protect the interests of other stakeholders in the corporation.

The primacy of shareholder interests in corporate law manifests itself in a variety of critical ways when it comes to the tools for curbing excessive risk-taking. Short of insolvency, courts generally hold that directors lack any duty in corporate law to look out for the interests of other stakeholders in the corporation (*N Am Catholic Programming Found Inc v Gheewalla* 2007). Reinforcing this narrow view of duty, the law grants to shareholders, and not to other stakeholders, standing to sue for breach of duties under corporate law – at least unless the corporation is insolvent.[66] Also, shareholder approval can significantly lower the degree of scrutiny applied by the court to the compensation of directors.[67] Last, but certainly not least, corporate law places the power to select the directors in the hands of the shareholders.[68]

This is not to say that those creating corporate law think corporations and their managers should ride roughshod over the interests of others on whom corporate actions have an impact. Instead, the issue is whether these are problems that corporate law should address, rather than problems for other laws to handle. Pervasive in corporate law is the notion that, except for certain abuses of limited liability,[69] the protection of other stakeholders is the job of other laws.[70] Hence the overriding view of those creating and enforcing corporate law is to leave it to employment, labor and occupational safety laws to protect workers; to consumer protection and contract laws to protect customers; to environmental and other laws to protect the community; and to banking laws to protect depositors.

Indeed, given the free choice regime for state corporate law, it is difficult to see how the system could be otherwise. After all, who chooses the state of incorporation? While directors may desire a state law regime that grants them discretion to consider the interests of stakeholders beyond the shareholders, directors are unlikely to favor a regime which increases their potential problems by adding to those who might sue directors for breach of duty or might claim the right to vote on their removal.

Moreover, to the extent corporate law protects anyone other than directors in the decision of where to incorporate through the right to vote, or to vote with one's feet, it is the shareholders. In the case of a reincorporation of a firm incorporated in one state to become a corporation organized under the laws of another state – a common route by which Delaware corporations are formed when companies go public, or later (Romano 1987) – it is the shareholders, not other stakeholders, who get a vote (Bebchuk 1992, note 143). It is the prospective shareholders who can refuse to invest based upon undesirable corporate law – a prospect arguably made realistic, even for the prospective shareholder ignorant of the intricacies of various state corporate law rules, by the impounding of the expected impact of these rules into the price of shares traded on efficient markets.[71] Hence, state corporate law inexorably must focus on shareholder interests to the extent that the law does not bow before management interests.

All of this produces a system in which corporate law rules are permissive in the sense that they become viewed largely as default rules that shareholders can contract around.[72] Section 102(b)(7) of Delaware's *General Corporation Law* is a good example. As discussed above, this provision played a critical role in the dismissal in *Citigroup*, and provides a much weaker approach to liability for inattention than found in banking law. It became the governing law for Citigroup because the shareholders of Citigroup (or its predecessors) voted to amend its certificate to add a waiver allowed by section 102(b)(7) or purchased shares in a corporation that had the waiver in its charter. Yet, before the shareholders could make this choice, they made another: They either voted to become a Delaware corporation or bought into a Delaware corporation. Section 102(b)(7) stems from a third choice as well: knowing that shareholders and those who would be directors decide where to incorporate, the Delaware state legislature voted to amend the state's corporate law to add section 102(b)(7).

Of course, section 102(b)(7) is not without limits. Shareholders cannot waive claims for breach of the duty of loyalty or for acts not in good faith. On the other hand, one strongly suspects that shareholders who agree to waive liability for actions in which directors acted disloyally or in bad faith must not have understood the impact of the waiver. Hence this limit may be little more than the corporate law equivalent to the notion that commercially unreasonable terms buried in the fine print of an adhesion contract that no one reads may not be enforceable (Alperin and Chase 2009, § 191). Also, section 102(b)(7) excludes claims for excessive dividends and the Delaware Supreme Court has stated that knowingly approving illegal conduct by a corporation violates the duty to act in good faith (*In re Walt Disney* [2006], p. 67) – both of which establish some protection of non-shareholder interests through corporate law that shareholders cannot waive. The instance of excessive dividends, however, is an elementary abuse of limited liability and it is presumably not worth the political capital to lobby for shareholders to possess the ability to waive corporate claims against directors who get caught engaged in illegal actions.

The various manifestations of shareholder primacy relevant to the tools of limiting excessive risk would be well and good if we assume that shareholder interests with respect to acceptable risk in a financial institution are consistent with societal interests. This, however, brings us back to the earlier discussion of the necessity for regulation of banks and other financial firms rather than relying on the shareholders' self-interest in avoiding failure as sufficient protection against excessive risk. As discussed previously, underlying the existence of banking and other financial firm regulation is recognition of disconnects between shareholder and societal interests with respect to acceptable risks.

5 CONCLUSION

In comparing state-created and enforced corporate law with banking and other national regulatory regimes, it is important not to fall victim to a 'nirvana fallacy' of assuming the other system is always better. In fact, banking and financial regulatory regimes performed poorly in the years leading up to the financial crisis (Posner 2009d) and some of this failure, no doubt, reflects structural weaknesses. Specifically, banking and other regulatory regimes are subject to industry capture resulting, among other factors, from the revolving door phenomenon of individuals moving from the regulated private sector to regulatory agencies and back to the regulated private sector again (Boone and Johnson 2009), and from campaign contributions to elected officials from the regulated firms (Rich 2009).[73] More fundamentally, it may be asking too much for regulatory agencies, whose heads are political appointees, and whose budgets are subject to political process, to maintain rigorous enforcement in the face of a pervasive deregulatory philosophy among elected officials and the electorate at large (Strumpfer 2009).

Perhaps the ultimate conclusion is that there are structural weaknesses in both state corporate law as well as banking and regulatory regimes that render each a poor reed on which to rely to prevent excessive risk-taking by financial firms. If so, then the conclusion may simply be that societies are doomed to endlessly repeat the cycle of excessive risk-taking and financial panic that stretches back at least 800 years (Reinhart and Rogoff 2009). In that event, the contribution of this chapter is an entirely academic, but not unimportant, one of contributing to our understanding of the inherent limits of the law.

On the other hand, the traditions of this form of scholarship demand a normative proposal rather than simply a depressing pathology. Therefore let us assume that changes can be made in order to avoid excessive risk-taking so that next time will be different. The question then becomes which law provides a better platform on which to work to make such changes. Put differently, in which law, corporate or banking, are the problems less structural and the necessary changes less difficult, with less potential for unintended consequences?

There have been proposals in the past to end the 'race to the bottom' in corporate law by enacting a national corporate law regime (Nader et al. 1976). There have also been proposals to change the shareholder focus of corporate law by establishing duties toward other stakeholders in the company (Greenfield 2002). This could change the underlying structure of corporate law, which currently renders it inherently weak in using available tools to curb excessive risk-taking by financial firms. On the other hand, there are strong arguments against adopting such proposals for corporations generally (Romano 1993). While the exploration of these arguments is well beyond the scope of this chapter, their existence seemingly counsels for a more focused approach: If the problem lies with financial firms, then a solution limited to financial firms (in other words using banking law) seems wise.

By contrast, while also getting well beyond the scope of this chapter, the problems of regulatory capture might be addressed, for example, by greater limitations on revolving door regulator-to-regulated employment (Boone and Johnson 2009); by an overlap of regulatory jurisdiction (Cox

2009); or even by borrowing a page from corporate and securities law and facilitating private enforcement actions. Of course, these actions might have unintended negative consequences,[74] but the question is a relative one of whether the potential untoward consequences are less than those possible from upending the key traditions of general corporate law for all companies.

Moreover, having banking law use all the available tools to curb excessive risk-taking, because state general corporate law is inherently weak, does not mean that banking law must provide the exclusive source of law. One could, as Congress did in enacting section 1821(k), leave corporate law in play for those cases in which perhaps corporate law is more aggressive in curbing excessive risk than banking law.

The bottom line is that banking legislation and banking regulators should move aggressively to use all the tools to curb excessive risk-taking rather than rely on state general corporate law. To see how this might play out in concrete examples, we return one last time to *Citigroup*.

Beginning with compensation that promotes excessive risk-taking, cynics might suspect that the Delaware Chancery Court in *Citigroup* had in the back of its mind forestalling federal action in the area when it allowed the claim to proceed on the ex-CEO's termination package. Regardless, the lesson of this chapter is that the Federal Reserve was wise, in its recent proposal to regulate compensation, not to wait on state corporate law to address the problem.

Turning to the subject of liability for unreasonable risk-taking, Congress already moved to a fair extent in this area in section 1821(k) of the FIRREA. As discussed above, this section creates a minimum national standard for imposing liability on grossly negligent directors in actions brought by the FDIC on behalf of failed banks. Significantly, part of the motivation for this provision lay in Congress's concern about states watering down liability standards in the wave of state corporate law legislation of which section 102(b)(7) of the Delaware General Corporation Law was a part. This was pointed out in *FDIC v McSweeney* (1992), discussing the legislative history of section 1821(k) of the FIRREA (pp. 537–8). The problem is that section 1821(k) does not go far enough. It leaves the matter with state corporate law until the FDIC asserts an action in the right of a receiver of a failed bank or when FDIC money is used to save the bank. Even putting aside liability for directors and officers of a holding company (as in *Citigroup*) rather than a bank, by waiting to trigger the federal standard until the bank fails or the FDIC saves the bank, the statute leaves a gaping hole when a financial firm is bailed out by the Treasury Department or the Federal Reserve (rather than the FDIC) on the grounds it is 'too big to fail.'[75] Indeed this avoidance of more liability-conducive federal standards may compound the moral hazard problem in the 'too big to fail' notion.

Finally, and most radically, perhaps it is necessary to rethink the importation for financial corporations of the corporate law norm that shareholders possess the exclusive power to elect directors. Germany and some other nations use a system in which employees have the right to elect a certain number of directors to the board (Gevurtz 2006, pp. 63–5). Perhaps a system in which bondholders, depositors or the like can elect a certain number of directors could temper the moral hazard afflicting financial corporations. For instance, Indiana law permits depositors in mutual building and loan associations to elect directors (*Indiana Law Encyclopedia* 2009, vol. 4, § 8).

NOTES

1. Federal Reserve Chairman Ben Bernanke, in an address to the American Economic Association, blamed the real estate bubble on mortgages that should not have been extended.
2. Richard Posner (2009a) ('the basic responsibility for the depression rests with the private sector – with decisions such as Citigroup's to increase the amount of risk in its lending'); Hill and Painter (2010) (excessive risk-taking at financial institutions led to financial crisis); Fanto (2009) (arguing that failure of risk management in financial corporations contributed to the financial crisis).
3. For example, Citigroup, in a couple of major transactions in 2007, acquired billions of dollars worth of subprime loans from financially troubled subprime lenders to package into CDOs.
4. Martin and Morgenson (2009) referred to allegations in a class action lawsuit that Citigroup recycled older CDOs into new CDOs because it could not find buyers for the old CDOs.
5. It appears from the plaintiffs' complaint in *Citigroup* that a staggering $25 billion face value of CDOs – around half of the CDO inventory upon which Citigroup incurred losses – came from CDOs returned to Citigroup under liquidity puts: *In re Citigroup Inc Shareholder Derivative Litigation*, Second Amended Complaint, para 68.
6. For example, the senior risk officer at Citigroup who was responsible for overseeing risks involved in Citigroup's CDO operations had long-standing friendships both with the head of the division undertaking the CDO operation and with the Citigroup executive who oversaw the buildup in Citigroup's inventory of CDOs and related securities. This relationship, according to accounts, raised eyebrows of those concerned about risk controls at Citigroup and it was said that Citigroup traders who wanted to undertake profitable but risky deals could take advantage of this relationship to convince the senior risk officer that the risk was worth taking (Dash and Creswell 2008).
7. At one point the risk managers not only reported to the senior risk officer but also reported to the head of the division undertaking the CDO operation – which placed the risk managers in the awkward position of reporting to the person whose division's risk-taking they were supposed to be keeping in check. Keep in mind that the purpose for having risk managers is because traders and the manager of their division have an incentive to take excessive risk (*ibid*).
8. *Ibid.*
9. *Ibid* (Citigroup CEO Charles Prince never questioned the risk entailed in Citigroup's

CDO operation before an emergency meeting when it was too late to avoid huge losses, because no one had warned him); Eric Dash (2008a) (reporting on pressure for the chairman of the Audit and Risk Management Committee of Citigroup's board of directors to resign for failing to oversee Citigroup's risk management practices and that, according to people familiar with the matter, some Citigroup directors were not aware of Citigroup's CDO loss exposure until huge write-downs started piling up).

10. 12 USC § 24 (2006) (preventing national banks from underwriting most types of securities); 12 USC § 335 (2006) (extending the prohibition on underwriting to state banks); 12 USC § 377 (2006) (preventing affiliation of banks with firms engaged in underwriting securities).
11. *Gramm-Leach-Bliley Act* (1999) (repealing 12 USC § 377, thereby allowing affiliation with underwriters, but not underwriting of securities, by banks).
12. Lipton (2009) referred to proposals before Congress to require independent risk committees responsible for the establishment and evaluation of risk management practices to be formed at large financial companies.
13. This observation is commonly known as the 'Berle–Means thesis' after the authors of the classic work which pointed out the phenomenon: Berle and Means (1932).
14. One might also ask whether the self-interest of the financial institution's creditors will lead creditors to prevent the institution from taking excessive risk. Writers sometimes blame deposit insurance for creating moral hazard by removing the insured depositors' incentive to monitor banks against dangerous risk-taking. See, for example, Macey and O'Hara (2003). The problem, of course, is that the threat of a bank run by ill-informed depositors, who might be reacting as much to the danger of the run as they are to poor investments of the bank, seems a crude tool to discourage excessive risk-taking that the depositors will be the last people to discover (Mülbert 2009). For an explanation as to why bondholders in the bank lack sufficient incentives to address excessive risk-taking, see Bebchuk and Spamann (2010), pp. 266–7.
15. General corporate law has some, largely minimal, capital rules. See the *Model Business Corporation Act* §§ 6.21 (no capital requirements in issuing shares), 6.40 (2003) (prohibiting distributions that leave assets less than debts and liquidation preferences of senior shares, or leave the corporation unable to pay its bills as due). Traditional statutes, as in Delaware, complicate things with references to par value of stock as a minimum price for shares upon issuance by the corporation and a constraint on dividends; but par is simply a number in the certificate of incorporation subject to reduction or elimination by amendment of the certificate: *Delaware General Corporation Law*, §§ 102(a)(4), 153, 154, 170, 242(a)(3) (2011).
16. By contrast, reserve requirements – in other words, the requirement that some portion of the bank's assets from deposits or capital be held and not loaned out – serve somewhat different functions. One is a matter of monetary policy as such reserves reduce the amount of money in circulation. The other is to address a timing problem. Banking involves a mismatch between the bank's assets in the form of long-term loans and the bank's obligations in the form of short-term deposits. Reserves provide a cushion to help ensure banks can cover withdrawals of short-term deposits despite the delays entailed in waiting for payments on their long-term loans (Pollard and Daly 2009, § 11.03). None of this, however, is really relevant to the general riskiness of the financial institution's investments and lending.
17. The impact of capital requirements on moral hazard may be particularly important given the presence of deposit insurance, since the existence of such insurance may allow banks with little or no capital – where the moral hazard problem is the greatest – to still attract deposits (Macey and O'Hara 2003, p. 98).
18. Adjusting the capital requirements for the riskiness of the bank's assets should decrease this incentive – albeit this increases the complexity problem with capital requirements.
19. Walker (2010) pointed out that incentive compensation schemes are designed to deal with the problem of excessive conservatism by managers.
20. It is also worth noting that the opaque quality of a bank's assets can render it difficult

for those outside management to judge the degree to which increased earnings reported by management seeking a bonus simply resulted from increasing the risk profile of the assets as opposed to superior acumen.

21. For a description of the major studies that potentially cast doubt on the impact of executive compensation in leading to excessive risk-taking by financial firms, see Bhagat and Romano (2009), note 3; Friedman (2009). For a contrary view of the significance of these studies, see Bebchuk and Spamann (2010), pp. 270–72.
22. Applying Judge Hand's famous formula from *United States v Carroll Towing Co* (1947), adjusted for investments rather than accident avoidance, if the magnitude of gain expected from an investment decision multiplied by its probability of occurring exceeds the magnitude of loss risked by the investment decision multiplied by its probability of occurring then the investment is reasonable (ignoring the opportunity costs of competing investments).
23. Court implied a private right of action for violation of the SEC rule against false statements in proxy solicitation, in part, to aid enforcement by catching violations the SEC lacks the resources to detect.
24. See also Mülbert (2009), pp. 22–3, citing evidence of favorable correlation between financial expertise of board chair and bank performance.
25. Dash and Creswell (2008) (quoting a former Citigroup executive as saying that Charles Prince 'didn't know a CDO from a grocery list').
26. *Model Business Corporation Act* § 7.28 (2003) (for corporations generally); 12 USC § 71 (2000) (for national banks).
27. *McDermott Inc v Lewis* (1987) (defining the scope of the internal affairs doctrine, under which the state of incorporation provides the governing corporate law rules, as covering the relationships *inter se* of the corporation, its directors, officers and shareholders).
28. Indeed, a treatise in the area has the title 'The Corporate Law of Banks . . .' (Malloy (1988)).
29. Many other nations, especially those following civil law traditions, provide some minimum capital, and sometimes even capital maintenance, requirements in their general company laws (Gevurtz 2006, pp. 35–8).
30. See note 15 above.
31. 12 USC § 1842(a)(1), (2) (2006).
32. 12 USC § 1831p-1 (2006) (authorizing federal regulatory agencies to promulgate regulations for safety and soundness of FDIC insured depository institutions). See also 12 USC § 1818(b)(3) (2008) (authorizing the Federal Reserve Board to issue cease-and-desist orders against bank holding companies engaged in unsafe or unsound practices on the same basis as applied to state banks that are members of the Federal Reserve System and have federally insured deposits).
33. 12 USC § 1831o (2006).
34. *Citigroup* (2009), p. 118 (liability for excessive risk and claims based upon excessive compensation resolved by Delaware law for Delaware corporation); *McDermott v Lewis* (1987) (issue of who can vote to elect directors resolved by law of state of incorporation).
35. Delaware courts do not have exclusive jurisdiction in cases involving the internal affairs of Delaware corporations and, indeed, a securities fraud action pending in New York also asserted claims for breach of fiduciary duty against Citigroup directors and officers, based upon the CDO losses. Nevertheless, the Delaware Chancery Court in *Citigroup* refused to stay the Delaware action, in part because Delaware law would control: *Citigroup* (2009), at pp. 115–19.
36. Bebchuk and Spamann (2010), pp. 259–60 (the biggest banks in the United States are not stand-alone banks but subsidiaries of bank holding companies, and major strategic decisions are taken at the holding company level).
37. 12 CFR § 7.2014 (1996) (replaced former 12 CFR § 7.5217(a)) (Office of the Comptroller of the Currency regulation allowing national banks to include indemnification provisions in their articles if the provisions substantially reflect general standards of law as

evidenced by the law of the state in which the bank is headquartered, the law of the state in which the bank's holding company is incorporated, or else the relevant provisions of the *Model Business Corporation Act*).

38. *Joy v North* (1983) (applying Connecticut corporate law to fiduciary duties in Connecticut commercial bank); *Jones v HF Ahmanson & Co* (1969) (applying California corporate law to fiduciary duties in California savings and loans).
39. *Atherton v FDIC* (1997), p. 228 (Congress enacted section 1821(k) against a background of failing savings and loan associations, large federal payments to insured depositors, and recent changes to state law designed to limit preexisting director and officer liability).
40. 12 USC § 1818(i) (2008).
41. 12 USC §1818(b)(3) (2008) (treating a holding company like a state FDIC insured bank for purposes of section 1818(i)).
42. 12 USC § 1818(i)(2)(B)(i), (C) (2008).
43. 12 USC § 1831p-1(c) (2006).
44. 12 USC §§ 24, 71 (2008).
45. 12 USC § 1818(b)(3) (2008) (treating a holding company like a state-insured bank for purposes of section 1818(e)).
46. 12 USC § 1818(e) (2008).
47. 12 USC §§ 1818(e)(1)(A)(ii)–(iii) (2008).
48. 12 USC §§ 1818(e)(1)(C)(i)–(ii) (2008).
49. 12 USC § 1817(j) (2009).
50. Felsenfeld (2006), pp. 88–110 (decline in regulation of interest rates on deposit accounts), pp. 145–202 (liberalization of activities for bank holding companies), pp. 225–34 (allowing inter-state banking), pp. 245–302 (allowing holding companies to engage in securities business).
51. Malloy (1991), pp. 223–4 (arguing that prevalence of FDIC insured institutions combined with federal regulation of such institutions has substantially federalized bank regulation).
52. 12 USC § 1831p-1 (2006) (authorizing federal regulatory agencies to promulgate regulations for safety and soundness of insured depository institutions, with no indication that such regulations are optional for the bank's owners).
53. Fed R Civ P 23.1; Del Ct R 23.1.
54. Admittedly, as discussed earlier, section 1818(i) imposes a more demanding standard of culpability (reckless or knowing) before imposing financial penalties on officers or directors who engage in unsafe or unsound banking practices in a bank that does not fail. This, however, seems to reflect the difference between what Congress viewed as a tort-like recovery provision (12 USC § 1821(k) (2006)) and what Congress viewed as a criminal-like penal provision (12 USC § 1818(i) (2008)). Specifically, section 1821(k) provides recovery for losses suffered by the bank (and, therefore, the FDIC), whereas section 1818(i) provides a flat fine for each day of continuing violation. Most significantly, however, it was section 1821(k), not 1818(i), that Congress enacted because of its dissatisfaction with state law developments, along the lines of section 102(b)(7) (2011) of the *Delaware General Corporation Law*, which made it more difficult to recover against grossly negligent bank corporation directors.
55. *Bates v Dresser* (1920) (bank president ignored a number of warnings of bookkeeper's dishonesty).
56. In *Caremark Int'l Inc* (1996), the claim involved the board's failure to detect and prevent violations by employees of Medicare rules limiting the payment of referral fees.
57. Bainbridge (2009) (arguing that *Citigroup* is inconsistent with *Caremark Int'l Inc* (1996) and Delaware law in possibly rejecting a duty to monitor business risks as opposed to just for misconduct).
58. *Unisuper Ltd v News Corp* (2005) (held that a complaint for breach of an oral agreement was adequate under notice pleading standard despite the lack of details regarding the contract).
59. *FDIC v McSweeney* (1992) (action brought by FDIC without anyone arguing that demand was required).

60. *Brehm v Eisner*, p. 262 (applying waste standard to compensation approved by disinterested directors); *Beard v Elster* (1960) (compensation approved by disinterested directors entitled to deference under the business judgment rule).
61. The plaintiffs noted that under the contract Ovitz would actually do better financially by being terminated, so long as it was not for cause, than he would by staying on the job. The court responded that Ovitz hardly appeared to be trying to get himself dismissed but without giving cause within the meaning of the contract. The more subtle incentive problem – that such a contract gave Ovitz little incentive to provide optimum performance – is not an argument the court even recognized: *Disney Co.*
62. Federal statutes have effectively nationalized various aspects of corporate law for public companies. For example, the *Sarbanes-Oxley Act* imposes requirements with respect to the audit committees of public companies: 15 USC § 78j-1 (2002) (amending section 10A of the *Securities Exchange Act*). Despite these inroads, however, corporate law is predominately state law, particularly in the areas relevant to curbing excessive risk – liability for excessive risk-taking, limits on compensation and selection of directors and officers: *Santa Fe Indus Inc v Green* (1977). The primary exceptions of relevance relate to the selection of directors. Here, there is federal regulation of proxy solicitations for public corporations under section 14(a) (15 USC § 78n(a) (2002)), and federal regulation of tender offers under section 14(d) and (e) (15 USC §§ 78n(d) and (e) (2002)), of the 1934 *Securities Exchange Act*. Indeed, pursuant to its authority to regulate the solicitation of proxies, the SEC recently responded to the financial crisis by proposing to require that companies provide greater disclosures about their risk oversight practices, including information as to the board's role in risk management and the qualifications and experiences of directors and director nominees: Lipton (2009). Whether such disclosure will actually change who gets elected to the board or the risk practices of the board, however, is another matter – and beyond the power of the SEC under section 14(a).
63. *Model Business Corporations Act* § 3.02(10) (2003); *Delaware General Corporation Law*, Del Code Ann tit 8, §§ 101(a), 102(a)(2) (1998). By contrast, many continental European nations traditionally operated under the view that corporations must be formed in the nation in which the company had its headquarters – variously called the *siege social, siege real*, or seat theory. Under this view, a nation would reject the effort to incorporate under its law if the corporate headquarters would be in another nation, and a nation in which a firm had its headquarters would refuse to recognize the firm as a corporation – meaning, for example, the firm would lack the capacity to sue in that nation's courts and its owners might face personal liability – unless the firm incorporated under that nation's, rather than another nation's, law (Roth 2003, pp. 180–85).
64. Restatement (Second) of Conflict of Laws § 302 (2009); *Model Business Corporations Act* § 15.05, official cmt (2003).
65. Cary (1974), pp. 683–4 (pointing to the Delaware Supreme Court's decision refusing to find liability upon inattentive directors in *Graham v Allis-Chalmers Mfg Co* (1963) as evidence of the Delaware Supreme Court's seeking to attract corporate charters).
66. Fed R Civ P 23.1 (granting shareholders standing to bring a derivative action on behalf of the corporation).
67. *Michelson v Duncan* (1979) (shareholder approval of compensation reduces review to the waste standard).
68. *Model Business Corporation Act* § 7.28 (2003) (for corporations generally); 12 USC § 71 (2000) (for national banks).
69. The doctrine of piercing the corporate veil is used to protect creditors from the abuse of limited liability through fraud, removal of assets from the corporation and, for tort victims, externalization of accident costs through inadequate capitalization (Gevurtz 1997).
70. Macey (1991). But see Macey and O'Hara (2003), p. 102 (advocating a different rule for banks under which bank directors would have a fiduciary duty toward fixed claimants, such as depositors).

71. Winter (1977), p. 277. Perhaps publicly traded bonds might have a similar effect, but such an impact seems less plausible as one starts dealing with bank depositors.
72. Easterbrook and Fischel (1989). But see Eisenberg (1989), p. 1480 (arguing that mandatory rules should govern some aspects of public corporations, such as fiduciary duties).
73. Rich (2009) observed that financial reform has been embattled on Capitol Hill where the financial industry spent $344 million on lobbying in the first three quarters of 2009.
74. Choi (2004), arguing that private securities fraud class actions are often meritless and brought to extort settlement.
75. As discussed earlier, the tiered financing of the Citigroup bailout meant that the use of FDIC money depended on the depth of Citigroup's losses.

REFERENCES

Articles, Books, Reports and Press Releases

Alperin, Howard J. and Roland F. Chase (2009), *Consumer Law Sales Practice and Credit Regulation*, St Paul, MN: Thomson West.

Bainbridge, S. (2009), 'Caremark and enterprise risk management', *Journal of Corporation Law*, **34** (4), 967–90.

Bebchuk, L. (1992), 'Federalism and the corporation: the desirable limits on state competition in corporate law', *Harvard Law Review*, **105** (7), 1435–510.

Bebchuk, L. and H. Spamann (2010), 'Regulating bankers' pay', *Georgetown Law Journal*, **98** (2), 247–88.

Berle, Adolph A. and Gardiner C. Means (1932), *The Modern Corporation and Private Property*, New York, NY: Commerce Clearing House.

Bhagat, S. and R. Romano (2009), 'Reforming executive compensation: simplicity, transparency and committing to the long-term', available at http://ssrn.com/abstract=1506742 (accessed 2 June 2011).

Boone, P. and S. Johnson (2009), 'The recession is over – for now', *New York Times*, 20 September 2009.

Bratton, W. and M. Wachter (2010), 'The case against shareholder empowerment', *University of Pennsylvania Law Review*, **158** (3), 653–728.

Calomiris, C. (2009), 'A recipe for ratings reform', *Economists' Voice*, **6** (11), Article 5.

Cary, W. (1974), 'Federalism and corporate law: reflections upon Delaware', *Yale Law Journal*, **83** (4), 663–705.

Cassidy, J. (2009), 'An economist's invisible hand', *Wall Street Journal*, 28 November 2009.

Choi, S. (2004), 'The evidence on securities class actions', *Vanderbilt Law Review*, **57** (5), 1465–526.

Comizio, V.G. and S. Swartz (2000), 'Show me the money: federal banking regulation of executive compensation and benefit matters', *Annual Review of Banking Law*, **19**, 271–327.

Cox, J. (2009), Address at the University of the Pacific, McGeorge School of Law Symposium, 'Local to global: rethinking spheres of authority after a world financial crisis', 16–17 October 2009.

Dash, E. (2008a), 'Citigroup director expected to quit key committee', *New York Times*, 8 April 2008.

Dash, E. (2008b), 'Citigroup to halt dividend and curb pay', *New York Times*, 24 November 2008.
Dash, E. and J. Creswell (2008), 'The reckoning: Citigroup saw no red flags even as it made bolder bets', *New York Times*, 23 November 2008.
Dobbs, Dan B. (2000), *The Law of Torts*, St Paul, MN: Thomson West.
Easterbrook, F. and D. Fischel (1989), 'The corporate contract', *Columbia Law Review*, **89** (7), 1416–48.
Ebrahimi H. (2009), 'France's Nicolas Sarkozy: traders must wait three years to cash in all of their bonuses', *Daily Telegraph*, London, 26 August 2009.
Eisenberg, M. (1989), 'The structure of corporation law', *Columbia Law Review*, **89** (7), 1461–525.
Eisenberg, M. (1990), 'The duty of care of corporate directors and officers', *University of Pittsburgh Law Review*, **51** (4), 945–72.
Fanto, J. (2009), 'Anticipating the unthinkable: the adequacy of risk management in finance and environmental studies', *Wake Forest Law Review*, **44** (3), 731–56.
Felsenfeld, Carl (2006), *Banking Regulation in the United States*, Huntington, NY: Juris Publishing.
Friedman, J. (2009), 'Bank pay and the financial crisis', *Wall Street Journal*, 28 September 2009.
Gevurtz, F. (1994), 'The business judgment rule: meaningless verbiage or misguided notion?', *Southern California Law Review*, **67** (2), 287–337.
Gevurtz, F. (1997), 'Piercing piercing: an attempt to lift the veil of confusion surrounding the doctrine of piercing the corporate veil', *Oregon Law Review*, **76** (4), 853–908.
Gevurtz, Franklin A. (2000), *Corporation Law*, St. Paul, Minnesota: West Group/Gale Cengage.
Gevurtz, F. (2002), 'Getting real about corporate social responsibility: a reply to Professor Greenfield', *UC Davis Law Review*, **35** (3), 645–65.
Gevurtz, Franklin A. (2006), *Global Issues in Corporate Law*, St Paul, MN: Thomson West.
Gordon, J. (2002), 'What Enron means for the management and control of the modern business corporation: some initial reflections', *University of Chicago Law Review*, **69** (3), 1233–50.
Greenfield, K. (2002), 'Using behavioral economics to show the power and efficiency of corporate law as regulatory tool', *UC Davis Law Review*, **35** (3), 581–644.
Hanks, J. (1988), 'Evaluating recent state legislation on director and officer liability limitation and indemnification', *Business Lawyer*, **43** (4), 1207–54.
Hau, H. and M. Thum (2009), 'Subprime crisis and board (in-)competence: private vs. public banks in Germany', available at http://ssrn.com/abstract=1360698 (accessed 2 June 2011).
Heineman, B. (2009), 'Shareholders: part of the solution or part of the problem?', *The Atlantic*, 28 October 2009.
Hill, C. and R. Painter (2010), 'Berle's vision beyond shareholder interests: why investment bankers should have (some) personal liability', *Seattle University Law Review*, **33** (4), 1173–200.
Hilsenrath, J. and L. Di Leo (2010), 'Fed chief edges closer to using rates to pop bubbles', *Wall Street Journal*, 4 January 2010.
Kulpa, A. (2009), 'Minimal deterrence: the market impact, legal fallout, and

impending regulation of credit default swaps', *Journal of Law, Economics & Policy*, **5** (2), 293–314.
Lapine, Kenneth M., Dennis Lassila, Burton V. McCullough, Paul S. Pilecki and Harold Weisblatt (1997) (Supp 2008), *Banking Law*, Albany, NY: Lexis Nexis Matthew Bender.
Levitin, A. (2009), 'The crisis without a face: emerging narratives of the financial crisis', *University of Miami Law Review*, **63** (4), 999–1010.
Litan, R. (2009), 'Whither financial reform?', *Economists' Voice*, **6** (11), Article 8.
Macey, J. (1991), 'An economic analysis of the various rationales for making shareholders the exclusive beneficiaries of corporate fiduciary duties', *Stetson Law Review*, **21** (1), 23–44.
Macey, J. and G. Miller (1987), 'Toward an interest-group theory of Delaware corporate law', *Texas Law Review*, **65** (3), 469–524.
Macey, J. and M. O'Hara (2003), 'The corporate governance of banks', *FRBNY Economic Policy Review*, **9** (1), 91–107.
Malloy, Michael (1988), *The Corporate Law of Banks: Regulation of Corporate and Securities Activities of Depository Institutions*, Boston, MA: Little, Brown.
Malloy, M. (1991), 'Seeing the light: savings association conversions and federal regulatory realignment', *Annual Review of Banking Law*, **10**, 189–224.
Malloy, Michael (2004) (Supp. 2009), *Banking Law and Regulation*, New York, NY: Aspen.
Malloy, Michael (2009), *Banking Law and Regulation (Cum. Supp. No. 2)*, New York, NY: Aspen Publishers.
Manne, H. (1965), 'Mergers and the market for corporate control', *Journal of Political Economy*, **73** (2), 110–20.
Martin, A. and G. Morgenson (2009), 'Can Citigroup carry its own weight?', *New York Times*, 1 November 2009.
Mülbert, P. (2009), 'Corporate governance of banks', available at http://ssrn.com/abstract=1448118 (accessed 2 June 2011).
Nader, Ralph, Mark J. Green and Joel Seligman (1976), *Taming the Giant Corporation*, New York, NY: W.W. Norton.
Norton, J. (1989), 'Capital adequacy standards: a legitimate regulatory concern for prudential supervision of banking activities?', *Ohio State Law Journal*, **49** (5), 1299–364.
Paletta, D. (2009), 'Agencies in a brawl for control over banks', *Wall Street Journal*, 22 December 2009.
Philips D. (1984), 'Principles of corporate governance: a critique of part IV', *George Washington Law Review*, **52** (4&5), 653–704.
Pollard, Alfred M. and Joseph P. Daly (2009), *Banking Law in the United States*, Huntington, NY: Juris Publishing.
Posner, Richard (2009a), *A Failure of Capitalism: the Crisis of '08 and the Descent into Depression*, Cambridge, MA and London, UK: Harvard University Press.
Posner, R. (2009b), 'Capitalism in crisis', *Wall Street Journal*, 7 May 2009.
Posner, R. (2009c), 'Are American CEOs overpaid, and, if so, what if anything should be done about it?', *Duke Law Journal*, **58** (6), 1013–47.
Posner, R. (2009d), 'Financial regulatory reform: the politics of denial', *Economists' Voice*, **6** (11), Article 1.
Puzzanghera, J. and M. Zimmerman (2009), 'Bank bonuses are in Fed's cross hairs', *Los Angeles Times*, 23 October 2009.

Reinhart, Carmen M. and Kenneth S. Rogoff (2009), *This Time Is Different: Eight Centuries of Financial Folly*, Princeton, NJ and Oxford, UK: Princeton University Press.
Rich, F. (2009), 'Hollywood's brilliant coda to America's dark year', *New York Times*, 13 December 2009.
Roe, M. (2003), 'Delaware's competition', *Harvard Law Review*, **117** (2), 588–646.
Romano, R. (1987), 'The state competition debate in corporate law', *Cardozo Law Review*, **8** (4), 709–58.
Romano, Roberta (1993), *The Genius of American Corporate Law*, Washington, DC: The AEI Press.
Roth, W-H. (2003), 'From Centros to Ueberseering: free movement of companies, private international law, and company law', *International and Comparative Law Quarterly*, **52**, 177–208.
Schooner, H. (1995), 'Fiduciary duties' demanding cousin: bank director liability for unsafe or unsound banking practices', *George Washington Law Review*, **63** (2), 175–220.
Scott, K. (2010), 'The financial crisis: causes and lessons', *Journal of Corporate Finance*, **22** (8), 22–9.
Seligman, J. (1976), 'A brief history of Delaware's general corporation law of 1899', *Delaware Journal of Corporate Law*, **1** (2), 249–88.
Sjostrom, W. (2009), 'The AIG bailout', *Washington & Lee Law Review*, **66** (3) 943–94.
Stiglitz, J. (2007), 'Multinational corporations: balancing rights and responsibilities', *American Society of International Law Proceedings*, **101**, 3–60.
Strumpfer, W. (2009), Address at the University of the Pacific, McGeorge School of Law Symposium, 'Local to Global: Rethinking Spheres of Authority after a World Financial Crisis', 16–17 October 2009.
Vitiello, M. (1997), 'Three strikes: can we return to rationality?', *Journal of Criminal Law and Criminology*, **87** (2), 395–481.
Walker, D. (2010), 'The challenge of improving the long-term focus of executive pay', *Boston College Law Review*, **51** (2), 435–72.
Williams, Julie L. (2009), *Savings Institutions: Mergers, Acquisitions and Conversion*, New York: Law Journal Seminars Press.
Winter, R. (1977), 'State law, shareholder protection, and the theory of the corporation', *Journal of Legal Studies*, **6** (2), 251–92.

Jurisprudence

Aronson v Lewis, 473 A (2d) 805 (Del 1984).
Atherton v FDIC, 519 US 213 (1997).
Bates v Dresser, 251 US 524 (1920).
Beam v Stewart, 845 A (2d) 1040 (Del 2004).
Beard v Elster, 160 A (2d) 731 (Del Ch 1960).
Brehm v Eisner, 746 A (2d) 244 (Del 2000).
Briggs v Spaulding, 141 US 132 (1891).
Dodge v Ford Motor Co, 170 NW 668 (Mich 1919).
Erie Railroad Co v Tompkins, 304 US 64 (1938).
FDIC v McSweeney, 976 F (2d) 532 (9th Cir 1992).
Graham v Allis-Chalmers Mfg Co, 188 A (2d) 125 (Del 1963).

Hoye v Meek, 795 F (2d) 893 (10th Cir 1986).
In re Am Int'l Group Inc, 965 A (2d) 763 (Del Ch 2009).
In re Caremark Int'l Inc Derivative Litig, 698 A (2d) 959 (Del Ch 1996).
In re Citigroup Inc Shareholder Derivative Litigation, 964 A (2d) 106 (Del Ch 2009).
In re Citigroup Inc Shareholder Derivative Litigation, Second Amended Complaint.
In re Walt Disney Co Derivative Litig, 825 A (2d) 275 (Del Ch 2003).
In re Walt Disney Co Derivative Litig, 906 A (2d) 27 (Del 2006).
In re WorldCom Inc Securities Litig, 346 F Supp (2d) 628 (SD NY 2004).
JI Case Co v Borak, 377 US 426 (1964).
Jones v HF Ahmanson & Co, 460 P (2d) 464 (Cal 1969).
Joy v North, 692 F (2d) 880 (2d Cir 1982), cert denied, 460 US 1051 (1983).
Louis K Liggett Co v Lee, 288 US 517 (1933).
McDermott Inc v Lewis, 531 A (2d) 206 (Del 1987).
Michelson v Duncan, 407 A (2d) 211, at 217 (Del 1979).
N Am Catholic Educ Programming Found Inc v Gheewalla, 930 A (2d) 92 (Del 2007).
Santa Fe Indus Inc v Green, 430 US 462 (1977).
Smith v Van Gorkom, 488 A (2d) 858 (Del 1985).
Steiner v Meyerson, 1995 WL 441999 (Del Ch 1995).
Stone v Ritter, 911 A (2d) 362 (Del 2006).
Unisuper Ltd v News Corp, 2005 WL 3529317 (Del Ch 2005).
United States v Carroll Towing Co, 159 F (2d) 169 (2d Cir 1947).

Statutes and Regulations

12 CFR § 7.2014 (1996).
12 USC § 71 (2000).
12 USC §§ 24, 335, 377, 1821(k), 1831o, 1831p-1, 1831p-1(c), 1842(a)(1), (2) (2006).
12 USC §§ 24, 71, 1818(b)(3), 1818(e), 1818(e)(1)(A)(ii) and (iii), 1818(e)(1)(C)(i) and (ii), 1818(i), 1818(i)(2)(B)(i), 1818(i)(2)(C) (2008).
12 USC § 1817(j) (2009).
15 USC §§ 78a, 78j-1, 78n (a), (d), (e) (2002).
Banking Secrecy Act, 31 USC § 5318 et seq. (2006).
Del Ct R 23.1.
Delaware General Corporation Law, Del Code Ann tit 8 (1998).
Delaware General Corporation Law, Del Code Ann tit 8 (2011).
Glass-Steagall Act, or the Banking Act of 1933, Pub L 73-66, 48 Stat 162.
Gramm-Leach-Bliley Act, Pub L No 106-102, § 504, 113 Stat 11439 (1999).
Fed R Civ P 23.1.
Financial Institutions, Reforms, Recovery, and Enforcement Act of 1989 (FIRREA) 12 USC § 1821(k).
Indiana Law Encyclopedia (2009), Vol 4: Building and Loan Associations, Thomson West.
Model Business Corporation Act (2003).
Restatement (Second) of Conflict of Law (2009).
Sarbanes-Oxley Act of 2002, Pub L No 107-204, 116 Stat 745 (2002).
Securities Act of 1933, 15 USC § 77a et seq.

Web Resources

Allen, F., E. Carletti and R. Marquez (2009), 'Credit market competition and capital regulation', 9 September 2009, available at http://blogs.law.harvard.edu/corpgov/2009/12/11/credit-market-competition-and-capital-regulation/#more-5965 (accessed 2 June 2011).

BIS (2006), Bank for International Settlements, 'Basel committee on banking supervision: enhancing corporate governance for banking organisations', available at http://www.bis.org/publ/bcbs122.pdf (accessed 2 June 2010).

Citigroup Inc (2009), 'Citigroup's 2008 annual report on form 10K', available at http://www.citigroup.com/citi/fin/data/k08c.pdf (accessed 2 June 2010).

Lipton, Martin (2009), 'Risk management and the board of directors', 17 December 2009, available at http://blogs.law.harvard.edu/corpgov/2009/12/17/risk-management-and-the-board-of-directors-2/#more-5811 (accessed 2 June 2010).

Morphy, James (2009), 'Fed proposes incentive compensation policies for banking organizations', 3 November 2009, available at http://blogs.law.harvard.edu/corpgov/2009/11/03/fed-proposes-incentive-compensation-policies-for-banking-organizations/ (accessed 2 June 2010).

PART III

Corporate governance and globalization

9. How public regulation changes corporate governance practice – corporate board reform in Taiwan

Yu-Hsin Lin

INTRODUCTION

This chapter takes the example of the legal transplantation of US-style independent directors into Taiwan and explores how public regulation affects (or does not affect) corporate governance practice. Taiwan's corporate law traditionally follows a two-tier board system where the board of directors is the decision-making institution and the statutory supervisor is the monitoring institution. However, most statutory supervisors of Taiwanese public companies have long been controlled by the controlling shareholders and failed to act as corporate monitors. Since 2002, Taiwan has gradually introduced independent directors into corporate boards in order to strengthen the internal governance of public companies.

As of September 2011, 43.92 per cent of the companies listed on the Taiwan Stock Exchange (TSE) had at least one independent director on their board. In other words, 56.08 per cent of TSE-listed firms chose not to have any independent directors. Only 6.8 per cent of TSE-listed companies had established audit committees to replace statutory supervisors. In summary, few Taiwanese public companies have made a complete switch to the US-style board structure. The majority of firms have stayed with the original structure and preferred not to have independent directors on their boards. This chapter focuses on companies that, whether voluntarily or not, introduce independent directors onto their boards and assesses the effectiveness of these new independent directors.

THE CORPORATE BOARD REFORM

Board Structure

Corporate board structure around the world has two major styles: the Anglo-American style and the German style; also known as the 'one-tier system' and 'two-tier system' respectively. In general, the 'Anglo-American style' board structure, notably that of the United States and the United Kingdom, relies on the board of directors and several sub-committees to monitor the management; the German structure relies on a supervisory board to monitor the management board while the management board focuses on managing the company. The structure of a board is clearly path dependent in relation to the given country's political and economic conditions. Many Asian countries follow the German-style governance structure because they first transplanted their corporate law from European legal systems.

The corporate board structure of Taiwan generally follows the Japanese-style governance structure, which is a modified version of the German structure. The governance structure in Taiwan and Japan differs from the typical German model in that the statutory supervisor position in Japan and Taiwan is weaker than its German counterpart, the supervisory board. In Germany, the supervisory board has the right to appoint or remove directors; however, in Japan and Taiwan, supervisors are nominated by the board and elected by the shareholders. In addition, the statutory supervisors in Taiwan do not act collectively as a board as does their German or Japanese counterpart; rather, they act individually. According to the *Company Law* of Taiwan, a supervisor is an independent supervisory institution responsible for auditing the business conditions of companies and evaluating the performance of companies' boards of directors and managers. However, in Taiwan, a supervisor has the right only to audit board meetings, not the right to vote. In addition, the pre-reform law set no qualification for supervisors. In practice, many supervisors are relatives or friends of the founding family, the controlling shareholder, directors or top managers. Therefore, most statutory supervisors of Taiwanese public companies are criticized as being just 'rubber stamps'.

The Reform

In the aftermath of Enron and other high-profile corporate fraud cases, the US Congress, in enacting the *Sarbanes-Oxley Act* of 2002 (SOX), placed great reliance on outside/independent directors and audit committees as a means of monitoring both firms' internal control systems and the integrity of their financial reporting systems. Following the passage of SOX, many Asian countries, such as China, Japan, South Korea and Taiwan, initiated corporate board reforms to be in alignment with the US-style governance structure. In response to local corporate fraud scandals, Taiwan's financial authority considered introducing the institution of independent directors to enhance corporate monitoring functions. In 2002, the TSE began taking a leading role in requiring all newly listed companies to have at least two independent directors and one independent statutory supervisor. However, the TSE is still hesitant to apply such requirements to all listed companies owing to fierce opposition from industry. Instead, the TSE adopted the 'comply or disclose' approach requiring all listed companies to disclose the TSE-defined 'independence' of their directors and supervisors. Since then, more and more public companies have voluntarily inducted independent directors and independent supervisors.

The Taiwan government's proposal for corporate board reform has triggered much debate among scholars in Taiwan. The most prominent issue is whether or not Taiwan should introduce independent directors and abandon the institution of statutory supervisors. The Taiwanese Congress finally settled the dispute by revising the *Securities and Exchange Law* in 2006 to give public companies the option to have independent directors. Public companies also have the option to establish audit committees. And if they do, the law requires the companies to abandon the institution of statutory supervisor. The amendment basically resembles the 2002 Japanese board reform, which also granted corporations the freedom to choose between the US-style board structure and the traditional board structure.

What distinguishes Taiwan's reform from Japan's is that the financial authority of Taiwan may deprive the choice of Taiwan's public corporations whereas that of Japan may not. Specifically, Taiwan's law grants the Financial Supervisory Commission (FSC) the right to mandate that public corporations (1) have independent directors on their corporate boards, or (2) replace statutory supervisors with audit committees made up of at least three independent directors, with at least one possessing financial expertise. Hence, the policy goal in Taiwan is to align all public firms' board structures with the unitary board model and strengthen the monitoring function of corporate boards. Since March 2006, the FSC has mandated that all public financial firms, and those non-financial listed firms with equity value over NT$50 billion (US$1.6 billion), should have at least two independent directors on their board and the total number of independent directors should be no less than one-fifth the number of board members.

Table 9.1 Breakdown of TSE-listed firms that have independent directors

Number of independent directors in each firm	Number of TSE-listed firms	Percentage (%) of total TSE-listed firms
1	13	1.7
2	197	25.5
3	113	14.6
4	14	1.8
5	3	0.4
Total	340	43.9

Source: Taiwan Stock Exchange and Market Observation Post System, October 2009.

On 22 March 2011, the FSC further expanded the mandate to firms with equity valued at over NT$10 billion (US$345 million).

As of September 2011, there were 340 TSE-listed companies whose boards had a combined total of 817 independent directors. That is, 43.92 per cent of the TSE-listed companies had at least one independent director on their board. Only 6.8 per cent (53 out of 774) of TSE-listed companies adopted the US-style board structure voluntarily by establishing audit committees and abolishing statutory supervisors. Still, 56.08 per cent of TSE-listed firms did not have any independent directors. Table 9.1 shows the breakdown.

Under current regulation, there are three types of board structure in Taiwanese public companies: (1) with independent directors and an audit committee (but no statutory supervisor); (2) with independent directors and statutory supervisors (but no audit committee); (3) with statutory supervisors only. In general, large companies (that is, with equity valued over NT$10 billion (US$345 million)) and newly listed companies, which are generally much smaller in size, should have at least two independent directors on the board. Other companies have the option to choose among the three types.

CHARACTERISTICS OF CORPORATE GOVERNANCE IN TAIWAN

Corporate Ownership and Control

The corporate environment in Taiwan is very different from that in the US. Yeh, Lee and Woidtke (2001) found that corporate ownership in Taiwan was concentrated and family-dominated. The largest sharehold-

Table 9.2 Comparison of board composition and ownership structure between financial firms and non-financial firms in Taiwan

	Financial firms	Non-financial firms
Panel A: board composition		
Percentage of largest shareholders as directors	59.18	62.69
Percentage of largest shareholders as statutory supervisors	57.48	49.55
Number of board members	11.80	7.13
Number of statutory supervisors	3.29	2.57
Panel B: ownership structure		
Control (voting) rights of largest shareholders	24.95	29.81
Cash-flow rights of largest shareholders	17.17	22.13
Excess control (control rights – cash-flow rights)	7.78	7.68
Pyramidal structure	0.46	0.18
Cross-shareholding	0.34	0.33

Source: Yeh and Ko (2006), pp. 294–5.

ers of the non-financial firms in Taiwan control 62.69 per cent of the board seats and 49.55 per cent of the statutory supervisors. Hence large shareholders in Taiwan not only own public firms, they also manage and control public firms. Yeh and Ko (2006) found that the average control rights of the largest shareholders in non-financial firms was 29.81 per cent; however, the average cash-flow rights were only 22.13 per cent. The data are shown in Table 9.2. This discrepancy provides an incentive and opportunity for controlling shareholders to mine corporate assets at the expense of minority shareholders.

Before the introduction of independent directors in 2002, many corporate boards in Taiwan functioned like paper meetings. The board members were either founding family members or top executives. Typically, family members were deeply involved in the management of the company.

For example, Procomp Informatics Ltd, the subject of Taiwan's largest corporate fraud case in 2004, was controlled by Su-Fei Yeh and her brother. Ms Su-Fei Yeh was the chairperson and CEO of Procomp and her brother, Meng-ping Yeh, was the vice chairperson. Among the five board members, the Yeh family held two seats and the remaining three seats were all held by top executives of Procomp. In practice, the Yeh family controlled the board and, in turn, the firm. Similarly,

Table 9.3 Excess control of Procomp and Infodisc

	1999	2001	2003	2004
PROCOMP				
Percentage of board seats controlled by largest shareholders (A)*	55.5%	55.5%	100%	100%
Percentage of shareholding by largest shareholders (B)	15.48%	13.23%	10.32%	7.83%
Excess control (A/B)	3.6	4.2	9.7	12.8
INFODISC				
Percentage of board seats controlled by largest shareholders (A)	100%	100%	80%	80%
Percentage of shareholding by largest shareholders (B)	34%	19.5%	9.9%	6.9%
Excess control (A/B)	2.9	5.13	8.1	11.6

Note: * Percentage of board seats controlled by largest shareholders refers to the percentage of directors that are largest shareholders, family members of the largest shareholders, or company employees.

Source: Yeh 2005, p. 144.

Xue-Ren Lu and his wife held two of the five board seats of Infodisc Technology Corp, the subject of the second-largest corporate fraud case in 2004.

In theory, controlling shareholders with major shareholdings monitor management more effectively and greatly reduce agency costs as long as their interests are in line with outside investors. Under this scenario, the interests of minority shareholders would not be sacrificed when the controlling shareholders dominate the board. However, if the control rights of the controlling shareholders exceed their cash-flow rights, as in the case of Taiwan and most other countries, the interests of controlling shareholders deviate from those of minority shareholders, creating a danger that minority shareholders could be expropriated.

This is exactly the danger in Taiwan's corporate governance system. For example, in 2004, Ms Su-Fei Yeh of Procomp and her brother controlled all five board seats while they only held 7.83 per cent of Procomp's shares. Similarly, Mr Lu of Infodisc controlled 80 per cent of the board seats in 2004 while owning only 6.9 per cent of the shares. In both companies, the control rights of the largest shareholders far exceeded their cash-flow rights, and such deviation reached its peak before the corporate debacles. Table 9.3 shows the increasing pattern of such deviation over the years for Procomp and Infodisc.

Business Groups

Another characteristic of Taiwan's corporate ownership structure – namely, the prevalence of business groups – provides a further channel for expropriation. Business groups control most of the firms in Taiwan and contribute a very large part of the revenue to the economy of Taiwan. The top 100 business groups in Taiwan owned more than 6300 affiliated firms and hired more than 3 million employees in 2007. The total revenue of the top 100 business groups was 7.8 times that of Taiwan's government in 2007. Their revenue growth in 2007, 16.01 per cent, also far exceeded that of the GNP of Taiwan. Among the top ten business groups, nine were in the financial industry. Family businesses continue to dominate Taiwan's economy. In terms of total asset value, family business groups account for 73.56 per cent of the top 100 business groups. Seven major families in Taiwan control almost 40 per cent of the total assets of the top 100 groups. The major families include the Tsai family of Cathay and Fubon groups, the Wu family of Shin Kong and Tai Shin groups, the Wang family of Formosa Plastics Group, the Gu family of China Trust, Chailease and Taiwan Cement Group, the Kuo family of Foxconn Group, the Hsu family of Far Eastern Group, and the Hsu family of Chi Mei Group.

Given the importance of business groups to Taiwan's economy, the corporate governance of business groups becomes vital. One of the key issues therein is the fairness of the transactions among group firms. While sometimes these transactions facilitate the growth of business groups, they also provide channels for controlling shareholders to mine corporate assets. Several business practices in Taiwan further provide controlling shareholders easy access to corporate assets without much oversight being in place. For example, cross-shareholding between public parent companies and subsidiaries keeps public companies in stable management. Huang (2001) suggested that cross-shareholding might help corporations to (1) maintain stable control of management; (2) facilitate human capital investment; (3) enhance the operational efficiency of strategic alliances with other firms; (4) diversify risks; and (5) facilitate financial arrangements among group firms.

Controlling shareholders can further control the board by electing subsidiaries as institutional directors or statutory supervisors, provided the subsidiary assigns an individual representative to perform its duty. Article 27 of the *Company Law* provides:

> Where a government agency or a juristic person acts as a shareholder of a company, it may be elected as a director or statutory supervisor of the company

> provided that it shall designate a natural person as its proxy to exercise, on its behalf, the duties of a director or statutory supervisor.
>
> Where a government agency or a juristic person acts as a shareholder of a company, its authorized representative may also be elected as a director or statutory supervisor of the company; and if there is a plural number of such authorized representatives, each of them may be so elected.

Individual representatives of such subsidiaries can also be elected as directors or statutory supervisors. Furthermore, more than one such individual representative can be elected as a director or statutory supervisor. Hence, through cross-shareholding, controlling shareholders can literally appoint anyone they choose to serve as directors and statutory supervisors. Controlling shareholders could embezzle corporate resources through appointees without any internal oversight.

THE RESPONSIBILITIES OF INDEPENDENT DIRECTORS

Statutory Responsibilities

In general, Taiwanese law requires independent directors to pay attention to internal audit procedures; material corporate transactions; matters on which directors or statutory supervisors have conflicts; securities offerings; and the retention or dismissal of outside auditors or internal accounting, financial and auditing officers. Article 14-3 of the *Securities and Exchange Law* provides:

> When a company has selected independent directors as set forth in paragraph 1 of the preceding article, then the following matters shall be submitted to the board of directors for approval by resolution unless approval has been obtained from the Competent Authority; when an independent director has a dissenting opinion or qualified opinion, it shall be noted in the minutes of the directors meeting:
>
> 1. Adoption or amendment of an internal control system pursuant to Article 14-1.
> 2. Adoption or amendment, pursuant to Article 36-1, of handling procedures for financial or operational actions of material significance, such as acquisition or disposal of assets, derivatives trading, extension of monetary loans to others, or endorsements or guarantees for others.
> 3. A matter bearing on the personal interest of a director.
> 4. A material asset or derivatives transaction.
> 5. A material monetary loan, endorsement, or provision of guarantee.
> 6. The offering, issuance, or private placement of any equity-type securities.

7. The hiring or dismissal of an attesting CPA, or the compensation given thereto.
8. The appointment or discharge of a financial, accounting, or internal auditing officer.
9. Any other material matter so required by the Competent Authority.

However, independent directors do not have the right to veto these decisions. They can only ask the board to keep their dissenting opinion on file. The board can still decide by majority vote even if independent directors have dissenting opinions.

In practice, dissenting opinions from independent directors are rare. Nevertheless, once the companies make such opinions public, the market and the government will watch carefully. Such opinions usually have signaling effects. For example, one interviewee in the study (and only one), who serves in the financial industry, reported that he once filed a dissenting opinion concerning the appointment of the CEO of a subsidiary. Although a majority of the board members voted for that candidate, the government authority overseeing the financial industry asked the firm to reconsider the appointment after reviewing the dissenting opinion. In the end, the firm withdrew the appointment.[1]

The Practice

> Most of the independent directors I know actively participate in corporate matters. However, their participation is usually limited to attending all the board meetings, actively participating in board meetings, and reading material in preparation for meetings. I think most of the independent directors just do that much. I don't think anyone would visit the firm if nothing came up. And I don't think anyone would look into the details of the pre-meeting materials.[2]

The above quite fairly reflects the reality of independent director participation in Taiwan. The standard tasks of independent directors are to attend board meetings, review meeting materials before the meeting, and review internal audit reports every month. In general, board meetings of firms in the financial industry are held once a month, while those in other industries are usually held every two to three months. Most interviewees included in the study made for this chapter admitted that they didn't spend much time reviewing materials before the meeting. However, if attending board meetings is the only major task for independent directors, the effectiveness of board meetings becomes crucial. Despite the fact that some independent directors are just too busy to preview the material,[3] sometimes it is because firms prefer not to provide all the detailed information outside the meeting for confidentiality reasons.[4] Nevertheless, these confidentiality concerns could compromise the readiness of independent directors, who already are not that familiar with daily corporate matters, to judge the fairness of board decisions effectively.

In addition to attending board meetings, independent directors in Taiwan also review internal audit reports every month as required by Regulations Governing Establishment of Internal Control Systems by Public Companies. Although some with accounting backgrounds pay more attention to the internal control systems, most interviewees revealed that such review is usually cursory and superficial. Some directors might not even have a clue about how to review an internal audit report.

> To be honest, I personally feel that the system of requiring independent directors to review an internal audit report does not achieve much of its goal. For example, one company provides me with a report that lists every item as 'no material irregularity' every month. To be honest, I really don't know what to question further. On the other hand, the other company provides me with a very detailed report about what the internal auditor found and what he plans to do. My feeling is that on the one hand, I feel much better when I see the more detailed report; on the other, I don't know what to question because you already handled all the issues.[5]

In addition to directors' individual abilities, the independence and ability of the internal auditor also influences the effectiveness of independent directors in overseeing the internal control process. Traditionally, the internal audit departments of most public companies in Taiwan are supervised by general managers and thus are not as independent. On 19 December 2005, the FSC of Taiwan revised the Regulations Governing Establishment of Internal Control Systems by Public Companies requiring the internal audit departments of all public companies to be directly supervised by the board. The revision formally enhances the status and independence of internal auditors and provides a better structure for internal auditors to ensure the functioning of the internal control system.

In summary, the participation of independent directors generally is limited to attending board meetings and reviewing monthly internal audit reports. In companies that have adopted the board committee system, independent directors, as members of the audit committee, play a more active role in overseeing the financial condition of the company. Nomination committees and compensation committees are still few in Taiwan. In addition, since the Taiwanese court has not adopted the business judgment rule and has not deferred to the decisions of independent board committees in situations involving conflicts of interest such as mergers, acquisitions and shareholder derivative suits, independent directors in Taiwan have not played an active role in reconciling matters that involve conflicts of interest. Therefore, the contribution of independent directors to companies is less valued in Taiwan than in the United States.

SOCIAL TIES

'Guan Xi' (Connections or Relationships)

To avoid joining a 'bad' company, independent directors screen the firms beforehand. The key criterion used by independent directors in Taiwan is the integrity of the controlling shareholders and managers.

> How do I decide whether to take on the position? First thing is the integrity of the leader. If the leader or the management team always follows the rules, the job of the independent director becomes easier because the cost of monitoring is not high.[6]

Potential candidates usually judge such integrity from the personal relationships between the leaders in companies. More than 55 per cent of the interviewees had personally known the chairman/CEO or major shareholder of the firm for more than ten years. The trust was built on a long-term understanding of one another. The strong personal trust in controlling shareholders alleviates the concern of independent directors about transparency and information asymmetry.

> If you doubt every report presented to you, it would be endless. If everything needs to be redone, the cost would be too high. I think the trust towards the management should be built on the long-term personal understanding and trust in the integrity of that person. In addition, the company should perform well. Based on these two assumptions, the independent directors can monitor (the company) and make a reasonable judgment.[7]

The strong personal ties between independent directors and controlling shareholders may be an inevitable result of the introduction of a new outside institution into a controlled or family-dominated board. However, such close relationships in turn raise concerns over the independence of the 'independent' directors.

Just as an independent director is afraid of joining a 'bad' company, a controlling shareholder is also worried about inviting a 'bad' outsider to the board. Different controlling shareholders might provide different definitions for a 'bad' independent director. Controlling shareholders would then, according to their own criteria, screen their own 'good' independent directors. A firm that truly honors corporate governance would seek a truly 'independent' director and provide him/her with abundant resources to do his/her job. For example, Taiwan Semiconductor Manufacturing Company (TSMC), a leading company in promoting corporate governance, searches for candidates through law firms and accounting firms instead of finding someone the executives personally know; they look for candidates who are established in their respective fields of practice and have expertise that is helpful to the company. On the contrary, a firm that only wants a window-dressing director would find someone who is willing to be a rubber stamp for board decisions.

The reality is that, except in a few large companies, most leaders of public companies in Taiwan generally seek independent directors who they know personally. As mentioned, controlling shareholders would seek their own 'good' independent directors. There is also information asymmetry between candidates and controlling shareholders about the quality of independent director candidates. *Guan xi* (relationship) has been an important source of reliable information in Chinese society. Therefore, it is no surprise that controlling shareholders would first invite someone who has the *guan xi* to join the board. Nevertheless, *guan xi* might compromise independence. Commentators in several regions, such as China, India and Taiwan, have cast doubt on the independence of independent directors. Their close relationship with controlling shareholders is definitely one of the major concerns.

> In many companies, the so-called independent directors are invited by the controlling shareholders. In addition, many of them maintain a good relationship with the major shareholders and executives. They [the independent directors] might politely remind the management [of some pitfalls] to a certain point. However, I think the role of these [independent] directors is limited.[8]

Among the 40 independent director interviewees, 19 of them used the term 'very close friend' to describe their relationship with the controlling shareholders or CEOs, and 14 of them personally knew the controlling shareholders or directors but were not very close friends. Only seven of the interviewees did not know the controlling shareholders or other inside directors before they were invited to join the board. Although the statistical results cannot be generalized due to the limited number of samples, most interviewees agreed that independent directors usually had some *guan xi* with the controlling shareholders.[9] The question would then be, 'Does *guan xi* matter with regard to director independence?'

Structural Bias

It is a common concern that an independent director might be biased in making decisions if he/she has *guan xi* with controlling shareholders. Such concern is underpinned by the theory of structural bias, which suggests that even if an independent director does not have financial or employment ties with the firm he might still be biased in making decisions because of the social pressures generated by his personal relationship with the management or controlling shareholders. The US scholars Brudney (1982) and Cox and Munsinger (1985) have long been aware of the social and psychological causes of bias that could impair independent directors' impartiality. Hwang and Kim (2009) examined the social ties among board directors of Fortune 100 firms and the impact of social ties to executive compensation. They identified social ties by mutual alma mater, military service, regional origin, discipline and industry and found that the percentage of independent boards dropped from 87 per cent to 62 per cent when screened by social ties. In addition, the CEOs of socially independent boards received significantly lower compensation than those of non-independent boards, suggesting that social ties and structural bias do matter in corporate governance.

However, the US Delaware courts believe that most friendships are not at the level where they create bias in decision making. In *Beam ex rel Martha Stewart Living Omnimedia, Inc v Stewart* (2004), the Delaware Supreme Court stated:

> But, to render a director unable to consider demand, a relationship must be of a bias-producing nature . . . Allegations of mere personal friendship or a mere outside business relationship, standing alone, are insufficient to raise a reasonable doubt about a director's independence . . . [S]ome professional or personal friendships, which may border on or even exceed familial loyalty and closeness, may raise a reasonable doubt whether a director can appropriately consider demand. This is particularly true when the allegations raise serious questions of either civil or criminal liability of such a close friend. Not all friendships, or even most of them, rise to this level . . . (p. 1050)

In determining the independence of directors in shareholder derivative actions, the Delaware court has applied a case-by-case approach – it has presumed the independence of a director, and posed a demanding standard in refuting such independence. However, in addition to financial interests, the Delaware courts do rebut the independence of directors if they find close social or professional relationships among directors. In *Biondi v Scrushy* (2003), the court questioned the independence of the two members of the special litigation committee because of their long-standing personal ties with the defendant director. Furthermore, in *In re Oracle Derivative Litigation* (2003), the court found that the members of the special litigation committee lacked independence because of the ties among several directors with Stanford University.

More challenges based on personal relationship have been raised recently to question the independence of directors in cases involving demand excusal in a derivative suit or the application of the business judgment rule in the US. It is expected that the extent to which personal relationships compromise director independence will continue to develop in US Delaware case law. Furthermore, American scholars Davis (2005) and Velasco (2004) have called for more judicial power in reviewing the substantive merits of independent directors' decisions in cases involving structural bias.

However, from an economists' point of view, Fama and Jensen (1983) suggest that directors will try hard to avoid such bias in order to preserve their reputation in the independent director market. Therefore, even if bias could arise from friendship, it is avoidable. While the above reputation argument is based on an assumption that directors are well aware of their biases, contemporary psychological research studies recognize another prototype of bias – 'unintentional bias'. Unintentional bias concerns bias that results from unconscious cognitive processes. Unconscious bias could exist in every stage of the cognitive processes – from the starting point, reasoning, to information processing. Because such bias is 'involuntary' and 'unconscious,' it can occur even when the decision maker intentionally seeks to avoid biases. Page (2009) argued that since decision makers are not aware of such bias, the reputation argument supported by economists cannot be sustained.

Given the existence of unintentional bias and the increasing awareness of the impact of personal relationships on director independence in US Delaware courts, the issue of structural bias deserves more attention in countries which have transplanted the institution of independent directors from the US. The close relationship between independent directors and controlling shareholders is not a unique phenomenon in Taiwan; rather, it is a common issue faced by most Asian countries. For example, in India, truly independent directors are rarely found in Indian companies because of the fact that board members are selected by the promoters on the basis of existing contacts.

In Taiwan, as in many other Asian countries, a sophisticated commercial court and complementing legal system does not exist to provide the kind of *ex post* judicial review found in the US. For example, a shareholder derivative suit is almost unheard of in practice owing to the various procedural hurdles set in the *Company Law* of Taiwan. In addition, the business judgment rule has yet to be accepted by the Taiwanese court. Because of these very different local conditions, *ex post* judicial review of director independence does not exist in the current legal system, and is unlikely to develop in the near future. On the flip side, the Taiwanese legal system has yet to recognize the role of independent committees in resolving conflicts of interest, which in turn limits the function of independent directors and the value they can create. This is exactly the danger of legal transplantation. While the country that receives the transplant is yet to have the soil to nurture the precious seed, it must either fertilize the soil or plant another seed that fits in order to let the flower blossom.

CONCLUSION

Public regulation does change the landscape of corporate governance in Taiwan. As of September 2011, 43.92 per cent of the TSE-listed companies had at least one independent director on their board. However, among these companies, very few truly welcome independent directors and expect them to actively participate in corporate matters. It is fair to say that the new regulation has created a market for independent directors in Taiwan. But it does not change much of the substantive corporate governance practice there.

Compared with the US, the participation of independent directors in Taiwan is relatively limited. The value of independent directors in reconciling conflicts of interest issues has not been recognized by Taiwanese public companies. The existence of statutory supervisors further weakens the monitoring function of independent directors. Furthermore, there is significant information asymmetry between independent directors and controlling shareholders; in particular, the shareholder managers. To overcome the problem of information asymmetry, independent directors in Taiwan generally choose to join boards with which they are familiar. The interview results reveal that independent directors generally maintain close social relationships with the controlling shareholders. Thus, there is concern that bias arising from social ties could hinder the independence of directors.

Transplantation is a long process whereby new legal measures grind against pre-existing local conditions. Taiwan is still in a transition period, where less than half of listed companies operate under a dual board system with independent directors on the board. Independent directors are put on advising boards for some monitoring tasks, while another institution, the statutory supervisor, is still in charge of corporate oversight. In addition, without complementary judicial deference to the decisions of independent boards, the value of independent directors to corporations is greatly diminished. These existing local conditions present challenges to the new legal device and hinder the transplantation process.

NOTES

1. Interview with Anonymous Independent Director (AID) No 25 (1 March 2009).
2. Interview with AID No 4 (7 October 2008).
3. Interview with AID No 29 (21 October 2009).
4. Interview with AID No 30 (22 October 2009).
5. Interview with AID No 26 (12 October 2009).
6. Interview with AID No 7 (12 October 2008). Also in the interview with AID No 14 (11 November 2008) it was stated: 'I have my own criteria, that this person must be the one whom I can trust and with a good reputation, otherwise, I do not dare to join . . . I think the attitude of the key leader is very important. Basically, it is the personal trust towards the key leader.' Similarly in the interview with AID No 3 (30 September 2008), I was told: 'When I'm considering accepting this position [as an independent director], I will first see who invites me to join the board. He should be the one whom I can trust because I need to be extra cautious when taking on such responsibility.'
7. Interview with AID No 7 (12 October 2008).
8. Interview with AID No 18 (18 February 2009).
9. Interview with AID No 3 (30 September 2008); Interview with AID No 4 (7 October 2008); Interview with AID No 18 (18 February 2009); Interview with AID No 20 (19 February 2009); Interview with AID No 21 (25 February 2009).

BIBLIOGRAPHY

Articles and Books

Brudney, V. (1982), 'The independent director – heavenly city or Potemkin village?', *Harvard Law Review*, **95** (3), 597–659.

Cosenza E. (2007), 'The holy grail of corporate governance reform: independence or democracy?', *Brigham Young University Law Review*, [2007], 1–51.

Cox, J.D. and H.L. Munsinger (1985), 'Bias in the boardroom: psychological foundations and legal implications of corporate cohesion', *Law & Contemporary Problems*, **48**, 83–135.

Davis, K.B. (2005), 'Structural bias, special litigation committees, and the vagaries of director independence', *Iowa Law Review*, **90**, 1305–58.

Fama, E. and M. Jensen (1983), 'Separation of ownership and control', *Journal of Law and Economics*, **26** (2), 301–25.

Fink, R.A. (2006), 'Social ties in the boardroom: changing the definition of director independence to eliminate "rubber-stamping" boards', *Southern California Law Review*, **79**, 455–96.

Gilson, R.J. and C.J. Milhaupt (2005), 'Choice as regulatory reform: the case of Japanese corporate governance', *American Journal of Comparative Law*, **53** (2), 343–77.

Huang, M.J. (2000), 'Gong Si Jan Kong yu Jan Cha Ren Jye Du Gai Ge Ren

[Innovation of Taiwan's corporate auditor system – a corporate governance perspective]', *National Taiwan University Law Journal*, **29** (1), 159–208.
Huang, M.J. (2001), 'Jiao Cha Chi Gu v Gong Si Jian Kong [Cross-shareholding v corporate governance]', in *Gong Kai Fa Shin Gong Sh Fa Zhi yu Gong Si Jian Kong* [Public Company Regulation and Corporate Governance], Taiwan: Angle Publishing, pp. 194–203.
Hwang, B.H. and S. Kim (2009), 'It pays to have friends', *Journal of Financial Economics*, **93** (1), 138–58.
Lin, K.C. (2001), 'Jian Cha Ren Xiu Zheng Fang Xiang zhi Jiang Tao [Review of the reform of statutory supervisors]', *The Taiwan Law Review*, **73**, 47–59.
Liu, L.Y. (2003), 'Jian Quan Du Li Dong Jian Shi yu Gong Si Ji Li zhi Fa Ji Yang, Jiu [Research on building a sound legal system on corporate governance and independent directors and statutory supervisor]', *The Taiwan Law Review*, **94**, 131–54.
Page, A. (2009), 'Unconscious bias and the limits of director independence', *University of Illinois Law Review*, **1**, 237–94.
Tseng, W.R. (2003), 'Wo Guo You Guan Gong Si Zhi Li ji Xing Si [Some thoughts on corporate governance in Taiwan]', *The Taiwan Law Review*, **103**, 61–76.
Velasco, J. (2004), 'Structural bias and the need for substantive review', *Washington University Law Quarterly*, **82**, 821–917.
Wang, W.Y. (2005), 'She Li Du Li Dong Jian Dui Gong Si Zhi Li de Ying Xiang [The impact on corporate governance of introducing independent directors and statutory supervisors]', *The Law Monthly*, **56** (1), 45–64.
Yeh, Y. H. (2005), *Zhengfa de Guwang* [The Disappearing King of the Stock Market], Taiwan: Sunbright Publishing.
Yeh, Y.H. and Chen-En Ko (2006), 'De Ri Mei Han Geguo Duli Dongshi, Shenji Weiyuan Hui ji Jita Zhuanmen Weiyuan Hui Fazhi Guifan ji Shiwu Yunzuo Qingkuang [The law and practice of independent directors, audit committees and other functional committees in Germany, Japan, United States, and Korea]', Taipei: Financial Supervisory Commission of Taiwan.
Yeh, Y.H., S. Lee Tsun and Tracie Woidtke (2001), 'Family control and corporate governance: evidence from Taiwan', *International Review of Finance*, **2** (1–2), 21–48.
Yu, S. M. (2002), 'Taiwan Shin Gong Si Fa yu Du Li Dong Shi (Shang) [New Taiwan corporation law and independent directors (1)]', *FT Law Review*, **123**, 63–77.

Jurisprudence

Beam ex rel Martha Stewart Living Omnimedia, Inc v Stewart (2004), 845 A.2d 1040, 1050 (Del).
Biondi v Scrushy (2003), 820 A.2d 1148 (Del Ch).
In re Oracle Derivative Litigation (2003), 824 A.2d 917 (Del Ch).

Statutes and Regulations

Company Law, Art. 218 (2011) (Taiwan), available at http://law.moj.gov/tw/eng/LawClass/LawAll.aspx?PCode=J0080001 (accessed 2 November 2011).
Regulations Governing Establishment of Internal Control Systems by Public

Companies, Art. 15 (2009.3.16), available at http://eng.selaw.com.tw/FLAWDAT0201.asp (accessed 25 November 2009).
Sarbanes-Oxley Act of 2002, Pub L No 107-204, 116 Stat 745 (2002).
Securities and Exchange Law, Art. 14-2, 14-3 (2010) (Taiwan), available at http://law.moj.gov/tw/eng/LawClass/LawAll.aspx?PCode=G0400001 (accessed 2 November 2011).

Web Resources

Chailease Finance Co Ltd (2008), 'Taiwan Dichu Dashing Chituan Chiye Yanjiu [Research on large business groups in Taiwan]', available at http://www.chailease.com.tw/ugC_NewsCenter_Detail1.asp?hidID=65&hidPage1=1&hidShowType=his (accessed 16 October 2008).
'Financial Supervisory Commission of Taiwan 294 (January 2006)', available at http://www.fsc.gov.tw/news_detail2.aspx?icuitem=3365703 (accessed November 2009).
Infodisc Technology Co Ltd 'Annual Report 8 (2003)', available at http://newmops.tse.com.tw/ (accessed 25 November 2009).
Murali, D. (2009), 'Truly Independent Directors, a Rarity', *The Hindu Business Line*, available at http://www.thehindubusinessline.in/2009/01/22/stories/2009012250220900.htm (accessed 18 May 2011).
Procomp Informatics Co Ltd, 'Annual Report 7 (2003)', available at http://newmops.tse.com.tw/ (accessed 25 November 2009).
Taiwan Stock Exchange, 'Market Observation Post System', available at http://newmops.tse.com.tw/ (accessed 2 November 2011).
Taiwan Stock Exchange, 'Statistical Highlights of Listed Securities', available at http://www.twse.com.tw/ch/statistics/statistics_list.php?tm=04&stm=004 (accessed 2 November 2011).
Wang, Hui H. and Huang Guo D. (2007), 'Lai Yin-Zhao: Duli Dongshi Weibi Duli [Independent directors are not necessarily independent]', available at http://pro.udnjob.com/mag2/fn/storypage.jsp?f_ART_ID=31087 (accessed 5 February 2007).
'Wanshan Shangshi Gongsi Duli Dongshi Zhidu de Jianyi [Suggestions for the Institution of Independent Directors for Public Companies]' (2009), available at http://news.cnyes.com/dspnewsS.asp?cls=listnews24hr&fi=\NEWSBASE\20090418\WEB357 (accessed 18 April 2009).
Zhao Fen Kao (2008), 'Diaocha: Guonei Baida Chiye 2007 Nian Yingshou Chengzhang 16.01% [Survey: the top 100 business groups feature revenue growth of 16.01% in 2007]', available at http://www.cna.com.tw/SearchNews/doDetail.aspx?id=200810160059 (accessed 16 October 2008).

10. Corporate law reform and corporate governance in Malaysia – responses to globalization

Aishah Bidin

INTRODUCTION

Reforming company law is an important part of the corporate law program in Malaysia. The objectives of the reform program are the creation of a legal and regulatory structure that will facilitate business, promote accountability and protect corporate directors and members, taking into account the interest of other stakeholders in line with international standards. Malaysian corporate law reform has taken on a different dimension recently. This chapter provides an overview of the reforms currently in progress in Malaysia. It has a special focus on corporate rehabilitation and restructuring. A new regime on rehabilitation is currently under parliamentary process in Malaysia and the chapter explains how it has been influenced by the models in Singapore, Australia and the UK.

Since the Malaysian *Companies Act 1965* came into force, it has been amended more than 30 times. The approach taken has been on a 'piecemeal basis' and has lacked a systematic and coherent review of corporate law and practice. To ensure that the reform program is effective and objective, cross-jurisdictional studies were carried out for the purpose of identifying international corporate initiatives and trends. Further, these studies helped ensure that the reforms will be in tandem with global standards and enable Malaysian businesses to compete internationally.

This chapter outlines the approach taken by the Malaysian Corporate Law Reform Committee (CLRC) in its efforts to modernize corporate law and practice in Malaysia.[1] It explains the basis of, justifications for, and effect of reforms in other jurisdictions such as the UK, Australia, New Zealand and Hong Kong – which have provided an important benchmark in determining the changes and responses to be included in corporate law reform in Malaysia. The chapter also establishes that, within the context of globalization, modernization of corporate law would not be complete without considering the advances achieved in information and communication technology (ICT) and their impact.

MODERN COMPANY LAW

The modern company is the most important business vehicle in Malaysia. It has facilitated economic development of the country for more than a century by enabling incorporated businesses to raise capital and attain economies of scale. In Malaysia, companies are incorporated under the *Companies Act 1965*. Company law in Malaysia allows a person to invest his or her money in a company and become the joint owner of the shares of the company, together with other persons who have similarly invested their money, without the burdens of unlimited liability and management responsibilities being imposed.

The limited liability company remains the primary vehicle for commercial expansion and economic advancement. The three basic elements which have made limited companies popular and successful as vehicles for generating capital are limited liability, perpetual succession and transferability of securities.

The number of companies incorporated over the years has increased tremendously. Thirty years ago there were fewer than 20 000 companies registered in Malaysia. As of 31 December 2009, the number of companies on the register of Suruhanjaya Syarikat Malaysia (SSM), or the Companies Commission of Malaysia,[2] stood at 882 843 (SSM 2009). In the 1980s, the annual increase in the number of new companies incorporated ranged between 9000 and 15 000. In 2009 the incorporation of new local companies dropped marginally by 0.05 per cent compared with 2008 despite the difficult economic conditions in the first nine months of 2009. Temporary reduction of incorporation fees by SSM served to encourage the formation of new companies to participate in various domestic activities, with impetus from the government's RM67 billion economic stimulus package.

REGULATORY LAW FOR CORPORATIONS IN MALAYSIA

The first law on companies implemented in Malaysia was the *Companies Enactment 1897*, which was largely borrowed from UK law. This enactment was repealed and replaced by the *Companies Enactment No 20* of 1917. Ten years later, the *Companies Enactment 1927* was introduced to replace the 1917 statute.

The 1927 enactment continued in force until 1946 when the *Companies Ordinance 1940* of the Straits Settlement was extended to apply to all Federated Malay States. This ordinance was in force until 15 April 1966 when the *Companies Act 1965* (the *Companies Act*) was implemented. The *Companies Act* is not the only piece of legislation regulating corporate activities. Malaysia has a comprehensive legal framework which governs corporate activities. Other than the *Companies Act*, the framework includes:

1. *Securities Commission Act 1993*
2. *Capital Market and Services Act 2007*
3. *Malaysian Code on Take Over and Merger*
4. *Malaysian Code of Corporate Governance*
5. Bursa Malaysia Listing Requirements, and
6. The common law.

English common law, derived from the decisions of the English courts, has been adopted by the courts in Malaysia, which is a member of the British Commonwealth. The evolution of the British commercial revolution in the last 160 years has seen considerable development in the principles of common law and equity relating to companies. Some examples of common law principles include the general rule in *Foss v Harbottle* (1843),[3] which is subject to certain limited exceptions. The proper claimant in an action for a wrong alleged to have been done to a company is the company itself. Second, if the alleged wrong is a matter which it is competent for the company to settle itself (the internal management principle) or in the case of an irregularity, which can be ratified or condoned by internal procedure (the irregularity principle), no individual member may bring action.

Other instances are the duty of directors to act *bona fide* in the interests of the company (*Allen v Gold Reefs of West Africa Ltd* 1900); the rule which required a company's share capital to be kept intact for the benefit of its creditors (*Trevor v Whitworth* 1887); and the rules on the separate legal personality of the company and the circumstances in which this could be disregarded (*Salomon v Salomon & Co Ltd* 1897).

These English common law principles have been the foundation of company law and the decisions of the Malaysian courts. The *Companies Act* consists of 374 sections divided into various subsections and has nine accompanying schedules. The Act requires companies to maintain certain registers with SSM.[4] These are:

- Register of members (section 158)
- Register of substantial shareholders (Division 3A of Part IV and section 69L)

- Register of debenture holders (section 70)
- Register of holders of interests other than shares and debentures (section 84)
- Register of directors, managers and secretaries (section 141)
- Register of directors' shareholdings (section 134), and
- Register of charges (section 115).[5]

Apart from these registers, all companies are required to lodge an annual return signed by a director, manager or secretary with the Registrar within one month of their annual general meeting (*Companies Act*, section 165). The matters to be stated in the annual return are prescribed in the 8th Schedule for companies with share capital and in section 165(6) for companies without share capital. A company having share capital is required to attach a copy of its last audited balance sheet and profit and loss account unless it is an exempt private company.[6]

THE EVOLUTION OF CORPORATE GOVERNANCE PROVISIONS UNDER THE *COMPANIES ACT 1965*

The *Companies Act 1965*, since it was implemented in 1966, has been amended more than 30 times to keep pace with developments in the corporate sector. In the past, officials of the Registrar of Companies,[7] in drafting the proposals for amendments, have relied to a certain extent on the work and recommendations of the Jenkins Committee (1962) in the UK and the Eggleston Committee (1967) in Australia. Many of the recommendations of these two committees, particularly those dealing with accounts and audit; disclosure of interests by directors and substantial shareholders; substantial property transactions with directors; and insider trading were adopted through amendments to the Malaysian *Companies Act* in the form of sections 132A to 132E as well as Division 3A of Part IV relating to disclosure by substantial shareholders.

These provisions are generally designed to prevent corporate abuses through related party transactions involving substantial acquisitions or disposals of property (section 132C) and substantial property transactions (section 132E). Section 132G, which has proved to be controversial, was included in 1992 in an environment where asset shuffling was a common practice among companies. Many companies were found to transfer recently acquired assets to other companies in which the controlling shareholders or directors, or persons connected with them, had an interest. The transactions were usually done at excessive prices far above market value.

Section 132G has been branded by lawyers, accountants, corporate planners, consultants and merchant bankers as 'inhibiting genuine transactions.' The regulatory body, the Companies Commission of Malaysia (SSM) was not totally unaware that section 132G may prevent some genuine transactions, but the policy is intended to strike a balance between protecting minority shareholders and investors and allowing genuine transactions to proceed. This led to the introduction of subsection (6) to section 132G to provide clear cut exemptions for *bona fide* transactions, as defined, from the prohibition applied under the section. Nevertheless, due to various issues and abuses of the section, it was finally repealed as a result of an amendment made to the Malaysian *Companies Act* in 2007.

As can be seen, the amendments made to the *Companies Act* over the years have strengthened the governance structure in the corporate sector to ensure the sustainable and healthy growth of companies. Since the beginning of the financial crisis in 1997, the *Companies Act* has been amended five times and new provisions have been introduced allowing share buybacks (section 67A), extending the maximum period of stock options from five to ten years (section 68), imposing limitations on payment of dividends (section 365), strengthening rules on disclosure of substantial shareholdings (section 69D), and improving existing provisions intended to curb abuses of restraining orders against troubled companies to protect the interests of their creditors (section 176(10A)).

As a regulator responsible for maintaining and regulating the integrity of corporations as business vehicles that form an integral component in the economy, SSM has the view that there is a real need to review the *Companies Act.* The continuing debate on corporate governance, developments in information technology, the financial crisis, and experience with the existing framework on insolvency law have exposed some weaknesses and inadequacies in the current provisions of the *Companies Act*.

CORPORATE LAW REFORM PROGRAM – AN OUTLINE

Suruhanjaya Syarikat Malaysia defined a strategic objective to initiate, develop and implement a comprehensive regulatory framework in tandem with the changing business environment. It has adopted a two pronged approach in its attempt to achieve this strategic objective. The first is a near-term plan to implement the Recommendations of the High Level Finance Committee on Corporate Governance,[8] while the other approach is a long-term plan for a fundamental review of the core company law provisions currently in force. The long-term plan is better known as SSM's Corporate Law Review Program.

Apart from a near-term plan to amend the *Companies Act 1965*, SSM has embarked on its Corporate Law Reform Program as a part of its comprehensive agenda to modernize the company law framework and strengthen corporate governance in Malaysia. It is expected that this initiative will provide an environment conducive for companies and businesses, in order to improve Malaysia's competitive edge in attracting investments.

The timing of the reform program is quite appropriate as Malaysia can now learn from the experience of other jurisdictions and adopt principles and techniques best suited for the Malaysian corporate environment. For example, the Corporate Law Economic Reform Program (CLERP) of Australia was identified as a source of guidance on the way to simplify and modernize the style of drafting legislation as well as the way to create rules that balance strict legal principles with economic and commercial needs.

The UK Department of Trade and Industry's reform program, aptly named 'Modern Company Law for a Competitive Economy,' was another resource. It has provided valuable insights in the reformulation of the existing principles in the *Companies Act 1965*, which are essentially a legacy of the 1948 UK *Companies Act*. Hong Kong and Singapore had their own corporate law reform programs, and this has also assisted Malaysia in designing a modern company law that accords with international standards yet is suitable for the local corporate and business environment.

On 17 December 2004, SSM established the Corporate Law Reform Committee (CLRC) to undertake the review program. The objectives of the program were to enable corporate and business activities in Malaysia to function in a cost effective, consistent and transparent manner in a competitive business environment while balancing the obligations, responsibilities and protection of corporate participants in line with international standards of good corporate governance. The review also took into consideration the needs of the domestic business environment and prevailing international standards.

The CLRC's efforts were spearheaded by a Steering Committee responsible for the overall supervision of the review to be conducted by CLRC. It was intended that the committee would ensure that the CLRC was able to achieve its objectives within set timelines. The Steering Committee was assisted by five working groups. Each working group was assigned the task of reviewing a specific core area of company law outlined below:

- Group A: Company Formation and Private Companies and Alternative Forms of Business Vehicles
- Group B: Fund Raising and Capital Maintenance
- Group C: Corporate Governance and Shareholders' Rights

- Group D: Corporate Securities and Insolvency, and
- Group E: Enforcement and Sanctions.

The working groups were empowered to create sub-committees. Group D was concerned with corporate securities and insolvency, which are the subjects of this article. It had seven sub-committees. The Steering Committee and the working groups were supported by a full-time secretariat and a research team provided by SSM.

FORMULATING A CORPORATE REHABILITATION FRAMEWORK

The primary aim of any corporate rehabilitation regime is to provide mechanisms for the restoration and revival of the business of a financially distressed company (see, for example, Ministry of Economic Development (2002)). It must be pulled back from the brink of collapse with a view to continuing its existence and keeping trading, if only to maximize recovery for its creditors. A corporate rehabilitation framework has proven to be beneficial,[9] as compared to the drastic approach of liquidation. Rehabilitation facilitates the continuation of business with the hope of achieving the following:

- preservation of the economic value of the distressed company by keeping it as a going concern that can serve all stakeholders;
- minimizing the losses for creditors, employees and others who deal with the insolvent company from loss of employment and business opportunities and having to reestablish relationships with another entity; and
- facilitating more measured distribution of the assets of the company if it does eventually fail, thus increasing the returns to all creditors.

There are, nonetheless, costs associated with corporate rescue regimes. These include the cost of credit as a result of creditors' inability to enforce contractual rights during the moratorium period, and the risk that allowing the company to trade may further erode its value and reduce the amount available to pay creditors.

Current Legal Framework on Corporate Insolvency

Under the current law in Malaysia, there are several methods of dealing with company insolvency. An overview of the existing law and its limitations is important in defining the path of reform.

Receivership where creditors may appoint a receiver and manager

Most often the company will be wound up and its assets hived off and sold separately. Receivership procedures are common in several jurisdictions. The primary purpose of receivership is not to act in the collective interest of all the creditors of the company but rather to realize the company's assets under a debenture trust in the interest of the debenture holders. Receivership is not designed to rescue or rehabilitate the company.

Winding up

Winding up enables proper closure of a company that either may not want to continue its business or may be unable to do so. Winding up may be carried out voluntarily (through a members' or creditors' voluntary resolution) or by an application to the court for a winding-up order. The two categories of winding up, namely compulsory winding up by the court and voluntary winding up (either by members or creditors), currently are the options available for insolvent companies in the event they decided to terminate the company. Otherwise, if there is still an opportunity to save the company, they might attempt to adopt a rescue mechanism – namely, a scheme of creditors' arrangement.

A scheme of arrangement under section 176 of the Companies Act

While section 176 is not intended specifically as a corporate rescue mechanism, it has proved useful for companies facing financial difficulty. The procedures under section 176 were amended in 1998[10] following criticism from the market, but the remedy under section 176 is still seen as costly, cumbersome and slow in procedures and implementation. These problems are especially felt when the arrangement mechanism is used for corporate rehabilitation or rescue purposes. This is for a number of reasons, which include:

- delays in the court system
- the company which is the subject of the proceeding must identify and divide the creditors into separate classes, and the court may refuse to approve a scheme if it considers that the creditors have not been properly classified
- creditors are restrained from enforcing their security for unduly long periods because of restraining orders, which are initially for a maximum period of 90 days; the court may extend the period provided the company has fulfilled the requirements under section 176 (10A) of the *Companies Act*, and
- a real lack of protection for the company since the stay is effective only from the date the notice of the proposed compromise was

given whereas, to be most effective, the stay should apply during the period the proposal is being developed.

Pengurusan Danaharta Nasional Berhad Act

In response to the problems faced by the banking sector in Malaysia in the wake of the 1997 financial crisis, a new formal insolvency process of 'special administration' was introduced under the *Pengurusan Danaharta Nasional Berhad Act 1998* (*Danaharta Act*). This was meant to complement the existing options in insolvency law and the restructuring process.[11]

One of the remarkable features of special administration under the *Danaharta Act*, as compared to the scheme of arrangement process, is that it is a non-court-based procedure. Special administration operates on commercial principles by adopting a market-driven approach, despite the fact that it is a government entity. Time is of the essence in the formulation of a workable restructuring plan. The appointment of a special administrator ensures that the development and implementation of the plan are carried out within a period of three to six months after the appointment. This is speedier than the procedures under section 176 of the *Companies Act*, where the court process usually takes much longer to complete.

The restructuring plan initiated by the special administrator requires only the approval of the secured creditors and not the shareholders of the company or its unsecured creditors. Once approved, the plan binds the company, its shareholders and all creditors. This is a distinction from the scheme of arrangement procedure, which requires approval of 75 per cent in value and a simple majority in the number of each class of creditors and shareholders present and voting. The creditors under a scheme of arrangement are divided into classes according to their interests.

Corporate Debt Restructuring Committee

Another informal corporate rescue mechanism introduced following the 1997 financial crisis was the Corporate Debt Restructuring Committee (CDRC), which functions under the auspices of the Central Bank of Malaysia. The CDRC sets specific criteria to be met by an applicant company, such as having a potentially viable business and more than RM50 million worth of debt with more than one financial institution. The CDRC acts as a secretariat and supervises and facilitates negotiations between the creditors, banks and debtor companies.

Corporate Rescue/Rehabilitation Frameworks in Other Jurisdictions

Singapore

Prior to the amendment of Part VIIIA of the *Singapore Companies Act* (the SCA) in 1987,[12] an insolvent company in Singapore could only rely on section 210, which provided for a scheme of arrangement for entering into a compromise or arrangement with its creditors or shareholders. Such schemes were often proposed when a company was in financial difficulties and the members or creditors considered that there were some advantages in the company continuing its business. Otherwise, the creditors could initiate legal proceedings or petition for the winding up of the company. The scope of the scheme of arrangement in Singapore is similar to Malaysia.

In order to allow a fundamentally viable company some breathing space to reorganize its business and become more cost-effective and profitable, the SCA was amended in 1987 by including a new Part VIIIA based on the provision of administration under Part II of the UK *Insolvency Act 1986*. The amendment made to the SCA in 1987 has given ailing companies an opportunity to be rehabilitated and turned around to become more profitable. An application must be made to the court for an order placing the company under judicial management. The judicial management order will allow a financially troubled company to get court protection from any threat of liquidation or potential suits from its creditors during a moratorium period. This allows the company to carry out a restructuring scheme to revitalize its operations and recover financial health.

Australia

Prior to the inclusion of Part 5.3A of the *Australian Corporation Law* in 1993, financially troubled companies had several options to compromise or arrange their debts with creditors to avoid the threat of liquidation. These options were:

- A scheme of arrangement under section 411 of the *Corporations Act 2001*. The key features of the scheme of arrangement are similar to those in other jurisdictions in the British Commonwealth. They are seen as relatively inflexible, expensive and time consuming, as implementation requires sanction from the court.
- To enter into official management if a company appears to be unable to pay its debts in full. The procedure requires a resolution of its directors affirming that the company is unable to pay its debts as and when they fall due, and the convening a meeting of creditors

to decide by special resolution to place the company in official management. The effect of official management is that management functions are transferred to an official manager appointed by the creditors with the aim of restoring the company's financial health. Other than this, the resolutions of the creditors are binding on all the creditors irrespective of the support of individual creditors for the decisions, and a statutory moratorium applies to legal proceedings against the company.

The Harmer Report on General Insolvency Inquiry (1998) recommended the introduction of a new procedure for the voluntary administration of insolvent companies. This was meant to align Australia with the development of bankruptcy and company law and practice in other jurisdictions.[13] The official management mechanism, described earlier, was abolished by the *Corporate Law Reform Act 1992* because of its infrequent use and its potential overlap with the voluntary administration regime. The primary purpose of the Australian voluntary administration (VA) procedure is:

> [T]o provide a flexible, easily initiated and relatively inexpensive procedure that gives a company the benefit of a debt moratorium. This allows the company to attempt a compromise or arrangement with its creditors aimed at saving the company or the business and maximizing the return to creditors. If creditors agree to the arrangement, it will be set out in a deed of company arrangement which binds the company and its creditors. If these attempts fail, the legislation facilitates the transition to winding up. (Australia Joint Parliamentary Committee 2004, p. 14)

The Australian voluntary administration regime does not require court involvement in the process. The administrator is appointed by the board of directors, or by a person or group of persons having a charge over all or substantially all of the property of the company, or by a liquidator. The administrator has control over the company's business. There is an automatic stay of legal proceedings against the company and its property, although in some limited situations the secured creditors and the owners or lessors of property possessed, used or occupied by the company are not bound by the stay. A period of five days is given for the administrator to call the first creditors' meeting. This is intended to enable the creditors to decide whether or not to appoint a committee of creditors or to replace the administrator. A second creditors' meeting must be called within 21 days of the appointment of the administrator, who must report to the creditors on the company's affairs and financial situation. The second creditors' meeting is to enable the creditors to decide whether the company should execute a deed of company arrangement and end the administration, or wind up the company.

The deed of arrangement, if executed, is binding on all unsecured creditors, secured creditors who have voted in favor of the deed, owners or lessors of property who have voted for the deed, the company and its officers and members, and the deed administrator. Secured creditors and owners or lessors of property who did not vote in favor of the deed may also be bound by its terms if the court so orders. In actual fact, the VA scheme is an interim form of administration which may be invoked by a company pending a determination of its future by its creditors. It is not a complete insolvency procedure that provides for the resolution of all the affairs of an ailing company.

United Kingdom

The UK *Companies Act 1985* had a scheme of arrangement similar to section 176 of the Malaysian *Companies Act 1965*. Sections 425–7 of the UK *Companies Act 1985*[14] (UK CA 1985) provided a procedure for a company to make an arrangement or compromise with its creditors, which is similar to the provision in Malaysia. Prior to the enactment of the UK *Insolvency Act 1986*, section 425 of UK CA 1985, which dealt with schemes of arrangement, was the only provision relating to the rehabilitation of ailing companies in UK company law. The section allowed companies to enter into binding compromises with creditors provided the company obtained consents from each creditor. This proved to be a burdensome and costly procedure.

Unlike a Company Voluntary Arrangement (CVA), an Administration Order (AO) under the UK *Insolvency Act* is a court-based procedure. A CVA is a composition in satisfaction of the company's debt or a scheme of arrangement resulting from the acceptance of a proposal by the directors to the company and its creditors. Normally the directors remain in control of the company and continue to have power to carry on the business and realize its assets.

Section 8 of the *Insolvency Act* specifies four alternative requirements, at least one of which must be fulfilled by a company before an AO can be granted by the court:

- survival of the company and/or its business
- approval of a CVA
- entering into a compromise or a scheme of arrangement with creditors under section 425 of UK CA 1985, or
- more advantageous realization of the company's assets than winding up.

The administration procedure under the *Insolvency Act* has been criticized as being expensive from the initial stage of preparation of affidavits and reports by the prospective administrator through to implementation. This has been a hindrance for small- and medium-size companies, discouraging some directors of companies in financial difficulties from taking early steps to use the administration procedure. This is one of the reasons why the procedure has not been as successful as hoped. To overcome the weaknesses in the administration procedure, the UK *Enterprise Act 2002* (UK EA) made changes to corporate insolvency procedures.

The amendment of the insolvency procedures in the UK is in Part 10 of the UK EA. It aims at facilitating company rescues wherever possible and seeks to achieve this by restricting the use of administrative receivership to shift the balance in favor of administration, which is a collective procedure that takes into account the interests of all creditors. The UK EA introduces a streamlined system of administration that focuses on the following five substantive changes to the administration procedure:

- the purpose of administration
- the entry route into administration
- the administrator being authorized to make distributions to creditors
- clear time-limits, and
- exit options to end the administration.

Under the UK EA, it is now possible to put a company under administration without a court order. The appointment takes effect from the date and time a notice of appointment is filed with the court. The overall limit for the administration is one year, in contrast to the former situation when the Administration Order was open-ended. The one-year time limit may be extended by the consent of the creditors or the court. It is also possible to apply to the court for an AO. The rationale for having two entry routes into the administration procedure is that the existing court order route may still be suitable for complicated cases.

Corporate rehabilitation – the process and content of reform in Malaysia

Referring to the experience of the other Commonwealth jurisdictions, discussed above, Malaysia has attempted to chart its course of reform. The underlying issues and the direction of reform are outlined below. The first issue concerns the deficiencies perceived in the existing framework described earlier. The following are some major issues considered by the working group of the Corporate Law Reform Committee in Malaysia concerning insolvency. The present framework is inadequate as there is no focus on a rescue mechanism or attempts to rehabilitate companies. For example, where money is lent to a company without debentures (which is often the case with listed companies), there is no recourse to the creditor to force management to restructure. Usually the only option available is liquidation. Receivership is not available where there are no debentures. Court receiverships are few and far between. Even when receiverships are granted by the court the purpose of the exercise is not restructuring, which is socially better; for example, the rehabilitation of abandoned housing projects.

Under the current provisions of the *Companies Act 1965*, a company in financial difficulties can only restructure under section 176. By allowing the management of the company to remain in the hands of the board of directors, it caters for situations where there is confidence in the existing management. But there is no suitable mechanism when there is lack of confidence in the incumbent management.

The *Pengurusan Danaharta* scheme and the Debt Restructuring Committee efforts, discussed earlier, have been effective, but these were established to deal with a specific set of circumstances arising out of the financial crisis. There is a need to establish corporate rescue mechanisms that are applicable in general in diverse situations.

The working group on corporate securities and insolvency was of the view that the rehabilitation process should recognize the cause of the financial distress that has led to the need for restructuring. There may be cases where external circumstances have caused the financial distress of a well-run company. Equally, there may be cases where financial distress is due to mismanagement.

When there is lack of confidence in the management of a distressed company, it should be possible to appoint an independent party with sufficient powers to manage the company and simultaneously seek a suitable restructuring option. With this goal, it is proposed to enable aggrieved creditors (secured and unsecured) to make an application to the court to place the management of the company in the hands of a qualified independent person. At the same time, while managing the company, the independent person must also develop a restructuring option acceptable to the creditors. The system should facilitate rehabilitation by ensuring that the process is managed by a person with the necessary skills and experience and by providing the person with necessary powers to implement the restructuring plan effectively. This is the judicial management scheme proposed in Malaysia.

Where there is confidence in the management of a troubled company, it may be expedient to allow the restructuring to proceed with minimal court intervention. The scheme may be initiated by the company or any of its creditors by filing a notice. This scheme, designated as a Company Voluntary Arrangement (CVA), enables a company in financial distress to obtain protection while the directors manage the company. At the same time, a qualified insolvency practitioner supervises the restructuring plan. It may be argued that a CVA is somewhat similar to section 176 of the *Companies Act* in that the directors continue to manage the company while a restructuring plan is being developed. One of the concerns about CVAs is the fact that the directors are in control of the management of the company during such a scheme. In such situations the directors, whether acting recklessly or negligently or even intentionally, might expose the business to the risk of liabilities on account of wrongful and fraudulent trading.

In addition, in line with international standards (World Bank 2001),[15] it has been recommended by the working group on corporate securities and insolvency that a corporate rehabilitation system for Malaysia should include the following important features:

1. Clear rehabilitation plans: the system should provide for a rehabilitation plan that is easily understood and implemented.
2. A realistic time frame: the new procedure should encourage rehabilitation by providing a realistic timeframe within which the proposal must be prepared, approved and implemented.
3. Moratorium: the system should provide a moratorium period to enable the proposal to be formulated and implemented without threat of liquidation or creditors' action that may frustrate the rehabilitation process.
4. Safeguarding creditors' interests: similarly it is necessary to safeguard creditors' interests by imposing a moratorium against dissipation of the debtor company's assets or funds; adequately providing for creditors' voting; and providing for dissemination of information among the creditors concerning the company and its rehabilitation plan.
5. Involvement of insolvency practitioners: the involvement of qualified and competent insolvency practitioners will ensure that there are no unnecessary delays in implementing the restructuring plan.
6. Involvement and supervision of the court: in addition, the new system must, as an additional safeguard, determine the level and extent of court involvement in the initiation, implementation and supervision of the rehabilitation plan.

The recommendations made by the working group on insolvency, summarized above, have been accepted by the Malaysian Government.

They are currently under legislative process and within the purview of the Ministry concerned. The parliamentary procedure is expected to be completed soon.

CONCLUSION

Company law regulating corporate behavior has been in existence in Malaysia for more than a century. It has evolved tremendously in this period into a sound legal framework which has worked well. The framework and its systems have contributed significantly to the economic growth of Malaysia, which has been facilitated by a responsive legal framework that is relevant to the business environment. The initiatives by Suruhanjaya Syarikat Malaysia (SSM) in its near-term plan to amend the *Companies Act 1965* and implement the recommendations of the High Level Finance Committee on Corporate Governance, and its long-term plan under the Corporate Law Reform Program, are not to put any new system in place but merely to develop, strengthen and improve the existing system further to keep pace with the rapid changes taking place globally. This shall remain the primary agenda of SSM, which is aware that the economy of the nation is driven by companies which are the engines of growth. Suruhanjaya Syarikat Malaysia is the statutory body vested with the power to regulate companies and initiate changes to corporate laws, in addition to its registry functions. It is fully committed to ensuring that corporate vehicles in Malaysia will continue to generate profits for economic advancement, and be equally guided by the principles of transparency and accountability. By doing so, it protects shareholders' interests. As stated in the Cadbury Report, '[t]he country's economy depends on the drive and efficiency of its companies. Thus the effectiveness with which their boards discharge their responsibilities determines the country's competitive position' (1992, para. 1.1).

Globalization is influencing legal systems in Asia as elsewhere in the world. Legal change and globalization are integral to the development of market-based societies. This has been recognized in many Asian jurisdictions where law reform and corporate governance have been major governmental priorities. The Asian economic crisis gave birth to a new international consensus about the need for greater and more-timely information to sustain developing markets. This is in accordance with one of the terms of reference of the CLRC – namely, to consider any legal and regulatory changes that need to be made in order to modernize company law in Malaysia so as to accommodate changes in information and communications technology and to meet the current and future needs of business.

In Malaysia, law reform has been largely led by the state with little evidence of concerted lobbying from business. The globalization of corporate law in Malaysia has also taken the form of adopting international standards developed by multilateral bodies such as the World Bank, IMF, OECD and UNCITRAL. This is evident from the breadth of the scope of corporate law review and reform exercises undertaken since the onset of the financial crisis in the late 1990s until today.

The social, political and economic environment in Malaysia encourages significant state influence on business, whether directly as a corporate owner or indirectly through the persuasive powers politicians have over companies and business leaders. This has resulted in situations of conflicts of interest. In certain cases it is difficult for regulators, appointed by the executive branch of the government and answerable to it, to apply the laws and regulations created by the same executive-dominated parliament or regulators.

The Malaysian Government has been proactive in implementing development-oriented policies and using the law as an instrument of social change and control. This trend has also led to extensive and wide discretionary powers being given to the authorities in the name of transparency and accountability. The combination of using law and legal reform as a tool of economic development, and the complex relationship between law and economic efficiency, has given rise to some other sensitive issues. For instance, the differences in shareholding structures as well as economic, political and cultural differences mean that the nature of the problems and solutions will vary across markets. In particular, in a corporate framework the excessive powers of controlling shareholders create the biggest agency problems. In addition, cultures and value systems, the quality of legal institutions, issues related to access to courts, and the influence of politics in business affect the development process.

Legal reform in the globalization era, and transplanted laws, will evolve as they interact with elements in the local environment. This evolution need not necessarily result in changes in the substantive law. Often, there will be differences in the way the law is used, administered and enforced. The historical character and the economic setting of the Malaysian corporate sector are special; here, the government has always played a dominant role in legal, social and economic reform. This is evident from the setting up of special vehicles by the government to protect special interests and assuming of authoritative power through legislation. The need for political and institutional transparency in corporate governance should not be underestimated. As global changes continue to affect Malaysia, developing effective new laws requires proper understanding of the socio-cultural environment in which they are meant to be applied. The constraints discussed here suggest that law reform in this part of the world is still a long and winding road yet to be travelled.

NOTES

1. The Corporate Law Reform Committee (CLRC) was established on 17 December 2003 and forms a strategic part of the direction in providing an environment that is conducive to company and business operation. During its term, the CLRC circulated 12 consultative documents to the public and related stakeholders and finally submitted the final recommendation report to the government in early 2008.
2. SSM, or the Companies Commission of Malaysia, was established on 16 April 2002. It serves as an agency to incorporate companies and register businesses in Malaysia. SSM also serves as a depository and custodian of corporate and business information and currently serves as the regulatory body for companies in Malaysia.
3. For further reading see Aishah Bidin (2003a) 51–6.
4. Not every company needs to maintain all the registers listed here. For example, private companies are not required to maintain a register of substantial shareholders.
5. Section 115(2) including foreign companies registered in Malaysia under section 118. This register is to be distinguished from the register of charges maintained by SSM under section 111.
6. 8th Schedule, Part II – definition of 'exempt private company' is stipulated in section 4 of the Act.
7. In Malaysia the *Companies Act 1965* is administered by the Companies Commission of Malaysia through its Chief Executive Officer who is also known as the Registrar of Companies (ROC). The principal function of the ROC is to ensure that companies and their officers comply with the provisions of the *Companies Act*. It also performs some other administrative functions.
8. The High Level Finance Committee on Corporate Governance was established on 24 March 1998 after an announcement by the Minister of Finance. Its main function is to establish a framework for corporate governance and setting best practices for industry. The Committee is chaired by the Secretary General of the Treasury, who is the Minister of Finance. Its members comprise the governor of the Central Bank of Malaysia, the chairman of the Securities Commission, the chairman of the Kuala Lumpur Stock Exchange, the chairman of the Financial Reporting Foundation and representatives of various industry organizations.
9. Empirical studies in Australia have shown that the eventual returns to creditors after voluntary administration are slightly higher than the returns if a company is wound up straight away. See McColl (2001).
10. *Malaysian Companies (Amendment) Act (No 2) Act A1043 1998*. The amendments to section 176 aimed to ensure that the process of obtaining a restraining order was more transparent, and that creditors were better protected by providing stricter time periods for applications for an extension of the restraining order and preventing the company from disposing of its assets during the period of a restraining order. See Aishah Bidin (2004).
11. Prior to the financial crisis in South-East Asia in 1997, the only formal corporate rescue process in Malaysia was the scheme of arrangement under section 176 of the *Companies Act 1965*. See also Aishah Bidin (2003b).
12. Part VIIIA of the *Singapore Companies Act* (Chapter 50) was superseded via the *Companies (Amendment) Act 1987*, which came into effect on 15 May 1987 vide GN No. S 137/1987. It is largely based on Part II (Administration Orders) of the UK

Insolvency Act 1986, which came into force on 29 December 1986. See also Aishah Bidin (2005).

13. The provision for corporate voluntary administrations came into force on 23 June 1993 in the Australian *Corporate Law Reform Act 1992*.
14. Recommendations made in the consultative document and in the final document of the CLRC Report were originally based on the UK *Companies Act 1985*. Nevertheless, the CLRC has taken cognizance of the ongoing process of reform in the UK and amendments made to the UK *Companies Act* at the time, culminating in the UK *Companies Act 2006*.
15. World Bank (2001), Principle 17, states:

> To be commercially and economically effective, the law should establish rehabilitation procedures that permit quick and easy access to the process, assure timely and efficient administration of the proceeding; afford sufficient protection for all those involved in the process, provide a structure that encourages fair negotiation of a commercial plan, enable a suitable majority of creditors in favor of a plan or other course of action to bind all other creditors by the exercise of voting rights (subject to appropriate minority protections and the protection of class rights) and provide for judicial or other supervision to ensure that the process is not subject to manipulation or abuse.

REFERENCES

Articles, Books and Reports

Australia Joint Parliamentary Committee (2004), Committee on Corporations and Financial Services, 'Corporate Insolvency Laws: a Stocktake', available at http://www.aph.gov.au/senate/committee/corporations_ctte/completed_inquiries/2002-04/ail/report/ail.pdf (accessed 12 May 2011).

Bidin, Aishah (2003a), 'Legal issues arising from minorities shareholders remedies in Malaysia and United Kingdom', *Journal of Law and Society* (Malaysia), **7**, 51–69.

Bidin, Aishah (2003b), 'Review of the Corporate Debt Restructuring Regime and Insolvency Law in Malaysia', presented at the Conference on Companies and Securities Law, Asia Business Forum, Kuala Lumpur.

Bidin, Aishah (2004), 'Insolvencies and corporate rescues in Malaysia', *International Commercial and Company Law Review*, **15**, 334–55.

Bidin, Aishah (2005), 'Corporate Debt Restructuring and Corporate Insolvency: Jurisdictional Analysis', presented at the Corporate Debt Restructuring Conference, Asia Business Forum, Kuala Lumpur.

Cadbury Report (1992), 'Committee on the financial aspects of corporate governance', Gee Publishing, available at http://www.econsense.de/_CSR_INFO_POOL/_CORP_GOVERNANCE/images/cadbury_report.pdf (accessed 12 May 2011).

Companies Commission of Malaysia, Corporate Law Reform Committee, 'On company liquidation – reforms and restatement of the law', Consultative document 4, available at http://www.ssm.com.my/clrc/cd4.pdf (accessed 16 May 2011).

Companies Commission of Malaysia, Corporate Law Reform Committee, 'Reviewing the corporate insolvency regime', Consultative document 10, available at http://www.ssm.com.my/clrc/CD10.pdf (accessed 16 May 2011).

Harmer Report on General Insolvency Inquiry (1998), Australian Law Reform Commission, Canberra, available at http://www.austlii.edu.au/au/other/alrc/publications/reports/45/ (accessed 16 May 2011).

McColl, S (2001), 'Voluntary administrations: how well are they working?', *Australian Journal of Corporate Law*, **12** (3), 194.

Ministry of Economic Development (2002), *Business Rehabilitation*, Discussion document, New Zealand.

World Bank (2001), *Principles and Guidelines for Effective Insolvency and Creditors Rights Systems*, available at http://www.worldbank.org/ifa/ipg_eng.pdf (accessed 16 May 2011).

Statutes and Regulations

Capital Market and Services Act 2007 (Malaysia).
Companies Act 1965 (Act 125) (Malaysia).
Companies Act 1985 (UK).
Companies Act 2006 (UK).
Companies (Amendment) Act 1987 (Malaysia).
Corporate Law Reform Act 1992 (Cth) (Australia).
Corporations Act 2001 (Cth) (Australia).
Enterprise Act 2002 (UK).
Insolvency Act 1986 (UK).
Malaysian Companies (Amendment) Act (No 2) Act A1043 1998 (Malaysia).
Pengurusan Danaharta Nasional Berhad Act 1998 (Malaysia)
Securities Commission Act 1993 (Malaysia).
Singapore Companies Act 1967 (Singapore).

Jurisprudence

Allen v Gold Reefs of West Africa Ltd [1900] 1 Ch 656.
Foss v Harbottle (1843) 67 ER 189.
Salomon v Salomon & Co Ltd [1897] AC 22.
Trevor v Whitworth (1887) 12 App Cas 409.

Web Resource

Suruhanjaya Syarikat Malaysia (SSM) (2009), data on companies and businesses registered in Malaysia, available at http://www.ssm.com.my/en/statistics.php (accessed 12 May 2011).

PART IV

Corporate ethics and responsibility

11. Public regulatory encouragement to the adoption of private ordering systems to achieve environmental protection through sustainable commerce

Peter A. Appel and T. Rick Irvin

INTRODUCTION

Sustainable commerce provides an underappreciated source of environmental improvements. By sustainable commerce, we mean products and practices that minimize environmental impacts and optimize commercial value while realizing both public and private environmental benchmarks (Irvin et al. 2008, p. 562). The term includes means of improving the environment described under names such as sustainable development, greentech, cleantech, and the like. Current corporate governance structures allow for the adoption of programs to achieve sustainable commerce, but firms often underperform from an environmental standpoint. Sustainable commerce solutions employing private/public partnerships that encourage the application and enforcement of private ordering systems can result in faster and more economical environmental improvements than reliance on traditional command and control regulatory systems alone.

Environmental challenges pose difficult problems for human communities at every level from the local to the global. Basic understanding of economic incentives in the context of group action and the unique risks presented from environmental exposure provide some insights into understanding why the conundrums that environmental threats create resist easy solutions. Environmental threats often operate at a subclinical level of impact in humans, so that exposure to a toxic chemical may not cause a recognizable reaction or present a diagnosable condition until years after the exposure. Even then, scientists may not fully understand the mechanism of how the substance produces a particular effect (e.g. cancer) so that the particular hazardous material or environmental assault may escape blame. People in the potentially affected community may thus underestimate the possible effect of their exposure to a substance and may not take action against it (e.g. suing the party causing the exposure or lobbying for corrective legislation). To complicate matters further, even if an individual correctly calculates her risk of danger from exposure, she may nevertheless rationally choose to rely on others or free-ride on their efforts (either other private actors or the government) to obtain protection against the potential danger (Olson 1965). Although in a world without transaction costs, individuals would bargain for an efficient solution to resource conflicts (Coase 1960), the world is full of transaction costs and other impediments to free bargaining and resolution of conflict. As a result, markets do not provide accurate and up-to-date signals to economic actors that induce them to anticipate negative externalities. The actors should internalize (or protect against) these negative externalities either through proactive abatement (or prevention) activity or insurance.

As important economic actors comprised of multiple stakeholders, corporations face additional difficulties in internalizing the signals of the market and taking proactive steps to prevent against creating environmental problems. Rules that limit the potential liability of corporate actors (shareholders and officers and directors) insulate these actors from the effects of their decisions. Shareholder liability is limited for corporate actions in all but the rarest of cases; shareholders stand to lose their investment in a particular corporation but their other assets are not available to satisfy the debts or liabilities of the firm. Shareholders are also a heterogeneous lot. Looking just at the length of expected investment, shareholders range from day traders seeking to maximize share value over extremely short time periods to pension funds that might have very long investment horizons.[1] In the US, officers and directors have legally enforceable fiduciary obligations to their shareholders but not to other communities involved in and affected by corporation action. Moreover, the extent of officer and director liability to shareholders is tempered by rules that protect them from liability for every possible misstep. These rules create an incentive for individuals to hold these positions and room to take calculated risks on behalf of the corporation and its stakeholders. The basic corporate structure, with shareholders and officers and directors, creates principal/agent problems arising from unshared goals and asymmetric information that are well known and widely discussed in the literature, with disputes over the overall amount and form of executive pay (e.g. shares versus stock options versus performance bonuses versus deferred compensation) offering a prominent example.

When the difficulties of responding to environmental problems coincide with the principal/agent problems inherent in the corporation, environmental catastrophe can predictably ensue. Well known and dramatic examples include:

- Love Canal, a contaminated area in New York State sold for residential use where homeowners lacked information about potential environmental threats and the polluting company did not reveal its activities;
- The 1952 London Great Smog, in which individuals underestimated the potential health impacts on themselves, and corporate polluters underestimated their individual impacts on the environment and collectively did not have mechanisms to control the overall emissions to a safer level;
- Bhopal, India, where a chemical company did not adequately design its plant or alert the surrounding communities of the potential hazards posed by the manufacturing at the facility.

If one applies these examples from the precursors to a massive and complicated problem such as global climate change (GCC), the outlook is not particularly bright. Control of greenhouse gases (GHGs) will certainly not occur at levels that will correct the emissions causing this phenomenon, let alone have any possibility of reversing the accumulation of these substances in the atmosphere where their residence time is typically measured in decades. Although some effects from GCC are already being seen (e.g. melting glaciers in the Arctic), most of the more significant predicted effects will occur not immediately but in the mid- to long term. Stakeholders interested in short-term corporate profits or share value will eschew adopting GHG abatement measures that cut into bottom lines.

Informational asymmetry also hampers a response. Although general patterns of GCC impacts can be predicted, specific events are harder to link to it, and the effects of GCC will be felt in diffuse areas, often far from the site of the sources of the pollution. Thus, affected populations cannot target particular individual sources of GHGs, sue them to abate their emissions or lobby for corrective legislation, and expect localized redress or response. Firms will have an incentive to free-ride on the efforts of others if they can maximize their output of GHGs as cheaply as possible while hoping that the goodwill efforts of their competitors correct GCC. And to the extent that a global legal solution is required, the lack of effective legal regimes (especially in the near term) renders a true top-down solution nearly impossible.[2]

None of this is to say that corporate actors have not responded to environmental problems generally or the potential threats of GCC specifically. Many corporations have made sustainability a goal for their management.

Indeed, given the incentive structure just described, the efforts undertaken to date are impressive. Nevertheless, relying on self-correcting corporate responses as the complete solution for environmental problems will predictably fall short of publicly shared environmental goals, and history is rife with examples of these predictable failures. Some levels of regulation will be necessary.

In the US, government has historically and primarily responded to environmental destruction through comprehensive command-and-control regulations. Although these regulations have resulted in dramatic environmental improvements and recovery, they often meet with resistance by members of the regulated community (e.g. corporations) because of the costs imposed by the regulations (especially as contrasted in some instances to the benefits gained). These regulations emerged from a more adversarial vision of government relations with private enterprise, one that fundamentally mistrusted the willingness of the private sector to act in an environmentally protective way even when these actions were ultimately in the long-term best economic interest of the firm. That vision was probably a correct assessment of most corporations' responses to environmental challenges and still captures the attitude of many firms. The recent sustainability efforts of major corporations present a hopeful opportunity that private efforts at sustainable commerce, leveraged through public encouragement and assistance, can achieve further environmental gains more quickly and more economically than traditional command-and-control regulation alone.

Sustainable commerce, especially as achieved through public/private partnerships, presents an underutilized strategy for further environmental gains. Private ordering systems can provide means of achieving systematic improvement of environmental performance, and public actors can through encouragement and regulation create positive incentives for private actors to adopt these means. Through these public–private partnerships, environmental problems can be averted more successfully than through pure regulation alone.

GREEN MEANS GREEN: ENVIRONMENTAL IMPROVEMENT AND THE CORPORATE BOTTOM LINE(S)

Despite the pessimistic prediction that firms will avoid environmental obligations, corporations do not routinely ignore these duties. Environmentally sound performance is essential to a corporation's financial success. At a bare minimum, compliance with enforceable rules and regulations forms an essential part of every business's objectives. Uncorrected environmental problems can also result in tort or tort-like liability for corporations. Every year, corporations pay millions of dollars in compensatory (and sometimes punitive) damages for negligently exposing people to harmful chemicals and substances such as asbestos, industrial chemicals, and food-borne chemicals such as pesticides. The federal Superfund law in the US, *Comprehensive Environmental Response, Compensation and Liability Act* (CERCLA), mandates that present and past owners and operators must contribute to cleanup costs at contaminated sites along with those who arranged for disposal of hazardous substances at the site. The liability under this law is without regard to traditional tort requirements of negligence or causation of harm. Thus, whether they take the form of a punitive measure or a compensatory one, these expenses, possibly ruinous in amount, provide an incentive for corporations to engage in cost-avoidance. Nevertheless, the possibility of paying billions of dollars in compensation for wrongs does not necessarily provide sufficient incentive for all cost avoidance. The recent oil calamity in the Gulf of Mexico from the *Deepwater Horizon* oil rig has already caused BP, one of the world's largest companies and one that worked on developing a reputation for being forward-thinking on environmental issues ('Beyond Petroleum' as it said in one ad), to expend billions on cleanup and restoration, not to mention compensation for the lives of the workers lost on the drilling rig when it exploded.

Command-and-control regulations provide their own positive and negative requirements for improved performance. For example, the US law governing hazardous waste disposal, the *Resource Conservation and Recovery Act* (RCRA), imposes a massive regulatory burden for generators of such waste. The generators must monitor the waste from its creation, store it for only a short period of time, ship it with an approved transporter to an approved treatment, storage or disposal facility, all the while maintaining records of the waste and being liable to report any irregularities to the Environmental Protection Agency (EPA) and to report overall discharges of toxic chemicals into the environment. This regulatory burden provides a great incentive for a firm to avoid these costs altogether and devise means to reduce or eliminate the generation of hazardous waste.[3] The same is true for other laws in the command-and-control panoply. Although compliance costs are often high, liability for violations is even higher. In the US, fines for environmental violations typically run at $37 500 per violation, and every day that a problem remains uncorrected counts as a violation.[4] Individual corporate actors as well as corporations themselves are also subject to criminal penalties under US environmental laws.[5]

In addition to these pure penalty-avoidance strategies, many corporations have learned that environmentally sound practices can enhance their profitability. Several authors have catalogued a variety of examples in which corporations have saved money by decreasing energy consumption. For example, the delivery giant UPS has adopted many measures to reduce its fuel consumption. One recent case study details how UPS's use of management information science (MIS) solutions has improved UPS's financial and environmental performance. Fuel for its delivery trucks constitutes a significant expense for UPS, and over the years UPS has deployed many informatics solutions to lower these costs. The now-familiar handheld devices that UPS drivers use to collect information resulted in fuel savings to UPS by reducing idle times for the trucks. Employing proprietary firmware, UPS experimented with using informatics to reduce energy consumption and tested a program to collect information on its routes, the patterns the drivers took, the idling times they experienced, and the fuel used. With this information, UPS adjusted the routes periodically by determining traffic patterns and flows. UPS can also use this information to reduce the idling time of its vehicles, which considerably increases overall fuel efficiency and reduces emissions. It can also target repairs to its vehicles on an as-needed basis rather than running repairs on a lockstep maintenance schedule, thereby reducing waste from disposing of parts that still have useful life (Watson et al. 2010).

Firms have also saved money by decreasing outputs of toxic chemicals in their products. Not only can companies avoid possible penalties, liability for cleanup, and negative publicity, but switching from toxic chemicals to less hazardous inputs can yield positive results. The 3M Corporation has had several noteworthy successes from its 3P Program (Pollution Prevention Pays). Underlying this program is a simple philosophy that waste is waste. In other words, that anything not in a product is money lost. Some of the overall financial benefit firms experience by decreasing toxic inputs is caused by regulation. For example, the Interface Corporation has opened several markets for its carpets by reducing the amounts of chemicals in them, allowing the company to compete in the European market in light of the now-applicable Registration, Evaluation, Authorisation and Restriction of Chemicals (REACH) Regulations.[6]

Environmental innovation can also improve profitability. Automobiles provide an example. US auto manufacturers excelled in producing sport-utility vehicles (SUVs), but lagged behind competitors in producing fuel-efficient cars that were popular in the marketplace. When petroleum prices spiked in 2006, the market plummeted for gas-guzzling SUVs. The American manufacturers were caught flat-footed; General Motors, once the largest corporation in the world, filed for bankruptcy and secured financial guarantees from the US government. Symbolically, GM has discontinued the Hummer line of SUVs and a prospective deal with a Chinese company that contemplated producing the vehicles has fallen through. Meanwhile, other car manufacturers (notably Japanese manufacturers such as Toyota and Honda) rolled out cars based on hybrid technologies to much acclaim and longer-term market success. To the extent that technological improvement builds market share (e.g. the development of hybrid technology for cars), the patent system provides its own rewards for these inventions. Ford Motor Company now builds hybrid vehicles that are based on the Toyota hybrid platform.

The literature discussing these means for firms to improve profitability through environmental improvement is extensive (Elkington 1997; Esty and Winston 2006; Gibson 1999; Hoffman 1997; Savitz and Weber 2006). Primarily, it has as its target audience the firms themselves and it encourages environmental improvement as a form of corporate self-improvement. In particular, voluntary environmental improvement is often analyzed in the corporate social responsibility (CSR) literature. Much of the CSR literature itself mostly forms a reaction to the strong position staked out notably by economist Milton Friedman that the only social responsibility of a business is 'to use its resources and engage in activities designed to increase its profits so long as it stays within the rules of the game, which is to say, engages in open and free competition without deception or fraud' (Friedman, 1962, p. 133; Friedman, 1970). In this view, social responsibility activities are counterbalanced by activities that actually enhance profits.

Although the overwhelming majority of commentators agree that corporations *may* legally engage in activities within the CSR agenda, many observers concede this point only grudgingly because they believe that these activities are a waste of firm resources because they are not remunerative and that the financial benefits from environmental improvements must be overstated. 'Agitating for corporations to engage in responsible conduct that increases their profits,' they say, 'is a lot like saying there are $20 bills lying on the sidewalk that they have missed. Maybe sometimes they have missed them, but they already have ample incentives to recognize and act on such profit-maximizing opportunities' (Elhauge 2005, p. 15).[7] In analyzing environmental improvements in the CSR context, critics not only underplay the real economic gains available through sustainable commerce, but also frame the legal question arising from these actions as whether a corporation may elect to engage in sustainable commerce. Most observers agree that directors of a corporation can permissibly direct the firm to engage in sustainable commerce activities just as the firm may engage in other projects under the CSR umbrella such as improving working conditions for workers in overseas factories or supporting the arts. It is for that reason that much of the literature touting the potential profitability for firms to take environmentally beneficial actions reads like corporate self-improvement work, much like diet and exercise books for individual improvement. This literature does not provide an agenda for creating greater incentives for firms to improve their environmental performance but only positive encouragement for companies that have made the choice to operate in more environmentally friendly ways or have environmental improvement as a feel-good strategy.

WHY MANY CORPORATIONS OVERLOOK SUSTAINABLE COMMERCE

If sustainable commerce presents financial opportunities for firms, why do so many firms underperform environmentally, let alone eschew sustainable commerce improvements? In short, if UPS can adopt information systems that save energy and cost, what will it take for its competitors to do the same? Is it, to borrow the phrase, the only firm seeing the $20 bills on the ground? Of course, if the fuel savings and environmental improvements UPS realizes are extensive, the financial advantages it will enjoy over competitors (which can benefit many corporate stakeholders in different forms: savings it can pass on to customers, dividends to shareholders, bonuses to management) will give it advantages in the marketplace. But the marketplace does not immediately correct imperfect behavior by actors and the advantage that UPS enjoys from its improvements in fuel consumption may be overshadowed by its underperformance in another area.

Apart from the pressures of the marketplace however, impelling a corporation to adopt sustainable commerce practices through standard corporate governance rules is almost out of reach. Outsiders can encourage corporations to pursue sustainable commerce through market activities such as favoring environmentally preferred companies or boycotting polluters. The effectiveness of these tools is subject to considerable debate. In addition, potential shareholders may have limited ability to determine the environmental performance of firms that they consider investing in. Efforts such as the Carbon Disclosure Project (CDP) have met with cooperation from some firms but have also met with resistance from others. For example, many firms refuse to cooperate with these efforts citing securities rules as a reason to withhold information (Appel and Irvin 2008, pp. 413–14).

Shareholders also enjoy limited means of dubious efficacy to request environmental improvement by the corporations in which they hold an interest. Even if management exposes a firm to great financial liability by ignoring an environmental problem, courts will insulate this decision of management through the business judgment rule. In one typical formulation of this rule:

> It is a presumption that in making a business decision the directors of a corporation acted on an informed basis, in good faith and in the honest belief that the action taken was in the best interests of the company. Absent an abuse of discretion, that judgment will be respected by the courts. The burden is on the party challenging the decision to establish facts rebutting the presumption. (*Aronson v Lewis* 1984)[8]

These examples lead to the conclusion that shareholders cannot successfully sue corporate management for failing to adopt cost saving measures or environmentally advantageous practices such as those found in sustainable commerce except in the rarest circumstances.[9]

To be sure, some observers argue that greater insulation of managerial discretion through the business judgment rule can improve environmental performance by proactive corporations. For example, the American ice cream manufacturer Ben and Jerry's has had a long commitment to several social causes including support for environmentally sound practices. Some of these commitments, such as the firm's support for the World Wildlife Fund, have no tangible relation to the firm's financial performance (unlike the energy savings experienced by UPS); others such as the company's use of recycled paperboard for its ice cream containers represents a sustainable commerce practice that can help the bottom line, depending on the economics of the paperboard industry. In 2000, the international firm Unilever purchased Ben and Jerry's and the founders claimed at the time that management did not resist the takeover for fear of a shareholder lawsuit based on the refusal because the deal was, overall, beneficial to shareholder. Ben and Jerry's has maintained an active CSR agenda since its acquisition by Unilever, but the message is muted from its original levels of commitment (Werther and Chandler [2006] 2011, pp. 374–6). Our estimation is that such instances of activist corporations having their progressive agendas curtailed by the business judgment rule form the exception rather than the rule and that the business judgment rule more often than not insulates corporations that have rejected sustainable commerce measures rather than companies that have pursued these measures too aggressively.

For publicly traded corporations in the US, the securities laws create additional means for shareholders to address sustainable commerce, but these means are also of limited efficacy. Under Securities and Exchange Commission ('SEC') Rule 14a, shareholders of a certain amount can request that a corporation consider adoption of corporate policies by placing a proxy proposal on the agenda for the annual meeting. The rule has standards of who can submit such a request and a corporation that wants to avoid a vote on the resolution and omit the request from its proxy materials must inform the SEC of its intent. The rule provides several reasons for which a corporation may legitimately turn down the request, including that the request presents an issue of special interest 'which is not shared by the shareholders at large' or that the request relates to a matter of 'ordinary business operations' (Shareholder Proposals, 1998). If the SEC agrees with the corporation's decision not to include the request, it issues a no action letter indicating that it will not take action against the firm. Since the late 1990s, investors ranging from pension funds to labor unions to activist groups have filed hundreds of requests to include GCC-related resolutions and requests for change on corporate agendas. Interestingly, the SEC has issued many no action letters either on the ground that the shareholders' proposal for action involves a matter of special interest or because the proposal involves a matter of ordinary business operation. Nevertheless, socially responsible investor groups still use the petition route to attempt to spur corporate reaction. The Investor Network on Climate Risk (a project of the Ceres network of environmentally concerned investors) has announced that in 2010 and 2011 just over 100 such resolutions were filed each year with publicly traded corporations (Ceres 2010). It remains to be seen how many of these resolutions will be presented in proxy statements to shareholders, how often the requested corporations will seek no action letters from the SEC and what impact, if any, the adoption of any of these resolutions will have on individual corporate behavior or GCC. In addition, INCR reported that support among large mutual funds for such resolutions has waned in 2011, when they actually reach the stage of presentation to the shareholders (Berridge and Cook 2011). With all of these conditions it suffices to say that, although this is an available means, it remains insufficient for the task of righting corporate behavior and making a significant dent in GHG emissions.

ADOPTING SUSTAINABLE COMMERCE THROUGH PUBLIC–PRIVATE PARTNERSHIPS

Because the current system of corporate governance has limitations in inspiring the adoption of sustainable commerce, environmental protection requires innovative means of encouraging or impelling the production of sustainable goods and the adoption of sustainable practices. Many of the advances in sustainable commerce have involved private efforts of one firm creating pressure on other firms to meet private environmental targets as well as public environmental objectives.

Case Study: Murray Industries

One case study we have reported before (Appel and Irvin 2008, pp. 407–8) provides an example. The UK home improvement firm B&Q has sustainability objectives that all potential suppliers must meet before B&Q will purchase their products. Murray Industries of Lawrenceburg, Tennessee, is a manufacturer of power lawn equipment and wished to sell its goods to B&Q; securing B&Q's business would not only open the UK but also the EU to Murray. Before it could do so, Murray had to demonstrate its environmental sustainability to B&Q's satisfaction. Murray undertook a complete overhaul of its production systems to meet this challenge. The resulting manufacturing process created linkages between the design team and the manufacturing team so that the design decisions would not inadvertently create environmental problems on the production and manufacturing end. Key to Murray's success was obtaining certification under the ISO 14000-series of environmental standards. This series of company practices, which is created by the private International Standards Organization, creates an iterative process for firms to analyze their activities, plan for how to correct them, implement the changes, evaluate and check to see whether the changes actually reach the desired goal and to review the end result in a form of constant evaluation and improvement. Murray's ISO 14000 certification allowed it to become a B&Q supplier and secure this market. It also improved Murray's environmental performance within the US to the benefit of its local community and domestic customers.

Case Study: Wal-Mart and GHG Reduction

A similar process will be at work with the world's largest retailer. In a recent announcement, Wal-Mart has announced that it aims to reduce carbon emissions from its global supply chain by 20 million metric tons. In establishing this goal, Wal-Mart collaborated with the NGO Environmental Defense, which identified the supply chain as a potentially large source of GHGs. The project also involves the major accounting firm PricewaterhouseCoopers, ClearCarbon Inc, a consulting firm that helps corporations measure their carbon footprint, the CDP and the Applied Sustainability Center ('ASC') at the University of Arkansas. These other actors will certify that the targeted reductions actually take place. According to the Wal-Mart press release, 'This team will identify projects, quantify reductions, engage suppliers and ensure proper procedures are followed for each GHG reduction claim' (Wal-Mart Stores 2010). The process that Wal-Mart and its partners will follow resembles the Murray model: Wal-Mart will first identify products with the highest levels of embedded carbon (with the assistance of the ASC). Wal-Mart will then act on these findings. For a project to be included as part of this goal, it must reduce GHGs from a product in either the sourcing of raw materials, manufacturing, transportation, customer use or end-of-life disposal. Wal-Mart must demonstrate it had direct influence on the reduction and show how that reduction would not have occurred without Wal-Mart's participation. Wal-Mart and its partners will then evaluate whether the reductions occurred and the project is successful:

> ClearCarbon will perform a quality assurance review of those claims to ensure methodology, completeness and calculations are correct. When the claims meet the quality assurance check, PricewaterhouseCoopers will assess under consulting standards whether the defined procedures were followed consistently to quantify the reduction claim. (Wal-Mart Stores 2010)

Wal-Mart's announcement does not indicate whether this will be a continuous process of improvement after the goal of 20 million metric tons of reduction is met. Although Wal-Mart's effort targets only carbon reduction among its suppliers, the effect of this new policy could be substantial given Wal-Mart's size and position in the marketplace.

A Public Model

Public actors could function in the same way as B&Q and Wal-Mart. Public entities are major purchasers of products from automobiles for public fleets to office supplies for governmental functions. Governments have taken baby steps in promoting sustainable commerce through procurement. For example, many government offices require the purchase of recycled paper. Nevertheless, a public requirement that all public suppliers must meet ISO 14000 certification would go a long way to the adoption of sustainable commerce practices. ISO 14000 requires that the suppliers of suppliers also act in an environmentally responsible manner, so imposing this requirement would have consequences that would trickle down through the supply chain. Public entities can also use their debarment authorities to enforce these requirements. Debarment bans a particular company from contracting with the government; most debarment actions occur as a response to an environmental violation. If a corporation cannot contract with the government, management must report that fact to shareholders, who will then put pressure on management to correct the violations (either through selling stock with the effect of decreasing the value of the shares or by petitioning for a correction to the problem).

The ports of Los Angeles and Long Beach provide another example of how public–private partnerships succeed in achieving sustainable commerce in comparison to traditional regulation. These ports combined account for 40 per cent of the goods imported into the US. The ports produce a great deal of carbon emissions and other air pollution, especially ozone and particulate matter. The sources of this pollution not only include the cargo ships themselves (which burn very dirty fuel), but also the emissions from related activities at the port itself, namely: tugboats; out-of-port long-haul trucks; onsite short-haul trucks; and trains. Some of the onsite trucks provide drayage services at the ports, which move containers at the ports and take the goods away from the ports to transshipping facilities or their eventual destination.

The ports adopted measures to reduce emissions and address the pollution. Although the ultimate target is not GHGs, reductions in other targeted emissions will also reduce GHG emissions. The federal *Clean Air Act* establishes a process for the federal government to identify air pollutants that affect public health, and requires that the states adopt State Implementation Plans to achieve the federally established ambient air quality standards. The EPA has classified the Los Angeles area as an extreme nonattainment area for ground-level ozone, a pollutant that has significant public health impacts, including exacerbating lung disease and asthma. Ground-level ozone is formed primarily through the photochemical reaction of pollutants, importantly, motor vehicle emissions (hydrocarbons and nitrogen oxides) in the air. Diesel fuel is a primary fuel source for most of the ships and vehicles at the port. To the extent that an area achieves improvements in its ozone and particulate matter emissions through reduction of motor vehicle emissions, emissions of GHGs will also decrease in that area. EPA has also taken initial regulatory steps to address GHGs under the *Clean Air Act*. Whether or not that act or a new, comprehensive scheme to address GHGs will eventually become the regulatory regime, earlier GHG reduction will assist a geographic area to be on target for meeting initial regulatory goals. In addition, reductions in co-pollutants such as ozone and particulate matter from the program have positive public health impacts in the surrounding community even without regard to GHG reductions.

The ports have adopted a comprehensive plan to reduce emissions and clean up the air at the ports and their surroundings, namely the San

Pedro Bay Ports Clean Air Action Plan (CAAP). The CAAP sets emission requirements on each of the five sources of pollution at the ports, and the overall design of the CAAP is traditional command-and-control regulations. One component of the CAAP is the Clean Trucks Program. The Clean Trucks Program bans trucks with engines built in 1993 or before that date; trucks with engines built between 1994 and 2003 must be retrofitted with filters that cost between $20 000 and $25 000 per truck. These emission limitations ratchet down over time; as of 1 January 2012, all trucks must meet 2007 federal emissions requirements. Since retrofit technology for older trucks is unavailable, this rule essentially requires trucks to have engines from 2007 or later. In addition, the original CAAP contained a concession agreement for licensing trucks allowed to serve the ports. Part of this concession program attempted to reshape the supply market of drayage services at the ports. Because much of the drayage services were supplied by small operators or independent contractors, the ports sought to phase these truckers out in favor of larger entities who would, in the view of the ports, operate more safely and cleanly (*ATA v LA* 2009).

Complicating the design of the CAAP is the relationship between the federal government and the states in the US. As a general matter, the federal government's laws are supreme over those of the states, especially where Congress speaks directly to the issue. Congress has addressed the question of local control over transportation at ports through a provision of the *Federal Aviation Administration Authorization Act* (FAAA Act) of 1994. Specifically, the FAAA Act of 1994 prohibits states from enacting any law, regulation or other provision having the force and effect of law related to a price, route or service of any motor carrier (FAAA Act 2006). The FAAA Act provides an exception, however, for state regulations of motor vehicle safety.[10]

The concession agreement of the Clean Trucks Program was the target of litigation by the American Trucking Associations ('ATA'), a trade group representing many small and independent truckers. The ATA contended that the concessions agreement exceeded the ports' authority to regulate services at the ports because of the preemption provision of the FAAA Act; the ports contended in response that the concession agreements were motor vehicle safety regulations within the authority specifically preserved in the FAAA Act. The litigation was extensive, resulting in several published court opinions[11] and undoubtedly expensive. As of this date, the courts have entered a preliminary injunction against the application of major portions of the concession agreements.

Another part of the CAAP is the Technology Advancement Program ('TAP'), which takes a very different approach to the control of emissions at the ports. Under this program, the Port of Los Angeles seeks to develop new zero-emission technologies for implementation at the port. The Balqon Corporation applied for a grant from the Port of Los Angeles to develop and manufacture an electric truck capable of providing drayage services at the port. The Port of Los Angeles has taken delivery of 25 of Balqon's trucks already (Port of Los Angeles 2011). The Port of LA has become a partner of Balqon's as well through its initial grant to the company. Balqon pays a royalty to the Port of LA for every electric truck sold and it has located its manufacturing plant in Los Angeles to provide jobs to local residents. The Balqon trucks have also been ordered internationally for use in other ports, such as Singapore.

Balqon produces electric trucks for both onsite and offsite transportation. The onsite trucks are meant to transport containers around shipping ports and large warehouses, short-haul yard usage. The primary onsite model carries loads up to 60 000 lb, and has an effective range on a single charge (Balqon 2011). These vehicles are not meant for highway use, as they do not go fast enough or far enough because of their limited battery life (Herron 2009). Nevertheless, the Balqon trucks are perfectly suitable for short-haul transport around a shipyard or marine terminal, which is a significant part of the drayage at the port. The Port of Los Angeles has also recently begun negotiations with Vision Industries about that company's zero-emission hydrogen fuel cell hybrid electric truck (Port of Los Angeles 2011). These trucks have a longer range than the Balqon trucks and could therefore supply some off-port drayage. Depending on the success of these programs, eventually all the trucks could be replaced by zero-emission vehicles.

The Balqon/Port of Los Angeles partnership provides a compelling example of sustainable commerce at work. Rather than resorting to expensive, time-consuming litigation that ultimately did little, if anything, to improve the air quality at the port and in the Los Angeles area, the partnership offers a means for ports to improve the environment, make money for an individual company and the governmental entity. Notably, the Port of Los Angeles and Balqon can (and have already) teamed up to export the drayage truck technology to other ports and thus improve local environments elsewhere and make a small dent in GHG emissions. This provides a positive example of a means to environmental improvement other than through command-and-control regulation. This is not to say that command-and-control regulation played no part in the development of the electric trucks. Without the federal *Clean Air Act* and its requirements to lessen harmful emissions, the Port of Los Angeles may not have had the impetus to develop the Clean Trucks Program. Nevertheless, the partnership between the Port and Los Angeles and

Balqon provides a positive example of sustainable commerce that can then create pressure on other corporations to seek similar positive partnerships.

CONCLUSION AND THE PATH FORWARD

We do not believe that no form of governmental regulation is necessary for the environment or that corporations will make all necessary corrections to their practices on their own. While there are hopeful examples, the counter-examples are legion. Rather, we contend that governments need not reflexively react with command-and-control regulation and ignore other means of achieving environmental improvement. Instead, governments working with firms can require information exchange and disclosure, set aggressive standards in the procurement for potential governmental suppliers (see McCrudden 2007), and become actual partners with suppliers, thereby harnessing the power of the market to impel improvement without costly and time-consuming regulation.

Although we have catalogued examples of how sustainable commerce has now taken place, other situations present themselves. For example, a public–private partnership could more quickly implement the gains from the UPS experiment and make those improvements available across other firms and sectors. Governments could develop a standardized system of measuring and reporting information relevant to traffic flows, and pass on the information to participating companies in real time to corporations seeking to reduce wasteful energy consumption from traffic delays. The SEC could more effectively require disclosure of information related to the environment to facilitate environmentally concerned investors to reallocate their investments towards environmentally friendly firms more rapidly than the present market allows. All of these improvements would ultimately harness the power of the marketplace to encourage environmental improvement; they can be implemented without a huge new command-and-control system; and will therefore achieve benefits more rapidly and cost-effectively than traditional regulation. Although we do not call for the end of the command-and-control system, the sustainable commerce incentives we have will augment the success of the existing legal regime.

Relying on traditional corporate governance structure has produced some environmental gains, but supplemental government regulation is needed for more rapid environmental improvements to be seen within the corporate sector. Sustainable commerce provides a means of achieving economic growth and environmental improvement.

NOTES

1. This variability among shareholders simply on their expected returns from the stock – ranging from increase in share prices to payment of dividends – can affect managerial behavior. Institutional investors such as mutual funds and pension funds often exert power through their investment decisions and proxy voting. They too have responsibilities to their investors and will seek strong share prices, which in turn can affect managerial behavior.
2. The recent negotiations in Copenhagen on the extension and amendment of the Kyoto regime, which itself implemented the Framework Convention on Climate Change, illustrate this point. Most commentators agree that the disorganized conference yielded nothing of significance in terms of enforceable limits on major GHG emitters. To the extent that it did, each of those nations would have to implement the agreed-to limits. The US, which is a major source of GHGs, has so far failed to produce a legislative response to its emissions.
3. Michael Gerrard makes this point. '[T]he remarkable reduction in hazardous waste generation was not dictated by a command-and-control statute; it stemmed in no small part from the costly liability scheme of CERCLA, the costly land disposal restrictions of RCRA, and the publicity penalties of [the Emergency Planning Community Right-to-Know Act]' (Gerrard 2007, p. 44). Enacted in the wake of the Bhopal disaster and a similar occurrence at a plant owned by the same corporation in West Virginia, the *Emergency Planning and Community Right-to-Know Act* requires those who emit toxic substances to report on an annual basis the amounts of their emissions into the air, the water, and on land. Although not a command-and-control regulation per se, it does not limit emissions; it merely requires public disclosure of them. This federal regulation operates through negative incentive, that is, puts pressure on firms to avoid the bad publicity of disclosing their emissions of toxic substances.
4. The *Clean Water Act* provides an example of federal enforcement tools available. The act provides administrative penalties that the Administrator of the US EPA can pursue against a violator. These penalties vary depending on the severity of the offense involved. The act also provides for civil penalties that can be pursued in court, as well as criminal penalties. The offenses can range from actually discharging pollutants into water without a permit, to violating the terms of a permit, to submitting a false statement or failing to maintain required records, to interfering with monitoring equipment. The statutes usually put the maximum amount of the penalty at $25 000 per day. Under the *Federal Civil Penalties Inflation Adjustment Act of 1990*, as amended by the *Debt Collections Improvement Act*, EPA and other agencies are directed to adjust for inflation the statutory civil penalties that may be assessed for violations of the statutes that they administer. The EPA's most recent schedule of civil penalties appears at Civil Monetary Penalty Inflation Adjustment Rule.
5. See: *Toxic Substances Control Act*, *Clean Water Act*, *Resource Conservation and Recovery Act*, *Clean Air Act*, *Comprehensive Environmental Response, Compensation and Liability Act*.
6. For more on Interface Corporation, see its website at www.interfaceglobal.com.
7. Forest Reinhardt similarly claims that '[a]ny story in which the voluntary provision of public goods contributes to shareholder value must invoke market failures besides environmental externalities' (2005, p. 158). He claims that 'in order to make the claim that "it pays to be green," one must implicitly or explicitly invoke some other market failure besides the environmental externalities' (Reinhardt 2005, p. 158). Included in his list of possible culprits is 'asymmetric information.' Thus, although Reinhardt does not state this explicitly, one of the problems inherent in corporate governance, namely asymmetric information, can be seen as a reason that one can predict that corporations will not act in an environmentally beneficial manner even when that behavior would produce profit (through, for example, enhanced revenue, better productivity, or reduced costs).

8. The Delaware Supreme Court overruled *Aronson* with regard to the standard of review applied to lower court decisions on motions to dismiss, see *Brehm v Eisner*, but *Aronson*'s statement of the business judgment rule remains good law.
9. There is a considerable wealth of literature on whether shareholder primacy or board primacy is better for corporate management (see for example Bebchuk 2007; Blair and Stout 1999). This chapter does not take a position on this debate. Rather, the purpose here is to point out the many obstacles that exist in generating pressure for corporations to adopt sustainable commerce measures. All of the stakeholders in a corporation may have an interest in environmental improvement but each one of them has limited leverage to accomplish that task.
10. Specifically, the FAAA Act provides that it does not restrict the safety regulatory authority of a state with respect to motor vehicles, the authority of a state to impose highway route controls or limitations based on the size or weight of the motor vehicle or the hazardous nature of the cargo, or the authority of a state to regulate motor carriers with regard to minimum amounts of financial responsibility relating to insurance requirements and self-insurance authorization (FAAA Act 2006).
11. For example: *ATA v LA 2010, ATA v LA 2009, ATA v LA 2008*.

REFERENCES

Articles, Books and Reports

Appel, P.A. and T.R. Irvin (2008), 'Changing intellectual property and corporate legal structures to promote the U.S. environmental management and technology systems industry', *Boston College Environmental Affairs Law Review*, **35** (3), 397–418.

Bebchuk, L.A. (2007), 'The myth of the shareholder franchise', *Virginia Law Review*, **93** (3), 675–732.

Blair, M.M. and L.A. Stout (1999), 'A team production theory of corporate law', *Virginia Law Review*, **85** (2), 247–328.

Coase, R. (1960), 'The problem of social cost', *Journal of Law and Economics*, **3** (1), 1–44.

Elhauge, Einer R. (2005), 'Corporate managers' operational discretion to sacrifice corporate profits in the public interest', in Bruce L. Hay, Robert N. Stavins and Richard H.K. Vietor (eds), *Environmental Protection and the Social Responsibility of Firms: Perspectives from Law, Economics, and Business*, Washington, DC: Resources for the Future Press, pp. 13–76.

Elkington, John (1997), *Cannibals with Forks: the Triple Bottom Line of 21st-century Business*, Oxford, UK: Capstone Publishing, Inc.

Esty, Daniel C. and Andrew S. Winston (2006), *Green to Gold: How Smart Companies Use Environmental Strategy to Innovate, Create Value, and Build Competitive Advantage*, New Haven, CT and London, UK: Yale University Press.

Friedman, Milton (1962), *Capitalism and Freedom*, Chicago and London: University of Chicago Press.

Friedman, M. (1970), 'The social responsibility of business is to increase its profits', *New York Times Magazine*, 32.

Gerrard, M.B. (2007), 'What the law and lawyers can and cannot do about global warming', *Southeastern Environmental Law Journal*, **16** (1), 33–64.

Gibson, R.B. (ed.) (1999), *Voluntary Initiatives and the New Politics of Corporate Greening*, Peterborough, ON: Broadview Press.
Hoffman, Andrew J. (1997), *From Heresy to Dogma: An Institutional History of Corporate Environmentalism*, San Francisco: The New Lexington Press.
Irvin, T.R., P.A. Appel, J.M. McEntire and J.C. Rabon (2008), 'Kyoto comes to Georgia: how international environmental initiatives foster sustainable commerce in small town America', *Georgia Journal of International and Comparative Law*, **36** (3), 559–613.
McCrudden, Christopher (2007), *Buying Social Justice: Equality, Government Procurement, and Legal Change*, New York and Oxford: Oxford University Press.
Olson, Mancur (1965), *The Logic of Collective Action: Public Goods and the Theory of Groups*, Cambridge, MA: Harvard University Press.
Reinhardt, Forest L. (2005), 'Environmental Protection and the Social Responsibility of Firms: Perspectives from the Business Literature', in Bruce L. Hay et al. (eds), *Environmental Protection and the Social Responsibility of Firms*, pp. 151–83.
Savitz, A.W. and K. Weber (2006), *The Triple Bottom Line: How Today's Best-Run Companies Are Achieving Economic, Social and Environmental Success – and How You Can Too*, San Francisco: Jossey-Bass.
Watson, R.T., M.-C. Boudreau, S. Li and J. Levis (2010), 'Telematics at UPS: en route to energy informatics', *MIS Quarterly Executive*, **9** (1), 1–11.
Werther, William B. Jr. and David Chandler (2011), *Strategic Corporate Social Responsibility: Stakeholders in a Global Environment*, Thousand Oaks, CA: SAGE Publications.

Jurisprudence

American Trucking Associations, Inc v City of Los Angeles (2008), 577 F Supp (2d) 1110 (CD Cal) [*ATA v LA* 2008].
American Trucking Associations, Inc v City of Los Angeles (2009), 559 F (3d) 1046 (9th Cir) [*ATA v LA* 2009].
American Trucking Associations, Inc v City of Los Angeles (2010), 596 F (3d) 602 (9th Cir) [*ATA v LA* 2010].
Aronson v Lewis (1984), 473 A (2d) 805 (Del Sup Ct).
Brehm v Eisner (2000), 746 A (2d) 244 (Del Sup Ct).

Statutes and Regulations

Civil Monetary Penalty Inflation Adjustment Rule, 73 Fed Reg 75340 (11 Dec 2008), corrected, 74 Fed Reg 626 (7 Jan 2009).
Clean Air Act, USC 2006, c 42 s 7401.
Clean Water Act, USC 2006, c 33, s 1251.
Comprehensive Environmental Response, Compensation, and Liability Act, USC 2006, c 42, s 9601.
Debt Collections Improvement Act, USC 2006, c 31, s 3701.
Emergency Planning and Community Right-to-Know Act, USC 2006, c 42, s 11001.
Federal Aviation Administration Authorization Act (FAAA Act), USC 2006, c 29, s 14501.

Federal Civil Penalties Inflation Adjustment Act of 1990, USC 2006, c 28, s 2461.
Regulation (EC) No 1907/2006 of the European Parliament and of the Council of 18 December 2006 concerning the Registration, Evaluation, Authorization and Restriction of Chemicals (REACH), 2007 *Official Journal of the European Union* (L 136) 3.
Resource Conservation and Recovery Act, USC 2006, c 42, s 6901.
Shareholder Proposals, CFR 1998, c 17, s 240.
Toxic Substances Control Act, USC 2006, c 15, s 2601–92.

Web Resources

Balqon Corporation, 'Nautilus XE20', available at http://www.balqon.com/product_details.php?pid=1 (accessed 21 April 2011).
Berridge, R. and J. Cook (2011), 'New Ceres survey data: U.S. mutual funds backtrack in supporting climate resolutions in 2010', available at http://www.ceres.org/resources/reports/new-ceres-survey-data-u.s.-mutual-funds-backtrack-in-supporting-climate-resolutions-in-2010/view (accessed 21 April 2011).
Ceres (2010), 'Climate and energy resolutions 2011', available at http://www.incr.com/resolutions (accessed 21 April 2011).
Herron, D. (2009), 'Balqon introduces a zero-emission heavy-duty electric truck meant for short-haul delivery', Examiner, available at http://www.examiner.com/green-transportation-in-national/balqon-introduces-a-zero-emission-heavy-duty-electric-truck-meant-for-short-haul-delivery (accessed 21 April 2011).
Interface, Inc (2008), 'Interface', available at http://www.interfaceglobal.com/ (accessed 21 April 2011).
The Port of Los Angeles (2011), 'Port of Los Angeles Electric Trucks', available at http://www.portoflosangeles.org/environment/etruck.asp (accessed 21 April 2011).
Wal-Mart Stores (2010), 'Wal-Mart announces goal to eliminate 20 million metric tons of greenhouse gas emissions from global supply chain', available at http://walmartstores.com/pressroom/news/9668,aspx (accessed 21 April 2011).

12. Codes of ethics and corporate governance – a study of New Zealand listed companies

Trish Keeper

INTRODUCTION

Corporate ethics and codes of ethics have received a great deal of attention in recent years; years that have been colored by numerous high-profile corporate scandals and changes. These events emphasize that compliance with the law does not guarantee ethical behavior and that 'moral responsibility in the corporate domain cannot be reduced to obeying the law' (Kaptein and Wempe 2002, p. 23). As the Enron collapse illustrated '[w]hatever law, and whatever kind of law, is put in place for controlling business, it is mined for opportunities for circumvention' (McBarnet 2006, p. 35). However, while society, and for the most part companies and those who manage them, now accepts that corporations should behave ethically, there continues to be a degree of ambivalence with regard to attributing corporations with ethical responsibilities for wider stakeholder and societal interests (Kaptein and Wempe 2002, p. 39). Primarily, this reluctance flows from a theoretical disagreement as to the nature of a company. Those who advocate that a company's principal objective is to maximize the return to shareholders contend that it is unethical for a company to consider the rights and interests of any other group (Friedman 1970). On the other side are those who reject this strict profit maximization approach in favor of some wider responsibility.

Among proponents of the viewpoint that corporations do have ethical responsibilities beyond share value maximization (either as a normative belief, or under the banner of stakeholder theory or corporate social responsibility), there is, however, a diverse range of views on that wider accountability. There are also conflicting views as to how, and to what extent, ethics should be formalized into business policies, practices and processes. As Milton-Smith observed in 1997 with respect to Australian and New Zealand companies, 'although directors clearly recognize ethics is a priority issue, they still have problems in conceptualizing how they should deal with it' (Milton-Smith 1997, p. 1492).

Within this context, the chapter begins by providing an overview of the incentives or motivations for changing attitudes towards corporate ethical behavior since the 1970s. It argues that these are largely identical to the forces that have driven corporate governance reforms during the same period and that the business ethics movement has largely been subsumed into a more general focus on the governance of corporations. For example, the obligation for directors, managers and employees to act ethically and for a company to have issued a corporate code of ethics is now considered orthodox corporate governance practice in most jurisdictions. The chapter then overviews the central aspects of recent research on ethics and its relationship with corporate governance, including critical theory researchers who argue that the hegemony of the adoption of ethical codes within corporate governance has resulted in the institutionalization or capture of ethics – a result, critical theorists assert, which forecloses discussion on the nature of ethical behavior for particular organizations.

The second half of the chapter reviews the changing regulatory incentives for codes of ethics and examines the requirements with respect to ethical decision making and codes of ethics for companies listed on the New Zealand Exchange's principal exchange (NZSX). It also sets out the findings of disclosure practices with respect to codes of ethics for NZSX companies. The findings indicate that New Zealand companies, which are only listed on the NZSX, appear not to place a high degree of importance on ethical practices. The results suggest that, comparative to overseas jurisdictions, New Zealand listed companies have a low level of adoption of corporate codes of ethics, although it is not possible to form a conclusive opinion on this point.

BUSINESS ETHICS

The Rise of Business Ethics

The origins of corporate or business ethics as an identifiable movement have been traced to the mid-1970s, although commentators differ as to the reasons for its genesis at that time. Kaptein and Wempe (2002) identified six interlinked factors; in their view the most influential was the emergence of the information age (pp. 31–9). The rise of information technology not only allowed business to be involved in high-level globalized information exchange, but also encouraged shareholders and other stakeholders, through media such as the internet, to monitor corporate activities more actively. The rise of the information age was also causal in the shift from the highly centralized, regulated social order of the 1950s and 1960s to one that was comparatively decentralized – a society that required the adoption of 'a new or different type of business ethic' in that the 'trend to decentralization [had] brought greater social responsibility for business' (ibid., p. 32). Additionally economic changes since the 1980s associated with the collapse of eastern European socialist or communist economies and increased privatization in western nations, together with the sustained growth of multinational corporations, changed the traditional regulatory power of the state (ibid., p. 33). Non-governmental organizations representing environmental interests or human rights groups also started to have a stronger role, supported by technology developments – in particular, the internet. Similarly, a study of the codes of ethics of transnational corporations stated that the source of a more comprehensive global business ethics program was the increasing internationalization of business, together with pressure from non-governmental organizations (Carasco and Singh 2003, p. 71).

Kaptein and Wempe (2002) further argued that a consequence of these developments was a growing mistrust of business. However, at the same time as corporations became more decentralized, flexible and multi-jurisdictional, employees had greater opportunities for autonomy and the exercise of discretion. Businesses needed to become increasingly reliant on trust, rather than the traditional methods of supervision and monitoring of managers and employees. Accordingly, Kaptein and Wempe contended that the combination of technological and economic changes resulted in the decline of centralized regulatory authority, increasing reliance on trust and therefore the need for corporations to adhere to good ethical practices. The final factor they identified was the increasing costs of corporate irresponsibility, not just in terms of fines but also in terms of corporate reputation and customer and supplier loyalty (pp. 37–8). Stevens (2008) identified that corporate scandals proliferated in the US after the Watergate incident and the resignation of President Nixon in 1974, and continued for several decades thereafter. This was a key factor in the public's mistrust of corporations. She argued that the scandals resulted in corporations turning to ethical codes to promote and publicize both their integrity and merits (p. 601), although Stevens has acknowledged that their benefits other than enhancing reputation continue to be debated. Brickley and others observed that uncertainty over what behavior was accepted as 'right', owing to social and technological changes, together with changing standards of acceptable behavior 'brought about by movements as disparate as civil rights and women's rights, on the one hand, and corporate restructuring and stakeholder theory, on the other' (Brickley et al. 2005, p. 112), led to growing doubt as to what was acceptable behavior. Corporations, especially in the US, responded by creating formal codes of ethics to eliminate the uncertainty about ethical standards and setting down in writing the expected norms of behavior.

Comparatively little research in New Zealand on attitudes to business ethics has been carried out. Milton-Smith (1997), writing on the state of business ethics in Australia and New Zealand, was of the view that the 'perceived excesses' of the 1980s had led to the increased focus on business ethics. He commented that in this decade every state in Australia had a Royal Commission on some aspect of corruption. He identified the stock market crash of 1987, especially in New Zealand, as a 'catalyst for creating new ethical responsibilities' (p. 1486). In his view, international factors such as globalization and rising community expectations with respect to corporate social responsibility applied equally to Australasian companies. At the time of the study, in comparison to Australia, he considered that New Zealand businesses 'placed less emphasis on ethical standards and protection' (ibid., p. 1487), although he indicated that attitudes were beginning to change in New Zealand. He referred to a survey undertaken in 1993 of New Zealand's top 200 companies (Kazi 1993).[1] The survey results suggested that a majority of companies gave 'relatively low priorities to ethical value' (ibid., p. 435) and instead prioritized objectives such as a superior rate of return, superior customer service and market share. Interestingly with respect to codes of ethics, more than half the respondents stated they published a code of ethics, and in general there was strong support for published codes of ethics (ibid., p. 436). In a subsequent 1999 study of middle- and lower-level managers, Kazi also found that New Zealand companies gave low priorities to ethics compared to other corporate values (Kazi 1999).

This conclusion was echoed in a recent study by Transparency International New Zealand. In February 2010 it published a report on the disclosure of codes of ethics by companies listed on the NZX 50 index with specific focus on approaches taken by companies to bribery and corruption. The research found that 'many of New Zealand's largest listed businesses don't pass some fundamental best practice ethics tests' (Transparency International New Zealand 2010, p. 2).

Business Ethics: Contested Territory

As discussed in the introduction, corporate or business ethics continues to be contested territory and the intention of the following paragraphs is merely to provide an overview of ongoing debates and more recent criticisms. Milton Friedman is commonly represented as the 'poster boy' of the opponents of business ethics and corporate social responsibility. Friedman stated that in a free economy

> [T]here is one and only one social responsibility of business – to use its resources and engage in activities designed to increase its profits so long as it stays within the rules of the game, which is to say, engages in free and open competition, without deception and fraud. (Friedman 1962, p. 113)

From the beginning of the business ethics movement, statements of business ethics and codes of ethics have been subject to the criticism that they are little more than a form of risk management, both in terms of reputational advantages and as an instrument of agency control on the scope of directors' and managers' discretion. For some, the utility of a code of ethics as a form of control system on management discretion is the only valid justification for its adoption (Trevino and Weaver 2003, pp. 89–123). Sacconi in *The Social Contract of the Firm* argued that corporate codes of ethics are economically rational as they provide a form of social contract between the constituents of a corporation, which reduces corporate governance problems caused both by the opportunism of agents and incomplete contracts (Sacconi 2000). According to his social contract justification, compliance with the principles of such a code is the only rational option for persons interacting within the firm (ibid., pp. 16–18). Others have also argued that a business code can be 'seen as a description of the social contract between corporations and their stakeholders. Such a code shows how the rights of stakeholders should be respected' (Kaptein and Wempe 2002, p. 272). They define a business code as a document that 'indicates the basic corporate responsibilities toward stakeholders, and that formulates virtues and principles applicable to the entire corporation' (ibid.). Social contract theorists have gained some support in recent years, but in general the debate about the theoretical foundation of business ethics continues.

Codes of Ethics

Irrespective of this theoretical debate and the lack of 'convergence regarding the precise moral duties owed by company managers' (du Plessis et al. 2005, p. 347), the reality is that, internationally, business ethics and the adoption of a code of ethics have become an accepted part of business. Starting from the mid-1970s, an increasing number of corporations, especially in the US, adopted codes of ethics or conduct as well as appointing ethics officers and establishing ethics training programs (Chew and Gillan 2005, p. 103). In the US over 90 per cent of large corporations had a code of ethics by 1992, while in Canada over 85 per cent had a code by 2000 and in Germany and the UK a majority of the largest corporations had codes by the late 1990s (Schwartz 2002, p. 27). One consequence of the increasing number of corporations with codes of ethics has been an intensified research focus on codes of ethics or conduct.

A great deal of the initial research examined why companies decided to adopt codes and how specific codes were formulated and implemented. This type of research appears to have largely disappeared in recent years, no doubt in part due to the fact that codes of ethics are now generally accepted, if not required, as part of a company's corporate governance processes. In addition, although research results have not been unanimous, the 'corpus of ethical code research has yielded sufficient data to show that codes are effective' (Stevens 2008, p. 606), which may also explain why such research has declined. More recent research, as published in management literature as well as in the growing number of publications exclusively devoted to business ethics, has focused on the effectiveness of codes and the related question of whether business ethics does in fact influence or militate corporate and employee behavior (Kaptein and Wempe 2002; Trevino and Weaver 2003; Campbell and Kitson 2008). Associated studies have considered the content of ethical codes, either normatively or descriptively. Normative approaches to codes of ethics operate on the assumption that codes need to go beyond requiring compliance with legal requirements but should encompass universal moral standards such as trustworthiness, respect, accountability or responsibility, fairness, and caring in the sense of avoiding unnecessary harm (Schwartz 2002, p. 29). Schwartz (2002) has also argued that factors such as prioritization of values, comprehensibility, and avoiding vague statements in favor of clear identification of expected behavior, length and achievability are relevant considerations. Descriptive business ethics describes the ethical beliefs or practices of various business entities and attempts to rationalize them.

Emerging critical theory research on business ethics and codes of ethics asserts that current approaches are both narrow and predetermined (Parker 1998; Crane and Matten 2004; Jones et al. 2005). Jones, Parker and ten Bos are representative of a growing critical approach to business ethics as it exists today. They argue that a great deal of business ethics, as it is currently perceived, is no more than common sense, or a set of excuses for being unpleasant (Jones et al. 2005, p. 3). Further, they claim that current business ethics has been given a narrow and restricted scope, thereby foreclosing discussion and confining its application to certain prescribed areas. The authors detail six problems or foreclosures with business ethics in its current state, but their essential criticism is that business codes of conduct, by designating certain things as ethical, by implication create a perception that things which are excluded from such codes do not involve ethical considerations. Their complaint is that 'other things are treated, explicitly or implicitly, as if they do not involve ethical questions' (ibid., p. 5). Similarly, if the idea of ethics is to challenge and question, it should include considerations of the underlying business and political structures. That business ethics currently operates within market economies without challenging or even attempting to challenge the distribution of wealth and power illustrates how the current state of business ethics forecloses discussion of the appropriateness of existing corporate governance rules as well as political systems (ibid., pp. 6–7).

CORPORATE GOVERNANCE

Development

The corporate governance debate can be traced in history as far back as the South Sea Bubble (1720). This chapter focuses on developments since World War II. It is during this period that institutional shareholders and multinational and transnational corporations emerged. Additionally, during the post-war period theoretical challenges to orthodox views of the role of the company emerged out of a sense of dissatisfaction with the existing managerial capitalist approaches based on assumptions of dispersed shareholding and share value maximization. The subsequent intense focus on the rules that govern corporations, and on those who manage them, resulted in a plethora of governmental commissions and industry-led reviews focusing on 'good' governance. This focus also led to the development of corporate governance as a separate discipline (Clarke 2007, p. 1, citing World Bank 2000). Tricker stated that the significance of the field of corporate governance research, as separate from the study of company law, had only been recognized relatively recently (Tricker 1994). He considered this emphasis on the study of corporate governance was a result of the activities of certain high-profile corporate predators in the previous decade and the emergence of new forms of corporate structures (ibid., pp. xi–xii) – structures which are both multi-jurisdictional and massively complex. Farrar suggests that the managers of leading companies in the 1990s started to turn their attention to the promotion of self-regulation to 'ward off the increasing politicization of reform of corporate law, to combat increased shareholder activism and simply out of self protection' (Farrar 1999, p. 266).

Clarke in *International Corporate Governance – A Comparative Approach* suggests the current focus on corporate governance can be explained by a number of factors, many of which mirror events or changes that have been identified as drivers in the development of business ethics (Clarke 2007). He identified the vast growth of deregulated capital markets as well as massive expansion in the activities of multinational corporations – to the extent that they can determine the prosperity of national economies. Additionally, because of the rapidly increasing proportion of individual wealth held by institutional investors such as pension funds, there has been an increasing awareness of the need to ensure such investments are secure through monitoring and improved standards of governance. Finally, he argues that there is a general trend in society 'facilitated by new technology and social awareness, towards developing greater openness, transparency and disclosure' (ibid., p. 1), which again has been a key force in the development of business ethics.

Position in New Zealand

While some of the factors with respect to corporate governance reform, discussed above, have greater applicability to events and developments in the US, Europe and the UK, it is important to keep in mind that the underlying themes in the history of corporate governance are of an 'international nature' (Farrar 1999, p. 260). Historically, international developments have shaped the rules that regulate New Zealand's capital markets and undoubtedly will continue to be influential in the future. As Farrar stated with respect to New Zealand and Australia, the rules regulating the governance of companies and financial markets 'owe much to their colonial inheritance and are currently influenced by North American ideas and yet do business with South East Asia where many of the legal systems are of a different background and history' (ibid.).

Definition of Corporate Governance and Its Link to Ethics

There are many definitions of corporate governance. For the purpose of simplicity, the Organisation for Economic Co-operation and Development (OECD) definition is provided:

> Corporate governance involves a set of relationships between a company's management, its board, its shareholders and other stakeholders. Corporate governance also provides the structure through which the objectives of the company are set, and the means of attaining those objectives and monitoring performance are determined. Good corporate governance should provide proper incentives to the board and management to pursue objectives that are in the interests of the company and its shareholders and should facilitate effective monitoring. The presence of an effective corporate governance system, within an individual

> company and across an economy as a whole, helps to provide a degree of confidence that is necessary for the proper functioning of a market economy. As a result, the cost of capital is lower and firms are encouraged to use resources more efficiently, thereby underpinning growth. (OECD 2004, p. 1)

The definition not only focuses on the existence of certain structures within companies, but also on how objectives are to be achieved and performance is to be monitored. It is not sufficient to have in place policies and procedures that comply with 'best practice' governance standards if they are not enforced or monitored. Good corporate practices require a culture of openness and honesty within an organization. As Campbell and Kitson state, 'the values regarded as important by the "corporate governance" approach are derived from a view of the everyday business virtues that make business life possible. These include openness, honesty in dealings and compliance with what is regarded, within the business community, as good business practices' (Campbell and Kitson 2008, p. 25).

Furthermore, many writers and commentators contend that if companies adopt an ethical approach to corporate governance policies and practices, in contrast to a legal approach, this avoids a tick-box or legalistic mentality towards compliance with the policies and practices. Arjoon states:

> [T]he difficulty with legal compliance mechanisms is that many abuses that have enraged the public are entirely legal, for example, companies can file misleading accounting statements that are in complete compliance with Generally Accepted Accounting Principles (GAAP). (Arjoon 2005, p. 344)

Arjoon (2005) makes a distinction between a legal approach and an ethical approach to ethics. Under a legal approach, ethics is regarded as a set of limits or something that has to be done, with the objective of preventing unlawful conduct. The legal approach emphasizes rules and requires monitoring and penalties to enforce these rules, based on deterrence. In contrast, an ethical approach views ethics as a set of principles to guide choices, with the aim of achieving responsible conduct. An ethical approach views ethics as permeating every part of an organization's business practice and is based on individual and communal values (pp. 347–9).

Inherent in the legal approach is a capture or institutionalization of moral principles within 'best practice' or 'standard' corporate governance codes. It was recently stated, after reviewing the corporate governance codes developed in the US, UK and Canada, that while generally encouraging 'economic wellbeing and corporate profit pursuits, [these] standards of [corporate governance] have generally grounded ethical values and notions of good corporate behavior within such codes' (Bhimani 2008,

p. 137). This in itself may not seem controversial, but as Bhimani points out, the US and UK codes of best practice give support to and are based on agency theory and transaction cost economics theoretical approaches. He states 'they are underpinned by certain common assumptions concerning the wealth maximization objectives of enterprises, human motivation and managerial self interest. These assumptions have, in turn, led to corporate governance codes reflecting concerns relating to transparency, disclosure and trust' (ibid., p. 140). The danger for business ethics being so closely intertwined within corporate governance processes based on certain theoretical perspectives is the potential for undermining ethics and the independence of thought that is critical for ethical judgment.

These concerns aside, the chapter at this point examines how codes of ethics now form part of codes of corporate governance practice both internationally, with reference to the US and Australia, and in New Zealand.

REGULATORY REFORMS

Increased Disclosure

As set out above, large corporations adopting codes of ethics or corporate conduct has been orthodox practice in overseas jurisdictions, especially the US, for many years, although the incentives for this practice have changed in the last decade. Since the large-scale corporate failures that marked the final years of the twentieth century and the first years of the twenty-first century, many countries have enacted measures to increase disclosure of information relating to the financial and non-financial performance of companies. Increased disclosure enhances the accountability of corporate officers and operates to ensure the independence of advisers. In addition, many countries and organizations have formulated 'soft laws' such as codes of corporate governance practice. Stock exchanges have also augmented listing requirements with respect to corporate governance policies and practices and included rules on ethical decision making and codes of ethics.

United States

A crucial change with regard to codes of ethics was the enactment in the US of the *Public Accounting Reform and Investor Protection Act* (commonly known as the *Sarbanes-Oxley Act* (SOX)) in 2002. In terms of discouraging unethical practices, SOX introduced a number of measures to reduce conflicts of interest among board members and enhance audit independence as well as augment existing independent director rules. For codes of ethics, the only significant change SOX introduced was to require public companies to adopt and publish codes of ethics for senior financial officers. The SOX reforms were followed by changes to NYSE (2011) and NASDAQ (2009) listing rules. They also resulted in changes to the Federal Sentencing Guidelines (USSC 2010) in the US (known as the 'Corporate Sentencing Guidelines'), which are designed to encourage companies not merely to have a code of ethics but also to ensure that employees are adequately trained and compliance is monitored. Sentences given to corporate offenders may be reduced or mitigated if a court is convinced that the offending was caused by an employee acting alone, contrary to the practices and culture of the corporation.

Comparing codes of ethics in US corporations both before and after SOX and the introduction of the amended Guidelines, Canary and Jennings stated that, post-SOX, 'the rote checklist of components . . . no longer suffice[d] for lack of culpability because managers and organizations [were] held accountable for both dissemination and understanding among employees (Canary and Jennings 2008, p. 264). This approach was reinforced by a subsequent United States Justice Department Memorandum, which outlined the principles of federal prosecution of business organizations (Thompson 2003). This Memorandum affirmed that it was not sufficient that corporations had established some form of compliance program, but that it must be 'designed and implemented in an effective manner' (ibid.). Only when a prosecutor is satisfied that 'a corporation has adopted and implemented a truly effective compliance program . . . may [it] result in a decision to charge only the corporation's employees and agents' (ibid.).

Position in Australia

Australia has chosen to adopt the UK Cadbury Code approach, whereby companies are given the opportunity to comply with best practices formulated in a code (Cadbury Committee 1992). If a company decides to not follow all or some parts of the code, it must explain why it has not done so. Australian Stock Exchange (ASX) Listing Rule 4.10.3, with regard to annual reports, requires disclosure by an entity of the extent to which it has 'followed the best practice recommendations set by the ASX Corporate Governance Council during the reporting period. If the entity has not followed all of the recommendations, it is required to identify those recommendations it has not followed and give reasons for not following them' (ASX 2008).

The ASX Corporate Governance Council (ASX CGC) was set up in

2002 and is now 'the main contributor to corporate governance policy and practice in Australia' (Psaros 2009, p. 45) as it is responsible for the development and monitoring of ASX's Corporate Governance Principles and Recommendations (ASX CGC 2010). The ASX CGC is made up of 21 representatives from the legal and accounting professions, business groups and the financial sector. Principle 3 of the Governance Principles and Recommendations provides that 'companies should actively promote ethical and responsible decision-making'. To this end, it is recommended that companies establish a code of conduct and disclose either the entire code or its summary as it relates to:

- the practices necessary to maintain confidence in a company's integrity;
- the practices necessary to take into account the legal obligations of companies and the reasonable expectations of their stakeholders; and
- the responsibility and accountability of individuals for reporting and investigating reports of unethical practices.

In addition, there is a recommendation that companies establish and disclose a trading policy applicable to executives, directors and employees when trading in the company's securities. The commentary attached to Principle 3 suggests the minimum content requirements for ethics codes, including (1) statements about the core values and aspirations of the company, (2) the company's perceptions of responsibilities to its stakeholders, (3) its approach to the community, and (4) the company's employment practices. In addition to corporate social responsibility disclosures, the commentary suggests that disclosures should reflect a company's commitment to compliance with its legal obligations. These include compliance with legal requirements, avoiding conflicts of interest and measures to promote disclosure of unethical conduct, including whistleblowing procedures. Finally it is recommended that the means by which a company monitors and ensures compliance with its code are disclosed.

Regulatory Requirements in New Zealand

Alignment with international practices

New Zealand during the last decade has also institutionalized codes of ethics within the 'best practice' corporate governance rules. The NZSX Listing Rules were amended in 2003, and in February 2004 the Securities Commission of New Zealand published its *Corporate Governance in New Zealand: Principles and Guidelines* (*NZ Principles and Guidelines*). These measures were part of a deliberate policy to align New Zealand with international developments by including within the corporate governance best practices framework explicit expectations of ethical decision making and personal behavior (Securities Commission of NZ 2004). As stated in November 2002, '[c]onvergence with international best practice in financial reporting, corporate governance, and market regulation will enhance the reputation of our capital markets' (Securities Commission of NZ 2002).

New Zealand Securities Commission's Principles and Guidelines

The *NZ Principles and Guidelines* set out nine Principles with the intention that once the Principles had been implemented by directors and boards 'through their structures, processes, and actions' and by demonstration in public reporting and disclosure, this would foster high standards of corporate governance in New Zealand (Securities Commission of NZ 2004, p. 3). The Securities Commission's approach relies heavily on disclosure of corporate governance practice, principally in annual reports, and was not intended to create an additional or dual reporting regime. It opined that for listed companies or issuers with high standards of governance and disclosure requirements under the listing rules, adoption of the Principles and Guidelines would 'not impose any new requirements or additional reporting' (ibid., p. 7).

The Securities Commission of NZ (2004) identified as Principle One that 'directors should observe and foster high ethical standards' as ethical behavior. This is treated as 'central to all aspects of good corporate behavior' (ibid., p. 9). The Guidelines associated with Principle One state that boards should adopt a code of ethics for the entity that sets out 'explicit expectations for ethical decision making and personal behaviour' (Securities Commission of NZ 2004). The Guidelines also detail the matters which should be included within such codes. These include dealing with conflicts of interest, using company property, safeguards against insider trading, fair dealing with third parties, policies for dealing with gifts and bribes, compliance with the law, and reporting unethical decision making. Additionally, the Guidelines state that the code should contain procedures for dealing with breaches, requirements to communicate the code to employees, employee training, and the adoption of policies to review the code and monitor adherence to it. Finally, the Guidelines recommend that the code be published together with the policies relating to review and monitoring.

The *NZ Principles and Guidelines* state that issuers should disclose in their annual reports how they achieve the Principles, but there is a substantial degree of non-compliance with this expectation. As discussed later in this chapter, only a minority of the companies solely listed on the NZSX in fact make any explicit reference to the *NZ Principles and Guidelines* in their governance disclosures. With specific respect to codes of ethics disclosures, the Securities Commission states that entities should report how they achieve the Principles. Distinct from the Guidelines, there is no expectation that companies report against individual matters within the Guidelines, such as the adoption of a corporate code of ethics. Finally, in terms of surveillance of corporate disclosures, at the time of writing the Securities Commission only regularly reported on its surveillance of financial reporting by issuers in prospectuses, continuous disclosure notices and sections of annual reports. There was irregular surveillance of other corporate governance disclosures (Chen and Cotton 2006; Securities Commission of NZ 2010).

New Zealand Stock Exchange (NZSX) Listing Rules

The NZSX Listing Rules also incorporate requirements for ethical behavior and codes of ethics within its corporate governance rules. It has also adopted a self-regulatory approach whereby it is up to issuers to disclose compliance with such rules. Rule 10.5.5 of the Listing Rules applicable to issuers listed on the NZSX (main board) and NZDX (debt securities) provides that each issuer's annual report must contain certain information (NZSX 2009). With regard to corporate governance, an annual report must contain:

(h) a statement of any corporate governance policies, practices and processes, adopted and followed by the issuer; and
(i) a statement on whether, and if so, how the corporate governance principles adopted and followed by the issuer materially differ from the Corporate Governance Best Practice Code or a clear reference to where such statement may be found on the issuer's public website.

Appendix 16 to the Listing Rules contains the NZSX Corporate Governance Best Practice Code (NZSX Code). With reference to codes of ethics, the NZSX Code provides (NZSX 2009):

A. Background: Pursuant to NZSX Listing Rule 10.5.5(h), Issuers shall disclose in their annual reports the extent to which its corporate governance processes materially differ from the principles set out in the NZX Corporate Governance Best Practice Code ('the Code').
B. Preamble: The Code sets out principles to enhance investor confidence through corporate governance and accountability. The Code is composed of flexible principles which recognise differences in corporate size and culture.

1. Code of Ethics
1.1 An Issuer should formulate a code of ethics to govern its conduct
1.2 The code of ethics should address ethical issues, establish compliance standards and procedures, provide mechanisms to report unethical behaviour and ensure that disciplinary measures are in place for any violations.
1.3 When drafting the code of ethics, the Issuer should consider the following matters:

> conflicts of interest; and
> receipt and use of corporate information; and
> receipt and use of corporate assets and property; and
> Directors giving proper attention to the matters before them; and
> a general obligation to act honestly and in the best interests of the Issuer as required by law; and
> compliance with any other applicable laws, regulations and rules.

These rules give rise to a number of concerns. Firstly, the failure to adopt consistent language between the Listing Rules and the NZSX Code creates confusion as to what must be disclosed. Rule 10.5.5(h) requires disclosure of all corporate governance 'policies, practices and processes', which appears to require issuers to disclose in detail their day-to-day corporate governance rules. The term 'policy' is defined in the *Concise Oxford Dictionary* (ed. Allen 1990) as a course or principle of action adopted or proposed by a government, party, business or individual. 'Practice' is defined as including the actual application or use of an idea and also a customary, habitual or expected procedure or way of doing something. Finally, a 'process' refers to a series of actions or steps taken in order to achieve a particular end. In addition, Rule 10.5.5(i) requires disclosure of a statement as to the corporate governance 'principles' of the issuer, which at best could be the issuer's policies, but would be something different than its practices and processes. This statement must disclose whether such principles differ and, if so, how they differ from the Best Practice Code in the Appendix to the Rules. Things become more complicated as the NZSX Code requires disclosure of the extent to which an issuer's corporate governance 'processes' materially differ from the principles set out in the Code.

As a second point, the Listing Rules requires issuers to disclose whether, and if so how, the issuer's corporate governance principles materially differ from the NZSX Code. Appendix 16, clause A, simply requires disclosure of the extent to which an issuer's practices differ from the Code. Accordingly neither requirement demands that an issuer provide an explanation as to why a company has chosen not to follow 'best practice' as set out in the NZSX Code. This is a less onerous requirement than the 'comply or explain' approach prevailing in the UK and Australia.

Further, the required and suggested contents of a code of ethics detailed in Appendix 16, clauses 1.2 and 1.3, are less demanding than those of the ASX CGC and the Securities Commission's *NZ Principles and Guidelines*. It is unclear whether a code should include all the matters detailed in clauses 1.2 and 1.3 or just the minimum requirements of clause 1.3. This is important because clause 1.2 appears to take a wider approach to the content of codes of ethics, whereas clause 1.3 provides a limited list of matters an issuer should consider for inclusion and, at least in respect of directors, does not significantly extend beyond matters that are already regulated by the New Zealand *Companies Act 1993* or the common law. Although research to date has not examined in detail the content of the codes of ethics, initial analysis has revealed that in a minority of the companies surveyed the codes of ethics do not include matters beyond the matters specified in clause 1.3. However, as the NZSX Code does not require issuers to publish their code of ethics, it is not possible to reach any firm conclusion on the content of codes.

Analysis of NZSX issuers

The research initially involved analysis of the corporate governance disclosures with respect to ethical practices and codes of ethics for all companies with securities listed on the NZSX and the alternative exchange (NZAX), as on 1 March 2010. Analysis is based on information taken from the latest annual reports for each company available in the Investment Research Group database,[2] supplemented by corporate governance information on individual company websites. Although 148[3] securities were listed on the NZSX and 27 companies on the NZAX on this date, the corporate governance practices of only 94 issuers have been considered for the analysis. The securities that were excluded fall into three categories, as explained below.

Exclusions

Funds and multiple securities. First, the securities of traded funds such as AMP Investments World Index Fund, the Australian 20 Leaders Fund and the four NZX Index Funds were excluded given the governance structures of such funds. Secondly, as the focus was on the ethical practices of issuers, it was irrelevant if an issuer had more than one class of securities listed on the NZSX. A number of securities were discounted for this reason.

Overseas issuers The most significant category of excluded companies comprised those also listed on an overseas exchange (overseas companies). In this category are companies that are domiciled in New Zealand but also listed on an overseas exchange, and companies domiciled overseas and also listed on the NZSX. These companies were excluded for two reasons. First, as such companies are subject to the listing rules of an overseas exchange, their corporate governance policies and codes of ethics disclosures should reflect the requirements of that jurisdiction. Companies listed on recognized overseas exchanges, such as the ASX, are deemed to comply with the NZSX Listing Rules provided such companies remain listed on the overseas exchange and comply with the Listing Rules of that Exchange. Accordingly, overseas companies are not subject to NZSX Listing Rules and the NZSX Code and do not need to disclose compliance or otherwise with the NZSX Code.

The second reason that overseas company were excluded is that applicable overseas codes or rules generally require a higher level of corporate governance disclosure than currently mandated in New Zealand. Accordingly, including overseas companies in the analysis would have distorted the results.

New Zealand Alternative Exchange (NZAX) It should also be noted that companies listed on the alternative exchange NZAX were also excluded. The NZAX is an alternative equity market introduced as a lower cost exchange for 'small to medium sized, fast growing businesses seeking a safe and efficient alternative capital raising facility' (NZSX 2008). Companies listed on the NZAX are required to comply with the NZAX listing rules. These are described by the New Zealand Exchange as having a 'more flexible corporate governance standard' (ibid.). The meaning of this phrase becomes evident when the NZAX rules are reviewed. NZAX Listing Rule 10.5 sets out the disclosures to be made in the yearly and half-yearly reports. Only one rule contains a reference to corporate governance. This is Rule 10.5.5(h), which provides that there shall be disclosed a statement of any corporate governance policies, practices or processes adopted or followed by the NZAX issuer. Accordingly, NZAX issuers do not need to have or disclose a code of ethics.

It should be noted that a small minority of NZAX listed companies referred to the NZSX Code, with one company disclosing compliance with the Code in its annual report. Two companies disclosed that they had some form of code of ethics. One had a code of conduct as part of a Directors Operating Manual and another had adopted the New Zealand Institute of Directors Code. The majority, however, made no disclosure regarding corporate governance practices other than the legal disclosure requirements for annual reports. These include disclosures about independent directors, entries in the interests register and specific statements by the auditor and directors about the financial statements.

Analysis

For each of the 94 companies included in the survey the data collected was checked against the following four criteria.

1. Whether the company stated that it complied, in part or in full, with the Securities Commission's *NZ Principles and Guidelines*.
2. Whether the company stated how its corporate governance practices materially differed, if at all, from the NZSX Code.
3. Whether the company stated that it had adopted a code of ethics or equivalent.
4. Whether the code of ethics or equivalent document was published in the annual report or website.

Analysis revealed an overall lack of uniformity in the disclosure practices of the companies within the data set. In terms of the four criteria set out above, exploration of the disclosure practices revealed 12 different compliance combinations. These combinations can be grouped into three general sets. The first group encompasses all companies that substantially complied with the four criteria. Companies with disclosure practices that complied with some of the four criteria were included in the second group and companies that disclosed only minimal compliance were included in the third group. Each of the three groups is discussed below.

Substantial compliance including published code of ethics

Thirty-six companies (38 per cent) listed on the NZSX fell within this group. These were companies that had adopted a code of ethics, disclosed the code and indicated compliance with the NZSX Code or the *NZ Principles and Guidelines* to some degree. The largest sub-group, consisting of 19 companies, disclosed compliance with all four criteria. A minority of these companies expressed that they had taken into account overseas corporate governance codes, such as the ASX CGC Code, in the formulation and monitoring of their codes of ethics or were considering doing so. Also included within this group are 14 companies that disclosed they had a code of ethics and also published the document. This subgroup either stated that their practices did not materially differ from the NZSX Code or referred to compliance with the Securities Commission's *NZ Principles and Guidelines,* but not both. A small number of companies (3 per cent) stated that they had a code of ethics and disclosed it, but did not make any statement with respect to the NZSX Code or the *NZ Principles and Guidelines*.

Mid-level compliance

A number of companies simply stated they had a code of ethics (or equivalent) but did not publish it or make it available on their website. This included one company which simply stated that it did have a code, but made no statement about how its corporate governance practices differed from the NZSX Code or the *NZ Principles and Guidelines*.

More problematic were those 18 companies that simply stated that their corporate governance practices 'do not materially differ', or 'comply in all substantial respects' or even 'generally follow' the NZSX Code, but made no express statement as to a corporate code of ethics. It is therefore unclear whether they had adopted a code of ethics, although on the basis that a failure to adopt a code of ethics would (hopefully) be seen as a material deviation from the NZSX Code, these companies did in fact have some form of code of ethics.

Also included within this second group were 23 companies that disclosed that they had a code of ethics, but did not publish it. However, all of the companies made some form of statement that the company complied with the NZSX Code (14 companies) or with the *NZ Principles and Guidelines* (1 company) or with both (9 companies).

The difficulty with all companies in this second group is gauging the level of compliance because of the vague language used in corporate governance statements and because companies are not required to publish codes of ethics. For example, a statement that a company 'generally follows the NZSX Code' or 'in most respects conforms to the NZSX Code' could imply that in some other respects it fails to conform to the Code. Accordingly, for the 45 per cent of companies that fall within this category, it is unclear whether they have codes and, if they do, what the codes contain.

Low-level compliance

Finally, 15 of the 94 companies analysed did not make any statement in their latest annual reports or on their websites as to compliance with the NZSX Code or the Securities Commission *NZ Principles and Guidelines*. They also did not refer to any code of ethics. Also included within this group is one company that referred to the *NZ Principles and Guidelines* but made no other statement as to compliance with the NZSX Code or the adoption or otherwise of a code of ethics. Accordingly, it is not possible to make any assessment about the corporate governance practices with respect to ethical behavior or codes of ethics for approximately 17 per cent of the companies within this category.

ANALYSIS AND CONCLUSION

The original objective of the research was to evaluate, based on disclosures, how companies listed on the NZSX approached ethics, through an analysis of their codes of ethics and statements as to ethical practices. A limitation of this approach is that any analysis based on corporate disclosures will always present an incomplete view of the value of ethics within an organization. However, it was not appreciated before the research was undertaken that a significant number of listed companies do not publish their codes of ethics as this is not a requirement of the NZSX Code. It is unclear why the NZSX does not require codes to be published, although it does suggest that the NZSX does not afford a high priority to non-financial corporate governance practices.

Recent research by Transparency International New Zealand (TINZ), which was limited to NZX 50 index companies, undertook analysis of the content of the companies' codes of ethics. This research focused specifically on policies on bribery and corruption and found that, even within the companies listed on the NZX 50 index, only 46 had a code of ethics. Of these, only 68 per cent made their policies public. The Report stated:

> A detailed examination of code of conduct policies among companies listed on the NZX 50 shows us that only 44% prohibit bribery. This figure is considerably less than that seen in comparable markets in other parts of the world and fails to meet the Securities Commission Corporate Governance Principles and Guidelines. Only 18% of the NZX 50 have policies on restricting (as opposed to prohibiting) facilitation payments. None of the companies identified as having a high risk exposure to corruption have policies that restrict facilitation payments. Less than half of the NZX 50 supply evidence of providing their employees with training on the company's code of conduct and most also don't report that they outline information to their stakeholders and the public regarding the systems in place for monitoring compliance with the code. (Transparency International New Zealand 2010, p. 5)

Transparency International New Zealand concluded that the ethical practices of the NZX 50 index companies were not measuring up to the international standards or regulators' expectations indicated in the Securities Commission's *NZ Principles and Guidelines*. It is contended that if TINZ excluded dual-listed companies, which make up a significant proportion of companies on the NZX 50 index, or included companies outside this list, there would be even greater disparity between practices in New Zealand and internationally.

In conclusion, the issue of corporate ethics and codes of ethics remains contested territory for many researchers. However, in general the ongoing debate is not about whether companies should take into account ethical responsibilities but what the rationale, nature and extent of that wider accountability is or should be. Furthermore, the adoption of a code of ethics is now a requirement of corporate governance best-practice codes in most developed countries. In New Zealand, although the Securities Commission's *NZ Principles and Guidelines* requires the adoption of a code of ethics, compliance with the *NZ Principles and Guidelines* is not mandatory, although the Securities Commission does review the disclosures of issuers from time to time. The NZSX Code also requires issuers to adopt a code of ethics and that code must address certain issues. However, the requirements as to content in the NZSX Code provide little or no guidance as to how issuers should deal with ethical issues. In addition, there is no express requirement on issuers to disclose their codes of ethics and for many issuers, given the conflicting disclosure requirements between the Listing Rules and the NZSX Code, it is not possible to even ascertain if an issuer has adopted a code of ethics. Accordingly, not only are the ethical practices of New Zealand issuers not measuring up to international best practice, but the rules regulating codes of ethics, their content and disclosure also fall below international standards in this area.

NOTES

1. In the study by Kazi (1993), survey forms were sent to either the secretary or chief accountant of 200 companies listed in the *Management Magazine* in December 1990. Of these, ten companies either could not be contacted or had closed, giving a sample size of 190. From this number 99 usable responses were received.
2. Investment Research Group is a company based in Auckland, New Zealand that maintains a database of information for investors.
3. This number does not include securities issued by any issuer that was suspended by the New Zealand Exchange at this date.

REFERENCES

Articles, Books, Reports and Press Releases

Allen, R.E. (ed) (1990), *The Concise Oxford Dictionary of Current English*, New York, NY: Clarendon Press.

Arjoon, S. (2005), 'Corporate governance: an ethical perspective', *Journal of Business Ethics*, **61**, 343–52.

Bhimani, A. (2008), 'Making corporate governance count: the fusion of ethics and economic rationality', *Journal of Management and Governance*, **12**, 135–47.

Brickley, J.A., Clifford W. Smith and Jerold L. Zimmerman (2005), 'Corporate governance, ethics, and organizational architecture', in Donald H. Chew and

Stuart L. Gillan (eds), *Corporate Governance at the Crossroads: A Book of Readings*, New York, NY: McGraw-Hill, pp. 103–14.
Cadbury Committee (1992), Committee on the Financial Aspects of Corporate Governance, *Report of the Committee on the Financial Aspects of Corporate Governance*, London, UK: GEE Publishing.
Campbell, Robert and Alan Kitson (2008), *The Ethical Organisation*, Basingstoke, UK and New York, NY: Palgrave Macmillan.
Canary, H. and M. Jennings (2008), 'Principles and influence in codes of ethics: a centering resonance analysis company pre- and post-Sarbanes-Oxley codes of ethics', *Journal of Business Ethics*, **80**, 263–78.
Carasco, E.F. and J. B. Singh (2003), 'The content and focus of the codes of ethics of the world's largest transnational corporations', *Business and Society Review*, **108** (1), 71–94.
Chew, Donald H. and Stuart L. Gillan (eds) (2005), *Corporate Governance at the Crossroads: a Book of Readings*, New York, NY: McGraw-Hill.
Clarke, Thomas (2007), *International Corporate Governance: a Comparative Approach*, London, UK and New York, NY: Routledge.
Crane, Andrew and Dirk Matten (2004), *Business Ethics: a European Perspective*, Oxford, UK: Oxford University Press.
Du Plessis, Jean Jacques, James McConvill and Mirko Bagaric (2005), *Principles of Contemporary Corporate Governance*, Melbourne, Australia: Cambridge University Press.
Farrar, J. (1999), 'A brief thematic history of corporate governance', *Bond Law Review*, **11** (2), 259–76.
Frances-Gomez, P. (2003), 'Some difficulties in Sacconi's view about corporate ethics', *Journal of Business Ethics*, **24**, 165–80.
Friedman, Milton (1962), *Capitalism and Freedom*, Chicago, IL: University of Chicago Press.
Friedman, Milton (1970), 'The social responsibility of business is to increase its profits', *New York Times Sunday Magazine*, 13 September 1970, reprinted in Walther C. Zimmerli, Klaus Richter and Markus Holzinger (eds) (2007), *Corporate Ethics and Corporate Governance*, Berlin, Germany and New York, NY: Springer, pp. 173–8.
Jones, Campbell, Martin Parker and Rene ten Bos (2005), *For Business Ethics*, Abingdon, UK and New York, NY: Routledge.
Kaptein, Muel and Johan F.D.B. Wempe (2002), *The Balanced Company: a Theory of Corporate Integrity*, Oxford, UK and New York, NY: Oxford University Press.
Kazi, F.A. (1993), 'Ethics in New Zealand organisations', *Journal of Business Ethics*, **12**, 433–40.
Kazi, F.A. (1999), 'Business ethics in New Zealand organisations: views from the middle and lower level managers', *Journal of Business Ethics*, **12**, 145–53.
McBarnet, Doreen (2006), 'Towards ethical compliance: lessons from Enron', in G.J. Rossouw and Alejo Jose G. Sison (eds), *Global Perspectives on Ethics of Corporate Governance*, New York, NY and Basingstoke, UK: Palgrave Macmillan, pp. 27–38.
Milton-Smith, J. (1997), 'Business ethics in Australia and New Zealand', *Journal of Business Ethics*, **16**, 1485–97.
Parker, Martin (ed.) (1998), *Ethics and Organizations*, London, UK and Thousand Oaks, CA: Sage.

Psaros, J. (2009), *Australian Corporate Governance: a Review and Analysis of Key Issues*, French Forest, Aust: Pearson Education Australia.
Sacconi, Lorenzo (2000), *The Social Contract of the Firm*, Berlin, Germany: Springer.
Schwartz, M. (2002), 'A code of ethics for corporate code of ethics', *Journal of Business Ethics*, **41**, 27–43.
Securities Commission of New Zealand (2002), 'Strengthening Confidence in New Zealand's Capital Markets: a Statement on Certain Aspects of Corporate Governance and Financial Reporting', Wellington, NZ: Securities Commission of New Zealand.
Securities Commission of New Zealand (2004), *Corporate Governance in New Zealand: Principles and Guidelines*, Wellington, NZ: Securities Commission of New Zealand.
Securities Commission of New Zealand (2010), *Review of Corporate Governance Disclosures by Selected Issuers*, Wellington, NZ: Securities Commission of New Zealand.
Stevens, S. (2008), 'Corporate ethical codes: effective instruments for influencing behavior', *Journal of Business Ethics*, **78**, 601–9.
Trevino, Linda K. and Gary R. Weaver (2003), *Managing Ethics in Business Organisations*, Stanford, CA: Stanford University Press.
Tricker, R. Ian (1994), *International Corporate Governance*, Singapore: Prentice Hall.
World Bank (2000), 'Corporate governance: a framework for implementation', in Thomas Clarke (2007), *International Corporate Governance: A Comparative Approach*, London, UK and New York, NY: Routledge.

Statutes and Regulations

Companies Act 1993 (NZ), 1993/105.
Sarbanes-Oxley Act (SOX), Pub L No 107-204, 116 Stat 745 (2002).

Web Resources

ASX (2008), Australian Stock Exchange 'Old ASX market rules (Prior to 01/18/2010)', available at http://www.asxgroup.com.au/media/PDFs/Chapter04.pdf (accessed 28 March 2011).
ASX CGC (2010), Australian Stock Exchange Corporate Governance Council, 'Corporate governance principles and recommendations with 2010 amendments', available at http://www.asx.com.au/documents/about/cg_principles_recommendations_with_2010_amendments.pdf (accessed 25 June 2011).
Chen, M. and M. Cotton (2006), 'Securities commission's principles and guidelines – an update', available at http://www.sec-com.govt.nz/speeches/2006/governance-principles-update/ (accessed at 28 March 2011).
NASDAQ (2009), 'The NASDAQ Listing Rules', available at http://www.nasdaq.com/about/Listing_Rules_041309.pdf (accessed 25 June 2011).
NYSE (2011), New York Stock Exchange, 'NYSE Rules', available at http://rules.nyse.com/NYSE/Rules/ (accessed 25 June 2011).
NZSX (2008), New Zealand Stock Exchange, 'About the AX', available at http://www.nzx.com/markets/nzax/about-the-ax (accessed 28 March 2011).

NZSX (2009), New Zealand Stock Exchange, 'NZSX/NSDX listing rules appendices markets, available at http:// www.nzx.com/market-supervision/rules/nzsx-and-nzdx-listing-rules (accessed 28 March 2011).

OECD (2004), Organisation for Economic Co-operation and Development, 'OECD Principles of Corporate Governance', available at http://www.oecd.org/dataoecd/32/18/31557724.pdf (accessed 22 June 2011).

Thompson, L.D. (2003), US Department of Justice, 'Memorandum to the heads of department components and United States attorneys, principles of federal prosecution of business organizations', available at http://www.usdoj.gov/dag/cftf/corporate_governance.htm (accessed 18 March 2010).

Transparency International New Zealand (2010), 'As good as we are perceived?', available at http://www.transparencynz.org.nz/index.php/indices-reports/new-zealand/report-qas-good-as-we-are-perceivedq (accessed 22 June 2011).

USSC (2010), US Sentencing Commission, 'Federal Sentencing Guidelines', available at http://www.ussc.gov/Guidelines/2010_guidelines/ToC_PDF.cfm (accessed 25 June 2011).

Index